*This book is dedicated to my husband and partner, Carlos,
for his help, support, and love.*

About the Author

Sue Plumley owns and operates Humble Opinions, an independent computer consulting firm that provides network installation, maintenance, and troubleshooting to small, medium, and large businesses in southern West Virginia. In addition to designing and supporting Microsoft, Novell, and LANtastic networks, Sue and her partner/husband Carlos help businesses configure and manage applications, printing, file distribution, e-mail and Internet access, and other useful tasks over the network.

Since 1992, Sue has also authored and co-authored over 65 books about operating systems, suites and individual applications, e-mail programs, groupware, networking, and so on. You can reach Sue via the Internet: splumley@citynet.net.

Documented NT Server

A Start-to-Finish Network Installation Plan

Sue Plumley

WILEY COMPUTER PUBLISHING

JOHN WILEY & SONS, INC.

New York • Chichester • Weinheim • Brisbane • Singapore • Toronto

Executive Publisher: Robert Ipsen

Editor: Marjorie Spencer

Managing Editor: Mark Hayden

Text Design & Composition: SunCliff Graphic Productions

This text is printed on acid-free paper.

This publication is designed to provide accurate and authoritative information in regard to the subject matter covered. It is sold with the understanding that the publisher is not engaged in rendering legal, accounting, or other professional service. If legal advice or other expert assistance is required, the services of a competent professional person should be sought.

Library of Congress Cataloging-in-Publication Data

Plumley, Sue.
    Documented NT Server: a start to finish network installation plan
  / Sue Plumley.
      p.   cm.
    Includes bibliographical references and index
    ISBN 0-471-19224-4 (pbk.: alk. paper)
    1. Microsoft Windows NT.   2. Operating systems (Computers).
  3. Client/server computing.   4. Computer networks.   I. Title.
  QA76.76.063P575   1997
  004.6'8--dc21   97-20682
                                            CIP

Printed in the United States of America
10 9 8 7 6 5 4 3 2 1

Contents

Part Two: Preparing and Installing NT Server 4.0   69

Part Three: Setting Up and Using NT Server 131

CHAPTER 6

Creating and Managing Users and Groups 133

CHAPTER 7

Managing Network Security Policies 163

CHAPTER 8

Managing Printing 189

Part Five: Application Management 271

CHAPTER 11

Using NT Server's Applications to Manage the Network 273

Part Six: Advanced NT Server 355

CHAPTER 14

Expanding the Network 357

CHAPTER 15

Using Multiple Domains 395

Acknowledgments

I'd like to thank the many people who contributed to this project. First and foremost my thanks go to Marjorie Spencer at Wiley. Marjorie's insight and advice have been invaluable throughout this project and others. Additionally, I'm grateful to Margaret Hendrey for her help, guidance, and patience. I'd also like to thank my agent, Lisa Swayne, for always being so cheerful, supportive, and helpful.

No book can ever be completed without the hard work of editors and reviewers. I appreciate those who have helped ensure that this book is technically accurate and those who make sure the text is consistent and the grammar is correct. Many others contribute to a book through typesetting, proofreading, indexing, and so on; thanks to you all.

Introduction

Whether you're considering installing a network or you've been using a network in your business for a while, you're most likely in need of some organizational help. Many people concern themselves with the hardware, software, and other logistical factors of networking while neglecting the design of the network; planning directories, security, group access, and so on are as important as installing the operating system. If you don't take the time to organize the network components, you may be establishing obstacles that bring down your entire system later.

Fortunately, Windows NT Server includes many features that can help you outline and plan your network. All you need to know is how to use them to best suit your circumstances. This book helps you plan your network and shows you how to use NT Server to actualize your designs. From planning to practicing, from upgrading your hardware to implementing the applications, *Documented NT Server: A Start to Finish Network Installation Plan* can help you effectuate the perfect network for your organization.

Who Should Use This Book?

Windows NT Server 4.0 is becoming the unparalleled networking choice of businesses since its release in 1996. Of the major networking solutions—Novell NetWare, LANtastic, Banyan Vines, Windows for Workgroups—Windows NT Server offers network security, ease of administration, fast and efficient connectivity to the majority of desktop clients in use today, and hardware and software compatibility.

Windows NT Server 4.0 is the perfect networking solution for any size business; however, many companies cannot afford to hire a full-time consultant or network administrator to plan, install, configure, and administer their network. As a result, they either avoid networking altogether or jump into networking without first planning their system, which ultimately wastes resources, time, and money.

Documented NT Server: A Start to Finish Network Installation Plan can help you plan, install, and configure an NT network using the author's skills, experience, and problem-solving techniques. Whether you're just starting to network your business or you need help organizing a network already in place, this book can help you.

Specifically, this book can help the following people to successfully implement an NT network:

- Owners, managers, or administrators of small, medium, and large businesses who are new to networking and need help installing and running NT Server and client computers.
- Anyone who is interested in planning the network—upgrading hardware and software, preparing users, planning directories, and so on—before installing the operating system.
- Businesses using a peer-to-peer network—such as LANtastic or Windows for Workgroups 3.11—who want to upgrade to a client/server network using NT Server 4.0.
- Network administrators searching for a more efficient solution to their current network organization.
- Computer systems consultants who have clients that want to start networking or upgrade their networks to NT.
- Certified NT specialists who need help planning network organization and implementing applications in a real-life networking situation.

Whether you're overseeing a small, medium, or large business or corporation, *Documented NT Server: A Start to Finish Network Installation Plan* can help you by introducing Windows networking concepts, offering solid advice for planning and deploying your network, explaining how to use NT-specific tools and utilities, covering client and server hardware requirements, presenting software alternatives, and much more. Any business can use this book as a guide to planning, installing, and administering a network, no matter the size or scale of the system.

How to Use This Book

This book is written to help you plan and design an NT network and implement the network. You will learn to outline a file and directory structure, organize users and groups, create security policies, and so on, before installing the operating system. Then, after the plan is in place, you learn how to implement the plan by installing NT, creating users and groups, managing printing, installing client software, and managing security. *Documented NT Server: A Start to Finish Network Installation Plan* takes planning a network a step further by covering use of the common NT accessories, explaining the installation and use of common applications, and discussing communications software. Finally, an advanced section of the book describes topics you can use to make decisions about expanding the network as your company grows.

The book contains six parts to help you plan and implement the network from start to finish. Part I, "Planning and Designing an NT Network," covers information about network models and hardware requirements. Chapters in this part present the benefits of networking business computers, potential problems with networking, and a general overview of the NT Server operating system. Also included in Part I are many real-life examples for organizing and administering a successful network plus multiple illustrations of network models. The last chapter in this part discusses the hardware requirements for both server and workstation, and software considerations for both.

Part II, "Preparing and Installing NT Server 4.0," helps you through the installation process. Included with installation instructions is information about backing up before installation, preparations and precautions about drivers and updated software, choosing a file system, and so on. When you are completely prepared, Chapter 5 leads you through the installation of the software, configuring the network, using the Control Panel, and solving installation problems.

"Setting Up and Using NT Server," Part III, guides you through setting up the server by creating groups and users, managing security policies, managing resources, and installing and configuring network printers. Naturally, more than one solution is offered for each of these procedures, so you can adapt your setup.

In Part IV, "Preparing and Managing Workstations," you learn to upgrade the hardware of existing workstations for use with the NT network, install and upgrade client software, and configure workstations for use with NT Server.

Part V, "Application Management," explains how to use the NT accessories, install and use applications, and use communications software. Most books about NT stop after giving information on server and client installation, and configuration. *Documented NT Server: A Start to Finish Network Installation Plan* goes several steps further by helping you decide how to install and implement your DOS applications (such as accounting or inventory programs), suite and individual applications (including word processing, spreadsheet, and database programs), and groupware applications (such as e-mail, scheduling, and an Internet browser).

The final part of the book, Part VI "Advanced NT Server," discusses when to add one or more servers to the network, the advantages and disadvantages of using multiple servers, server administration, and so on. Additionally, the text discusses using multiple domains and their use in a company that must expand offices over many floors, buildings, or sites.

At the end of the book are two appendices for reference. A glossary of networking terms in Appendix A provides definitions of common NT and networking terms. The troubleshooting guide in Appendix B contains problems and solutions you may encounter with installation, configuration, and running the network.

Conventions

Documented NT Server: A Start to Finish Network Installation Plan assumes you are familiar with the use of Windows, in general, and its common components (such as the mouse, maximize and minimize buttons, menus, and so on). However, you do not need to be familiar with Windows NT, specifically, to use this book. I will guide you concerning menu choice and explain options available to you so you can make your own decisions.

In the step-by-step instructions, I will tell you to choose a menu and command like this: Choose File, Open. Underlined letters on-screen are those that can be used as keyboard shortcuts; for example, to choose File, Open with the keyboard means you would press and hold the ALT key while pressing the F key. Then press the O to open the Open dialog box. Although I use the mouse in all operations, I will also give you keyboard shortcuts from time to time.

These shortcuts may be placed in tips scattered throughout the text. Tips also contain helpful hints on speeding your work or making a task more efficient or effective. Notes will also be included in the text to offer additional information that doesn't seem to flow with the other text. Finally, there are sidebars throughout the text that offer specific information about operating systems, other networking programs, and various applications.

PART

I

Planning and Designing an NT Network

1 *Understanding NT's Power and Potential*

A computer network physically connects your PCs so that your employees can share files and directories electronically, use e-mail, and share expensive equipment, such as CD-ROM drives, modems, and printers. Using a network in your business saves your company money, time, and energy. The advantages of a network are many; add NT Server to the mix and the advantages are incomparable.

Your company's computers may already be attached to a network or you may be considering whether to use a network in your business. This chapter explains the advantages of networking in general and the power of networking with NT specifically. Also, this chapter covers information about integrating NT with current networks and discusses some client considerations.

In this chapter, you'll learn about the following:

- Advantages of networking your office PCs
- Potential problems and solutions of networking
- Benefits to using NT Server
- Possibilities of integrating networks

Networking Your Office

Technology today offers many choices for networking an office. Because of the flexibility of available equipment and hardware, you can connect PCs within the same office, between floors or buildings, even among cities and countries. You can network as few as two computers or thousands, each sharing the same resources and data or by limiting data and equipment use. You can assign all computers on the network the same status, enabling each to use the others' resources or you can configure the networked PCs with stricter security limits, so only certain resources are shared.

Using a network benefits your company, your employees, and you as an administrator in many ways, which is the reason you'll want to network your office. Networking saves time, money, and labor for everyone connected; although you may question that if you're the administrator of the network. Naturally, the administrator must initially work more to get the network set up and running, but the time you'll save in other ways will more than make up for it.

Peer-to-Peer or Client/Server?

The most common type of network used in small- to medium-sized businesses is the LAN (Local Area Network). A LAN is a group of computers and associated peripheral devices connected by way of a communications channel and capable of sharing files and other resources. The connection can be through cables, phone lines, or a wireless signal of some sort; but generally, cables are used for the connections. There are basically two types of LANs in use: peer-to-peer and client/server or dedicated server.

Peer-to-Peer

A peer-to-peer network is a group of PCs linked together, each with the same status as the other; in other words, the drives, files, and printers on each PC can be made available to every other PC on the network. Each PC can still run local applications and the user can, in many cases, choose not to share files, directories, and/or resources. Some examples of peer-to-peer networks are Artisoft's LANtastic, and Microsoft's Windows for Workgroups 3.11 or Windows 95 peer-to-peer network. Figure 1.1 illustrates a peer-to-peer network.

Although a peer-to peer network may sound ideal, this network model includes many system management problems. Administration by one manager is difficult because each user controls his or her own workstation; if one user decides not to share a file or resource, remote management is not possible to enforce compliance. Additionally, the responsibility for system backup falls to each user. If a user fails to back up essential files and there's a system crash, those files are lost to everyone.

Other evident problems with peer-to-peer networks include security issues and system reliability. Users can easily use and misuse any files on the system. Accidental file damage, purposeful data destruction, and data loss are likely possibilities within a peer-to-peer network. Finally, a peer-to-peer network is generally small,

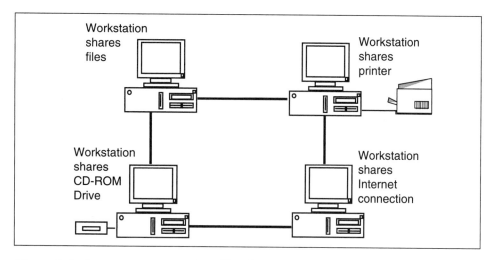

Figure 1.1 *A peer-to-peer network enables all workstations to share all data and resources with the others.*

often limited to 2 to 10 users. If your company requires more PCs than 10, you'd be better off using the client/server type of network.

Client/Server

The client/server network—also called a dedicated server—uses at least one central, often dedicated, computer as a server. The server is specially configured to enable easy storage and sharing of files and resources. A server is a data management center from which clients can access applications, files, and directories. Also, a server administers various shared resources—such as printers, modems, and CD-ROM drives—to the clients attached to the network. Figure 1.2 illustrates a client/server network. Two of the most popular examples of the client/server network are Windows NT Server and Novell NetWare.

There are also problems with the client/server type of network, including security issues, heavy network traffic, slow server response time, server crashes, and so on. Many of these problems, however, can be solved by the server operating system you use. NT Server, for example, incorporates various utilities and controls that help to alleviate these and other common client/server problems, as you will see throughout this book.

One feature NT Server offers to help you control security on the server is the administrative tool User Manager for Domains. With the User Manager, you control which users have access to particular resources on the server. You can, for ex-

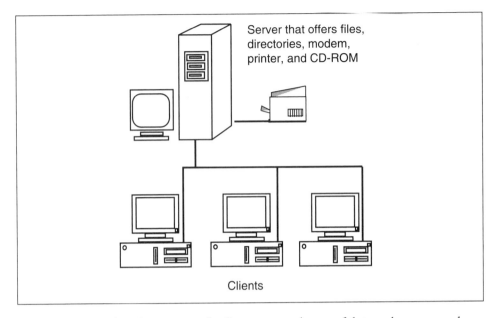

Server that offers files,
directories, modem,
printer, and CD-ROM

Clients

Figure 1.2 *In a client/server network, clients request the use of data and resources only from the server.*

ample, enable one or more users access to a directory of accounting files while denying access to those same files to others on the network. You can grant permission to some users to print to a color laser printer while denying those permissions to other users. The User Manager also offers many ways to make security administration easier; for more information, see Chapter 6.

NT also offers other administrative tools that enable you to track security breaches of the system, log system errors and application problems, monitor network usage, maximize server performance, and more. Using these NT features makes using the client/server model more efficient and effective.

In addition to using NT utilities and tools to alleviate possible problems with the client/server network model, a network can easily use more than one server to administer the clients on that network. Multiple servers provide a method by which you can divide services to lessen traffic and usage to any one server. Finally, the number of clients that can access any one server is limited only by the hardware and the operating system; NT's domain features make the use of multiple servers and clients reliable and practical. See Chapter 4 for information about some network options.

This book discusses the client/server network type and applies it specifically to the Windows NT Server operating system.

Note: Microsoft has two NT operating systems available: Windows NT Server 4.0 and Windows NT Workstation 4.0. NT Server is the server software that enables you to administer an entire network, set security policies, share resources, limit access, track network usage, and attach multiple clients as well as additional servers to the network. NT Workstation is also an operating system but for use on a client computer. NT Workstation is limited in its usage on the network and should not be used as a server. Although the two operating systems look similar and offer similar basic features, only NT Server has the server utilities needed to administer a network.

Benefits to Your Business

The reason you connect your PCs to a network is to benefit your business, to maintain a competitive edge. No matter what your business goals are, using a client/server system enables better information sharing, communication, and network organization. Following are some of the benefits of client/server networking.

Using the client/server model of networking enables your employees to collaborate easily and efficiently. In addition to sharing documents over the network, employees can also e-mail ideas, questions, and suggestions to each other; access sales, inventory, and manufacturing information; and gather, store, and share customer feedback. During all of this collaboration, you have the control of who is authorized to access information and data.

Networking also enables your employees to access current customer account records and service records to track customer needs and anticipate market trends. Productivity also improves immediately after e-mail and scheduling programs are made available to your staff. You might even want to establish an intranet (internal web site for your company's use only) on which you can publish and update information quickly and efficiently.

Following are a few more of the advantages to using a network in your business:

- Share files electronically. Whether your network users work with 1-2-3 or Excel, WordPerfect or Word for Windows, or Outlook or Organizer, they can share files of all types with each other over a network. You can store files on the server for quick and easy access by all users or just those you specify. Directories can be shared as well, with all or designated users.
- Share ideas, requests, questions, and so on. Using e-mail or an intranet within your company enables people to connect to each other when it's most convenient, providing a method by which individuals can exchange text files, image files, and others to one or more people on the network.

- Back up critical data electronically to the network. You can back up data on the server and/or data from individual workstations connected to the network. Back up to a tape drive, optical drive, network drive, or other data storage component.

- Share printers, CD-ROM drives, modems, and so on. You can connect expensive laser printers for example, to the network so everyone can access them; you also can share other peripherals over the network with those workstations that are connected.

- The administrator can limit access to shared data and resources so that users' access to critical or sensitive files and directories is limited. Additionally, reserve resources for use by specified personnel, if you want.

- The administrator can remotely support users of the network. You do not need to administer the network from the server; you can use a workstation from which to manage the network. In many cases, you can use dial-up remote access from outside of the office.

The Power of NT Server

The leading choice for networking business PCs is clearly client/server and the most flexible, efficient, and useful client/server network is NT Server 4.0. NT offers many advantages to networking within the familiar Windows environment; using the Windows graphical interface makes network administration quick and easy, especially if you're already familiar with Windows.

Advantages of NT Networking

Windows NT extends many Windows 95 features that you may already be familiar with—such as long file names, network protocols (including TCP/IP), and remote dial-up access. Additionally, training employees on the Windows interface will be easy, since they are probably already familiar with Windows. Graphical icons and toolbars make learning new tools simple.

Installation and configuration of Windows NT Server, security issues, tracking events, and other administration components are also effortless for anyone who is familiar with Windows and the network. For more information about installing Windows NT Server, see Chapter 5.

With NT Server, you can use one operating system to manage your critical business needs. NT Server is a high-performance file and print server, and a powerful applications server. Quick printing and file access improve the efficiency of your office and reduce the need for additional peripheral devices. Users can run applications on their local workstations or from NT Server safely and efficiently, making true application-sharing a reality in your network.

NT Server includes an e-mail application, protocol support for the Internet, a Web browser, and a World Wide Web server. Without purchasing additional software, you can use NT Server as an Internet web server, an intranet server in your company, and a communications platform.

Finally, consider the following advantages of NT Server:

- Windows is a common platform, which means your NT Server network performs well with many products from both Microsoft and other vendors, including Lotus, Symantec, and so on. Windows NT can also run DOS-based applications, 16-bit programs, and the latest 32-bit applications as well.

- NT Server works with a variety of client operating systems, including MS-DOS, Microsoft Windows 3.x, Windows for Workgroups 3.11, Windows 95, Windows NT Workstation, OS/2, UNIX, and Macintosh (see Figure 1.3).

- Microsoft's NT Server works with a variety of hardware types (including Intel, Alpha, MIPS, and RISC-based platforms), meaning you can probably upgrade your system to NT Server inexpensively.

- NT Server's scalability enables you to expand the number of servers and clients on your system while maintaining easy administrative control; thus,

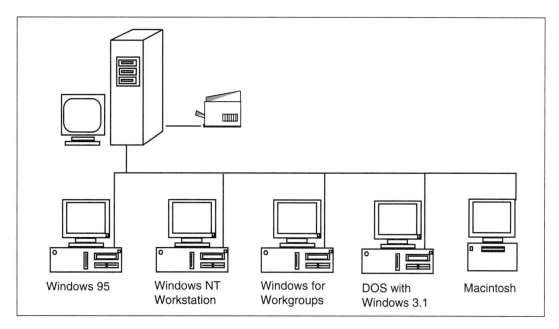

Figure 1.3 *NT Server can "serve" a variety of clients.*

your system can grow with your business from a single-site, single-server network to a multiserver, multiprocessor enterprise.

- You can use NT Server's built-in tape backup utility to back up your system onto tape.
- NT Server works with the Microsoft BackOffice suite of servers that enables you to add full enterprise-level network services when you need them.

Note: The BackOffice suite of servers includes several applications you can use to manage and administer your network. Included in the suite are the Internet Information Server, Microsoft Exchange Server, SQL Server, Microsoft Proxy Server, and more. These server applications enable you to attach to the Internet, create a firewall to protect your network from the Internet, use complex databases over your network, employ intricate e-mail services, and so on. For information about planning and installing BackOffice, see Sue Plumley's book, *Documented BackOffice: A Start to Finish BackOffice Installation Plan* (John Wiley & Sons, Inc.).

What Does NT Server Offer?

Now that you're familiar with the advantages of NT Server, let me describe some of the tools and utilities NT Server includes to ease network administration. These tools enable you to manage the users of the network, create groups to provide security and access throughout the network, manage printers and other resources, track and log security, manage files, attach to the Internet, and more. Many of these features will be covered in more detail elsewhere in this book; I've referred to the chapters for your convenience.

The User Manager for Domains is a tool you'll need to use immediately after installing NT Server. No one can access the network (except for you, the administrator) until you register each person with NT's User Manager. For each user, list a name, password, times he or she is allowed on the network, and other useful restrictions and permissions that define that user.

You also can place individual users within groups in NT. It provides several built-in groups—such as the Administrators group or the Print Operators group—and you can create your own groups. You assign individual users to a group, then give that group certain rights on the network, making administration of individuals easier and more effective. For more information about the User Manager for Domains, see Chapter 6.

Figure 1.4 shows the User Manager for Domains with the users connected to the network; notice the available built-in groups in the lower pane of the window.

User Manager - OPINIONS		
Username	**Full Name**	**Description**
Administrator		Built-in account for administering the computer/dor
AmarosDA	Drema Amarosa	Mgr/Sales
BenderHF	Hugh Bender	Asst Mgr
CarterJK	James Carter	Sales
CrowdeBA	Bob Crowder	Mgr. - Sales
DavisTL	Tim Davis	Mgr. PR
GartenJO	Jody Garten	Sales
Guest		Built-in account for guest access to the computer/d
IUSR_HUMBLE	Internet Guest Account	Internet Server Anonymous Access
JohnsoGR	Ginny Johnson	Training
PlumleSJ	Sue Plumley	Mgr/Director
ReynoGI	Gilda Reynolds	Art
SmithBB	Bessie Smith	Sales
TiltoMG	Marge Tilton	PR
WashiBA	Barb Washington	PR

Groups	**Description**
Account Operators	Members can administer domain user and group accounts
Administrators	Members can fully administer the computer/domain
Backup Operators	Members can bypass file security to back up files
Domain Admins	Designated administrators of the domain
Domain Guests	All domain guests
Domain Users	All domain users
Guests	Users granted guest access to the computer/domain
Print Operators	Members can administer domain printers

Figure 1.4 *Assign users to groups to make network security easier and more effective.*

NT Server also enables you to easily install and manage network printing. You can configure a variety of printers, share printers, and even manage individual print jobs using the NT Printers folder and print queue. Displayed in Figure 1.5 is a print queue with jobs waiting to be printed. See Chapter 8 for more information.

HP Color LaserJet - Paused					
Document Name	Status	Owner	Pages	Size	Submitted
9455 Report	Printing	Administrator	2	7.89KB/10.8KB	9:01:38 AM 2/26/97
554 Report		Administrator	2	10.8KB	9:01:54 AM 2/26/97

2 document(s) in queue

Figure 1.5 *Pause print jobs, cancel jobs, or rearrange the order in which jobs print in the NT Printers folder.*

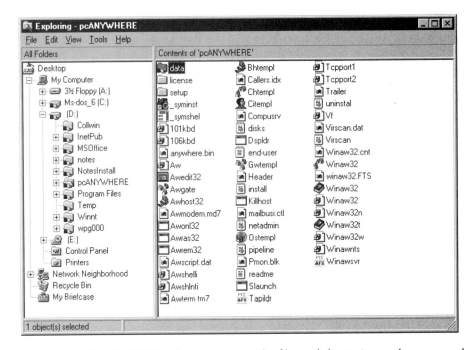

Figure 1.6 *Use the NT Explorer to manage the files and directories on the server and on the network.*

The Client Administrator included with NT Server enables you to create setup and installation disks for various client computers, including DOS, Windows for Workgroups, and Windows 95. Creating client software on a workstation is so easy, in fact, that you can let your users do it with the disks you supply. For information about installing and upgrading client software, see Chapter 10.

NT provides several applications you can use to manage files. The Windows NT Explorer enables you to display, copy, rename, delete, move, and otherwise manage files and directories. The Command Prompt also lets you view and manage files, but in a DOS-like environment. Figure 1.6 illustrates a directory structure of the server in the NT Explorer. Chapter 11 explains how to use both of these applications.

Communications is extremely important to most businesses today and NT Server provides the tools you need to manage internal e-mail and to access the Internet. Microsoft Exchange has long been a staple of Windows and it's also included in NT Server 4.0. With Microsoft Exchange, you can create a post office on the server that stores any e-mail messages sent using Windows Messaging. Users with Windows 95 or Windows NT Workstation will be able to communicate over the network.

Additionally, the Internet Explorer is a perfect Web browser. You can access Web pages, hypertext links, use search engines, and otherwise explore the Inter-

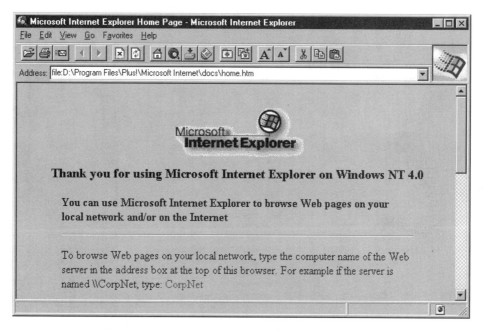

Figure 1.7 *Use the Internet Explorer for Intranets or Internets.*

net. Figure 1.7 shows the Internet Explorer. Chapter 11 describes how these two NT accessories work.

When problems occur on the network, NT records what it calls "events" in logs you can view in the Event Viewer. Using these logs, you can determine the cause of security problems, application errors, system faults, and so on. Figure 1.8 shows the Event Viewer in which you can sort and filter events so they're easier to organize and view. See Chapter 13 for more information.

As your business expands, so will your network. You'll probably want to add more servers to the network to handle various tasks and added services. You also can create multiple domains to help you organize your network users and servers. A domain can be a single computer, computers within a department, or all of the computers in one site. Generally, though, a domain is a convenient method of grouping computers on the network. The Server Manager, an administrative application in NT, enables you to manage multiple servers and domains. For more information, see Chapters 14 and 15.

Possible Problems and Solutions

As previously mentioned, naturally you'll see more problems with a networked system than with standalone PCs; when you add more hardware, software, and

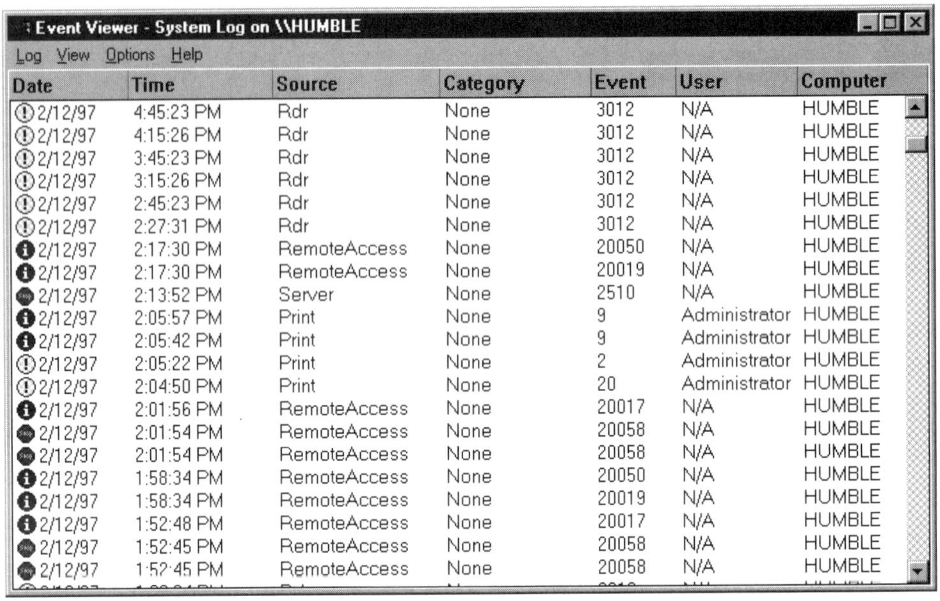

Event Viewer - System Log on \\HUMBLE

Log View Options Help

Date	Time	Source	Category	Event	User	Computer
2/12/97	4:45:23 PM	Rdr	None	3012	N/A	HUMBLE
2/12/97	4:15:26 PM	Rdr	None	3012	N/A	HUMBLE
2/12/97	3:45:23 PM	Rdr	None	3012	N/A	HUMBLE
2/12/97	3:15:26 PM	Rdr	None	3012	N/A	HUMBLE
2/12/97	2:45:23 PM	Rdr	None	3012	N/A	HUMBLE
2/12/97	2:27:31 PM	Rdr	None	3012	N/A	HUMBLE
2/12/97	2:17:30 PM	RemoteAccess	None	20050	N/A	HUMBLE
2/12/97	2:17:30 PM	RemoteAccess	None	20019	N/A	HUMBLE
2/12/97	2:13:52 PM	Server	None	2510	N/A	HUMBLE
2/12/97	2:05:57 PM	Print	None	9	Administrator	HUMBLE
2/12/97	2:05:42 PM	Print	None	9	Administrator	HUMBLE
2/12/97	2:05:22 PM	Print	None	2	Administrator	HUMBLE
2/12/97	2:04:50 PM	Print	None	20	Administrator	HUMBLE
2/12/97	2:01:56 PM	RemoteAccess	None	20017	N/A	HUMBLE
2/12/97	2:01:54 PM	RemoteAccess	None	20058	N/A	HUMBLE
2/12/97	2:01:54 PM	RemoteAccess	None	20058	N/A	HUMBLE
2/12/97	1:58:34 PM	RemoteAccess	None	20050	N/A	HUMBLE
2/12/97	1:58:34 PM	RemoteAccess	None	20019	N/A	HUMBLE
2/12/97	1:52:48 PM	RemoteAccess	None	20017	N/A	HUMBLE
2/12/97	1:52:45 PM	RemoteAccess	None	20058	N/A	HUMBLE
2/12/97	1:52:45 PM	RemoteAccess	None	20058	N/A	HUMBLE

Figure 1.8 *Investigate security problems, application errors, and system faults through the Event Viewer.*

users to your system, there are more possibilities of errors. Luckily, NT Server has built-in utilities and features that can help you avoid and/or alleviate many networking problems that can occur. This section briefly discusses some of those problems; see the references to other chapters in the book for more information.

Security

One of the largest problems with connecting computers together is security. Sensitive files, confidential directories, and resources that should be used for priority projects only are just a few of the problems that can occur when you network computers and people. NT Server provides several solutions to these and other security problems.

First, NT Server requires a security account for each user. This account consists of a user name, password, and use restrictions set by the administrator or his/her delegate. If a user doesn't remember or does not have a user name or password, then that user cannot gain access to the network or its resources.

Second, the administrator may create or use NT's built-in groups to assign rights to a collection of users. For example, the Administrators group has the most control over the network whereas the Users group has very little control over the network but can manage its own files, directories, and so on. The administrator of the network can assign rights to a group, then assign a user to the group, thus limiting the user's access to network resources.

Third, the administrator can also assign permissions that grant access to resources, such as a printer, file, or directory. There are different levels of permission access—such as read-only, execute-only, read/write, and so on—that can be applied to a single file or entire directory, to a single user or entire group.

Additionally, NT Server enables you, as the administrator of the network, to set up auditing and tracking of network events. For example, you can audit the use of any resource, then modify your policies to better suit the situation. For more information about users, groups, and other security issues, see Chapters 6 and 7.

Network Traffic

Another problem you may see with your network, especially as it expands, is increased network traffic. Many requests sent at the same time to the server or for a resource can cause a bottleneck, or network traffic jam, resulting in slow access for everyone connected. NT Server includes a performance monitor application in which you can search for specific performance problems, monitor disk and processor activity, as well as watch disk activity. With Performance Monitor, you can gauge your computer's efficiency and troubleshoot possible problems. Figure 1.9 shows the Performance Monitor; it's not an easy summary to read but it can help you sort through certain network problems.

Note: To start the Performance Monitor, choose Start, Programs, Administrative Tools, then Performance Monitor. If you need more information about running the Performance Monitor, see NT's on-line help or take a look at John Ruley's book, *Networking with Windows NT Server 4.0,* 3rd Ed. (John Wiley and Sons, Inc., 1997).

NT Server is a powerful operating system and, for the most part, you shouldn't have any trouble with network traffic. If, however, your network expands and you add services for the Internet, communications, and others, you may find your server is overtaxed by the amount of network traffic. If this happens, you can always add a server to take care of some of the load. It is common to add, for example, one or more member servers to your network; a member server doesn't authenticate users, as a primary domain server would. A member server may contain data, applications, print services, Internet connections, or other services to help extricate network traffic. See Chapter 2 for more information.

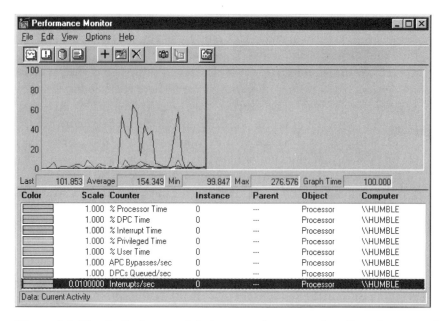

Figure 1.9 *Use the Performance Monitor to analyze network traffic and server performance.*

For clarification, the first NT Server you install to your network is a primary domain controller, which authenticates users no matter what else you assign the server to do—such as manage printing, distribute files, and so on. User authentication is a procedure performed by a network server in which the user's name and password are verified before the user is allowed to connect and access the network; also, the authentication process checks the user's rights and permissions and limits access based on the user's profile.

Server Crashes

When many people depend on the server for data, communication, printing, and other tasks, a server crash could be devastating to the entire company. Fortunately, NT server incorporates sever features that support fault tolerance (guarantees the server will continue to serve).

The server that authenticates users is called the primary domain controller; this server maintains a record of all users and their user accounts. When someone logs on to the network, the primary domain controller allows the user to access the network if the user account is authenticated. With NT Server, you can install a second server, called a backup domain controller, that maintains a copy of all user accounts. If something should happen to the primary domain controller, you can transfer users to the backup domain controller until the first server is repaired. NT

Server also supports directory replication, a process by which a backup server recreates the contents of the server's directories minute-by-minute, which is much better than a customary backup.

RAID (Redundant Array of Inexpensive Drives) is a method of using several hard disk drives in an array to provide fault tolerance in the event that one or more disks fail. In NT, RAID support is in the software as opposed to the hardware; therefore, all you need to do is install two or more drives and use the NT Disk Administrator program to specify RAID on those drives.

Another possible, and common, problem is a failed network adapter card in the server. Since NT Server supports multiple network cards, a card failure won't necessarily bring down the server.

Hardware Support

When you add or expand a network, you invariably discover hardware needs. You might upgrade your workstations and server, for example, by adding memory, hard drives, modems, CD-ROM drives, and other peripherals. You also will need network cards and cabling of some sort to connect your computers, if a network is not already in place.

NT does include a hardware compatibility list that helps you choose the items you will need for your network. Check for compatible network adapter cards as well as for CD-ROM drives, modems, and other peripherals. If you're sure to obtain the hardware that NT supports, you should have no trouble in that department.

The type of cables and network adapter cards you choose will depend on your network and how you want to configure it; if you can find someone in your area who is knowledgeable about installing network cards and cabling, you would be better off to hire that person to do the cabling for you than to try it yourself, especially if you're not experienced with working with cables. After the hardware is installed, however, you can easily install the software and configure NT Server for communications over the network with the help of this book.

Outside Support Expense

Included with the expense of cabling your network and installing network adapter cards are any other expenses you may incur for support of the network. As previously mentioned, hire someone to do the hardware installation and upgrades to the computers you may need before installing NT. Additionally, you will want that same person, if possible, to troubleshoot any problems you may have with hardware after the network is up and running. Network cards, cables, memory, and all hardware components can go bad at some point. You may also want to add more workstations or servers to the network, for which you'll need more cabling and network adapters. So keep in mind you'll need a hardware support person from time to time.

As for consultants, they generally help you plan and install the network operating system; configure users, groups, printers, and so on; and choose and install applications for network use. That's exactly what this book proposes to do; so save your money and read on.

User Training and Support

If you're already using a network in your company, you shouldn't have much trouble training the users connected to the network to successfully access data and resources; they already have an idea about how a network works. If your users are new to networking, you'll want to set aside a day or two to familiarize them with the network and help them find their way around drives, browsers, resources, and so on.

Fortunately, most people are already familiar with Windows and its graphical interface so you shouldn't have much trouble showing them how to manipulate Windows. If you've upgraded workstations, even from Windows 3.x to Windows 95 or Windows NT Workstation 4.0, the foundation is still the same. The changes are in the look of the program, not as much in the way it operates.

You can show users how to open the Network Neighborhood and access the server and its resources, discuss passwords, applications usage, security issues, and so on as an initial introduction. Figure 1.10 shows the open Network Neighborhood

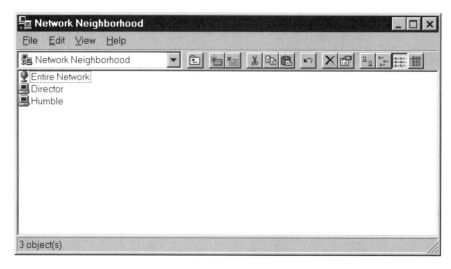

Figure 1.10 Use the Network Neighborhood to view network resources.

on a Windows 95 workstation. You might want to use some of the information in this book to share with your users; for example, tell the users how they'll benefit from NT, explain your security policies, identify the groups to which you've assigned the users, and so on. For more information about users and the network, see Chapters 9 and 10.

Users and Your Network

I've found that if you make sure your users understand, at least in part, what's going on with the network, you'll have less complaints and more cooperation. One thing you should be prepared for is that when an application isn't working for one reason or another, your users will most likely blame the network; as a matter of fact, application tech support people often blame the network as well.

There are many server problems that account for errors and failures, but users can often be the cause of problems as well. Users tend to fill the server's hard disk, for example, with duplicate files, backups, unnecessary application copies, and so on. Additionally, users often install software without asking for assistance; that often causes network problems as well as application problems on the individual's computer.

If you talk to your users, prepare them for the changes to come, and help them understand why it's necessary to follow a few guidelines, you can save yourself many hours of handling panic situations among users. Encourage users to ask questions, especially before they install software or save large amounts of data. Most importantly, however, you should establish some server-use procedures and guidelines.

First, delegate some of the network administration and maintenance to a few knowledgeable, competent employees. If you have help with the network and in tracking down problems, the transition and use of the system will be easier on you and your users.

Second, enlist the help of your network assistants to put together a booklet or at least a list of guidelines to distribute to the rest of your employees. Include information about how to use the network, how and where to save files, procedures to accessing printers and other resources, and so on. You might also want to establish a method of updating these guidelines, such as by e-mail, memo, or other notices.

Finally, let your network assistants train users in each department to help with network support. For example, show them how to manage print queues of printers in their department or how to access certain network services. These trained users can then help the others in their department when a minor network problem occurs without bothering you or your network assistants.

Application Compatibility

One consideration before you jump into setting up your NT network is the compatibility of your applications with NT. For the most part, you'll install off-the-shelf applications such as word processors to individual workstations instead of to the server. Other applications, however, may be more useful installed and accessed from the server. Check to make sure you have multi-user applications and licenses for every user.

Make sure you read the application's documentation carefully for any special installation instructions for network use. For example, you must install Microsoft Access differently to a network than to a standalone computer and with many Lotus products, you will use a shared directory on the server for network distribution.

Of more consequence, carefully check your vertical market applications before installing them to NT Server. A vertical market application is a program written specifically for your business, such as printing estimating programs or car part inventory applications. These programs may have been written just for your company or you may have obtained them from your corporate office or other source. Check with the person or company that produced the software to make sure it will run on NT and that the company will support the application if you do run it on NT. A good example is one application written specifically for Novell NetWare networks; it *will* run on NT but the technical support group will *not* support the program if you do not run it on NetWare. So painstakingly verify all applications' compatibility before switching to NT Server as your network operating system.

Day-to-Day Administration

You may think that being a network administrator will be hard work; well, you're right. There are a lot of day-to-day responsibilities that must be performed for the network to run smoothly and successfully. Users will forget their passwords and lose files somewhere in the system. Applications will lock up; workstations will crash; printers will refuse to print. The number of problems associated with a network in any one day's time can be overwhelming; but cheer up, sometimes everything will work perfectly.

I can offer you a partial solution to this problem: delegate. NT enables you to assign certain rights to individuals or groups that enable them to perform some of the administrative duties; take advantage of that. Consider training a small group of network assistants in handling some of your administrative duties.

Assign someone whose workstation is near the printer to be the print manager. That person can then be responsible for keeping jobs flowing smoothly through the printer. Let a member of your IS (Information Services) department manage users' passwords, login (logon) times, profiles, and so on. Designate some of your duties to responsible people who can manage specific areas of network administration; divide the work and make life a lot easier on yourself. Sure, you'll have to take some extra time to show these people how to perform their duties (give them a copy of this book with the chapter marked that they need to read). Just think of the time you'll save in the long run.

Note: It's especially important for the network administrator to delegate power over the network to others for many reasons; but if you're hesitant to relinquish some of your power, consider that you want someone else to be able to run the network so you can go on vacation.

Integrating Networks

The NT Server operating system represents a Microsoft Windows network. You will likely use the computer running NT Server as the server part of client/server and, as previously mentioned, connect a variety of clients to the network. If you're just starting to network your company, using NT Server is the best way for you to provide services, security, resources, and other benefits of networking to your users. You might, however, already have a network in place and you're considering adding or switching to NT Server. In this section, I'll address various ways you can handle integrating networks, describing options and recommending solutions.

Note: If you're installing a new network and NT Server as your server's operating system, you can skip this section. All the information you'll need will be in the next few chapters, including Chapter 5.

Moving from a Peer-to-Peer Network

If you're currently running a peer-to-peer network—such as LANtastic or Windows for Workgroups 3.11—you'll probably want to change over to an NT client/server network. Client/server offers many advantages over peer-to-peer, as mentioned earlier in this chapter.

When preparing to switch to NT, the first thing you'll need is a computer to use as a server. You cannot use one of your workstations as a server unless it meets all of the hardware requirements needed to run NT. An NT Server computer must be powerful, have enough RAM to run efficiently, and have adequate disk space for the operating system, shared files, applications, and so on. See Chapter 4 for specific hardware needs.

Most likely, your client computers will work well with the new client/server network with little or no hardware additions. You might, however, want to upgrade client computers to run Windows 95 or Windows NT Workstation so your users can get the most out of the network resources. See Chapters 9 and 10 for more information.

It's important to note that if you are currently using LANtastic, you'll want to remove the LANtastic software from your workstations before attaching them to the NT network. LANtastic software is not compatible with NT protocols and services. You'll also want to check the network cards you use for LANtastic networking with the hardware compatibility list that comes with the NT Server software. Often the network adapter cards will work with NT, but sometimes they're not compatible.

If you're using Windows for Workgroups or Windows 95 peer-to-peer, keep all client software intact unless you're upgrading; various Microsoft operating systems work very well together.

Integrating Client/Server Networks

There are various client/server networks you might be using and want to continue to use with your NT Server network. Basically, Microsoft networks and Novell NetWare networks are the only ones you can successfully integrate with an NT network. So if you're using Banyan Vines or some other such NOS (network operating system), consider leaving it behind and moving onto NT.

If you're using a LAN Manager 2.2 server, it can act as a member server of the NT domain; that means it can supply files and some other resources to the network users but cannot authenticate users. LAN Manager member servers can also assist in some network control functions, but not all. Using LAN Manager servers on the NT network means your primary domain controller server is still NT and NT runs the network as the first server. LAN Manager servers become add-on servers that support users in limited ways on the network.

If you're currently using a Novell NetWare network (3.x or 4.x), you can easily integrate that network with NT or migrate your network to NT completely. Integrating the two networks, you can use NT's Gateway to supply file and print services to clients on the NetWare network. NT clients can also share NetWare's resources. Running the two operating systems side-by-side offers many advantages and disadvantages.

The Gateway Service for NetWare enables Microsoft networking clients to access NetWare file and print resources. Say you use a NetWare network, but you've been contemplating the NT Server operating system and its features and benefits. So, you set up a computer to run Windows NT Server, for any of a multiple of reasons:

- You're thinking of migrating to NT but not really sure you want to move all users and data from NetWare to NT Server.
- You want to use NT Server with the Internet (set up a Web site, WINS or DNS server, and so on). See Appendix C for TCP/IP information.
- You want to set up a remote access server for your mobile users.
- You want the advantages of Windows 32-bit operating system.
- You want the benefits of using domains in your network.
- You need to attach to other NT domains in your corporation.

When using the Gateway Service for NetWare, your NT clients can access available NetWare resources using the NT server as a gateway, or bridge. As long as the users have permissions and rights to the NT server and to the NetWare resources, they can use NetWare files, directories, and printers. For more information about permissions and rights in NT, see Chapter 7.

Any client computer running MS-DOS, Windows for Workgroups, Windows 95, Windows NT Workstation 3.51 or 4.0, or Windows NT Server 3.51 or 4.0 can access resources through the Gateway. Using the Gateway Service may be frustrating for clients on the NT network, however, because Gateway access is slower than if they had the NetWare client software installed to their computers. For more information about using NT's Gateway Service and/or migrating from NetWare 3.x or 4.x to NT Server 4.0, check out my book, *Migrating from Novell NetWare to NT Server 4.0*, (John Wiley and Sons, Inc., 1997).

An alternative to installing NT's Gateway Service to the NT Server, if the workstations have enough memory and space, you can load the NetWare client and the IPX/SPX protocol supplied with Windows NT Workstation 3.51 and 4.0 and Windows 95 to help speed up the access. Using the NetWare client and protocol means you can access either the NetWare server and its resources or the NT Server and its resources from the client without much trouble at all. Simply open the Network Neighborhood and choose the server to which you want to connect. For more information about loading protocols and services and using the Network Neighborhood, see Chapters 5, 9, and 10.

Summary

This chapter has covered advantages and disadvantages of two different networking types: peer-to-peer and client/server. Also included was information about NT

Server and how it fits into the client/server networking model. As you continue reading this book, you will learn more about NT and how to implement NT to provide a successful, efficient network for you and your users.

2 *Exploring Network Models*

Before installing the NT Server software, you should plan your directory structure, decide security issues, and have a fixed idea about how you want to build your system in terms of files, applications, directories, and users. Often, a network server is in use before the administrator finds problems with the structure that impede security and workflow. Once you create your directory structure and make the server available to your company, the application and data files are more or less permanently established. Take the time now to plan and organize so you can save yourself time and headaches later.

This chapter will help you to do the following:

- Plan the organizational structure of your server's files and directories.
- Choose or create a server model that suits your company.
- Decide how you want to organize users and groups in your company.
- Consider security issues and determine an effective way to assign rights and permissions within your company.

Your Organizational Structure

Using a network will definitely change the way you do business by eliminating inefficiencies while promoting effective and profitable growth. During this transition and after the network is up and running, your responsibilities will change, some employees' roles may shift, and the way you do business will certainly reflect the improved conditions. Your first job, perhaps your most important job, is to plan your network by appraising your current situation and assessing the needs of your business, your customers, and your employees.

Before putting your server into use, you must make some plans for the organizational structure of your network. The server generally serves several purposes on a network and each component should be outlined before you even install your server. Consider the following tasks a server performs:

- Authenticates users by verifying a user name and password. Authenticated users are allowed access to the network and its resources according to any limits the network administrator sets; for example, a user may be allowed to open, read, and write to a report file stored on the server but not allowed to view accounting files on the server.

- Stores files and directories for company use. These files may or may not be made available to all users of the network; additionally, the network administrator can choose which individual files, and even entire directories of files, are made available to users. For example, a shared directory may hold all correspondence written by all users so that any one user can view any file; but, another directory may only be accessible to department managers.

- Manages resources attached to the network. Using NT Server tools and features, you can manage printers, CD-ROMs, modems, and other peripherals attached to the network by setting permissions for use of the resource. Permissions include such limits as days and hours the resource can be used as well as who may use the resource. Also, you can manage printers by rearranging, canceling, and pausing print jobs from the print server.

- Stores and runs applications for use by network clients. You can install network versions of many software programs that enable multiple users to run the program at the same time. Installing an application on the network gives the administrator more control over the application settings, files, and usage.

- Manages events and tracks network problems. You can track and log various network problems—application or system errors and security breaches, for example—so you can monitor system use and troubleshoot problem areas.

- Accesses the Internet. With a modem, an Internet connection, and the Internet Explorer, the server can not only access the Internet but also enable users to access the Internet through the server.

- Backs up files, directories, and other data on the network. NT includes a backup program that creates backups of the server's files as well as files on the client computers; you can, alternatively, use a third-party application to back up data. You can back up data to the server, to a member or backup domain server, or to a tape drive or other device.

- Stores and distributes e-mail for the network. NT includes Microsoft Exchange, which you can use to create a post office that stores users' e-mail.

Users will need a Microsoft mail program on their computers to make use of Microsoft Exchange, but then they can send and receive messages over the network.

- Enables the sharing of files and other data. Depending on your security policies, users can share files and data for easier collaboration.

- Enables you to create and implement an intranet within your network for collaboration and distribution of data to your users.

With these factors in mind, you must decide how you can organize your server to best suit the needs of your company and employees.

Understanding Network Models

A network model is a plan for your directory structure. You'll want to consider how to devise the structure so that it best suits your users' needs and your security requirements. Keeping your directory structure and file-naming conventions consistent within the server means less confusion for your users and network assistants. Also, keep the directory structure similar for all servers on your network; using a consistent structure makes it easier for you to change settings, modify users, and perform other network-wide tasks.

If at all possible, stick with the application's default directories and file-naming conventions; doing so will make it easier on you if you need to upgrade software, procure technical help, and find information about the program.

When you install NT Server, some directories are automatically created by the system. Others must be planned and created by the network administrator. Using your knowledge about your company and the work you do, you must determine the directory structure that best suits your company's needs and capabilities. Consider the following points when creating a network model:

- Think about your office philosophy—is most data available to everyone in the office or are some files shared only sometimes and to some people?

- When creating the structure, can you build the basic outline of directories, then let each person or department organize its own data within that directory; or do you want complete control over the server's directories?

- Determine which files can be stored on individual workstations. Will applications be run from the server? Will customer files, employee data, and files used on a daily basis be stored on the server or the workstations?

- Ascertain which files and directories are sensitive or private and structure the directories to prevent access by some and grant access to others.

- Consider creating separate directories for applications, configuration files, drivers, shared data, and personal directories, as well as any other categories that accommodate your business.

- Make sure you provide enough directories for file storage and that the structure is easy to understand and navigate.

- Do not create structures that go too deep; for example, creating a 10-layer directory structure may cause you problems when you discover that one group or department needs access to a file on layer 9 or 10.

- Consider which of your workstations use an operating system that allows long file names; you may want to create separate directories to store each operating system's type of files. (DOS and Windows 3.1 vs. Windows 95 or Windows NT, for example; or Macintosh users vs. DOS).

One way to approach your server organization is to consider your company's structure. Is the company divided into departments, such as Sales, Advertising, Production, Management, and so on? Are departments then divided into additional sections? For example, is the Advertising department partitioned into Newspaper, Radio, and Television?

Your company may consist of several offices, each with its own structure, or simply contain 10 employees, each with many duties and titles. If you outline the organizational structure of your company as a first step, you can use this outline later when you're deciding how to design your file system and create users and groups.

You can use an outline form or an organizational chart to detail your company's structure. Figure 2.1 illustrates a simple outline you might construct. Divide the company into departments, then list the people or sections within each department. You might also make a list of file types each user might save to the server, and any special security, application, or file storage issues you can think of. For example, will all users need access to files on the server or can some users store their files on their workstation hard drives instead?

Figure 2.2 shows a sample organizational chart from which you can plan a file and directory structure as well as organize users and groups. Using different sized rectangles, you can quickly change this chart into a directory structure, as described in the next section. Additionally, use arrows to indicate who must have access to which files; you'll use this information to set your security policies, as described later in the chapter.

Think about the previous list as you continue reading this section. Make notes about your own business as you read through the models. You may find a model in the next section that fits your company exactly, or you may need to adjust the organization to better suit your needs.

Customer Service (access to Sales but not Accounting)
    Debbie (access to Accounting)
    Shawn
    Todd
    Judy

Sales (access to only Sales directory)
    Dave
    Elaine
    Mary
    Lou

Accounting (access to all files)
    Marie
    Bob
    Gene

File types: word processing, database, spreadsheet,
illustration files--all departments, all users

Figure 2.1 Outline your company's organizational structure as a basis for file and directory design as well as security management issues.

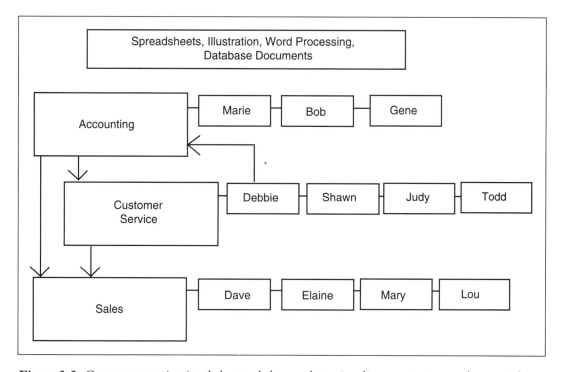

Figure 2.2 Create an organizational chart to help you determine directory structure and access rights.

Choosing a Server Model

A server model is simply a way of setting up a directory structure that best suits your business and the way you work. There are two basic models from which to choose a foundation for your server: global and departmental. One thing you must consider when setting up a directory structure is the security in your organization. Each model enables varying levels of security; however, you want to choose the model that will make your job as administrator easier while best serving the users. In addition, each model allows for many variations. The following structures are simply guidelines that should help you plan your own system.

TIP: Take a look at the directory structure on your own computer. Are you happy with how it is set up? Does it serve your needs or could the structure be improved? If you allowed other people to access your computer, how would the structure work for them? Would they be able to find the files they need?

The Global Model

A global model is based on the idea that all files are available to all users. If your company is open and most data is not sensitive, then you may want to implement this model. Naturally, you can still limit access to some directories and files within the global model; however, you'll want to carefully plan the structure in anticipation of your security issues. Figure 2.3 shows a sample directory structure that organizes files first according to the application, then into departments.

Users belonging to each department do not have personal directories on the server in this sample, although they could if it is necessary. User access to the directories and files will be discussed in a later section, "Users and Groups."

In the example shown, a directory is created for each type of document: word processing, spreadsheet, database, and illustration. The second layer of directories represents the company's departments: Sales, Customer Service, and Accounting. The third layer, shown in the figure for only the Sales department, contains directories to further organize the documents. In this particular example, the applications are stored on each workstation instead of on the server.

As an administrator, you can set up the directory structure to the first, second, or third level; you can let each department set up its own subdirectories; or you can vary this structure more to suit the needs of each department and user.

As far as security is concerned, each directory in the global model could easily be made available to all users. For example, a sales person might need to access a word processing report, a spreadsheet from accounting, and a customer service database. You can easily make all documents available to all users.

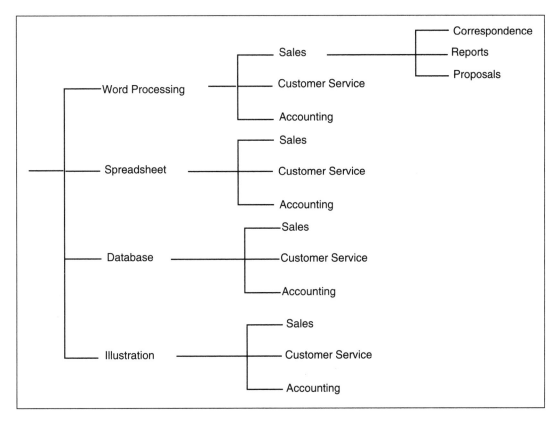

Figure 2.3 *The global model makes it easy to find specific file types.*

On the other hand, you could limit access to certain directories; for example, you could assign limited access to the Accounting subdirectories of all directories. However, other network models may be easier to use with limited access, as described in the following models.

You could, alternatively, add another first level directory (on the same level as Word Processing, Spreadsheet, Database, and Illustration) that contains Personnel files. This first level directory and all of its subdirectories can be marked as private so that only you, or certain people you designate, can view and use the data within.

Note: When making a directory accessible to some people and not others, you choose to share that directory with certain groups of people. Using NT Server's User Manager for Domains, you can set security policies that affect your directories, files, users, and groups, as described later in this chapter. For more information about the User Manager, see Chapter 6.

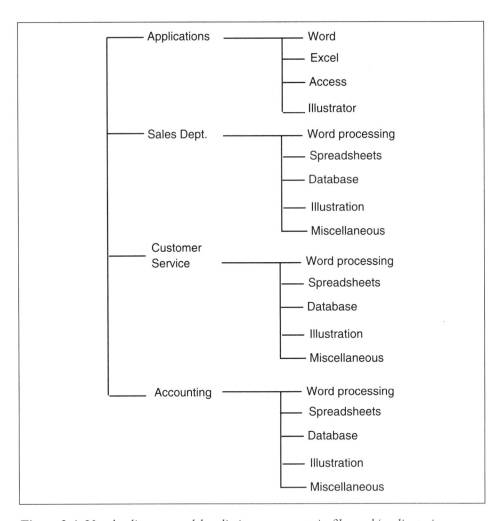

Figure 2.4 *Use the directory model to limit access to certain files and/or directories.*

The Department Model

The department model may suit your company's needs better if you have data that must remain confidential within the company. The department model is designed to limit access to other departments' directories and data. Figure 2.4 shows a sample directory structure, including a directory in which the applications are stored.

In this model, the application files are stored in one directory that is available to all users who need them. The other directories, however, limit access to the members of each department. The sales people, for example, can only access various files within the Sales Department directory. If a sales person needs a file from Customer Service, he or she needs to contact the system administrator to get a copy of that file. You, as system administrator, can at that point decide whether your sales person needs access to the Customer Service directory and all files contained or whether to copy one file and forward it to the sales person.

The members of the Accounting department, on the other hand, are granted access to all other department directories. Additionally, any one member of a department can be allowed access to any one file or directory. For example, in the earlier organizational chart, Debbie from Customer Service needs access to Accounting files; using the Department model, it would be easy to assign Debbie the rights she needs.

It's important that you set up the directory structure so as not to defeat your goal of easy administration. You don't want to constantly copy files from the Customer Service directory to give to your sales people; instead, move that directory of files to a shared directory from which the Customer Service and Sales Department can access the files they need.

Variations on a Theme

Using one of the two models as suggested may or may not work for your company. You'll want to consider the type of business you run, the type of data you use, and the organization of your employees. Be flexible when you design your network directory structure and, if at all possible, ask department heads and managers for their ideas before you set up the server.

Suppose your company deals with many, many clients, for example, as would a lawyer or doctor. You can apply either the global or the departmental model to a different type of directory structure.

Figure 2.5 shows a global model in which each customer is assigned a number and each number is a directory. Within each directory are subdirectories that contain various documents pertaining only to that particular customer. So, customer 98700's directory contains the subdirectories Proposals, Correspondence, and Quotations, as do the other directories on the list.

Additionally, two directories on the tree—Stephanie and Lisa—contain those documents pertinent to the staff members. These directories can also be made available to everyone or access can be limited to only the administrative staff, for example.

A different model can be used to organize the data in a different way. Using the department model, you can divide your directories into Proposals, Correspon-

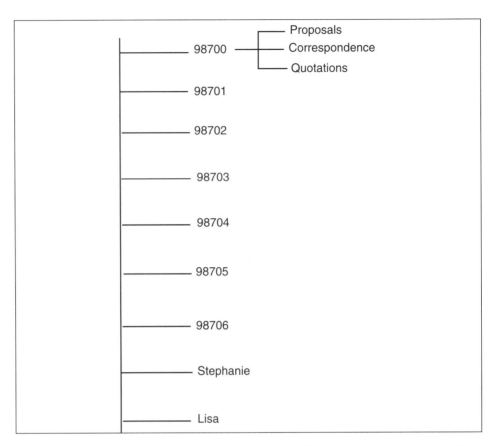

Figure 2.5 *A variation on a global model that accommodates customers or account numbers.*

dence, Quotations, and the like. Using this model, the second directory layer consists of the customer numbers and each customer number appears in each first level directory.

Therefore, all proposal documents related to customer 98701 appear in the Proposals/98701 directory. All letters pertaining to that same customer, however, would be found in the Correspondence/98701 directory. The advantage in setting up the network in this way is that only those people who need to see proposals have access to that directory (see Figure 2.6).

Again, you can easily grant access rights to individuals or groups of people so they have access to any or all directories on the server; your primary task here is to decide which structure works best for you.

Use these suggested models as a base for a structure that fits your company and your users. Sketch out several structures on paper before deciding on one.

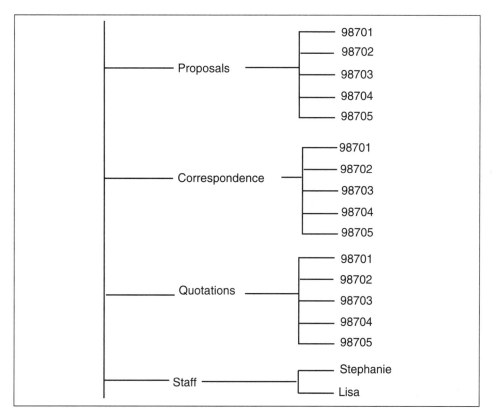

Figure 2.6 *A department model makes it easier to guarantee security for some documents.*

Organizing Files

After you decide on a directory structure, you'll also want to create standard naming conventions for the files on the system and choose where to store those files. Naturally, application files, server files, and other files installed by the system or any software programs have their own naming conventions and directory locations on the hard drive; you should never try to rename application and operating system files.

The files you will be naming, however, include the files you and the users of the network save to the server and to the workstation hard drives—documents, spreadsheets, databases, illustrations, accounting files, and others. Using a consistent file-naming convention throughout the network makes finding, backing up, deleting, and otherwise managing files easier and more efficient. Choosing where to store files makes it easier to keep track of documents, maintain tight security, and reduce network traffic.

Long File Names

It's important to discuss the long file names you can use with Windows NT 4.0 and Windows 95. In the past, DOS has limited the file name to an eight-character or less name with an optional three-character extension separated from the file name by a period (pronounced dot). Windows NT 4.0 (both Server and Workstation) and Windows 95 enable you to use up to 256 characters in a file name, including spaces. You cannot use the following characters in a long file name: \ | / ? : ★ " < >. Remember, the total number of characters you can use for a path and a file name is still only 260 characters, so keep that in mind when naming files. Here are some other facts about long file names:

- Long file names are the default format used in both Windows 95 and Windows NT Server and Workstation 4.0.
- If you copy a file with a long file name to a floppy disk, the long file name is preserved.
- Long file names aren't case-sensitive but they do preserve case.

When you specify a long file name without specifying an extension, the program that creates the file may add its own extension.

When you use long file names on your NT server, client computers running Windows 95 or Windows NT, and Macintosh computers can display and use those file names. However, any DOS-based client computers (including those running Windows for Workgroups) cannot use long file names.

Windows NT uses a set of rules, or algorithms, for converting the names to an 8.3 standard. First, all spaces are removed from the file name. Next, the first 6 characters of the long file name are used as the first 6 characters of the name (8). A tilde (~) is added and a number starting with 1 (up to 9) is also added. If necessary, 5 characters of the original name can be used, with the tilde, and the numbers 10 to 99. So the file name Marketing Analysis Report 1996 would become market~1.

For the extension, the first three characters after the period are used automatically. If, however, there is no period, there is no extension added. If a program adds its own extension—such as Word for Windows adds the DOC extension—that extension is used: market~1.doc, for example.

If by chance, the user on the DOS-based client changes a long file name to an 8.3 standard, the long file name is lost, even when it's used on an NT or Windows 95 computer.

Naming Files

There are many different ways to set up these standards for file naming. You must consider that with Windows NT Server, you can use long file names as well as the old DOS standard of 8.3 characters in a file name. Remember, though, if you have DOS or Windows 3.x clients on your network, they cannot read the long file names; only Windows 95, Windows NT Workstation, and Macintosh clients can recognize long file names.

You may also want to consider using application extensions within the file names—such as DOC for Word for Windows documents, 123 for Lotus 1-2-3 files, and so on. Although by default, Windows NT and Windows 95 do not show the extension in a file name, you can change that option within the program. Using the file extension makes searching for documents with wildcards easier as well as sorting file names easier. See Chapter 11 for more information.

Figure 2.7 shows the Windows Explorer with files listed and their extensions showing. The organization of files makes it easy to find the folder (directory) and the file you need quickly.

Note: To view the file name extensions in the Windows Explorer (in NT Workstation, NT Server, or Windows 95), choose View, Options. In the View tab of the Options dialog box, deselect the Hide MS-DOS File Extensions check box and click OK.

Wildcards

If you've used DOS much, you'll know how to use the wildcards for sorting and searching file names. You also can use those DOS wildcards in various Windows applications, including Windows Explorer, applications, and so on. The two wildcards used to help sort and search for file names are the asterisk (*) and the question mark (?). Use the asterisk as a replacement for several characters in a file name; for example, if you're looking for all files that end with the DOC extension, you represent it this way: *.DOC. The search feature will display files such as LET_Smit.DOC, 01-28-97.DOC, and so on. When looking for all files that start with LET, type LET*.* and the search feature will display LET_01sp, LET_SmithJake, LET_head.doc, and so on.

Use one question mark to replace one character in the file name when searching or sorting. For example, use LET_???.DOC to find file names such as LET_01s.DOC, LET_SMI.DOC, and so on.

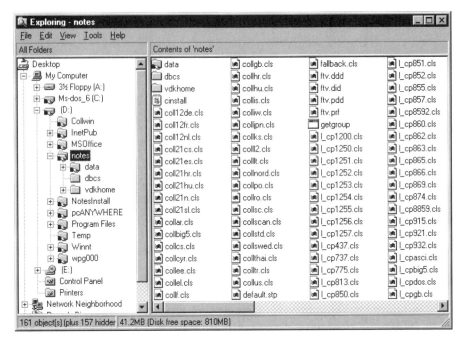

Figure 2.7 *Name your files for greater efficiency.*

You might use any of the following methods to name files network-wide or come up with your own ideas:

- *Date*: Use the day or month as part of the file name and/or add the last two numbers of the year; for example, advertising letters may be named 01-28-97 or 01_97. You could further distinguish between multiple files created on the same date by adding the initials of the creator, department abbreviations, additional numbers or code letters, and so on.

- *Customer's name*: Using a standard of the first five letters of a customer's last name works well in naming files, although you could use any number of letters, including first initials or names as well. You can also distinguish between multiple files in one customer's name by adding letters or numbers as codes; for example, name a file 01Smith, 02Smith, 03Smith, or 01PlumlS, 02PlumlS, and so on. Since Windows NT and Windows 95 do recognize uppercase and lowercase characters, you also can use this as a distinguishing factor.

- *Numbers* (customer, purchase order, invoice, case, and so on): Numbers work well for file names as long as users are careful to open and save the correct numbers; they can get confusing. So, you may want to use characters and numbers to help identify files; for example, PO909964 or PO909965 would help users differentiate pushes orders from these invoice numbers: IN099645 and IN099646.

- *More descriptive names*: Use names such as LET_Smith and LET_Pluml for letters to customers, REP_01-28 or REP_Qtr1 to identify reports, and JAN_news, JAN_radi, JAN_tele, and so on for January sales documents.

Whatever you decide, I recommend using the same number or characters to begin the file name for like files, so they'll be easier to locate and compare without opening every document. Also, if you can, use extensions that match the application in which the file was created. I don't recommend using 255 letters in a long file name just because you can; however, you should use enough letters to make the file contents easily recognizable. I also do not recommend letting each user choose his/her own way of naming files; after all, finding a letter you wrote to Jake Smith is much easier when viewing these files in a folder:

LET_DavisB
LET_PlumleS
LET_JohnsH
LET_SmithD
LET_SmithJ
LET_ThompD

than it would be to find that letter in the following list of files:

complainlet
1-28smith
dj28-smjd
letter-dj
smithomp1
smithomp2

Storing Files

The other part of storing files has to do with the location of the files. Do you want to store the files on the server or on individual workstations? Many factors contribute to the choice you make. Files stored on the server means more network traffic, thus the access to the files may slow at those times clients are accessing the most (such as first thing in the morning, right after lunch, and near the end of the day).

Disk space is another factor in deciding where to store files. If the server has plenty of space and the workstations have very little, you could create directories for each user on the server and let each user store his or her files there. If, however, there is enough room on the workstation for storing files personal to that user, I'd suggest letting each person create his or her own directory structure on his or her workstation's hard drive.

You may also want to limit the size and number of files a user can store on the server. Also, give users clear and concise instructions about how to keep their network space clean. Finally, consider archiving data on the server to an off-line storage area to help free disk space and prevent inevitable disk space problems.

You'll want to store files that must be accessed by two or more users on the server in a shared directory. You can, of course, designate which users may access that directory and those files, as explained later in this chapter. Furthermore, files that are confidential should be stored on the server as well, so you can keep your eyes our for security breaches (using the Event Viewer to view security logs).

Application Issues

Another consideration is whether you install your applications to the server for network use or to each individual workstation. First and foremost, check the applications you now have to see if they are labeled for network use and if they are compatible with Windows NT. Look in the application's documentation for licensing information, network and server installation, upgrade information, and so on. If you do not see these issues addressed in the application's documentation, call the manufacturer or technical support number listed in the paperwork to find the answers to the following questions:

Can I use this application on a server?

How many workstations can use the application when it's installed to the server?

Do I need to purchase additional licenses to use it on my network?

If not network compatible, what do I need to upgrade the application? Cost, equipment, and so on?

Are there any special installation instructions for server installation?

Will the company support (answer questions, solve problems) the software when it's installed to a network?

Note: Many applications also enable you to place them (often called network installation as opposed to server installation) on a server so your users can quickly install the applications to their workstations over the network instead of using disks or a CD-ROM. This saves time and work on your part and speeds installation in most cases; make sure, however, that you check licensing information and hardware requirements needed for the workstations.

Also consider the type of application before choosing where to install it. Database programs, accounting, and vertical (those written specifically for your business) programs often use shared files and need to be accessed by more than one person. These applications should be installed to the server for general use by the users that need them. On the other hand, a word processing program can easily be placed on the workstation hard drive and only the necessary document files may be stored on the server for sharing. If you do plan to install applications on the client computers, again make sure the application is compatible with the client's operating system (Windows 95, NT, or other OS).

Note: I don't recommend installing Windows 3.x on the server drive for use over the network to DOS machines; it would be slow, unwieldy, and tentative at best. Install Windows 3.x to the workstation computer. As an aside, Windows 95 and Windows NT Workstation are operating systems, unlike Windows 3.x, which is a program that runs on a DOS computer; so do not install either operating system onto the server for workstations to use through the network.

For more information about applications, see Part V, "Application Management," which includes Chapters 11, 12, and 13.

Users and Groups

In NT Server, you identify each user who is connected to the network. Give that user a user name and password, and create a user profile that describes how and when the user can access resources on the server. Groups are also included for easier administration and security uses.

A user is anyone who can log on to the network—an administrator, a guest, a user at a workstation, for example, anyone to whom you grant access. You can limit the access of any user by setting certain hours of the day for access, granting the user rights to perform tasks on the network and the server, or by giving the user permission to use files, directories, and other resources.

Using groups, both those built-in to NT and those you create, is an effective way of gathering users together and granting rights collectively. Suppose there are several people you want to enable access to the same printer and the same files on the server; instead of individually selecting each person and assigning those rights to each one, you can gather all of those people into a group and assign the rights to that group, once and for all. Then, any new users you want to have the same rights can be added to that group and voilà, their rights are granted; any one person you want to remove from the group has his rights canceled automatically. Groups are a great way of saving administrative time and organizing your users on the network.

Chapter 6 explains how you can create and manage users and groups in NT Server. In this section, I'm going to give you some ideas for organizing your users and groups.

Organizing Users

Your first task is to make a list of the users on your network and beside each person, list any restrictions you want to include in that user's profile. Remember in Chapter 1, I mentioned delegating some of your administrative power to others in your company? Now's the time to make note of those people and the power you want to delegate to them.

Note: The term *log on* means the user (including the administrator) must first enter the user name and password as assigned by the administrator before she or he can access the network or the server. Logging on to the server and logging on to the network are really the same thing, although technically you're logging on to the server. The only time you'll see a difference here is if there are multiple servers on the network; you can log on to each server, one at a time, to use the resources that server manages. For more information, see Chapter 14.

Table 2.1 presents a list of elements you can set for each user's account. Only the username and password are required; the rest of the elements are optional. Make a list of your users, passwords, and any special restrictions or other data you want to use for each account. Figure 2.8 shows the Users Properties dialog box in the User Manager for Domains, NT's application for managing users.

For now, use this information to group your users; later, you can use this information to create users in NT and set their rights and limits.

Organizing in Groups

In addition to creating user accounts in which you define a user and his or her limits, you can assign users to various groups to make administration of those limits easier. NT includes several built-in groups that I'll briefly describe. The built-in

Table 2.1 Account Elements

ELEMENT	DESCRIPTION
User Name	A unique log-on name, such as a combination of the user's last and first names (PlumleSJ, JohnsoGH, and so on); keep user names consistent throughout.
Full Name	The user's full name.
Description	Any text describing the account, such as Director or Sales.
Password	The user's confidential password; however, you probably won't want to assign the permanent password. For now, just use one general password and later the user can change the password to suit him or herself.
Logon Hours	The hours the user is allowed to log on to the server and use allotted resources; you may want to exclude weekends and evenings for some users.
Expiration Date	A date in the future when the account automatically expires; use this feature for temporary guests or users.
Profile	A file that determines the user's individual desktop settings (in Windows 95 and Windows NT Workstation only); you can control the user's colors, network connections, and other environmental elements so that everyone's desktop looks the same or some desktops differ for specific reasons.

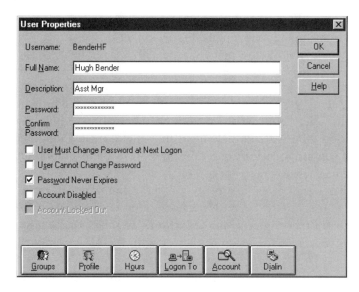

Figure 2.8 *Create a user's profile in great detail, if you want.*

Table 2.2 Groups

GROUP	DESCRIPTION
Administrators	Complete control over the network, from creating users to formatting the server's hard disk; limit the number of users you place in the Administrators group.
Server Operators	Less control over the server—can back up files, create groups, mark directories and printers as shared.
Account Operators	Creates and manages user accounts and groups.
Print Operators	Manage printing, stop printing, share printers.
Backup Operators	Back up and restore files on workstations and the server.
Users	No real rights on the server except to access it.
Guests	No rights on the server.

groups automatically grant the members of that group certain rights to perform tasks and procedures on the server. Additionally, you can add rights of different types to any of the groups. Chapter 6 deals more with the groups; for now, think about how your users fit into each group. You don't have to use all of the groups listed in Table 2.2; you can create your own groups if these aren't quite suitable to your needs.

TIP: While reviewing the following table, remember that you might want to delegate some of your administrative powers, especially as your network expands.

There are some general guidelines you might want to follow when assigning users to groups. There must be at least one member of the Administrators group; this is the person who is responsible for planning and maintaining network security. I suggest you assign at least one other person to the Administrators group to take care of things when you're not at work.

Rather than assign too many people to the Administrators group, you could assign two or so users to the Server Operators group as a backup, in case the members of the Administrators groups are not at work on the same day. The Server Operators can perform many tasks on the server until the Administrators get back to work.

If you want to delegate some authority, assign users who are responsible for hiring and firing employees to the Account Operators group. These users can create new users on the server and assign them to groups. Additionally, an Account Operator can remove users from the network prior to firing them, to prevent any transgressions by an angry ex-employee.

Assign qualified people to the Print Operators group, depending on how many printers are connected to your network. If you have only one printer, one or two Print Operators will do. If you have several printers and many print jobs circulating each day, you'll want to assign more Print Operators to manage the printers and print queues, and address printer problems quickly.

Your best bet is to train at least two people for every delegated responsibility, one as a backup. If you find you need more help with any task, you can always add more people to the group.

Miscellaneous Factors

There are just a few more things you might want to consider before continuing with your network. These are miscellaneous, unrelated issues but each is important enough to merit your attention.

Although network security is covered more fully in Chapter 7, here's another thought about your server. If files on the server are really critical, consider placing the server in a secured room, under lock and key if necessary. Another option would be to remove the keyboard from the server when you're not around or not using the server.

As for using the server as your own workstation, even though you certainly can, you probably shouldn't for several reasons. A dedicated server is much more efficient for handling file and print services than a server used as a workstation. Additionally, performing your personal work on the server leaves it open for perusal, security infractions, system or application errors, and so on.

Instead of using the server, consider installing NT Server to another computer as a member server—a server that doesn't authenticate but does manage printing, the Internet, or some other resource. You can use a less strategic server as your personal workstation.

In the client realm, I recommend against attaching a DOS client to your network. Even though it's possible and NT ships with a DOS client, the headaches you'll get from trying to keep the computer attached to the network just isn't worth it. Upgrade the hardware and go with a Windows 95 or Windows NT Workstation operating system, if at all possible. If you're really attached to your Windows for Workgroups 3.11 clients, you can successfully connect them to the network, but you'll lose security, network browsers, and other advantages. See Chapter 10 for more information.

Finally, as previously mentioned, you'll want to hire a hardware person to help you with your network adapter cards and cabling, if your computers are not already networked. If you're not sure of what the following things mean, ask your hardware person to check them for you. When networking client computers, keep the following facts in mind:

- Make sure your hardware is worth connecting to the network. Old computers that are already on their last legs shouldn't be upgraded; they should be replaced.

- Check to see that your workstations have an empty slot for the network cards; older machines might not have the room needed.

- If you have Pentium workstations and you're using 16-bit cards, make sure you have an open 16-bit slot; most Pentiums have a limited number of slots.

Summary

In this chapter, you've learned about various network models for organizing your server's directories, file-naming conventions, and information about organizing your users and groups of users before you install NT and set up your server. Remember, the more plans you can make now, the better off you'll be when the network is up and running.

3 *Requirements and Compatibility*

efore you can install NT Server, make sure you have the proper hardware to run the operating system. Use the appropriate processor and sufficient RAM, and check the compatibility of all peripheral devices so that when you install NT, you will not run into any surprises along the way. Also, you will need to check on your client computers—hardware, operating systems, and so on—see Chapter 9 for more information.

This chapter covers the following:

- Hardware requirements for an NT Server
- Considerations for peripherals to use with NT Server
- Network layout and design

Whether you're upgrading your present network, adding to an existing network, or starting a network for running NT, this chapter can help you plan for the computer hardware, printers and peripherals, and software you will use with NT.

NT Networking Architecture and Hardware Selection

Without going into all of the technical details of the NT operating system architecture, there are a couple of facts about NT's system design that will help you purchase hardware for its use. If you understand some of the basic components of the architecture, you can better plan and upgrade your system hardware.

One important question is how many servers will you need for your network? That's a difficult question to answer because it depends on the number of clients you have connected to the network, clients' needs for applications, peripherals, and other resources, and the services you want to offer to your clients. Considering NT's design may help you make your decision.

Another question you may have deals with the celebrated stories of NT's multiprocessing capabilities. Do you really need a server computer with multiple processors? Perhaps I can answer that question, as well.

Client/Server Computing

Basically, NT is designed for client/server computing. Servers offer services and clients consume those services. The server can service multiple clients at the same time and regulate their access to shared resources; but it is the client that initiates the exchange by requesting the service while the server passively waits for requests.

The server normally resides on a different machine than the client, across a network; clients can consist of various hardware or operating system software platforms. Additionally, client/server systems are scalable, meaning clients and servers can be added to the network to increase the number served and to enhance services.

Depending on the size of your network, you may need two or more servers to provide for your clients (see Figure 3.1). A computer running the NT Server software can perform many functions on the network, following are the most common:

- *Authentication server*: At least one network server must validate users' login information. Authentication usually involves comparing the user name and password to a list of authorized users. If a match is found, the user can log in and access the system in accordance with the rights and permissions assigned to the user's account. NT designates the primary domain controller (PDC) as the first server of the network, the server that authenticates users.

- *Backup server*: In NT, you can use a backup domain controller (BDC) as a backup for authentication of users. The backup domain controller keeps updated copies of all user accounts, rights, and permissions listed on the primary domain controller so that in case the PDC computer goes down, the BDC can continue services without disturbing the network or the users. See Chapter 4 for more information about PDCs and BDCs.

- *File server*: File servers store data—documents, images, drawings, accounting files, and so on—that clients can request over the network. The files on a file server are shared among the clients; shared files can be read, reviewed, and updated by more than on individual. Access to the files may be regulated by password protection or account or security clearance.

- *Print server*: A server that handles the printing for all users and all printers on the network. The server collects the print jobs and places them in a print queue on the hard disk, then routes them to one or more printers attached

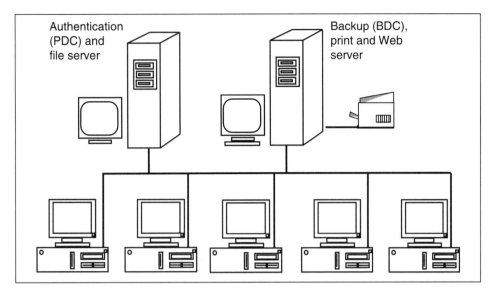

Figure 3.1 *Two or more servers on the network can share responsibilities and services.*

to the server or the network. The print queue is a list of documents waiting to be printed; one queue normally exists for each printer on the network.

- *Database server*: A database application that follows the client/server architecture divides the database application into two parts: a front-end running on the client computer and a back-end running on the server. The front-end collects and displays data while the back-end performs the computations, analysis, and storage of the data. An application server.

- *Web server*: A server that supplies documents to clients when requested. The Web server may provide services to your internal intranet of users, those attached to your LAN (local area network) only. A Web server may additionally or separately be attached to the Internet, thus serving clients over the World Wide Web. An application server.

- *Groupware servers*: Groupware applies to the distribution of mail, bulletin boards, images, and workflow to place people in direct contact with other people. Lotus Notes is an excellent example of a groupware application. Often, not only a specialized server is needed to manage groupware information, but a specially trained manager or administrator may also be needed. An application server.

You may or may not require all of the servers listed to run your network or you may want to start slowly and build your network as your business grows since purchasing the hardware, cabling, and operating systems for multiple servers can be quite expensive initially. For example, you could start with one server, the primary domain controller, and let that server handle file and print services. If your network is small (up to 50 users), one server can take care of many of your clients' needs.

As you depend more on your server and your network grows, you can add a backup domain controller, for example, to guarantee seamless networking and client authentication in case your primary server crashes. The backup domain controller can also be used for other tasks, such as a print server, Web server, even a groupware server. I suggest you start with the minimum number of servers and build onto your system, analyzing the performance and network demands as you go.

Multiprocessing/Multiple Processors

Most computers contain one processor, or central processing unit (CPU); a uniprocessor system can only perform one task at a time, even if it is using a multitasking operating system such as NT. The CPU switches between tasks quickly, so it appears to be performing two or more tasks at once, but it really only performs one task at a time.

Note: *Multitasking*, a term related to multiprocessing, is an operating-system technique for sharing a single processor among multiple threads of execution. The difference between the two is that a multitasking operating system only appears to execute multiple threads at the same time; a multiprocessing operating system does execute multiple threads at the same time.

In a multiprocessor system, one containing two or more processors or CPUs, multiple tasks can be performed simultaneously. For example, one processor may be running the operating system while another is accessing files for an application you are running.

Two types of multiprocessing exist: asymmetric and symmetric. Asymmetric multiprocessing assigns the tasks, sometimes in an unbalanced manner, that each processor runs; so one processor may be performing most of the tasks while another processor sits nearly idle. Symmetric multiprocessing, on the other hand, uses any available processor as needed, which helps to balance the computer's workload and provide fault tolerance (a design method that ensures continued system operation in case of an individual processor failure).

Serving Macintosh Clients

If you have Macintosh clients connected to your network, you won't need any additional hardware specifically to serve those clients. NT's architecture includes complete support for Macintosh networking. NT supports all Macintosh file system attributes, filenames, icons, and access permissions. Macintosh fully supports and complies with Windows NT security so that users can access files that reside on CD-ROM drives or other read-only media.

As the NT administrator, you can administer the services for Macintosh from the Control Panel. You can also create Macintosh-accessible volumes in the My Computer window. Administration and configuration of printing for Macintosh clients is simple since there is built-in printer support in Windows NT. For more information about Macintosh clients, see Chapter 9.

Windows NT is a symmetric multiprocessing (SMP) operating system. NT can support up to four microprocessors, speeding and improving performance, especially with applications designed with multiprocessing in mind.

Major applications that were designed for Windows NT will improve significantly in performance if your server computer has multiple processors; however, older 16-bit applications and applications that don't support multiprocessing may not show any performance improvement. Therefore, assess the applications you will be using to see if multiple processors in your server would benefit system performance. See the sidebar, "Networking Layers," later in this chapter for more information about NT's networking architecture.

Server Hardware Considerations

Windows NT Server is a versatile operating system that can operate on various hardware platforms, including x86-based microprocessor, Intel Pentium, or RISC-based microprocessor such as MIPS R4x00 or PowerPC. The following recommendations are for Intel processors; for information about RISC-based hardware requirements, see your NT documentation. As with any hardware you purchase for NT Server, check the hardware compatibility list (HCL) that comes with the operating system to make sure you purchase only equipment compliant with that list.

Using an Intel processor, you'll need a 32-bit x86-based microprocessor that is 80486/25mhz or higher for NT to run successfully. Alternatively, you can use an

Intel Pentium processor, which is highly recommended for efficiency and effective server operation.

NT also requires a VGA or higher resolution monitor. I suggest staying with an S3-based video accelerator; it may not be the fastest board but it is the most solid and less expensive than most. NT includes a S3 video driver you can use.

Although you can run NT Server with 16M RAM, you will want at least 32M on the server. Depending on your server needs—file and print server, remote access services (RAS), Internet connections, and so on—you may need even more RAM. Start with 32M, then determine whether you need more memory after running the server in your organization for a test period.

You will need 125M minimum of free disk space to hold the NT Server system files for an Intel processor. You may want to use a small computer system interface (SCSI)-based hard disk; NT supports most SCSI adapters although you should refer to the hardware compatibility list (HCL) before you purchase one. Using a SCSI-based system means you'll receive better fault tolerance; also, disk mirroring and RAID work best with a SCSI disk subsystem. Additionally, NT successfully supports integrated device electronics (IDE) drives.

Also, you will need a 3.5-inch floppy high-density disk drive plus a CD-ROM drive. Again, check the HCL before trying to install NT. If you do not have a CD-ROM drive on the server or if you only have a 5.25-inch floppy drive, you can install the software over the network.

A mouse or other pointing device is strongly recommended, as with any Windows program. You'll have better luck with a PS/2-type mouse than any other.

To use NT Server on a network, you will need a network adapter card. NT can support one or more network adapter cards; check the HCL for compatibility.

Peripherals and Printers

Before purchasing any peripherals—CD-ROM drive, modem, printer, or any other hardware attached to the server or network—make sure you check with NT's hardware compatibility list. If the hardware isn't on the list, it probably won't work with the NT operating system.

If you already have peripherals in place on your network, make sure they are compatible; if they are not, upgrade if at all possible. If you have older printers, for example, that are not worth upgrading, you might attach the printer to one workstation (such as a DOS computer) and use it as a local printer for that one client. This section reviews a few common peripherals and issues concerning them.

Drivers and Software

In addition to the actual hardware, you'll want to make sure you have all of the software you need to use your peripherals with the NT system. NT supplies many drivers for peripherals, but make sure you have the appropriate drivers and software for your devices. If the software isn't provided by NT, contact the peripheral's manufacturer to see if they have developed and distributed NT drivers for that specific device. You might also check the Internet for updated drivers and software. Check the software for the following peripherals:

- UPS (Uninterrupted Power Source)
- Backup Tape Drives
- CD-ROM Drives and/or Towers
- Sound Cards
- Optical Disk Drives
- Modems and/or Modem Servers
- Print Devices

Keep in mind that Windows NT 3.5x drivers are not compatible with Windows NT 4.0 and not all Windows 95 drivers are compatible either.

CD-ROM Drives

Windows NT supports the three basic types of CD-ROM drive controllers: ATAPI or IDE (integrated drive electronics), SCSI, and Proprietary. ATAPI/IDE CD-ROM drives connect directly to a conventional IDE controller since they are popular interface standards. Using this type of drive means less additional hardware to add to your server computer. Note that if you have an older BIOS on your computer (before January 1995), it may not recognize an ATAPI CD-ROM drive for what it is; the BIOS might assume the drive is a hard drive instead. NT will, however, recognize the CD-ROM drive and list it as such.

SCSI (small computer system interface) is a high-speed parallel interface used to connect the CD-ROM to the computer. You need a SCSI host adapter in your system to make use of the SCSI CD-ROM drive. This host adapter may already be a part of your system or can be installed as an adapter card. The main thing to watch out for with a SCSI CD-ROM drive is that it doesn't conflict with other devices. NT can automatically detect a SCSI CD-ROM drive.

A proprietary CD-ROM controller requires you set jumpers or switches to control the IRQ (interrupt request), DMA (direct memory access), or memory addresses they use. DMA is a method of transferring information directly from a mass-storage device, such as a CD-ROM, into memory without passing through the processor, which makes DMA a fast access method. A memory address is the exact location in memory that stores the data item.

Additionally, a proprietary CD-ROM controller will take up one of your expansion slots inside the computer, usually an ISA (Industry Standard Architecture) slot. Make sure you follow the card's documentation and instructions for setting jumpers and installing the drivers under Windows NT.

Video Cards

Most new video cards you purchase will include an NT driver, especially the popular brands. Also, NT includes support for most major brands of video cards. Make sure, once again, to check the hardware compatibility list before installing NT to your server computer.

Make sure you have the exact video card driver for your video card; some chipsets (S3, for example) have different types of drivers that may seem interchangeable, but are not. Check to be sure you have the exact name and manufacturer for the card.

Check the hardware settings of your video card in the card's documentation. If the card has jumpers or DIP switches that govern IRQs, make sure you adjust those hardware settings. A jumper is a small connector (either plastic or metal) that completes the circuit on the card itself. A DIP switch (dual in-line package) is the housing commonly used to hold an integrated circuit. Jumpers and DIP switches usually let you select one particular hardware configuration from a choice of configurations.

The IRQ (interrupt request) is one example of a hardware configuration; an IRQ signals that an event has taken place that requires the processor's attention. If you have trouble with your video card, you'll want to check to see that the IRQ being used on the video card is not being used by some other device.

NT is particularly sensitive to video cards and drivers after installation of the operating system; a failed or misconfigured video card can render NT unbootable. If, after installation of the operating system, your video card stops working or is configured using the wrong driver, you can choose the standard boot option: Windows NT 4.0 (VGA mode).

Note: The Windows NT 4.0 (VGA mode) option appears on a DOS-like screen during the NT boot process. In the *boot loader screen*, you can choose to start NT normally, special VGA mode, or boot to an alternate operating system such as

DOS. If your video driver isn't working, choose the VGA mode option to open NT and reconfigure the video card. For more information, see Chapter 5.

Modems

You may want to add a modem to your server to connect to the Internet or to use for RAS, which allows users to call in to the server and access network resources. NT makes modem installation and use fairly simple, by use of a Wizard. Wizards are step-by-step guides in the form of dialog boxes that lead you through installation and configuration processes in Windows. NT can autodetect your modem and configure it for you; or you can modify any configuration settings manually, if you prefer. As always, make sure the modem is on NT's hardware compatibility list before you install it to the server.

NT includes many modem drivers for various manufacturers and models. NT can manage a modem with speeds up to 57,600 baud, enables you to configure data bits, parity, and stop bits for the specific modem, and even lets you set error control and data compression options.

Printers

You can install printers locally or for network use. A printer installed locally means that only the computer to which it is attached can use it. You might, for example, want to designate a local printer to a computer that prints invoices or forms of some kind. A network printer may be attached to the server or to any computer on the network; when you install the network printer drivers to the NT server, you make that printer available to users of the network.

NT is extremely compatible with many printers—dot matrix, inkjet, and laser, for examples—and includes many drivers you can use with your printers. Check the HCL before buying a printer, however, and make sure any printers already in use are compatible as well. If you don't see the printer's manufacturer and the printer model in the HCL, check your printer's manual to see if it's compatible with another popular brand of printer. For example, an off-brand laser printer may be compatible with, or emulate, one of Hewlett Packard's LaserJet printers; you could then use the HP driver for your printer.

Note: After you install a network printer, you can control who can use the printer and even when they may use the printers. For more information about printers, troubleshooting printing, and print servers, see Chapter 8.

Compatibility Issues

Some general compatibility issues for Windows NT Server are listed here. For specific information, see the HCL that came with the NT software. You might also check the Release Notes readme file on the NT CD for more information. For an updated HCL, you can download from the Internet; see Microsoft's Web page at http:\www\microsoft.com. Note: since I'm only discussing x86 processors in this book, I've left out such items as MIPS RISC, Digital Alpha AXP RISC, and so on, in the following list.

The following list contains general information; for manufacturer's and specific models, see the HCL. Multiple manufacturers are represented for each device listed.

Hardware	*Specifications*
Processor	x86 architecture uniprocessor
	x86 architecture multiprocessor
	x86 PCMCIA (plus support for network adapters, add-in adapters, and modems, ISDN adapters, Serial and SCSI adapters for PCMCIA)
SCSI Adapters	CD-ROM, tape, scanners, fixed and removable drives
Non-SCSI	CD-ROM, tape drives
Display Adapters	640x480, 800x600, 1024x768, 1280x1024
Network Adapters	ISA, MCA, EISA, PCMCIA, PCI, VLB
Keyboards	102/102-key and IBM AT (84-key)
Pointing Devices	All versions of Logitech and Microsoft and those 100% compatible with these.

Additionally, multiple manufacturers are listed for various UPS, multimedia audio adapters, and multiple modems; plus a few manufacturers and models are listed for hardware security hosts, ISDN adapters, multi-port adapters, X.25 adapters, and third-party remote access servers. As for printers, NT includes many various drivers for nearly a thousand printer models. Finally, Windows NT includes many device drivers in the \DRVLIB directory on the Windows NT CD-ROM.

Considering Network Adapter Cards, Cabling, and Topologies

Earlier, I suggested you find a knowledgeable, competent consultant who can handle your network cabling and hardware installation, if you're not comfortable with performing those tasks on your network. I still believe that is the best way to go; however, I want to give you some information about network cards, cabling, and topologies—the inner workings of your network—so you can discuss your hardware setup with the consultant and help in making some of the more important decisions.

This section provides information about which network adapter cards you should use with your NT network, advice and information about the cabling schemes, and an outline of topologies you will want to consider.

Network Adapter Cards

Network adapter cards, or network interface cards, plug into your server or workstation to work with the operating system to control the flow of information over the network. The network card is connected to the cable, which in turn connects all the network interface cards on the network. Depending on the configuration of the network, you'll use hubs to connect multiple cables from the workstations. A hub modifies transmission signals, thus allowing the network to be extended to accommodate additional workstations. Each topology and adapter card requires a specific hub that is compliant with that type.

The network card(s) you choose for your server (and for your client computers as well) depends on several factors—speed, expense, and the topology of your network. Foremost, make sure the network adapter card you use is compatible with Windows NT Server by checking the HCL.

Match the network card you choose with the topology of the network. Topology is the map of a network—the direction in which the cables run between workstations, servers, gateways, and so on—and the path data takes to get from one user to another on the network. Topology is discussed more in the next section.

Basically, there are four types of network cards from which you can choose: 10Mbit (megabit—equivalent to one million bits), 100Mbit, fiber, and wireless. Each of these card types works with a specific topology; each has advantages and disadvantages.

The 10Mbit card is used with a 10BaseT topology and has been around for quite some time. Basically, the 10Mbit card is waning technology but it's okay for a small office to use. One definite advantage is that this type of card is relatively inexpensive. One disadvantage is that it's not really very fast, especially for sending large amounts of data or images over the network.

The 100Mbit card is used with 100BaseT topology. 100Mbit card is 10 times faster than the 10Mbit, so it's perfect for using with large data files, video or sound files, images, and so on. The 100Mbit card is more expensive than the 10Mbit card, both to purchase and to install. Installation of the cable is more expensive than the 10Mbit because with 100Mbit, the cable must be certified.

Also, you'll need to make sure the computer you're installing the 100Mbit card to has a PCI slot. PCI (peripheral component interconnect) is an Intel specification that defines a local bus, allowing up to 10 PCI-compliant expansion cards to be plugged into the computer. The PCI controller exchanges information with the computer's processor at either 32 or 64 bits.

Note: If your budget is tight but you would like to use the 100Mbit for your network, I'd suggest purchasing the 10/100Mbit cards to begin with; they can attach to either a 10Mbit or 100Mbit network. Use the 10Mbit hub to start with, as well. This will work fine and still be an improvement over using 10Mbit cards because when you need it, you can add the 100Mbit hub to your system to make it a 100BaseT network.

The fiber card uses a FDDI (fiber distributed data interface) networking method, which follows a ring topology. You'll need a PCI slot for the fiber card, as well as fiber cabling. The fiber card, fiber cabling, and fiber hubs are expensive to purchase and the cabling is expensive to install.

Finally, the wireless card is another choice. Wireless is a method of connecting the workstations to the network without using conventional cabling. Infrared is one method of wireless connections; infrared uses high-frequency light waves to transmit data between two computers up to 80 feet apart using an unobstructed path. Another method of wireless connection is through high-frequency radio signals, which can transmit data between computers up to 130 feet apart. Spread-spectrum radio is another method, but distances are limited to 110 feet and data rates are usually less than 1 megabit per second. The wireless card is expensive and probably slower than any of those previously mentioned. Wireless also uses the token-ring topology.

Topologies

LAN topologies refer to different methods of arranging and connecting the computers on your network. Each topology has advantages and disadvantages. Those topologies from which you'll choose include the star (or spanning tree) topology or ring network.

Star and Spanning Tree

The star topology connects computers through a central hub (see Figure 3.2) and the hub distributes signals to all connecting cables. The server(s) and workstations

When to Use Two Network Cards

NT Server enables you to use multiple network cards with different protocols; you would not normally need two cards in the server, however. You can use multiple protocols with one network card; for instance, use the NT Server to communicate with its clients using NetBEUI and the Internet using TCP/IP. You would only use two network cards when the NT Server needs to communicate with two different networks.

One example of when you might want to use two cards is if the NT Server is acting as a gateway, or router, between two networks—such as NetWare and Windows networks. Say the NT Server serves a group of Microsoft clients (Windows 95, Windows for Workgroups, and so on); you install one network card to run the NetBEUI protocol, for example, to communicate with these clients.

The NT Server also communicates with a NetWare network (NetWare server and clients connected to that server) using an IPX/SPX (Internet packet exchange/sequenced packet exchange) protocol. The IPX/SPX protocol is attached, or bound, to a second network adapter card so that the NT Server can communicate with both networks, at the same time, and even act as a bridge between the two.

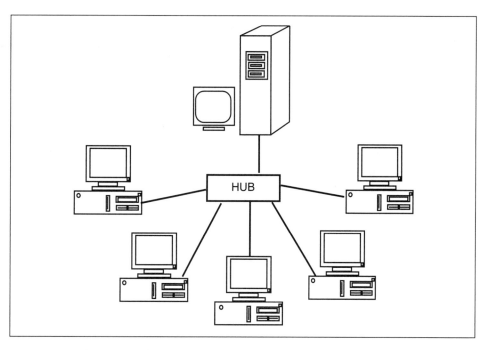

Figure 3.2 *The star topology helps protect each node from one bad cable on the network.*

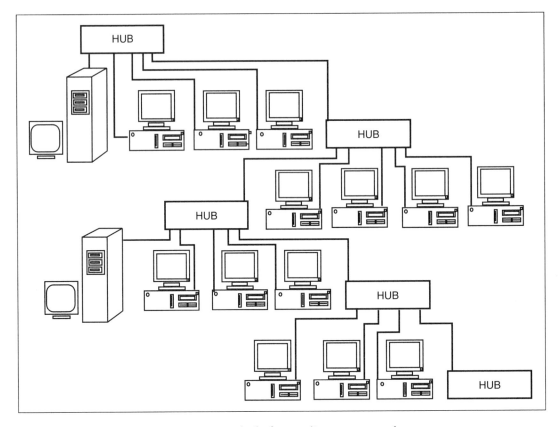

Figure 3.3 *Build a spanning tree as a method of expanding your network.*

are connected to the hub, each with a separate cable; the hub, then, modifies the transmission signals so each attached device receives input over the network.

10BaseT and 100BaseT use a modified star topology called the spanning tree. With the spanning tree topology, each hub and its connections form a star but also connect to other hubs in a branching design (see Figure 3.3). Using hubs, you can attach servers, workstations, and more hubs together, thus extending the network as needed.

The advantage of using a hub is that each cable connected to the hub is protected from all other cables; therefore, if one cable is damaged, only one computer on the network is affected. There are different sizes of hubs and varying numbers of devices that can be attached to a hub; one hub could connect to 8 computers or hubs and another may connect to 24, 48, and so on. The disadvantage of using the spanning tree is that central hub equipment can be expensive, especially for the 100BaseT hub.

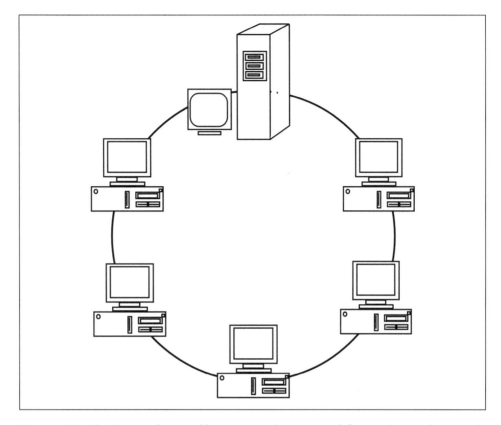

Figure 3.4 *The ring topology enables message tokens to travel from node to node, around the ring.*

Ring Topology

On a ring network, a computer sends a message, or token, that controls the right to transmit; the message is continuously passed from one node to the next, in one direction only, around the network. A node is any device connected to the network and capable of communicating with other network devices.

When a node has data to transmit, it captures the message, adds the message and destination address, then sends the token on, as shown in Figure 3.4. If the address matches a node's address, the message is accepted; if not, the node regenerates the message and places it back on the network where it travels to the next node in the ring. Ring networks can cover greater distances than star networks. Ring networks generally use some form of token-passing protocol, such as token-ring, to regulate network traffic.

The ring topology can use standard telephone wiring to connect up to 72 devices or shielded twisted-pair wiring to support up to 256 devices, or workstations. Although based on a closed-loop ring structure, a ring network uses a star-shaped cluster of up to eight nodes that are attached to the same wiring concentrator or MAU (multistation access unit). MAUs are then connected to the main ring circuit. The biggest disadvantage of token-ring topology is that if there's a failure somewhere on the network—wiring, network card, or other hardware problem—the token cannot pass until the problem is corrected.

Cabling

The cable you use to connect your network is of major importance. As previously mentioned, you might use a wireless form of connecting nodes; but for the most part, you'll probably use cabling instead. I'd recommend using wireless connections only in situations where you cannot run a wire or a long-range connection is too costly. Wires provide better security and throughput. You may hear the term *media* used to refer to methods of connecting nodes. Bound media is usually cabling and unbound media is the wireless form of connection.

Coaxial

Coaxial cable is fairly inexpensive, but I wouldn't suggest using it to cable your network. Coaxial cable isn't upgradeable; it will run at speeds no greater than 10Mbit. Also, if there's a cable problem anywhere on network, everyone on the network goes down. If you have to work on one node or move a node on the network, everyone on the network goes down. Finally, because of its very nature, coaxial cabling clutters the office with multiple cables, making an unattractive area anywhere a computer is attached.

Twisted Pair

Twisted-pair cable uses several pairs of wires braided together within a plastic sheath. Electrical signals travel on each wire and are protected from interference by the sheath. Shielded twisted-pair cable (STP) is cable with a foil shield and copper braid surrounding the pairs of wires. STP offers high-speed transmission for long distances and it's often associated with token-ring networks. Unshielded twisted-pair cable (UTP) is cable that contains two or more pairs (often four pairs) of twisted copper wires. UTP is easier to install than STP and less expensive; it does, however, limit the signaling speeds and uses shorter cable-segments.

There are several types of twisted-pair wires, but Category 3 and Category 5 are the most commonly used. Category 3 wire is less expensive but also less advanced as far as rate of transfer goes. Category 5 wire is best for high-speed networking. You can use Category 3 (sometimes called Cat 3) with 10BaseT; Cat 5 can be used with either 10BaseT or 100BaseT topologies.

Fiber Optic

Fiber-optic cabling is a cable using a thin glass filament that connects to optical equipment on either end. Fiber optic uses light rather than electrical pulses to carry the network signal. The advantage of fiber optic is in its signal strength and its immunity to electrical interference, which gives it the capability to transmit signals over long distances and at very fast speeds. The disadvantages to using fiber optic are that it's expensive and difficult to repair. For those reasons, fiber-optic cable is often used for high-speed backbones to the network; a backbone is a cable connecting two or more hubs or even two or more LANs.

Logical Network Communications

The logical layer of the network determines how the computers communicate with each other over the physical media, or cables. There are four common logical networks: Ethernet, Token-Ring, FDDI, and ATM. For example, when you choose to use a 100BaseT card and the unshielded twisted-pair cabling, you've chosen by default to use Ethernet network communications. On the other hand, if you choose token-ring cards, hubs, and topology, you've chosen the token-ring network communication. The following discussion is just to give you a bit more information about your network decisions.

Ethernet

Ethernet is a popular network protocol and cabling scheme with transfer rates of 10Mbits and 100Mbits per second. The adapters, hubs, and cabling that are used with Ethernet are fairly inexpensive and the 10Mbits speed is generally acceptable for most networks. Ethernet uses coaxial cable, fiber-optic cable, or twisted-pair wiring and works with the star, or spanning tree, topology.

Ethernet uses a Carrier-Sense Media-Access Collision-Detect (CSMA/CD) to determine when a computer can send data, which also prevents network failures when two devices try to access the network at the same time. Before a computer can send data, it listens on the wire to ensure no other computer is sending data; it can only send data when the wire is clear.

Token Ring

Token Ring was developed by IBM to run at 16Mbits. It is, however, more expensive than Ethernet because adapters and hubs for token-ring are more costly. Using the ring topology, token-ring computers take turns sending data. A token is passed between the computers, one at a time. A workstation passes the token, and any data it wants to send, to the next computer on the line.

FDDI

FDDI is not so much a topology as it is a method of communication over a topology. FDDI is specifically for fiber-optic networks transmitting at a speed of up to 100Mbits per second over a token-ring topology (refer to Figure 3.4). FDDI is perfect for connecting high-performance clients, such as engineering workstations, medical imaging, three-dimensional seismic processing, full-motion video, and so on. You could also use FDDI for linking two or more LANs successfully.

FDDI uses fiber-optic cable, which works well over distances of a mile or two. Fiber-optic cable is lighter and smaller than traditional copper cable and is immune to electrical interference. Fiber-optic also offers better security and has better signal transmitting than traditional cabling. FDDI could alternatively use shielded and unshielded twisted-pair cabling for shorter distances.

ATM

ATM stands for asynchronous transfer mode and is the high-speed networking option. ATM starts at 25Mbits and goes up to 155Mbits with speeds up to 2.2 gigabits per second possible. ATM is perfect for integrating disparate networks over large geographical distances; however, it is very expensive.

Protocols

In this discussion of networking components and NT architecture, it now seems like a good time to discuss networking protocols. The protocols discussed earlier in this chapter—such as Ethernet and Token-Ring—are communications protocols that are on the data-link layer of NT's networking architecture. The data-link layer provides transfer of data from one computer to another over the networking media (cabling and cards). Transport protocols—such as TCP/IP, NetBEUI, and IPX/SPX—exist in the transport layer of the architecture, which makes sure messages are delivered in the order in which they were sent, among other things. See the "NT Networking Architecture" sidebar for more information.

In NT, you can use any of three major transport protocols on your network: IPX/SPX, NetBEUI, or TCP/IP. You'll need to decide which protocol you're going to use before installing NT to your server. NT Server supports concurrent multiple protocols; meaning you can have TCP/IP, IPX, NetBEUI, and others loaded at the same time thereby connecting to the Internet, Windows clients, and NetWare clients, as well.

NetBEUI

Microsoft developed NetBEUI originally for its LAN Manager network operating system; but it's also included with Windows for Workgroups, Windows 95, and Windows NT. NetBEUI stands for NetBIOS Extended User Interface. NetBEUI is a protocol; NetBIOS (network basic input/output system) is a programming interface.

Note: NetBIOS is a programming interface for developing client/server applications. NetBIOS can communicate over NetBEUI, NWLink NetBIOS, or over TCP/IP through NetBT. NetBIOS also manages data exchange and network access, and provides an application program interface (API) with a consistent set of commands for requesting lower-level network services to transmit information from node to node. API defines the operating system functions available to an application—such as managing files, displaying data on the screen, and so on—and how the application should use those functions. In NT, API also supports icons, pull-down menus, and other components of the graphical interface.

NetBEUI is the default Windows protocol and will work fine for networks that are small- to medium-sized (20 to 200 computers) and in a single location. It's also easy to set up and performance is good. NetBEUI provides a fast protocol for your LAN. It's completely self-tuning, has good error protection, and uses only a small amount of memory.

NetBEUI is not, however, routable like TCP/IP and IPX, but it does support the Token-Ring form of routing. Routing is a process of directing message packets, or tokens, from a source node to a destination node, as is the case with the ring topology.

Following are some of the advantages of the NetBEUI protocol:

- Dynamically allocates the memory necessary to process requests made by clients, meaning it uses memory only when it's needed.

- Supports dial-up client communications with remote access service (RAS); so your users can dial the server from home or on the road and access the network and all resources for which they have permission.

- Provides connection-oriented and connectionless data transfer services.

- Can be used with programs that implement the following services: Net-BIOS, Network DDE (dynamic data exchange), RPC (remote procedure call) over NetBIOS, and so on.

Note: Network DDE enables users to use DDE over a NetBIOS-compatible network. DDE is a protocol that enables applications to exchange data; you may be familiar with DDE from earlier Windows versions, as it has often been used in conjunction with OLE (Object Linking and Embedding). RPC is a set of procedures that describes how an application initiates a process on another network node and how it retrieves the appropriate result.

TCP/IP

TCP/IP (transmission control protocol/Internet protocol) is a set of communications protocols that encompass media access, file transfer, electronic mail, and terminal emulation. TCP/IP is supported by a large number of hardware and software vendors and it's available on many different computers. NT's TCP/IP is 32-bit and therefore yields a high performance as well as being an industry standard designed for use with WANs (wide area networks).

Use TCP/IP if you plan to attach your network to the Internet, implement an intranet (a network that connects only your company's LAN networks), or if your network is very large or comprised of many different clients and servers. TCP/IP is routable, so it works well on the ring topology.

TCP/IP is not as easy to configure as the other transport protocols and you must design an addressing scheme to use this protocol, as explained in Appendix C.

A major advantage of using TCP/IP is that it uses Windows NT-based networking services, including:

- Domain name system (DNS), point-to-point protocol (PPP), and simple network management protocol (SNMP) agent for e-mail
- Supports TCP/IP network printing
- Supports wide area network browsing
- Includes connectivity utilities, such as finger, ftp, rcp, telnet, and others
- Supports FDDI, Ethernet, and Token-Ring

NWLink (IPX/SPX)

NWLink is an IPX/SPX (Internet packet exchange/sequenced packet exchange)-compatible protocol. IPX and SPX are generally thought of as Novell's NetWare transport protocols because NetWare uses the IPX to transfer data between the server and workstation, and SPX to provide additional capabilities over IPX, such as guaranteeing delivery of data. NWLink can, however, be used to connect computers running Windows NT Server or Workstation with computers running MS-DOS, OS/2, and Windows for Workgroups.

NWLink cannot, by itself, enable an NT computer to access files or resources on a NetWare server. To access files or printers, you must also use a redirector, such as the Client Service for NetWare (CSNW) on NT Workstation or the Gateway

---

NT Networking Layers

The NT architecture, or OSI (open systems interconnect) model, describes how the network is designed. Various functions are organized into groups, which are then allocated to a series of layers. Each layer offers services to the other layers and each layer builds upon the services offered by the other layers. So, the design of a set of layers and how the layers work with each other constitute the network architecture. In NT's OSI model, there are seven layers: physical, data-link, network, transport, session, presentation, and application. I'll describe these layers briefly so you can see how they connect.

The physical layer is the lowest, most basic level of the model. This layer defines the mechanical and electrical specifications of the network medium and network interface hardware, how they connect to each other, and how data is placed on and retrieved from the network medium. The data-link level organizes the physical layer's transmissions into logical groupings of information, detects errors, controls data flow, and identifies particular computers on the network.

Information is moved across a network made up of multiple segments by the network layer; the network layer determines which path the data takes. The transport layer ensures reliable data delivery and often compensates for lack of reliability in the lower levels. It is in the network and transport layers that the transport protocols reside.

The session layer adds control mechanisms to the data that establish, maintain, synchronize, and manage dialog between communicating applications. The presentation layer transforms that data into a format that can be understood by each application. Finally, the application layer specifies the communication interface with the user and manages communication between computer applications.

Naturally, this is just a brief summary of what each OSI layer can do; for more information about NT's architecture, see John Ruley's book *Networking Windows NT 4.0* (John Wiley & Sons, Inc., 1997).

Service for NetWare (GSNW) on NT Server. The GSNW is included with'the NT Server program and can be installed to help you connect to NetWare servers.

NWLink is only really useful if there are NetWare client/server applications running that use NetBIOS over the IPX/SPX protocol. You can run the client portion on the NT Server to access the NetWare server.

Summary

This chapter has given you a basis for understanding how networking and NT work using cabling, network cards, and protocols. Additionally, you've learned about the hardware requirements for using NT Server, and ideas for upgrading and purchasing new peripherals for your NT network.

PART
II

Preparing and Installing
NT Server 4.0

4 *Laying the Groundwork*

$\mathbf{B}$efore you install Windows NT Server to your system, you will need to prepare your system and data for the change. Whether you're upgrading your existing network to NT or preparing for a first-time installation of a network, you will want to protect existing data by backing up your system, decide on a file system, and choose various other networking options.

In this chapter, you will learn the following:

- How to outline a successful backup plan
- How to decide which file system is right for your network
- How to determine a domain model
- How to upgrade an exiting network to NT

Backing Up Your System and Data

Making regular backups of your data and files—such as accounting files, customer information, letters and reports, spreadsheets and databases, and so on—should already be a part of your daily work life. Before you embark on any change in your system, you should make sure everything is completely backed up, just in case you run into trouble. Various problems can occur when installing a new system—crashes, hard drive failure, damaged and destroyed data, and so on. A good backup prepares you for the worst case scenario.

In addition to backing up your data and files, you will want backups and records of other information about your system, such as drivers for your peripherals, IRQ addresses, and other configuration information. Some information you will copy to diskettes or tape and other information you will keep in a notebook or log.

Keeping Track of System Configuations

Every computer in your company has configuration files, drivers, and hardware settings that are specific to that particular computer. You should keep a log, or notebook, for each computer in your system with all of the configuration information recorded. Also, you should create a system disk for each computer and copy configuration files and drivers for CD-ROMs in particular, to that disk. Make sure you keep the log book up-to-date; if the computer's configuration changes in any way (say you add a new CD-ROM or hard drive to the computer), make sure you keep a record of those changes in the log.

The written information comes in handy when you need to configure network clients and protocols, add hardware—such as a modem or network card, for example—or update the computer's equipment. The system disk is useful for booting the computer after a system crash, providing drivers when the originals are damaged, and recovering from various system errors.

Log Data

In the log you keep for each computer, both workstations and servers, list all of the hardware configuration information you can think of, specific to that computer. Specifically, use the following list when recording information about your network computers:

- Computer's manufacturer, model, and serial number, operating system, installed applications, users' names, location of the computer, monitor brand and specs, mouse type, keyboard type.
- Computer's internal configuration: motherboard, processor speed, amount and type of RAM, number of hard disks and size of each, number of floppy drives and sizes, display adapters, hard disk and floppy disk controllers, CMOS information, and so on.

Note: A *motherboard* is a computer component that contains virtually all of the chips used by the system, including the CPU, memory, and the BIOS.

- CD-ROM drive specifications: manufacturer and model, location (internal or external), speed, drivers, port connections, and so on.
- Modem: manufacturer and model, location (internal or external), speed, drivers, port connections, and so on.
- Other attached peripherals: printers—manufacturer and model, specifications on memory, any font cartridges, printer fonts, ports and cables, and so on; UPS specifications; ZIP drives specifications; tape drive specs, and so on.

• Sound card, video card, network adapter cards: manufacturer and model, IRQ addresses, any jumper or DIP switch settings, and so on.

Make sure you also keep all manuals, receipts, warranties, and other vendor documentation to your computers, peripherals, and any hardware you acquire.

IRQs and I/O Port Addresses

A conflict in resource usage often results in all adapters and devices involved not functioning. You will need to identify which devices on the system have overlapping resources, then change the configuration of one or more of them until the conflict is eliminated. You can use MSD (Microsoft Diagnostics) or other software to help you detect the configuration and device conflicts. Windows NT includes a diagnostic program that lists system configuration for each device—WINMSD (choose Start, Programs, Administrative Tools, NT Diagnostics). Figure 4.1 shows NT's Microsoft Diagnostic dialog box.

The IRQ (interrupt request) is extremely important to note for any and all devices attached to your computer. There are a limited number of available IRQs and no two devices can share an IRQ. An IRQ conflict stops a device from working until the conflict is resolved. Following is a list of IRQs for common devices, although any computer may use different IRQs than those listed:

IRQ	Device
0	System timer
1	Keyboard controller
2	Second IRQ controller or floppy disk controller
3	COM2 (serial port)
4	COM1 (serial port)
5	Hard disk controller
6	Floppy disk controller
7	LPT1 (parallel port)
8	System clock
9	Available (network)
10–12	Unused
13	Math coprocessor
14	Hard disk controller
15	Unused

The unused IRQs can then be used for sound cards, network cards, or other added devices. Usually, when you're installing a new device, the computer's operating system detects and assigns an unused IRQ to the new device; however, conflicts can

(continues)

IRQs and I/O Port Addresses (*Continued*)

still arise. It's best if you know the IRQs for each machine so you can adjust them if possible.

I/O (input/output) port addresses act like mail boxes where data and commands are sent to and from an adapter. Each I/O port is exclusive, meaning it cannot be shared with any other adapter. Each adapter usually uses a group of sequential port addresses for communication; for example, the standard I/O port address used by disk controllers is 1F0–1F7h.

The only time you may encounter an I/O port conflict is when you're installing multiple disk controllers in a system. In that case, each controller will need a different I/O port address. At any rate, you should make note of any I/O ports being used by the system, just in case.

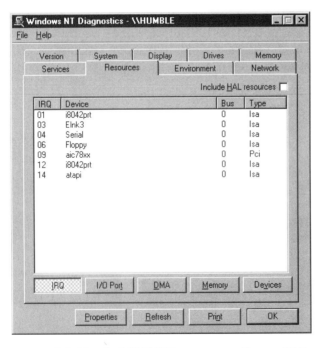

Figure 4.1 *Use the WINMSD program to discover IRQs and other hardware device settings on your server.*

System Disk

No matter what type of operating system a computer is running, you should have a system disk for each computer in your system. A system disk enables you to boot a computer that won't start on its own. In Windows 95 and Windows NT, a system disk is also called an emergency repair disk.

The system disk should contain certain files for you to be able to boot from it and examine your system. Whether you're using DOS, Windows 95, or Windows NT, your system disk should include the following:

Command.com: From the root directory of the computer, the command.com file loads instructions that make the computer run.

Configuration files: From the root directory, Autoexec and Config files may have different extensions. For example, in DOS-based computers, it's config.sys but in Windows 95 it's Config.win and Config.dos.

CD-ROM drivers: You should copy all CD-ROM drivers for a computer to a directory you create on a floppy drive using the exact same directory name. You can open and view the Config file, for example, and look for the statement that refers to your CD-ROM drive, such as `devicehigh=c:\qlogic\q151dos.sys`. Using this information, create the qlogic directory on your floppy disk, then copy everything in the qlogic directory on C: to the directory on A: or B:. You'll need these files to access the CD-ROM drive if anything happens to the system or the files become damaged.

Note: Make sure you add the CD-ROM drivers to an emergency repair disk created by Windows 95 or Windows NT; neither system adds those drivers to the disk automatically.

Backing Up Files and Data

The other information you'll want to back up from all of your computers is any data or files with which you work, such as word processing, spreadsheet, accounting, database files, and so on. You might want to back up your applications, one time, and keep the backup in a safe place. If you need to you can restore those programs quickly and any customized settings will also be restored at the same time.

You can back up files and data on diskettes if there's not much to back up; or you can use a tape backup for larger amounts of data. You may even be able to back up to an CD disk if you have a CD-writer device or you can always back up

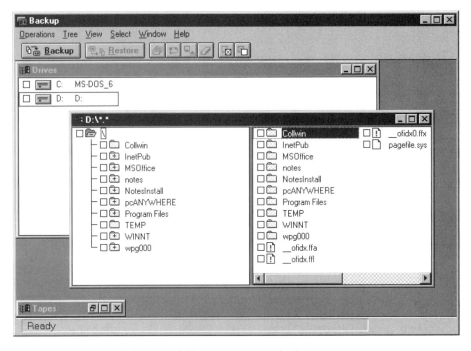

Figure 4.2 *Select the files and folders you want to back up.*

to the network (such as back up one client to another or to the server over the network).

NT includes a backup program, located in Start, Programs, Administrative Tools menu. and called Backup. Figure 4.2 shows the backup program window. You'll need a tape drive to use NT Backup. You can open any drive on the server and select the files and/or folders you want to back up by clicking the check box in front of the file or folder. After backing up files, it's just as easy to restore files and folders to your server's drive. For more information about Backup, see the on-line Help within the program.

Following are the types of backups you could make:

- *Full backup*: A complete copy of all selected files; the files are marked as having been backed up. If you need to restore the files, you can do so quickly from this one backup.

- *Incremental backup*: A backup of only the files that have been created or changed since the last full or incremental backup; files are marked as being backed up. If you need to restore files, you must first restore the last full backup you made, then restore each incremental backup made since that time.

- *Differential backup*: A backup of files created or changed since the last full backup. So to restore, you only have to restore the last full backup and the last differential backup. Files are marked as backed up.

You'll want to do a full backup of all files before you embark on a system or network change, to ensure that you have all of the files you need. Often, people will perform a full backup once or twice, then perform an incremental backup daily or weekly for months, even years, without ever performing a full backup again. What that means is that when you get ready to restore files, you have to first restore the last full backup, then restore each and every incremental backup you've made since that time. Performing an incremental backup daily saves time in backing up, but can cause nightmares when you have to restore the data.

It's also a good idea to make two full backups of your system and keep one backup as an insurance policy. You can update the one backup only every few months while you update the second full backup every week or two with incremental or partial backups every day.

What to Back Up in an Existing Network

In addition to your important data and files, you'll want to pay special attention to backing up the server in your network before changing to NT Server. Depending on the type of network you're currently using, consider backing up the following that apply to you:

- *Registry*: If you're already using a Windows NT 3.51 or Workstation computer as a server, back up the Registry before installing Windows NT Server 4. If something happens to the original Registry or setup and you need to go back to the way things were before the change, you can do so if you have this file.

- *Logon Scripts*: Logon scripts are files that define a user's account. If you've created logon scripts for your Windows or NetWare users, make copies of the scripts to use later.

- *Application files*: You might want to back up any specific application files such as vertical programs that are difficult to configure and set up.

- *User data*: You can back up the data in the users' folders. This is data the user saves to the server, usually on a daily basis.

Preparing the Hardware

The first step to preparing your hardware is to make sure all equipment you plan to use for NT Server is compatible with the operating system. Use the hardware compatibility list to make sure peripherals, printers, and hardware components you plan to use are listed. Also, check with the information in Chapter 3 to make sure your hardware meets the requirements to run NT; if necessary, upgrade any equipment before installing NT to save time, energy, and money.

The second step is to install networking hardware to your system. You will probably want to get some technical help with this preparation, using some of the information presented here and in Chapter 3 to communicate intelligently with your hardware consultant.

Purchasing and Upgrading Hardware

If you're purchasing a new computer on which to run NT Server, make sure the computer contains all of the components as listed earlier in this book and that those components are compatible with NT. Additionally, check the prices for larger hard drives, additional RAM, faster CD-ROM drives, for example, when you're quoted a price for a system; adding another gigabyte of disk space or an additional 16M of RAM may be inexpensive enough to make it worthwhile and thus save you time, money, and trouble later on.

I suggest you purchase your new server from a popular, known vendor as opposed to buying a built system from your cousin's friend or some little known mail order company. You want to check for warranties, technical support, full documentation included with the computer, spare parts availability, service manual availability, diagnostic software, system software, and so on.

If you plan to upgrade your existing hardware to NT standards instead of purchasing new equipment, make sure you use hardware that's compatible with your existing system. For example, if you're buying additional RAM, check the documentation for the exact type of RAM chips you need for your computer and be careful when specifying how much memory you need.

RAM most generally is purchased in the single in-line memory module (SIMM), a small board that plugs into the motherboard or a memory card. Since individual memory chips are soldered to the SIMM, removing or replacing individual memory chips is impossible; you must replace the entire SIMM if any part fails.

There are various sizes of SIMMs (8-, 32-, 9-, 36-bit, for example) and various capacities (4096K or 4M, 8192K or 8M, 16,384K or 16M) and even various speeds (60ns, 70ns). For this reason, you want to be as clear as possible when ordering RAM to ensure you get memory that will work with your system. Carefully check your computer's documentation before purchasing RAM.

If you're purchasing additional hard drives or CD-ROM drives, make sure you get what you need to match the controller in your computer; it's generally a good idea to buy the controller and hard disk at the same time from the same vendor so you're sure to get a match. A controller acts as a bridge between the device, such as a hard drive, and the computer. Since the PC cannot use the device directly, the controller communicates instructions to and from the device, usually through the BIOS. You also use controllers for floppy drives, CD-ROM drives, and the like.

Basically, NT uses either of two types of hard drives: IDE or SCSI. IDE (integrated drive electronics) is a popular hard disk interface. An IDE drive includes its own electronic control circuitry, thus eliminating the need for a separate hard-disk controller card. Placing the controller on the drive means the IDE drive is more reliable, performs well, and is relatively inexpensive. The disadvantages of an IDE drive include capacity and expandability. IDE drives aren't suited to large-capacity systems. Additionally, since the controller is mounted on the drive, to add a second drive you must disable its controller and have it use the controller from the first drive; therefore, you'll need to make sure both drives are from the same manufacturer to guarantee one controller is compatible with both.

Note: ESDI (enhanced small device interface) is another popular hard disk, floppy disk, and tape drive interface standard. ESDI is most often used with large hard disks and is perfectly compatible with Windows NT, as well. ESDI is a very high-speed interface, but most ESDI drives are limited in speed. The more popular, less expensive IDE drives have all but replaced ESDI.

SCSI (pronounces "scuzzy") stands for small computer system interface. The SCSI interface is high-speed and capable of connecting up to seven peripheral devices at a time using just one port. SCSI isn't exactly a disk interface, it's a system-level interface: This means you can use a SCSI controller to connect hard disks, tape drives, CD-ROM drives, and other mass storage devices, even scanners and printers.

When you purchase a SCSI hard disk, you're purchasing a drive, a controller and a SCSI adapter; so communications go through the SCSI adapter. Note, too, that SCSI standards are very specific when it comes to cables and connectors. When you purchase a SCSI hard disk, make sure you get the cables and connectors you need at the same time.

Finally, realize that by the time you upgrade memory, hard drives, motherboards, and controllers, you may as well have purchased a new computer. Weigh all of the possibilities before jumping into any purchases.

Networking Hardware

In Chapter 3, you read about network adapter cards and cabling as two types of networking hardware you will need to install or have installed before you can network your computers. This section addresses some issues you will want to consider, if not for use now then perhaps for use later as your network grows.

Note: The term internetworking refers to attaching two or more segments of a LAN together to extend the network and the resource usage. A segment is a network that doesn't contain any internetworking devices. Internetworking devices are hardware, and sometimes software, appliances that connect networks.

As your network expands, you'll find you need more power and higher performance from your system. Your users will want to send and receive data quickly and securely. As you know, networking basically serves to transfer data between computers attached to the network. Generally, the data travels from node to node in the form of data packets. A data packet is a unit of information transmitted over the network; data packets are a fixed maximum length and contain a header, a set of data, and error control information. Packets are reassembled if necessary, when they reach their destination.

Routers, bridges, and switches serve to make the delivery of data packets more efficient and productive by linking independent networks or by dividing large networks into smaller, more manageable segments for Ethernet, Token Ring, and FDDI.

Routers

The routing process enables the data packets to be delivered between networks or LANs. A router is an intelligent connecting device that can send packets to the correct LAN segment to take them to their destination. Routers operate at the Network layer, but have access to information from all three lower OSI layers—Physical, Link, and Network.

Routers use a set of routing protocols that govern the exchange of data between nodes. Both the sending node and the receiving node must use the same routing protocol to successfully communicate; alternatively, they can use a protocol converter that enables the two nodes to exchange packets. Routers enable data packets to be dispatched between dissimilar networks—Ethernet and Token Ring, for example—without being translated.

If there are a number of networks and routers between networks, each router between the sending and receiving nodes functions similarly—determining the

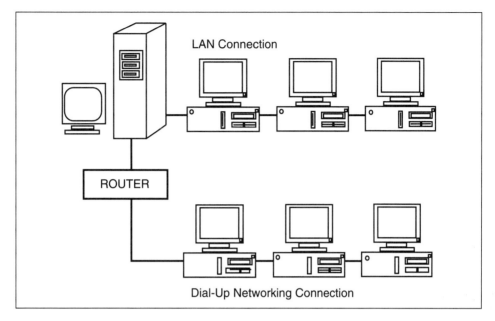

Figure 4.3 *The router can determine the destination of the packets and directs the packets in the right direction.*

destination of the packets and choosing the most appropriate route for the information to take.

You might use a router, for example, between your LAN and a remote telephone connection. The packets transmitted on the LAN are also transmitted to the router (also a node). The router determines whether the packets should go across the phone lines to a remote node; if the router determines the packets are not meant for the remote node, it passes the packets back to the LAN for distribution to the appropriate node.

Figure 4.3 illustrates the use of a router between a LAN connection and a remote dial-up networking connection. The router placed between the two networks determines if the packets are meant for the remote computers or for the computers attached to the LAN.

Bridges

A bridge is a hardware device used to connect two LAN segments so they can exchange data. Bridges are similar to routers, but are usually used to divide a too-busy network into separate segments. Bridges can work with networks that require different wiring or protocols and they operate at the data-link layer.

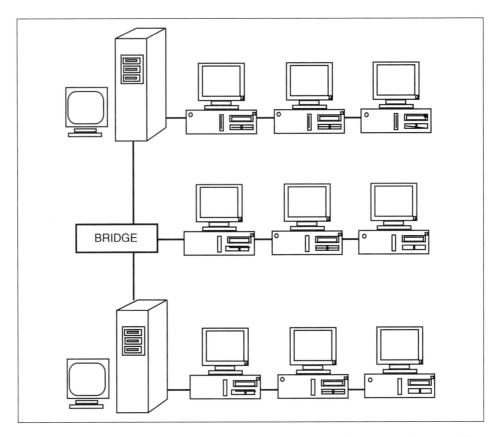

Figure 4.4 *Use a bridge to reduce network traffic by dividing a large network into smaller segments.*

Adding a bridge to a local area network effectively divides it into two networks. The local bridge reads packets and allows them to pass from one network to another only if the address is not in the local segment. Using a bridge reduces the amount of traffic on the LAN and improves performance. Also, remote bridges can transparently link distant networks over serial lines. Figure 4.4 illustrates a LAN divided into three more manageable groups by use of a bridge.

As explained previously, routers are also a device to assist in data exchange between networking segments. Routers differ from bridges in that they calculate the best path for the data to take and they can constantly adjust to changing network conditions. If you used a bridge between a LAN and a remote telephone connection, for example, the bridge would drop the packet if it determined it wasn't meant for the remote connection, instead of sending it back to the LAN, as the router would.

The decision on whether you'll use a bridge or router hinges on your specific needs. Routers are more processing-intensive than bridges and their processing speeds are not usually as high. On the other hand, routers are capable of much more sophisticated path selection, thus improving the efficiency of the network.

A *brouter* may be an alternative choice. Brouters are essentially routers that can also bridge. A brouter will first check a packet to see if it fits into the brouter's algorithms for choosing paths; if it doesn't fit, rather than dropping the packet, the brouter bridges the packet using layer 2 information.

Note: A gateway is a shared connection between a LAN and a larger system, such as another network or a mainframe computer. As your small network is physically integrated into a larger, perhaps heterogeneous network, you use a linking device, or gateway, to translate incompatible protocol implementations. Gateways are slower than a bridge or router, but perform a more complicated task.

You can, for example, use a computer running NT Server as a gateway by installing two network cards and binding each to a different protocol. Use one card for TCP/IP and an Internet connection, and use the other card for NetBEUI and the LAN connection. Clients on the LAN can go through the gateway, then, to access the Internet.

Switches

Switches are multiport devices that create temporary paths for routing information over a LAN. Switching provides better performance than routers because it provides more efficient use of the data-link layer and its technology. Additionally, only one communication at a time can take place in a routing environment; switching enables communications by allowing messages to be routed from one port on the switch to another, so there is no wait time. Unlike bridges and routers, switches don't have security, filtering, or WAN options; but they do deliver faster throughput than any bridge or router on the market.

There are three types of switching: Configuration, Frame, and Cell. Configuration switching is also called port switching; it operates at the physical layer and is transparent to upper-layer protocols. Configuration switching enables individual ports to be assigned, when the device is initially attached to the network, to individual segments within a multi-segmented network hub.

Frame switching operates in the data–link layer. It forwards the packet to the output port of the destination computer and supports both Ethernet and Token Ring. Ethernet frame switching supports shared or dedicated 10Mbps or 100Mbps connections. Instead of using conventional bridges to create logical boundaries between networks, the Ethernet switch gives a high-performance connection between multiple Ethernet networks while remaining inexpensive, simple to operate, and offering scalable high performance.

Cell switching, also called asynchronous transfer mode (ATM), is a high-speed transfer system designed to carry voice, video, and data traffic. Remember from Chapter 3, ATM is a switched networking technology that provides dedicated, high-speed connections to a nearly unlimited number of users. ATM switches can simultaneously support multiple transmissions, eliminating bottlenecks.

Choosing a File System

After choosing the hardware for the computer to which you will install Windows NT Server 4, you will need to choose the file system you want to use. During installation, NT offers you the FAT or the NTFS file systems from which to choose. Your decision depends on a number of factors, including security, your hardware platform, the size and number of hard disks you're using, and so on. You may even decide to use both file systems on the server, as explained later in this section.

FAT (File Allocation Table) File System

The FAT file system uses a table maintained by the operating system that lists all the blocks of disk space available on a disk. The table, located at the beginning of the volume, includes the location of each block and whether it's in use or damaged in some way. Since files are not necessarily stored in consecutive blocks on a disk, FAT also keeps track of which pieces belong to which file. Following are a few facts about the FAT file system:

- The server can access files on a FAT volume when it's running NT, Windows 95, MS-DOS, or OS/2.
- The maximum file size for FAT is 4G.
- With FAT, you cannot set any permissions on individual files and folders.
- FAT volumes are limited to the 8.3 file-naming convention.

Note: If you're using a RISC-based computer, the system partition must be formatted with FAT. You can use NTFS on the boot partition, however, but that partition must be large enough to hold all of the NT system components (at least 200 to 250M for the boot partition).

Volumes, Partitions, and Logical Drives

When working with hard disks and file systems, NT uses various terms to define capacity and function. A volume is the highest level of the file server directory and file structure. You can, for example, divide a large hard disk into several different volumes when you first install the operating system. For example, you might divide a disk into two volumes and use one volume for NT and the other for DOS and Windows 3.11, as explained in the section, "Using Both File Systems."

A partition is a portion of a hard disk that acts as a separate drive. The primary partition is formatted for a specific file system and assigned a drive letter. Generally, you would assign the drive letter C to the primary partition and install the operating system and boot files onto that partition. If you use multiple primary partitions, you can install a different operating system with a different file system on each, if you want. You can only use up to four partitions on a hard disk.

A system, or active, partition is the partition that contains the hardware-specific files for loading and initializing the operating system. Only a primary partition can be a system partition. A boot partition, on the other hand, can be located on a primary partition or a logical drive in an extended partition. The boot partition is the area that holds the files needed to start the operating system.

You can set up one extended partition on a hard disk. An extended partition is not formatted to a different file system and is not assigned a drive letter. Instead, you create one or more logical drives within an extended partition and each logical drive is formatted (for a different file system, for example) and assigned a drive letter. You use logical drives to add more than four logical areas to a hard disk as a method of avoiding the four-partition limit.

NTFS (New Technology File System)

The NTFS file system provides high performance and reliability for your server. It's designed especially for large disks and includes many advantages over the FAT file system. Security features are the biggest advantage of NTFS; it supports data access control, ownership privileges, individual folder sharing and individual file permissions, and more. Consider the following facts about NTFS:

- Maximum size of the drive is 16 exabytes (18,446,744,073,709,551,616 bytes); however, the practical limit for both a physical and logical volume is only 2T (terabytes).

- Enables a wide range of permissions for sharing files and security.
- Supports up to 256 characters for file names and uses an algorithm that enables DOS-based computers to use those file names by renaming them in the 8.3 convention.
- Offers a transaction log which allows Windows to complete any incomplete file-related tasks before continuing if the operating system is interrupted.
- Supports the FAT and HPFS (High Performance File System) used by OS/2.

Additionally, NTFS guarantees the consistency of a volume using standard transaction logging and recovery techniques, meaning the file system ensures the integrity of all NTFS volumes each time the computer is restarted. These logging and recovery techniques also guarantee that the NTFS volume structure won't be corrupted so that if you have a system crash, your files are still accessible.

Note: Important: Do not use any third-party DOS-based disk program to repair or defragment a FAT volume that is used by NT unless the program is specifically certified for NT version 3.5 or later. The program could corrupt the data. You can use the chkdsk utility at the command prompt in NT and in the FAT volume; chkdsk will do a surface scan if you include the /r switch, as in chkdsk /r.

Using Both File Systems

Perhaps your best option in the file system debate is to use both file systems on the server. You might, for instance, want to keep a small FAT partition to use with the larger NTFS partition. Keep the FAT partition to between 250 and 500M, depending on the overall size of the hard disk and use that partition as your system and boot partition. Format the rest of the disk as NTFS and use that partition for applications, data, and the NT operating system. The advantages of using both file systems are:

- You receive the NTFS security and disk recovery benefits.
- If you have a startup failure, you can use a DOS system floppy to troubleshoot the problem.
- You can run DOS programs and even run Windows 3.x on the FAT partition, if you want.
- When running Windows NT, you can move or copy files between FAT and NTFS volumes.

One major disadvantage of this method of using file systems is that you cannot use any compression or partitioning software, such as MS-DOS 6.22 DiskSpace, on the FAT primary partition or logical drive if you want to access it when running Windows NT.

If you choose to use both file systems (dual boot), you first create the FAT partition and install DOS to that partition. Then, when you're installing the NT operating system, Setup enables you to choose the partition and the file system you want to install. See Chapter 5 for more information.

Choosing One or Multiple Domains

Another choice you'll need to make before installing NT concerns domains. NT uses a domain structure to organize users in the database for naming and organizational purposes; a domain can describe one computer, a whole department, or a complete site. Additionally, the group of servers and computers that belong to a domain share common security policies; so that when a user logs on to a domain, he/she has access to each computer and server in the domain. Figure 4.5 illustrates a simple domain structure on an NT network.

You might, for example, divide various departments into domains for easier management; so Accounting, Sales, Publicity, Customer Service, and Production might each be a domain in your network. Alternatively, you might set up one domain in your office and, as your company grows, add domains in other offices within the building, in different buildings, or even in different cities. The advantages of the domain structure include the following:

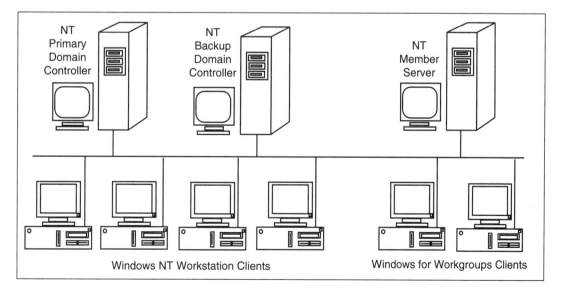

Figure 4.5 *A simple domain structure can include one or multiple servers.*

- A user can connect to many servers and resources with a single network logon.

- Users can access multiple network domains with one password and user name.

- Users must remember only one password to access available resources.

- Users, groups, and resources can be viewed from any workstation on the network for easier management of the network.

- The network and resources are easier to view and recognize when the entire network is grouped into domains.

- Administrators manage only one account for each user, for one or several servers, and for one or several domains, thus saving time and energy.

Domain Controllers

NT designates domain controllers as gatekeepers of all of the shared items in the domain. The domain controller simply keeps the database of security information and uses that information to validate requests for network resources from workstations.

A domain's master security database (that approves or rejects requests for resources on the network) is located on the *primary domain controller* (PDC). Any and all changes made to user accounts for the domain are made to the PDC. There is only one PDC per domain.

The responsibility of maintaining the directory database can be shared among multiple NT servers, also called *backup domain controllers* (BDC). The backup domain controller contains a copy of the database and periodically and automatically updates it with the PDC. Multiple BDCs can exist within a domain. If something should happen to the PDC, the BDC can be reassigned as a PDC and work continues on the network as if nothing has happened.

The first NT Server you install in a domain must be designated as the primary domain controller; the second should be a backup domain controller. See Chapter 5 for installation instructions.

Note: In addition to domain controllers, you may have other computers on your system that run the Windows NT Server software. These computers, called member servers because they do not contain the database of users, can be used as workstations, file servers, print servers, and so on.

Note: If your network is a small one—one or two servers and 20 to 100 or so users, for example—you can easily set up one NT domain for your entire system. You can install one primary domain controller (PDC) and one backup domain controller (BDC), and split the file, print, Web, and other services between the two servers; you could also install member servers to help handle multiple services, if necessary.

Single Domain Model

In a domain, users can reach all domain resources with one user name and password. Account administration is handled on the primary domain controller and changes made to the PDC affect all servers in the domain. In most cases, you'll want to use the single domain model (see Figure 4.6).

A single domain model enables you to centralize the management of your user accounts, thus making administration of the network easier. You can administer all network servers and domain accounts on the PDC. Technically, up to 26,000 users

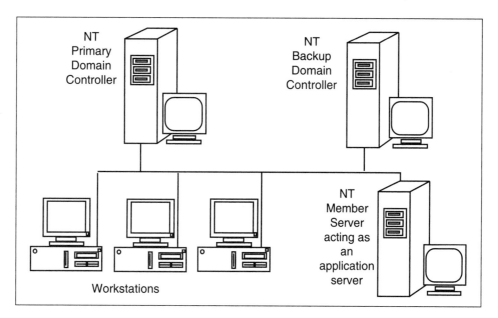

Figure 4.6 *A single domain model includes only one PDC, but may consist of a BDC, a member server, and multiple workstations.*

and groups can be successfully managed in a single domain, if you have enough servers capable of handling the network resources.

Multiple Domain Models

You may want to organize your network into multiple domains. Using multiple domains normally means you will need multiple administrators, one for each domain, because of work load. Before deciding, consider all of your network resources, servers, and workstations. Perhaps create a chart on how the current resources are used and how you plan to use them.

There are two methods of organizing multiple domains: the single master domain model and the multiple master domain model. The easiest method of organizing multiple domains in NT is to use a single master domain model. You can split the network into domains for organizational purposes using this model and you will still have centralized administration. The multiple master domain model is more difficult to administer and to guarantee security on because of the two-way trust relationships between domains. Trust relationships are links that combine two or more domains into one administrative unit that authorizes access to the resources on both domains.

NT's Directory Services provides two types of trust relationships: one-way and two-way. The one-way trust relationship represents one domain that trusts another to use its resources. The first domain enables users on the trusted domain access to resources, but its users are not trusted to use the second domain's resources. The two-way trust relationship enables users in each domain to access resources in the trusted domains. Naturally, using the resources in any domain is subject to permissions and rights. For more information, see Chapter 15.

Single Master Domain Model

The single master domain model consists of a master domain and one or more resource domains. The master domain contains all user and group accounts, and the resource domains share their resources—such as printers and file servers—with the users and groups in the master domain. All users log on to the master domain. All resources are located in other domains. The resource domains establish a one-way trust with the master domain which enables the users access to the resources.

One administrator can easily manage this one master domain as well as the resource domains. Alternatively, administration of each resource domain can be assigned to different administrators. Using the single master domain model, users only need to log on to the domain once but can still use all resources on the network. Figure 4.7 illustrates a single master domain model.

In summary, use the single master domain model when you need centralized account management, decentralized resource management is acceptable and per-

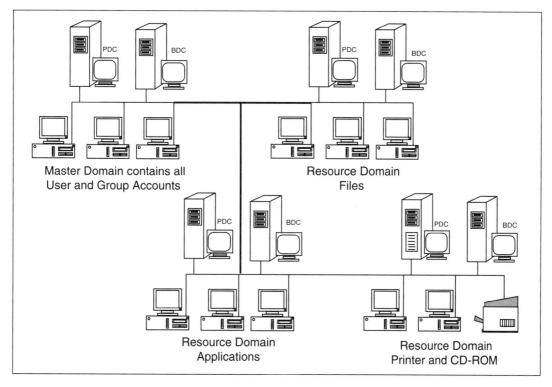

Figure 4.7 *A master domain contains all domain accounts and the resources are stored within other domains on the network.*

haps even preferred, and when resources can be grouped logically to correspond with local domains. The single master domain model can handle as many as 25,000 to 40,000 users and groups divided into as many resource domains as necessary and as permitted by your system resources.

TIP: If your company has an MIS (Management Information System) department that integrates data from all the departments, you might consider placing master domain administration in that department.

Multiple Master Domain Model

You could also use the multiple master domain model, in which you use two or more single master domains to serve as user and group account domains. Other domains on the network are resource domains, as in the single master domain model.

The trust relationships in a multiple master domain model differ from the single master domain model in that every master domain is connected to every other master domain in a two-way trust relationship. All resource domains have a one-way trust with each master domain, as well. With this model, every user account can use any master domain and any resource domain.

Generally, the multiple master domain model is used in organizations with 40,000 users or more; however, it can be adapted to networks with any number of users. You may also want to use this model if you have many mobile users, if centralization of administration doesn't matter, or if you want to share resources over a WAN as well as a LAN. For information about managing multiple domains, see Chapters 14 and 15.

Upgrading Your Network to NT Server 4.0

If you're already networking your computers but you want to upgrade to using NT Server 4.0, you'll find the process is easier than starting from scratch because you already know about networking. Your hardware, networking cards, and cabling are already in place and your users are acclimated to using a network.

Before you actually transfer your files and users, you will need to perform some preliminary work, as the following checklist suggests:

- Naturally, you will want to check your server's hardware for compatibility with NT and probably upgrade some of your server's equipment to better work with the NT operating system. You won't, for example, continue using the monochrome monitor you used with NetWare when you switch to NT.

- Check your workstations for hardware and operating system compatibility, as well. Note that included with the Windows NT Server 4.0 CD are clients you can use for DOS and Windows 3.x computers. See Chapter 10 for more information.

- Collect drivers and software for UPS, tape drives, CD-ROM drives and/or towers, sound cards, optical disk drives, modems and/or modem servers, print devices, and any other devices you currently use on the network.

- Collect software updates to enable any application you install to the server to work with NT; call the manufacturer for application updates or check out the Internet. Don't forget the all-important vertical application updates, as well.

- Back up, as described earlier in this chapter.

- Make a list of all users on your network, including their user names, passwords, and any other information specific to each user's account, such as login scripts, special permissions, and so on.
- List all administrators and/or managers for whom special permissions or rights will be granted.
- Make note of directories and files, perhaps even print the directory structure on the server(s). Note specific rights and attributes to the files you plan to transfer to the NT server.
- Record all drive mappings.

Migrating from NetWare

If you plan to migrate from NetWare 3.x or 4.x to Windows NT Server 4, you can use the Migration tool included with NT. With the Migration tool, you can choose directories and files, and users and groups to migrate, retaining many of the permissions and rights you assigned in NetWare.

When migrating your files, directories, users and groups, you can use the Trial Migration tool. The trial migration performs a mock migration and records all activity to logs you can view. In these logs, all transfers are recorded—both successful moves and errors—so you can study them and correct any possible problems you run across. Then, if you choose to migrate, you do not lose any data on the NetWare server, you simply transfer the data to the NT server. You can always go back to NetWare if you change your mind.

Even though NetWare's Directory Services do not directly migrate, you can use multiple domains to hold the users and groups within containers. However, if your network depends on a multi-layered directory services implementation, you'll want to fully understand how NT performs the same functions before determining if migration to NT is right for you. For more information on using the Gateway services and performing migrations, see Sue Plumley's book *Migrating from Novell NetWare to Windows NT Server 4.0* (John Wiley and Sons, Inc., 1997).

Using a Gateway Service with NetWare

NT also includes a Gateway tool that enables you to connect the NT and the NetWare servers together so that clients can access resources on both servers. You might try the Gateway service for several reasons. Perhaps you're considering a migration to NT but you're not really sure yet. The Gateway gives you a chance to work on the NT server and explore the possibilities before making a decision.

The Gateway Service for NetWare provides a bridge between the networks, enabling the NT clients to access NetWare resources without installing the Net-

Ware client software to the workstations. However, using the Gateway Service does tend to slow client access to NetWare resources.

Upgrading from a Windows Network

You may currently be using Windows for Workgroups or a Windows 95 peer-to-peer network from which you want to upgrade to NT Server. This is the easiest of all upgrades. If you're using a peer-to-peer network, you probably do not have one computer you're using as a server; therefore, you must purchase a computer that will be compatible with NT Server and that has enough power to be the server of your network. See Chapter 3 for information about hardware requirements.

After installing the NT operating system to your server, you can configure the server and the clients to use the same network protocol—NetBEUI, for example—and with little or no trouble, the clients can easily connect to the server and use the resources you install to the server. If you do have files, directories, or resources you want to move to the server, you can copy or move those items over the network using the My Computer window, the Explorer, or the Network Neighborhood. For more information about client computers, protocols, and other network-specific information, see Chapters 9 and 10.

Upgrading from Other Network Operating Systems

There are other NOSs (network operating systems) that you may be using: OS/2, LAN Manager, LANtastic, and so on. Basically, you follow the same steps as outlined earlier in this section for preparing and planning the migration or upgrade. There are only a few points to consider, as follows.

LAN Manager

If you're using LAN Manager, consider keeping the server and using it as a member server on the NT domain. NT is perfectly compatible with other Microsoft products, so LAN Manager 2.2 servers can serve your network, even though the LAN Manager servers will not be able to participate in all tasks and procedures.

LAN Manager can also serve as a Microsoft Network client redirector for Windows 95 and for 16-bit MS-DOS clients. A redirector intercepts application requests for file- and printer-sharing services and diverts them to the file server for action. Using LAN Manager servers, then, to direct your print services can alleviate some bottlenecks on other servers on the network.

LANtastic

When changing over from a LANtastic network, you must first check your network cards for compatibility with NT; not all LANtastic adapter cards are NT-compliant. Also, you must remove all LANtastic software before you install NT or configure the network components on the clients.

OS/2

Your OS/2 workstations can attach to an NT domain using either NetBEUI or TCP/IP and the NT Server client software. You also can connect to the NT print server from an OS/2 workstation; you use local print drivers on the OS/2 client when connecting to the network printer, much as you do when attaching from a DOS-based machine. Finally, NT 4 doesn't support OS/2 applications; you'll either need to do a dual boot on your workstation or update the applications to NT 4.

Summary

This chapter has covered information you need to know before installing the NT Server software. You'll want to prepare for the installation by making full backups of your system and configuration files. Then, you must make some decisions before installation, such as choosing the file system and domain model you want to use with NT. Finally, I've offered a few tips on upgrading or migrating from another network operating system to NT.

5 Installing and Configuring NT Server

When installing the operating system, NT offers many options for setup and configuration. This chapter helps you install the NT Server operating system to your server. It also covers many of the installation options, their consequences, and some possible solutions to problems you may encounter.

After you've installed and used the software for a while, you'll eventually need to configure additional network adapters, protocols, and so on, or add a modem, UPS, or other hardware. This chapter shows you the basics of how these configuration changes are made to the program. This chapter will present the following:

- Step-by-step instructions for installing the NT operating system
- Instructions for setting up the network components for the server
- Description of the Control Panel items
- Guidelines for adding and configuring hardware to the server

Preparing to Install

Before installing NT Server, make sure you have backups of any important files on the computer to which you plan to install. Check over the HCL included with your NT documentation to make sure your hardware—network card, video driver, sound card, CD-ROM, and so on—is compatible with NT. For an updated version of the HCL, access the World Wide Web at http://www.microsoft.com/ntserver/hcl/hclintro.htm. Additionally, make sure you have all of the device drivers and installation software for your applications, printers, modems, CD-ROMs, and any other devices you want to use on the server on diskette.

You'll need the following items to complete the installation of the operating system:

NT Server CD and three 3.5-inch setup disks

Computer name, workgroup or domain name, IP address (if you're using TCP/IP; see Appendix C)

The 10-digit CD KEY from the back of your CD case

IRQ addresses for any hardware on the server

One 3.5-inch 1.44M floppy disk for the Emergency Repair Disk

Refer to the previous chapters to confirm your server meets all of the system requirements for running NT. Remember, if you want a dual boot system on your server, you should first install MS-DOS or another operating system on one partition of your hard disk; then, you can choose to install NT to another partition or free space on the disk.

Note: I strongly recommend you create an Emergency Repair Disk. The disk is a bootable disk that contains the necessary data to reconstruct a configuration if your NT system is no longer able to boot; it helps when you forget your password, and when other configuration problems occur.

Installing NT Server

When you install NT, you will need a set of disks included with the NT Server package; the disks are labeled Setup Disk 1, Setup Disk 2, and Setup Disk 3. If you do not have those disks—as when installing over the network—NT will create them for you before installing the program. This section guides you through NT installation.

Beginning Setup

You're most likely installing the first server to your network—the primary domain controller. Follow the instructions, step-by-step, and choose the primary domain controller when prompted for server type, as described in the following directions. You may be installing a member server or a backup domain controller to your network; in which case you follow the same directions and just choose the appropriate server instead of the primary domain controller when prompted.

Problem? If you do not have the three 3.5-inch floppy disks needed to start NT setup or one of those disks is damaged, you can create them from over the network. To create the setup disks, attach to the network and change to the directory containing the setup files. At a MS-DOS prompt or in the Run dialog box from Windows, type winnt if the operating system of your server is anything other than a previous version of NT; type winnt32 if a previous version of NT is currently running. Follow the directions on-screen to create the disks; then you can pick up with the following instructions.

To install NT to the server, follow these steps:

1. Insert the 3.5-inch floppy disk labeled "Setup Disk 1" in the disk drive and turn the computer on. Setup begins automatically. As you're setting up NT, you press ENTER to continue Setup; if you need to quit the setup program, press F3 to exit, realizing Setup will not be complete and you'll have to start from the beginning to install NT at a later date.

2. When Setup prompts you to insert the disk labeled "Setup Disk 2," remove disk one, insert disk 2, and press ENTER. Setup loads various files, including the Setup program; video, floppy disk, and keyboard drivers; SCSI drivers; the FAT file system, and so on. A blue Welcome to Setup screen appears.

3. Read the information on the screen and do one of the following:

   1. To read about NT Setup, press F1. After you read about the Setup process, you can return to this screen to begin the installation.

   2. To set up NT, press ENTER. This begins the installation of the operating system.

   3. To repair a damaged or corrupted installation of NT, press R. If you previously installed NT and you experience system problems, you can use this option to reinstall and repair the operating system.

   4. To quit setup, press F3. If you exit the Setup, NT will not be installed.

   5. If you press ENTER to continue, a second blue screen appears.

4. You can enable Setup to automatically detect what NT calls *mass storage devices*, such as CD–ROM drives, SCSI adapters, drive arrays, and so on. You can manually select these devices, if you prefer; however, Setup is proficient at automatically detecting your devices. I suggest you press EN-TER to let Setup automatically detect your devices. If you prefer to man-

ually select the devices, press S and follow the directions on-screen. Choose the device driver or controller you want to use; if the device isn't on the list, you will need to use the manufacturer's disk to install the device.

Note: Don't worry if you do not see your hard disks listed. Setup detects all SCSI, IDE, and ESDI, even if they aren't included in the list.

5. Setup prompts you to insert the third disk, "Setup Disk 3." Remove disk 2, insert disk 3, and press ENTER. You may notice a period of inactivity while Setup searches for devices; don't disturb the process, even if it seems to take a while. After the third floppy disk, you can press F1 for help if you have questions about any screen in Setup.

Problem? If you think Setup is taking too long in any process along the way, wait another full five minutes to see if there's any disk activity. Some processes don't show disk activity. If you're convinced the Setup is stalled, put the first Setup disk into the floppy drive, turn the computer off, wait 10 seconds, then begin the process again. If Setup was past the three floppy disks and using the CD-ROM, remove all floppies from the drive before rebooting the computer and see if Setup will pick back up where it left off. If not, go back to disk 1 and start over.

6. When finished, NT displays a Setup screen that lists the devices it found and installed. If Setup missed a device, such as a CD-ROM drive, disk controller, or SCSI adapter, you can add the device by pressing S and following the directions on-screen. Otherwise, press ENTER to continue. Setup loads the necessary device drivers. You can also install additional devices after setup is complete (Start, Settings, Control Panel, choose the SCSI Adapters option).

Problem? If Setup was unable to locate your CD-ROM drive, it displays a screen telling you that Setup cannot continue. You must press F3 to exit setup. A screen appears telling you to remove any floppy disks from the drive and press ENTER to restart the computer. Insert the first setup disk in the drive and press ENTER. You'll need to go through setup again; this time, manually select your CD-ROM drive when prompted in step 4. If Setup still doesn't see your CD-ROM drive, then you might need an updated driver; check out the Internet or call the manufacturer of the device.

7. Setup displays a screen prompting you to format the drive if your disk is a new one or there is an operating system on the disk that is not compatible with NT. Setup warns you that continuing may erase data on the disk. Press C to continue Setup; press F3 to exit Setup.

8. Setup displays the licensing agreement for use of NT. You must press the PAGE DOWN key to continue. Press PAGE DOWN until you get to the end of the agreement. Press F8 to signify you agree to the licensing and you can continue. Press ESC to indicate you don't agree and exit Setup.

9. The next Setup screen displays a list of hardware and software components in your server, including the keyboard type and layout, mouse, and so on. To change any item, use the arrow keys to highlight the item, then press ENTER to display alternative choices. When the list is correct, highlight "The above list matches my computer" and press ENTER.

10. Next, the Setup screen displays a list of existing partitions and the space available for creating new partitions. Each drive and its file system is displayed in this list. You can install NT to any permanent hard disk with enough disk space (123M); however, NT must have access to the root directory of drive C (Disk 0) to be able to boot when you start your computer. If you want to use both MS-DOS and NT in a dual boot, thus using the FAT file system, install MS-DOS to the computer before installing NT; make your DOS partition only a part of the entire disk. Then you can install NT to the rest of the partition.

    If you want to use the entire partition for a FAT system and the disk has not been formatted, you can format it from Setup. If you want to use the NTFS file system, you can also format the drive to NTFS from Setup. Before you format a drive, you must delete the partition. Then you create a partition, specifying the size or accepting the default; then you can choose to format the drive.

    Highlight the item to which you want to install NT. If the space is unpartitioned, you can create a partition by pressing C. Delete an existing partition by pressing D. When you create a partition, Setup prompts you to enter the size of the partition, in megabytes. Setup also lists the minimum and maximum size you can designate for the new partition. Press ENTER to create the partition and Setup returns to the previous screen.

11. To install NT, highlight the partition or unpartitioned space and press ENTER. If the partition isn't formatted, Setup prompts you to format the partition. You can choose to format the partition in either the FAT or the NTFS file system. If the partition is formatted with the FAT system, you can skip the formatting process and continue with step 13.

12. Highlight the file system you want to use and press ENTER to continue. Setup formats the partition, displaying a screen that tracks the formatting progress.

13. Setup next displays the directory, or folder, to which it will install the system files. You can accept the default directory or enter another directory in which to install the system files; however, I suggest you keep the defaults for all installation directories in case you want to install other products that depend on NT's default file system.

    If you currently have Windows NT version 3.1, 3.5, or 3.51, Windows 95, or MS-DOS and Windows 3.x installed to the server, NT Setup detects the operating system and displays the directory in which one of these operating systems resides. You can either let Setup migrate the registry settings from the current system or you can create a dual boot. To create a dual boot, change the name of the directory to WINNT or something similar. Alternatively, let Setup overwrite the data in the selected directory to install NT.

    If you're running Windows 95, you must install Windows NT in a new directory; you cannot migrate the registry files from Windows 95 to NT because they are not compatible.

14. Setup next examines the hard disk. Although you can skip this examination by pressing the ESC key, I suggest you let Setup examine your disk to prevent problems later, after the operating system is up and running and users are attached. Press ENTER to continue; Setup doesn't examine the disk at this point but it will check it later in the process. Setup copies files to your hard disk and displays a screen to track the progress of the process.

15. When Setup finishes copying the files, it prompts you to remove any floppy disks from the drive and press ENTER. NT reboots your computer. During the process, you'll see the boot screen and a disk scanning screen. Don't respond to anything on-screen while Setup is checking and rebooting the computer. Setup may reboot your computer more than once; leave it alone until it prompts you with the next screen listed in the next set of steps.

Part Two of the Setup

Setup now shifts to a more Windows–like set of screens to continue setup. This part of Setup is completed through the use of a set of *Wizard* dialog boxes; wizards describe the process, give you choices, and let you go forward and/or backwards in the process. In any Wizard dialog box, choose the Next button to continue or the Back button to go to the previous wizard dialog box and change or check your options.

1. Setup displays the first Wizard dialog box, stating it will gather information about your computer; click the Next button.

2. When prompted, enter your name and the name of your organization; click Next or press ENTER.

3. Enter the 10-digit CD Key from the back of your CD case; click Next.

4. In the Computer Name dialog box, enter a name for your computer; that name can be up to 15 characters and it must be a unique name in the network. You can use spaces within the name. Click Next.

5. In the Server Type dialog box, choose the type of server you're installing: Primary Domain Controller, Backup Domain Controller, or Standalone Server (which is a member server). If this is the first server you're installing to your network, you must choose Primary Domain Controller. Click Next.

Problem? If your Pentium-based computer contains the faulty programming for performing the floating-point division, a screen appears next that offers the choice of letting NT turn off your computer's floating-point mode and run NT's floating-point operations instead. Choosing this option may slow the system considerably.

---

6. The Administrator Account dialog box appears; enter your password, then enter the password again to confirm it. Click Next.

7. Choose Yes in the Emergency Repair Disk dialog box to create a boot disk to use in case you forget your password, the server crashes, or some other catastrophe occurs. Click Next.

8. In the Select Components dialog box, choose the components you want to install to the server. To view the details of any component, select it in the Components list and click the Details button; select any of those components and choose OK to return to the Select Components dialog box. Click Next.

9. Setup displays the next dialog box in which you click Next to continue Installing Windows NT Networking. When prompted, choose the option that states the computer will participate on a network, then choose the method(s) of connection: Wired to the network (using a cable and network adapter) and/or Remote access to the network (using a modem). You can choose both options or just one.

   If you choose Remote access, you'll be prompted later for information about your client's remote use, installing a modem, and dialing information; if you're not prepared at this time to complete the RAS configuration, you can always add it later, after installation.

10. If you want to install the Microsoft Internet Information Server (IIS), make sure the option's check box is checked and click Next. The Internet Information Server is a Web server you can use to attach your users to the Internet or to create an intranet within your company that your users can take advantage of. Click Next.

    If you choose to install the Microsoft Internet Information Server, you'll be prompted later for information concerning the type of services you want to install, TCP/IP configuration, and so on; if you're not prepared to enter this information at this time, do not install the IIS now. You can always add the IIS later, after installation.

11. In the next Wizard dialog box, choose the Start Search button to enable Setup to detect your network adapter card(s). If Setup cannot locate your card, choose the Select From List button to select the card yourself. Click Next to continue.

12. Select the network protocols you want to install: TCP/IP, NWLink IPX/SPX-Compatible, and/or NetBEUI.

    If you choose TCP/IP, you will need to enter IP addresses and other configuration information; if you are unsure as to which addresses you should use, see Appendix C for more information. As with any installation item, you can install TCP/IP at any time after installation of the NT operating system.

13. In the next Wizard dialog box, you will select the Network Services. By default, all services are selected, and should be. Click the Next button to accept the defaults; if you click the Select From List button, you can choose additional services, such as the Gateway Services for NetWare, Microsoft DHCP Server, and so on. You can always add these services after installation is complete if you discover you need them. Click Next.

14. To begin installing, click Next again. If you selected a network adapter card to use to connect to the network, Setup displays a dialog box request-

Network Services

Network services support the network operations performed by NT. These services enable you to share files and printers over the network, enable automatic system backup, network monitor support, and so on. Following are descriptions of the network services; after installation, these services can be found in the Services tab of the Network dialog box:

Computer Browser: Keeps an updated list of computers attached to the network and provides the list to applications when requested.

NetBIOS Interface: A standard programming interface used to develop client/server applications; enables communications over various protocols between nodes on a network.

Remote Access Service: enables users at remote sites to use the network as if they were in the office, attached via LAN. With RAS, users attach via a modem and phone line.

RPC Configuration: Remote Procedure Call is a subsystem of NT that manages a name service database. Enables communications between remote systems, locates which server contains the requested service, and determines which communication mechanism to use.

SAP Agent: Service Advertising Protocol, provides a method for servers to advertise their services on the network; allows routers to create and maintain a database of current internetwork server information.

Server: Provides RPC support, file and print sharing, and so on.

Workstation: Provides network connections and communications.

Additional services you can add to the list are:

DHCP Relay Agent: Dynamic Host Configuration Protocol, supports obtaining an IP address from a DHCP server.

Microsoft Internet Information Server: Enables the use of the IIS, a Web, FTP, and Gopher server designed to work with NT. Use the server as an intranet or Internet server.

Gateway (and Client) Services for NetWare: Enables access to NetWare file and print resources to Microsoft networking clients.

Microsoft DHCP Server: Automatically provides IP addresses for WINS and DNS servers, and assigns IP addresses and other TCP/IP configurations to clients.

Microsoft DNS Server: Domain Name System, enables the server to locate other computers on the TCP/IP network using a distributed name resolution service. Similar to WINS.

Network Monitor Agent, Network Monitor Tools and Agent: Enables the computer running the Network Monitor—a tool that troubleshoots complex network problems—to attach to other computers on the network, or using RAS, to perform monitoring of network segments.

(continues)

Network Services (*Continued*)

Remoteboot Service: Enables NT Server to start and control MS-DOS and Windows computers over the network.

RIP for NWLink IPX: Routing Information Protocol, a router protocol that dynamically exchanges routing information with other routers running the RIP protocol when used with the NWLink IPX protocol.

Services for Macintosh: Enables Macintosh computers to share files and printers with PCs on the network.

Simple TCP/IP Services: Installs the server software that enables the server to respond to requests from other computers supporting TCP/IP services, such as a UNIX computer.

SNMP Service: Simple Network Management Protocol, allows you to administer the server remotely and to monitor statistics for TCP/IP services.

TCP/IP Printing: Enables the server to print to UNIX print queues or TCP/IP printers connected directly to the network.

Simple TCP/IP Services, SNMP Service, FTP Server, and TCP/IP Printing simplify integration into a UNIX network.

Windows Internet Name Service: WINS, enables the server to use dynamic name resolution to direct client requests for computers using the TCP/IP protocol.

---

ing the IRQ and I/O port address; enter the appropriate settings and click Continue. No matter what you type in the dialog box, Setup displays a message that it cannot verify the settings and asks if it should use them anyway. Choose OK.

15. Choose Next in the Wizard dialog box that states NT is ready to start the network. Click Next.

16. Setup displays the dialog box that asks if your computer is a member of a domain or a workgroup. Enter the Domain name in the text box provided. You choose the Create a Computer Account in the Domain if you're adding a computer, such as a member server, to the network. In this case, you don't need to check the check box for this option. Choose Next.

Note: A workgroup, as opposed to a domain, is a group of computers that share directories and other resources over the network but do not share a common directory database; therefore, members of a workgroup

Other Installation Options

Depending on the items you've chosen to install, you may see some of the following options and dialog boxes:

DHCP Server. If you've installed TCP/IP, cancel the DHCP server dialog box that appears. A DHCP server can automatically configure TCP/IP for you and NT has the capability of being a DHCP server; however, that option is not going to help you with this first server on your network. You must first have a DHCP server before you can use it to help configure TCP/IP settings. See Appendix C for information about setting up a DHCP server.

RAS: If you've chosen to install RAS, or remote access services, you'll be prompted to install a modem before the service can be configured. You can also install the modem later, after NT installation is complete, from the Control Panel. You may also need to configure RAS Server with the TCP/IP Configuration for clients to access your server; see Appendix C for information regarding TCP/IP.

IPX/SPX: If you've chosen to install IPX/SPX, you may need to configure the network number for the adapter to continue setup. The number is most likely 0000000; you can change the number to 000001 to continue.

TCP/IP: To install TCP/IP, you will need to enter an IP address, DNS, WINS, DHCP, and Routing information. See Appendix C for more information.

Microsoft Internet Information Server. If you've installed the Microsoft Internet Information Server, your computer name should also be a valid Internet host name; if it is not, Setup will display a dialog box warning you of the problem and offering solutions. Follow the directions on-screen.

You will also need to choose components in the Microsoft Internet Information Server Setup dialog box. Choose whether to install WWW services, Internet Service Manager, samples, and so on. Let NT create the directories required and it will load all of the necessary files.

---

cannot share resources with computers in a domain, only with members of their workgroup. For the most part, you'll want to assign your workstations to a domain instead of a workgroup.

If you had chosen to create a computer account, you would need to enter your user name and password to verify that you're allowed to create accounts on the network.

17. In the Finishing Setup option in the next Wizard dialog box, click the Finish button to complete the installation.

18. In the Date/Time Properties dialog box, choose your time zone, and verify the date and time. Click Close.

19. In the Display Properties dialog box, set the display type and test by clicking the Test button. Choose OK to continue setup. You won't be able to change fonts or color during installation; but you can change these settings later in the Display option of the Control Panel. Setup continues by copying files and saving system configuration.

20. When installation is complete, Setup displays a dialog box that prompts you to remove all floppy disks and CD-ROMs from your drives. Then click the Restart Computer button. NT shuts down and reboots.

Starting NT Server

Booting NT Server takes the computer through a series of startup processes. You can watch the process on-screen and at different points during the boot, change options to troubleshoot any startup problems you're having.

Booting the System

Initially, a x86 computer goes through its POST routine (Power On Self Test) which determines the amount of memory and whether certain hardware elements, such as the keyboard and mouse, are present. Next, each adapter card with a BIOS runs its own POST routine. Then, the system BIOS locates the startup disk, or the disk with the Master Boot Record and the Partition Table. First the system checks drive A; if there's no disk in A, it checks the first hard disk, usually C.

The system BIOS reads the Master Boot Record and loads it into memory and between the Master Boot Record and the Partition Boot Sector, the code starts the operating system.

Note: BIOS (Basic Input/Output System) is a set of instructions that lets the computer's hardware and operating system communicate with applications and peripheral devices, such as hard disks, printers, and video adapters.

As NT starts up, a boot loader (NTLDR) menu appears. The boot loader offers you the choices of the operating system you want to load. If you have a dual boot, you can use the arrow keys to choose the operating system you want to start, then press ENTER. NTLDR controls the operating system and hardware detection.

Notice NT has two choices, exactly the same except for the addition of [VGA mode] to the second choice. Use the first option to start NT. You use [VGA mode] only when you've loaded a video driver that isn't working. Choosing the [VGA mode] option from the boot loader menu starts NT with a standard, default video driver so you can see the screen and options. Open the Control Panel (Start, Settings, Control Panel) and double-click the Display option to change the video driver.

If you don't choose an entry before the counter reaches 0, NTLDR loads the default operating system, Windows NT Server Version 4.0.

Ntdetect.com next collects information about currently installed components—such as the computer ID, adapter type, video, keyboard, communication ports, and so on—and returns the information to the NTLDR.

The OS Loader V4.0 screen appears with the statement: "Press spacebar now to invoke Hardware Profile/Last Known Good menu." You press the spacebar if you've been having trouble with NT loading correctly; pressing the spacebar enables you to choose an alternate configuration for booting. Highlight the Last Known Good Configuration option to open Windows NT using the configuration that was used the last time it successfully started. Press ENTER to continue.

Otherwise, ignore the message and let NT continue to boot; it will only wait a few seconds for a response, then continue on its own.

The screen turns blue and the name and build of the operating system appear—MS (R) Windows NT (TM) Version 4.0 (Build 1345). This is the Kernel initializing. The kernal is the most fundamental part of the operating system; it stays resident in memory at all times and manages system memory, the file system, and disk operations.

Logging On

When the Kernel initialization finishes, the Begin Login dialog box appears. Press CTRL+ALT+DEL to log onto the server. In the Logon dialog box, enter the Administrator's password and press ENTER. I recommend you immediately create a User account for yourself with Administrative rights and save the Administrator user for emergencies. See Chapter 6 for information about creating users.

Configuring Network Components after Setup

Although you set up your network components during installation, you may find you need to modify settings, add an adapter or protocol, or otherwise change options after installation. This section gives you a brief overview of the Network dialog box.

To open the Network dialog box, choose the Start button, Settings, Control Panel. In the Control Panel, double-click the Network icon. The Network dialog box appears. The following sections describe each tab in the Network dialog box.

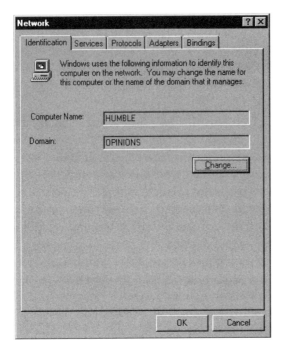

Figure 5.1 *The identification tab distinguishes the server on the network.*

Identification

The server must have a name to identify it on the network. You can change that name in the Identification tab (see Figure 5.1). You also can change the name of the domain; however, changing the domain name affects all other computers on the network. If you chose a workgroup instead of domain during installation, you can change to domain using the Change button, as well.

To change the computer or domain name, or to change from a workgroup to a domain, choose the Change button. The Identification Changes dialog box appears (see Figure 5.2). Enter the new name and choose OK to return to the Network dialog box. You can either choose OK to close the Network dialog box or choose another tab to configure. When you do close the dialog box, NT prompts you to restart the computer to allow the configuration changes to take place.

Services

Use the Services tab to view the list of network services installed to the computer and to add or remove services. Network services support specific operations on the

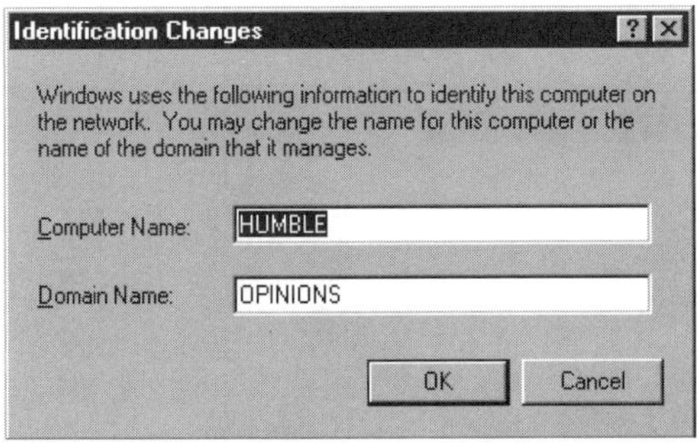

Identification Changes

Windows uses the following information to identify this computer on the network. You may change the name for this computer or the name of the domain that it manages.

Computer Name: HUMBLE

Domain Name: OPINIONS

OK   Cancel

Figure 5.2 *Change the computer name or the domain name.*

network, such as sharing files and printers, automatic backup, the Gateway Service for NetWare, and so on; see the sidebar, "Network Services," earlier in this chapter for a complete explanation of the services offered. Figure 5.3 displays the Services tab in the Network dialog box.

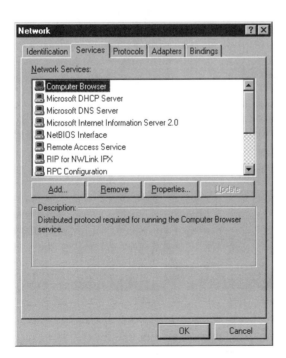

Network

Identification | Services | Protocols | Adapters | Bindings

Network Services:

- Computer Browser
- Microsoft DHCP Server
- Microsoft DNS Server
- Microsoft Internet Information Server 2.0
- NetBIOS Interface
- Remote Access Service
- RIP for NWLink IPX
- RPC Configuration

Add...   Remove   Properties...   Update

Description:
Distributed protocol required for running the Computer Browser service.

OK   Cancel

Figure 5.3 *Add or remove network services that enable network procedures to take place.*

Figure 5.4 *Add, remove, or configure devices to use for remote access services by choosing the Properties button in the Services tab.*

To add a service choose the Add button. NT displays a list of available services; select one and choose OK. You may need either a manufacturer's disk or the NT Server CD to complete the installation of the service.

To remove a service, select the service in the list and choose the Remove button. Be careful when removing services; you may stop the entire system.

To view the properties of any service, select the service and choose the Properties button. Some services do not display a properties dialog box. The properties enable you to configure the service, such as setting ports, addresses, and so on. Figure 5.4 shows the Remote Access Setup dialog box that appears when you view RAS properties.

You can either choose OK to close the Network dialog box or choose another tab to configure. When you do close the dialog box, NT may prompt you to restart the computer to allow the configuration changes to take place.

Protocols

The Protocols tab (see Figure 5.5) enables you to add, remove, and configure protocols. To add a protocol, choose the Add button. NT displays a list of available protocols in the Select Network Protocol dialog box (see Figure 5.6).

You also can add a protocol for which you have a manufacturer's disk; in the Select Network Protocol dialog box, click the Have Disk button. Select the protocol and choose OK.

To configure a protocol, select the protocol from the list and choose the Properties button. The protocol's Properties dialog box appears. Figure 5.7 shows the Microsoft TCP/IP Properties dialog box in which you can configure IP addresses, DNS, WINS, and other settings specific to TCP/IP. For more information about

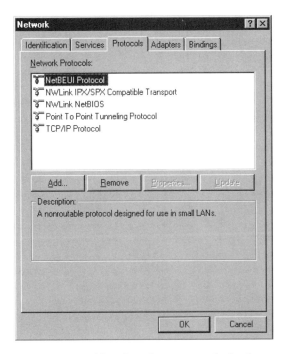

Figure 5.5 *Add and configure protocols for the server.*

TCP/IP, see Appendix C. Choose OK to close the Properties dialog box and return to the Network dialog box.

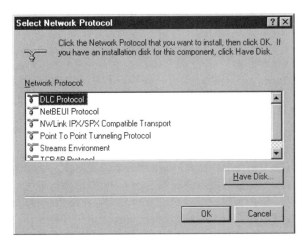

Figure 5.6 *Choose a protocol to add to the server.*

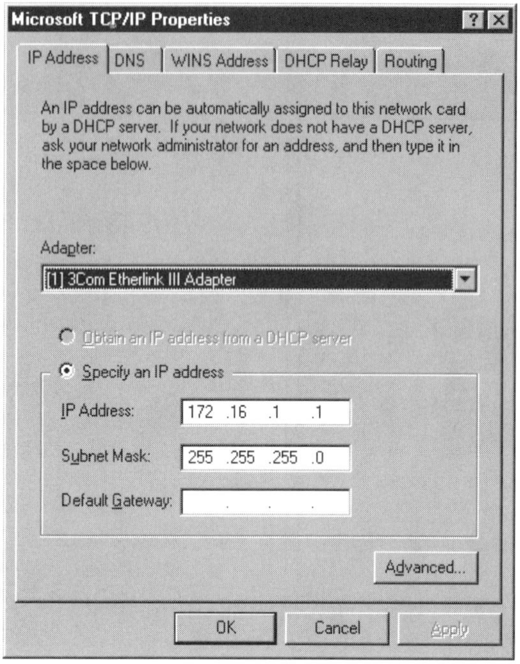

Figure 5.7 *Configure specific settings for a protocol.*

You can either choose OK to close the Network dialog box or choose another tab to configure. When you do close the dialog box, NT may prompt you to restart the computer to allow the configuration changes to take place.

Adapters

You most likely configured your network adapter card during the initial installation of NT; however, you can always add or remove an adapter, or change configuration settings in the Adapters tab of the Network dialog box (see Figure 5.8).

Add or remove adapters by clicking the appropriate button in the Adapters tab. NT includes many drivers for various manufactures and models of adapter cards; you can, alternatively, provide a manufacturer's disk to install the adapter's driver—make sure the adapter driver is compatible for NT Server 4.0 before trying to install it.

Figure 5.9 shows the Select Network Adapter dialog box. After you choose the adapter you want to add, choose OK to display the card's Setup dialog box. Set IRQ and I/Op port addresses for an adapter by selecting it or typing it in.

Alternatively, you can select an adapter in the Network Adapters list and choose the Properties button to configure various settings, including the IRQ and

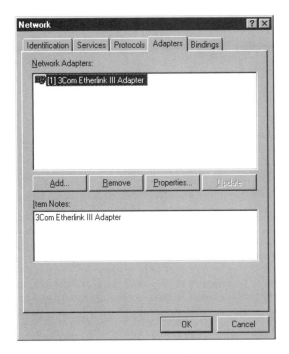

Figure 5.8 *Add, remove, or configure network adapters.*

I/O Port Address for the card (see Figure 5.10). Choose OK to close the dialog box and return to the Network dialog box.

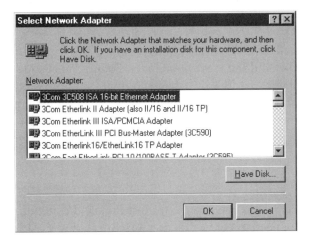

Figure 5.9 *Add an adapter to the server.*

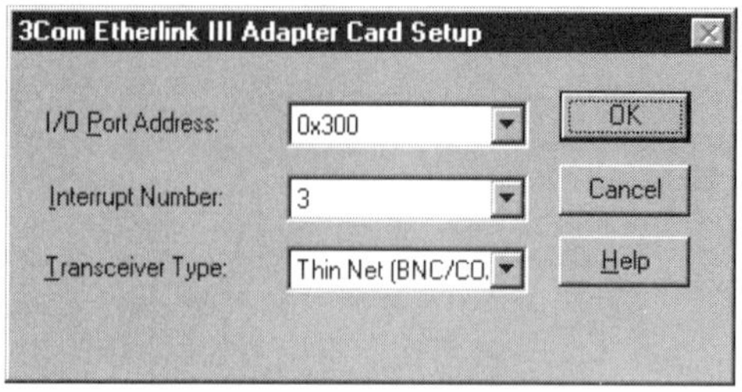

Figure 5.10 *Configure the network adapter card's settings.*

You can either choose OK to close the Network dialog box or choose another tab to configure. When you do close the dialog box, NT may prompt you to restart the computer to allow the configuration changes to take place.

Bindings

The Bindings tab shows a list of network services, protocols, and adapter cards, and the bindings that connect them. To view the bindings for any object in the list, double-click the object, then click any plus sign preceding the object in the list, as shown in Figure 5.11.

You can also choose to enable or disable a binding by selecting it and choosing the appropriate button; however, do not change the bindings unless you understand the effects of your actions. You could disable users' access to the server.

You can either choose OK to close the Network dialog box or choose another tab to configure. When you do close the dialog box, NT may prompt you to restart the computer to allow the configuration changes to take place.

Problem? If you install a service from the Network dialog box and the service doesn't start, double-click the Services option in the Control Panel and see if the service is listed in the dialog box. If it is, make sure that its Status is Started and its Startup is Automatic. You can change any of the Status or Startup options by selecting the service, then choosing the Start button and/or the Startup button.

Configuring Peripherals

NT offers many device drivers you can use for installing and configuring your drivers; however, you may need to contact the manufacturers of some devices you use and ask for updated NT Server 4.0 drivers, if NT doesn't supply then. You can install those drivers and configure the devices after the installation.

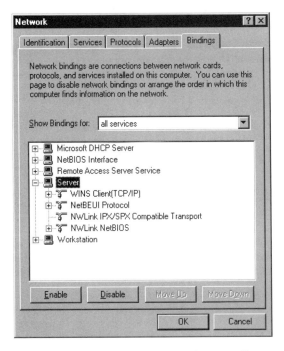

Figure 5.11 *View bindings to make sure all services are active and working.*

Before purchasing or installing any peripheral devices, check with the HCL to make sure the device works with NT. See Chapter 8 for information about installing and configuring printers attached to the NT network.

Control Panel Overview

You configure most devices in the Control Panel in NT. Figure 5.12 shows the Control Panel and the following list provides a brief explanation of each option, or icon, in the Panel. The following sections explain the options you can use in configuring devices in more detail. To open any option in the Control Panel, double-click the icon.

The contents of the Control Panel are as follows:

Accessibility Options: Enables you to configure keyboard, sound, and mouse settings to make the server more accessible for special needs.

Add/Remove Programs: Enables you to install and uninstall applications and run Windows NT Setup.

MS-DOS Console: Enables you to customize the command prompt window.

Date/Time: Set the date, time, and time zone of the server.

Figure 5.12 *You can configure most server settings in the Control Panel.*

Devices: Start or stop devices, such as the network adapter, CD-ROM, and so on. See following section for more information.

Display: Set wallpaper, screen saver, screen colors, and resolution. Be careful with screen savers and wallpaper on the server; those take precious memory away from the real tasks for which you need the server.

Fonts: Install and remove fonts from the system.

Internet: Sets a proxy server to access the Internet and act as a security barrier between your network and the Internet.

Keyboard: Set options for the server's keyboard, such as language, repeat rate, cursor blink rate, and so on.

Licensing: Lists client licensing mode; see Appendix A for information about licensing.

Mail: Enables the setup for MS Exchange settings and properties.

Microsoft Mail Post Office: Set up and configure a post office for the network, using MS Mail, Internet Mail, or other available program.

Modems: Install and configure a modem using the Wizard dialog boxes.

Mouse: Set button configuration, double-click speed, and so on.

MultiMedia: Set audio, video, MIDI properties, and view multimedia device properties.

Network: Configure and install network components.

ODBC: Add, delete, and configure data sources, such as SQL Server databases or a directory of dBASE files.

PC Card: Applies only to the PCMCIA card and controller.

Ports: Specify communications settings for selected serial ports.

Printers: Use to install and configure printers; see Chapter 8 for more information.

Regional Settings: Set time zone, currency, numbering, language, and so on for your area of the world.

SCSI Adapters: View list of adapters and their properties; see following section.

Server: Show the connected users, shared resources, network alerts, and so on.

Services: Displays the status of services, such as the Gateway Service, DHCP client, Event Log, and so on; see following section.

Sounds: Change the sounds you hear when certain errors or tasks are performed on the server.

System: Check performance, environment information, user profiles, and so on.

Tape Devices: Lists tape devices and enables you to add drivers; see following section.

Telephony: Enter information about your area code, phone system, and so on, and add telephony drivers to use NT with dial out utilities.

UPS: Configure the UPS service; see following section.

Setting Up Devices

You can control when many of the devices on the server start by using the Devices option in the Control Panel. Devices are hardware equipment such as the CD-ROM, disks, floppy drive, keyboard, mouse, ports, monitor, network adapters, and others; protocols, such as TCP/IP, RIP for NWLink IPX, NWLink, and so on; and services, such as WINS Client, Remote Access, NetBIOS Interface, and so on.

The Devices dialog box lists available devices and their startup type (see Figure 5.13). Startup can be Boot, System, Automatic, Manual, or Disabled. You may want to configure a device to start when the system boots or to start only when

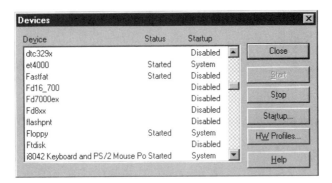

Figure 5.13 *View device startup status in the Devices dialog box.*

you choose to start it. Additionally, you can disable certain devices for troubleshooting purposes.

To start or stop a device, select the device and choose either the Start or Stop button. To configure startup types, select the device and choose the Startup button. Select the startup type you want to use from the list.

SCSI Adapters

Use the SCSI Adapters option in the Control Panel to view the properties of adapters and to add or remove drivers for SCSI adapters. SCSI (Small Computer System Interface) is a high-speed parallel interface used to connect a PC to up to seven peripheral devices at a time to just one port. You can use SCSI to connect hard disks, tape drives, CD-ROM drives, scanners, printers, and other devices.

Figure 5.14 shows the SCSI Adapters dialog box. The Devices tab lists the SCSI devices on the server.

In the Devices tab, select a driver and choose the Properties button. You can configure the following properties:

Card Info includes the type, manufacturer, and status of the device.

Driver Info lists the name, file, and status of the driver.

Resources list the IRQ, I/O, memory range, and so on.

Figure 5.15 shows the Resources tab of the adapter's Properties dialog box.

The Drivers tab enables you to add or remove drivers for the SCSI adapter.

Services

If you have problems with services or devices, check the status in the Services option of the Control Panel. The services you selected to install upon installation of

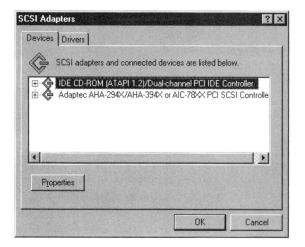

Figure 5.14 *View a list of SCSI adapters on the server.*

the operating system, or later chose in the Network dialog box, are some of the services that are listed in the Services dialog box. However, there are other services that help manage NT, including the Event Viewer (a utility for viewing logs that record system errors, security breaches, and so on), Plug and Play (a feature that enables you to use PNP devices with your server, and so on. Figure 5.16 shows the Services dialog box with the UPS service selected. If the UPS isn't functioning, you should make sure the service is configured to Automatic.

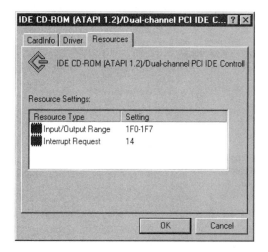

Figure 5.15 *View information about the device in the adapter's Properties dialog box.*

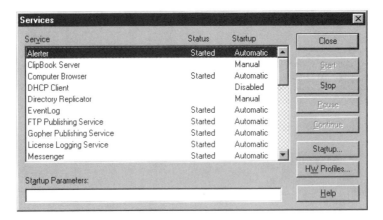

Figure 5.16 *View and configure services for certain devices.*

To change the service in question, select the service in the list and choose Start to start it manually, Stop to stop the service, Pause, or Continue. To change the Startup type, select the service and click the Startup button; choose Automatic, Manual, or Disabled.

Tape Devices

The Tape Devices option in the Control Panel enables you to view tape devices and install tape drivers. Figure 5.17 displays the Tape Devices dialog box. If no tape drives are listed, choose the Detect button. When the tape device appears in the list

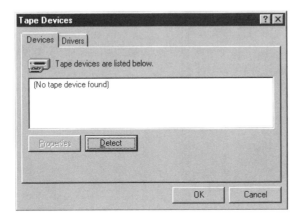

Figure 5.17 *Let the Tape Devices option detect your tape device.*

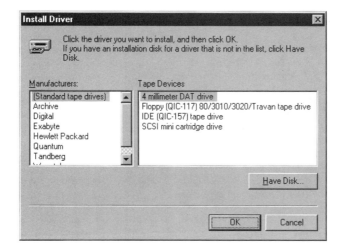

Figure 5.18 *Choose the driver for the tape device.*

on the Devices tab, select it and view the properties by choosing the Properties button.

Additionally, you can choose the Drivers tab to add or remove drivers. Figure 5.18 shows the list of NT's drivers; you can, however, insert a disk and choose Have Disk to install the manufacturer's NT-designed driver for the device.

UPS

NT supplies a UPS service you can use to notify your users of power outages and actions that will result from the power failure. In NT during a power failure, the UPS service pauses the server service to prevent new connections. Additionally, the service sends a message to notify users of the power failure. The service then waits the amount of time you specify before warning the users of the impending shutdown. If power is restored before the shutdown, the UPS service sends a message to users that the power is restored.

Some of the UPS service configuration options may not be available with your UPS. Additionally, setting the UPS service incorrectly for your hardware can cause problems with the UPS operation. Check your documentation for the UPS device before setting the UPS service in NT.

You should use the following services in combination with a UPS device on the server: UPS, Alerter, Messenger, and Event Log. See the previous section on Services to enable these.

You can configure the UPS service using the UPS option in the Control Panel. Figure 5.19 shows the UPS dialog box and Table 5.1 describes the options.

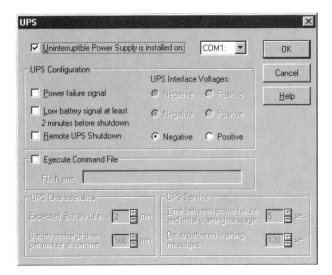

Figure 5.19 *Configure an uninterruptable power supply installed to the server.*

Table 5.1 UPS Options

OPTION	DESCRIPTION
Uninterruptable Power Supply Is Installed On	Select this option to activate the UPS service on the server and select the serial port to which the UPS is installed.
Power Failure Signal	Indicates whether the UPS can send a message in case of a power failure (corresponds to CTS cable signal).
Low Battery Signal	Indicates whether the UPS can send a warning when the battery is low (corresponds to the DCD cable signal).
Remote UPS Shutdown	Enable or disable shutdown of the UPS (corresponds to the DTR cable signal).
UPS Interface Voltages	Select either Positive or Negative for each option.
Execute Command File	Select and enter a file name to execute immediately before the system shuts down (the file must be able to execute and complete within 30 seconds).
Expected Battery Life	Enter the time, in minutes from 2 to 720, that the battery will sustain the system.
Battery Recharge Time	Enter the time, in minutes from 1 to 250, it takes the battery to recharge.
Time between Failure and Warning	Enter a time, in seconds from 0 to 120, before the first warning message is sent to users.
Delay between Warning Messages	Enter the time, in seconds from 5 to 300, you want to delay between warning messages sent to the users.

Note: Make sure that both the UPS and the serial cable are NT-compatible by checking the hardware compatibility list.

Modems

If you plan to use your server as a Web server for the Internet, as an Internet connection for your clients, as a remote access server to which clients can dial and access from home or another remote area, or as a dial-out server users can access to dial bulletin boards, on-line services, and so on, then you'll need to install one or more modems to your server.

Installing and configuring a modem is relatively simple because NT uses a Install New Modem Wizard to help you. Attach the modem(s) to your server and double-click the Modems icon in the Control Panel. If you've already added a modem, say during installation, the Modems Properties dialog box appears, as shown in Figure 5.20.

To add a modem, click the Add button and the Install New Modem Wizard appears. Follow the directions on-screen to install and configure the modem. To remove a modem, select it in the Modems Properties dialog box and click the Remove button.

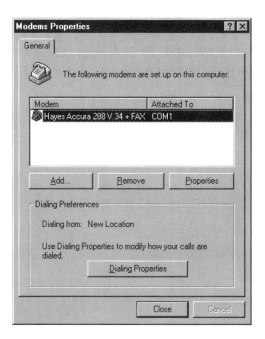

Figure 5.20 *Add or remove modems; configure existing modems on the server.*

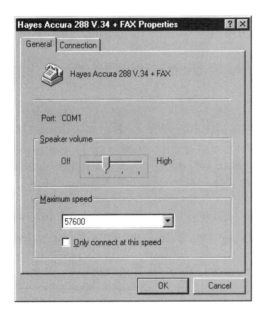

Figure 5.21 *Configure a modem's properties.*

To change or view the modem's configuration, select the modem and click the Properties button. Figure 5.21 shows the modem's Properties dialog box, from which you can set port, speaker volume, and maximum speed, as well as connection preferences such as data bits, parity, and stop bits.

Finally, you can set dialing properties for any modem by clicking the Dialing Properties button in the Modems Properties dialog box. Set such items as your area code, whether to use a calling card when dialing, and so on.

Display

You used the Display option in the Control Panel during installation of NT; however, you couldn't change anything in the dialog box but the display driver. After installation, you can open the Display option and change a variety of things. Figure 5.22 shows the Display Properties dialog box.

Following is a list of each tab in the dialog box and the types of settings it contains:

Background: Add a pattern or wallpaper to the screen using this tab; however, these items use extra memory and perhaps will subtract from the server's performance. It's better to use no pattern or wallpaper on a server.

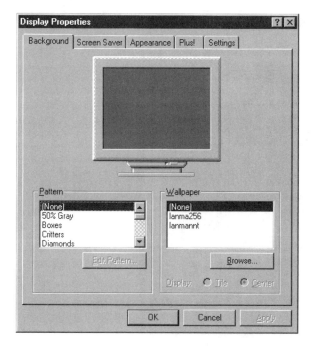

Figure 5.22 *Configure settings for your monitor in the Display Properties dialog box.*

Screen Saver: In this tab, you can choose a screen saver to use when the server is idle; however, a screen saver will subtract from your server's performance since the server will likely be working in the background all of the time. You shouldn't use screen savers with your NT server.

Appearance: Change color schemes, font format, and size in this tab.

Settings: Choose a color palette (256 colors, 65,536 colors, for example), desktop resolution, font size for the desktop, and refresh frequency (see Figure 5.23). You can also change the display type and driver in this tab; if you change the display driver and have trouble with it, choose the VGA option in the Boot Loader to load a generic driver, then come into this dialog box and change the driver.

System

Use the System icon in the Control Panel to view system information, hardware profiles, user profiles, environment, and other information about NT and your

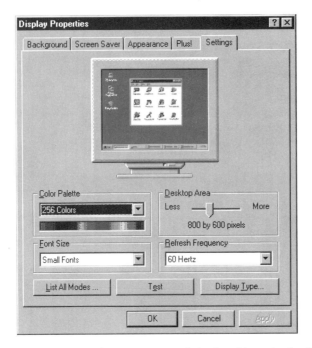

Figure 5.23 *Choose settings and display drivers in the Settings tab of the Display Properties dialog box.*

server. You will find the System Properties dialog box, shown in Figure 5.24, a most useful diagnostic tool.

Following is a list of the tabs in the System Properties dialog box and some of the information each contains:

General: Operating system version, registration information, and computer information, including RAM amount.

Performance: Enables you to specify the priority for foreground program relative to the background programs.

Environment: Lists system environment variables such as the operating system, default path, processor type, Windows directory, and so on.

Startup/Shutdown: Displays the list of programs that show in the NTLDR boot loader screen and enables you to change the amount of time the boot loader screen shows; default is 30 seconds. Also, enables you to direct the program in several recovery options, such as writing to the system log, alerting the administrator, automatically rebooting, and so on.

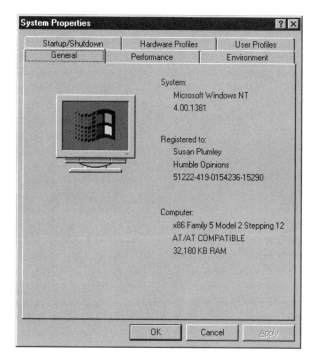

Figure 5.24 *View general information about your server in the General tab.*

Hardware Profiles: Display a list of hardware profiles used to boot the computer; profiles tell the system which drivers to load. You can create multiple profiles, configure their properties, and specify how to display the profiles choices when NT boots.

User Profiles: The user profiles describe those people who use the server; as administrator, your profile is listed along with any others you may add. You also can configure the properties of the selected profile.

Summary

This chapter covered installation of NT Server, including descriptions and advice about various options you must consider when installing the operating system. Additionally, you've seen how to configure and add various networking components, such as adapter cards, protocols, and services. Finally, this chapter described the contents of the Control Panel and configuration of some devices through the Control Panel.

PART

III

Setting Up and Using
NT Server

6 *Creating and Managing Users and Groups*

Windows NT Server includes administrative tools that enable you to create, edit, and manage users and groups on the network. Users are the people allowed to access the network and groups are sets of users that have the same level of security. A user account in NT, a security mechanism used to control access to the network, defines the user's name, password information, and information about any group to which the user belongs. You create and manage users and groups with the NT User Manager for Domains tool. This chapter shows how to do the following in NT Server:

- Create users
- Edit users
- Manage user accounts
- Configure the user's environment
- Manage existing groups
- Create and edit groups

Understanding Users and Groups

Thus far, you've seen how NT organizes computers into domains that can share network resources, such as files, directories, printers, and other peripherals. NT Server offers network users many services and benefits, including remote services, Internet access, applications-sharing, document-sharing, and more. With all of this sharing of data and resources, it stands to reason there has to be protection on the network for sensitive materials and limited resources. NT supplies the tools you need to guarantee security as well as access to the network resources—the User Manager for Domains.

You, as the network administrator, have control over the users on your network. You can enable users to open and change files, for example, or to connect to a specific printer only on certain days and times. You can grant these rights to individuals or entire groups of users. You control users' rights, group rights, and permissions for specific resources through the domain and domain controllers.

User Accounts

Within each domain is a primary domain controller that authenticates users. The PDC contains a database of all users on the network in the form of a user account. All users must have an account to log on to the server and use the resources within the domain.

The user account contains a name that identifies the user, a password, and a list of groups the user belongs to and the rights assigned to the groups and the individual user. When the user logs on to the network, the PDC checks the information against the database of users, verifies the user's rights, then enables the user to access only those resources for which he or she has rights.

Note: Each user account is assigned a unique security identifier (SID). When you create a user, NT assigns a SID; NT attaches the user's name, password, and other account information to the SID. If you delete the user's account, the SID is also deleted and the user can no longer log on to the network. If you change your mind and recreate that same user, a new SID is also created; you must, therefore, recreate the account information as well.

User rights determine what the user can and cannot do on the network. The network administrator, or someone delegated the authority by the administrator, decides which rights to assign a user. The administrator can assign rights to an individual; however, it's much easier to place individual users within groups, then assign an entire group rights. Editing and managing group rights then, is easier and more efficient than editing and managing each individual's rights.

Groups

NT includes several built-in groups, each with its own set of rights. For example, you're a member of the Administrators group, which entitles members the right to perform all tasks on the server. You can assign individual users to any group with the rights you want the individual to possess. NT enables you to edit the rights assigned to a group, as well; you can add rights or revoke rights to any built-in group.

You also can create your own groups and assign any rights to those groups that suits your purpose. Edit and manage groups you create just as you would the built-in groups; assign users to your own groups to limit their access to the network and its resources.

User Manager for Domains

In NT, the User Manager for Domains is the administrative tool for managing user accounts, groups, and security policies in domains. The network administrator controls all rights and permissions for user and group accounts to the resources on the domain. Object permissions refer to resources such as printers, files, and directories. In addition to granting a user rights dealing with the server or network, you can set permissions on a file, for example, and enable only certain groups to change that file. See Chapter 7 for information about object permissions.

Note: The User Manager for Domains is only available on a computer running NT Server and configured as a primary domain controller or a backup domain controller. On member servers and computers running the NT Workstation software, the utility is the User Manager and only enables you to control access to the computer on which you are working.

To open the User Manager for Domains, choose the Start button on the Taskbar, and select Programs, Administrative Tools, and User Manager for Domains. Figure 6.1 shows the User Manager for Domains on an NT Server, primary domain controller. Listed in the upper pane of the window are the individual users of the network; listed in the lower pane are groups.

The User Manager on a server running Windows NT Server looks similar to the User Manager in any client computer running Windows NT Workstation. The difference between the two tools is in the operating system running the computer. The User Manager on the server, called the User Manager for Domains, lets you manage user and group accounts on the local domain and on any domain to which you have access. The User Manager on a client or workstation enables you to manage only users and groups that access the workstation.

TIP: You can run User Manager for Domains on a computer running Windows NT Workstation if you've installed it using the Network Client Administrator so the server can be managed remotely from a workstation.

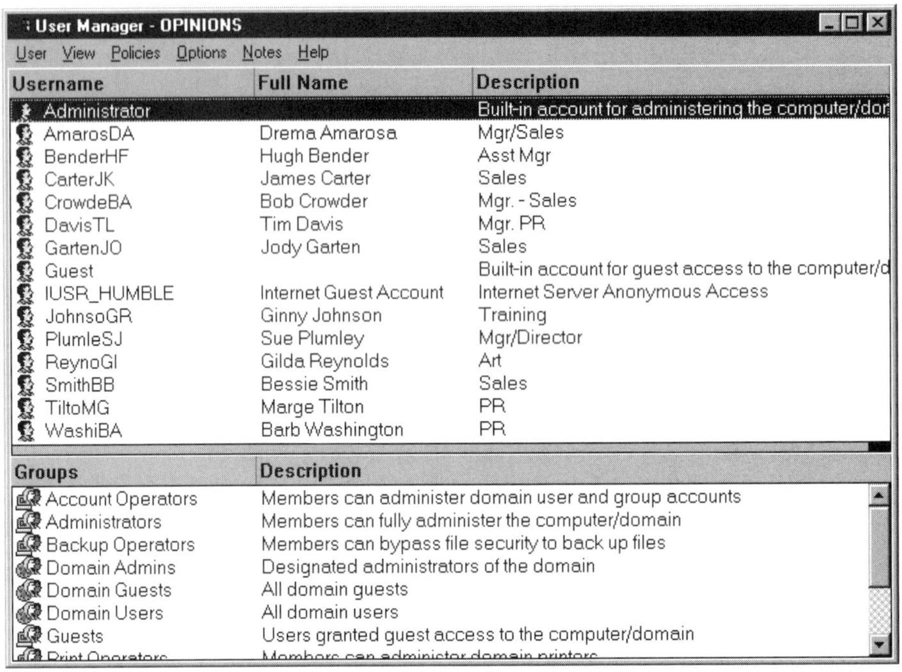

Figure 6.1 *View, edit, create, and otherwise manage users and groups in the User Manager for Domains.*

You'll notice, if your server is a member of more than one domain, that the domain name precedes the username to indicate where the user's account was created; for example BendeRH from the Product domain might appear as PRODUCT\BendeRH.

Single and Multiple Domain Information

In NT, a domain is a logical group of network servers and workstations that share common security and user account information. A domain may have one server or several, a few workstations or as many as 26,000, and as many as 250 groups. The number of accounts can be as much as 5000, depending on the power of the server.

For most organizations, a single domain is all you need. Administration and user management is easy within a single domain because one administrator can manage all network servers. You might, however, want to split your system into domains for organization purposes; this enables you to assign various administrators the task of managing their own department. For more information about multiple domains, see Chapter 15.

The possible computer members of a domain include primary and backup domain controllers, member servers, and workstations. You read about domain controllers earlier in the book; a domain controller is a computer running Windows NT Server that shares one directory database and manages all aspects of user-domain interactions. A member server is a computer running Windows NT Server software but has not been designated as a domain controller. Member servers don't have a copy of the directory database and cannot authenticate accounts; member servers usually serve as file, database, and/or print servers and can double as workstations.

If you use multiple domains, you'll need to understand trust relationships. A trust relationship is a link that combines two domains into one administrative unit that authorizes access to the resources on both domains.

NT's Directory Services provides two types of trust relationships: one-way and two-way. The one-way trust relationship represents one domain that trusts another to use its resources. The first domain enables users on the trusted domain access to resources, but its users are not trusted to use the second domain's resources. The two-way trust relationship enables users in each domain to access resources in the trusted domains. Naturally, using the resources in any domain is subject to permissions and rights. For more information about trusting domains, see Chapter 15.

User and Group Rights

The rights assigned to a user determine the actions the user can perform on the domain. If you're working on the domain controller and assign specific rights to a user, those rights apply to the domain controller and all other domain controllers in the domain and in trusted domains. If you're working on a member server or an NT Workstation computer, the rights you assign to a user apply only to access that one computer.

You can assign rights to individual users or to groups; it's generally more efficient to assign rights to groups, then add the user to the group that best defines the rights you want the user to have. Table 6.1 describes the rights you can assign to an individual or a group and the groups to which the right is assigned by default (rights used by the subsystem aren't included in the following):

Note: Important: Consider changing the Log on locally and Shut down the system rights so that Users, Everyone, and Guests cannot perform these tasks. See the section, "Editing Users," for more information.

Table 6.1 Users' Rights

RIGHT	GROUP	DESCRIPTION
Log on locally	Administrators, Backup Operators, Everyone, Guests, Power Users, and Users	Enables the user to log on to the server, from the server's keyboard
Shut down the system	Administrators, Backup Operators, Everyone, Power Users, and Users	Enables the user to shut down the server, and thus the system
Access this computer from the network	Administrators, Everyone, Power Users	Enables users to connect to the server, not necessarily to access the resources (Permissions govern this)
Back up and Restore files/directories	Administrators, Backup Operators	Enables the user to backup up and restore files and directories on the server, and on client computers
Bypass traverse checking	Everyone	Enables the user to change directorie and access files and subdirectories, even if the user has no permission to access the parent directory
Change the system time	Administrators, Power Users	Enables the user to set the time in the internal clock of the server
Force shutdown from a remote station	Administrators	Enables the user to shut down a remote computer
Load and unload device drivers	Administrators	Enables the user to install and remove device drivers
Manage auditing and security log	Administrators	Enables the user to specify which tasks can be audited and to view the log files
Take ownership of files	Administrators	Enables the user to take ownership of files, directories, printers, and other objects on the server

Creating and Managing Users

By default, there are two users in the User Manager for Domains—Administrator and Guest. If you've installed Internet services, you will also see the IUSR_ *SERVERNAME* user which acts like a guest account from the Internet connection. The Administrator has rights to perform all tasks and procedures on the server and network; the Administrator can manage the domain on the domain controller or on another computer with the domain. The Administrator is prompted to enter a password during Setup on the PDC. Guard this password carefully and make sure at least two people in your company know the password, in case one person leaves the company unexpectedly. Also, the Administrator's account cannot be deleted or disabled, so you cannot lock yourself out of the account unless you forget the password.

Note: You use the Administrator account when you first install and set up the server; you should create an account for yourself and anyone else to whom you want to assign Administrators rights. Add the Administrators group to these selected users' accounts to give them full rights on the domain. When administrative users have separate accounts, their actions can be audited on the individual user account name as opposed to the Administrative account.

The built-in Guest account enables those who do not have a user's account to log on to the domain. Additionally, a user whose account is disabled can also log on to the domain using the Guest account. No password is required. You can set rights and permissions for the Guest account; by default, the Guest account has no built-in rights. Also by default, the Guest account is disabled upon installation of NT; you will need to enable it, as described later in this section, if you want to use this account.

You can add as many users as necessary in the User Manager; for each user you add, you can set properties and rights. You can add one user at a time or you can add multiple users. Additionally, you can always delete a user when you no longer want that user on the domain. For a user to access the server, the network, and the domain resources, you must add an account for that user to the primary domain controller.

Note: When you add a user on the NT Server domain controller, you're adding the user to the domain; on the other hand, if you add a user from a member server or a workstation, you're adding that user only to the individual computer.

In Chapter 2, you were instructed to make a list of the users and network assistants who will be members of your network domain. You were to specify names and times the users would be permitted to use the server, as well as other information about each user. Now's the time you can use that information to create users in NT.

Adding Users

You must assign a *username* to any user you add to the domain. A username is not the same as the user's full name. Try to be consistent when adding usernames because NT presents the list of user accounts sorted by the usernames; using a standard for naming users means you can more easily find the user you want in the list. You might want to create usernames using the first four or five characters of the users' last name and their first initial, such as PlumlSJ, BendeRH, FrostAK, and so on. Or you can use some other standard that works for your company.

The username must be unique. The username can be as long as 20 characters and can contain any uppercase or lowercase characters except the following: " \ / [ ] ; : = + , ★ ? < > | .

You will also be asked to supply each user's full name; establish a standard for entering these names as well because you can sort users by their full name, too. The password is case-sensitive. You can assign a password, then give the user the right to change the password later, which is recommended. You don't need to know all passwords. The user should pick a word she or he can easily remember instead of trying to remember one you assigned. Besides, you will want to save your time for more important tasks than thinking up users' passwords. Finally, you may want to add a description of the user, such as "Manager" or "Network Assistant." Adding a description is optional.

To add a new user in the User Manager, choose User, New User. The New User dialog box appears, as shown in Figure 6.2. To add more than one user, enter the information for the first user, then choose the Add button; the text boxes clear, ready for the next user. Table 6.2 describes each of the options in the User Properties dialog box.

To continue configuring a user, you can choose any of the buttons at the bottom of the User Properties dialog box: Groups, Profile, Hours, Logon To, Account, or Dialin, as described in the following sections.

TIP: To change a username in the User Manager, select the user, then choose User, Rename.

Groups

The Groups button leads to the Groups Memberships dialog box (see Figure 6.3) which enables you to select the groups to which the user will be a member.

By default, every user is a member of the Domain Users group, as shown in the Member of list box. To add a group to the user's account, select the group in

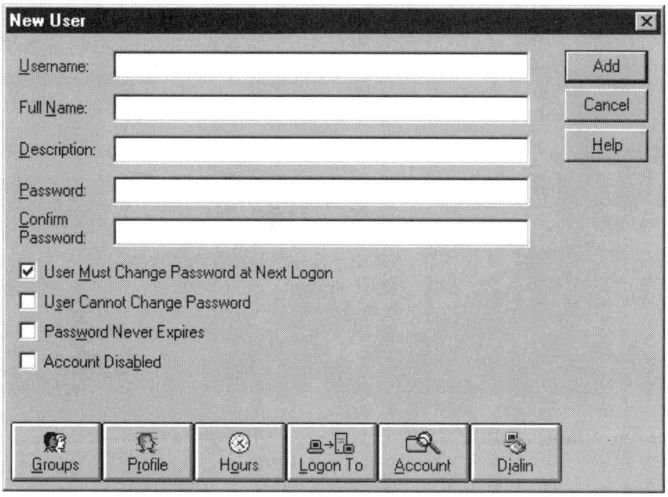

Figure 6.2 *Enter the information about the user in the New User dialog box.*

Table 6.2 User Properties

OPTION	DESCRIPTION
Username	The username used for logon purposes.
Full Name	Enter or edit the user's name as you want it to appear in the User Manager and on the user account; only the username is needed for logon to the network.
Description	Optionally, enter or edit the user's description.
Password	Enter the password the user must type to log on to the network; enter the password again in the Confirm Password text box to verify.
Password Options	From the check boxes, choose any or all restrictions for the user's password: User Must Change Password at Next Logon, User Cannot Change Password, and/or Password Never Expires.
Account Disabled	Select this option to prevent the user from accessing the network temporarily; the account remains in the database but cannot be used until you enable it again.
Account Locked Out	This option is grayed unless the account becomes locked out automatically; lockout occurs when a user fails to enter the appropriate password three times in a row.

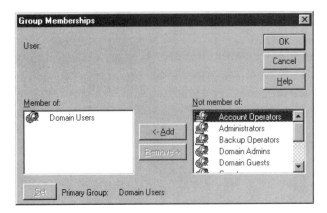

Figure 6.3 *Add or remove groups you want the user to belong to.*

the Not Member of list and choose the Add button. To remove a group from the user's group memberships, select the group in the Member list and select the Remove button. When you're done, choose OK to close the dialog box and return to the User Manager for Domains. For a list and description of built-in groups, see the section "Managing Groups," later in this chapter.

At the bottom of the dialog box is the Set button. Use Set only when the user is running the Macintosh client or POSIX applications. Set changes the primary group to which the user is a member.

Profile

Computers running Windows NT Server and Windows NT Workstation have user profiles that automatically create and maintain a user's desktop settings: screen colors, desktop items and settings, mouse settings, window size and position, and network and printer connections. No matter which workstation the user logs on to, the user's personal settings follow. The user profile is created when the user logs on to the workstation the first time. User profiles provide the user with a consistent working environment, even if the workstation is used by several people.

TIP: Profile is an optional setting; you do not have to configure the user's environment profile to create and use your Users and Groups on the server. You may want to wait until your server and network are up and running to work with these settings.

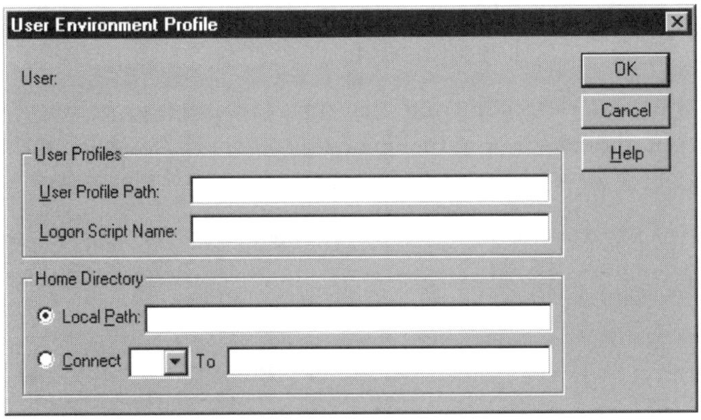

Figure 6.4 *Specify a home directory, path to a logon script, or enter a path to customize user's environment.*

Note: User profiles only apply to computers running Windows NT Server and Workstation; computers running MS-DOS, UNIX, or OS/2 are not affected. You can apply user profiles to computers running Windows 95, if you enable them. On the Windows 95 computer, open the Passwords icon in the Control Panel and choose to enable user profiles.

The User Environment Profile dialog box appears when you click the Profile button in the User Properties dialog box, as shown in Figure 6.4.

The User Profiles area of the dialog box designates the user's desktop environment information. Optionally, enter a path to the folder that contains the information in the User Profile Path text box in the following format: \\director\profiles\bendeh.

Note: The desktop environment includes screen colors, network connections, and other settings that the user has control over. You can, alternatively, designate a mandatory user profile. Open the Control Panel, System icon and choose the User Profiles tab. Copy the predefined user profile to the path location, then rename the NTUser.dat file to NTUser.man.

The Logon Script Name contains the path and name of the script file. You can use a BAT, CMD, or EXE file. Save the script file to the \\WINNT\SYSTEM32\REPL\IMPORT\SCRIPTS directory and enter this as the path in the User Environment Profile dialog box.

Logon Scripts

The logon script assigned to a user's account runs each time that user logs on to the network. You can assign a logon script to one user or to multiple user accounts by assigning the script to a group.

To create a logon script, use a text editor such as Notepad; then assign the script to users in the User Manager. Following are some special parameters you can use when creating logon scripts for multiple users:

%HOMEDRIVE%	Defines the user's local workstation drive letter that is connected to the user's home directory
%HOMEPATH%	Represents the full path of the user's home directory
%OS%	Represents the operating system of the user's workstation
%PROCESSOR_ARCHITECTURE%	Defines the processor type of the user's workstation
%PROCESSOR_LEVEL%	Defines the processor level of the user's workstation
%USERDOMAIN%	Represents the domain containing the user's account
%USERNAME%	Represents the username

The logon script is downloaded from the domain controller server that authenticates the user's logon request. If you have multiple domain controllers in the domain, you should copy all logon scripts for user accounts to every primary and backup domain controller since any controller could authenticate the user's logon request.

In the Home Directory, choose either the Local Path (local computer) or the Connect To (network) text box to enter the path to the user's home directory. In NT, the home directory is the user's own private space on the server. In NT, however, the home directory is used as a default directory for the Save As and Open dialog boxes of applications, for the command prompt, and so on. If you choose to place the home directory on the network and the directory does not already exist, User Manager for Domains creates it for you. If you do not assign a home directory, the default on the user's local drive is used: \USERS\DEFAULT.

• •

CAUTION: Important: If the home directory already exists when you assign it to a user, you must grant the user permission to his or her home directory before he or she can access it. In NT, grant object permissions from the NT Explorer. For more information, see "Assigning Object Permissions," in Chapter 7.

• •

TIP: If you're configuring multiple users, you can substitute %USERNAME% for the last item in the home directory path. NT will substitute the user name of the user account for you. If you're using the FAT file system, however, you cannot user %USER-NAME% because of the 8.3 limitation.

Hours

NT enables users to log on 24 hours a day, every day, by default; however, you can limit the logon hours in the User Properties dialog box by choosing the Hours button. As you can see in Figure 6.5, the Logon Hours dialog box contains a one week calendar with logon hours in one-hour increments. One box represents one hour in the calendar. The first box, for example, represents 12:00 A.M. to 12:59 A.M.; the last box represents 11:00 P.M. to 11:59 P.M.

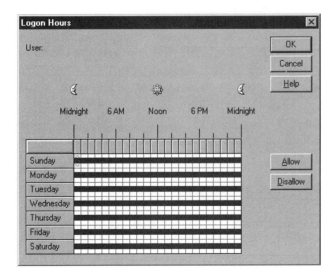

Figure 6.5 Set the logon hours to your business and your preferences.

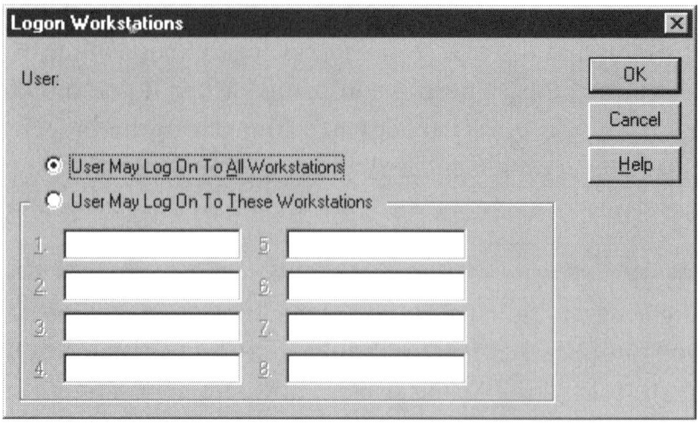

Figure 6.6 *Choose which workstations a user has access to.*

Filled boxes indicate the hours a user can connect to a domain server; empty boxes indicate hours of no access. If a user exceeds the set logon hours, NT Server responds by either disconnecting the user or by denying the user new connections. You set the response you want in the Account Policy dialog box (see Chapter 7 for more information). You set the hours in the calendar by first dragging the mouse across a time block to select it, then choosing the Allow or Disallow button.

Logon To

You use the Logon To button to specify which of the workstations on the network the user may access. Depending on the services set up in your network, different options may appear in the dialog box. Figure 6.6 shows the most common options on a server set up for domains in an NT network.

The default option, User May Log On To All Workstations, can be changed to User May Log On To These Workstations, then only certain computers can be named to enable access. If your network has additional services, such as one or more NetWare workstations, options to limit access to those services are included in the dialog box.

Account

NT also lets you determine such account information as an account expiration date and account type. Figure 6.7 shows the Account Information dialog box, opened from the User Profiles dialog box by choosing the Account button.

The default option in the Account Expires area is Never; however, you can change the data by choosing the option End of and adding the month, date, and year

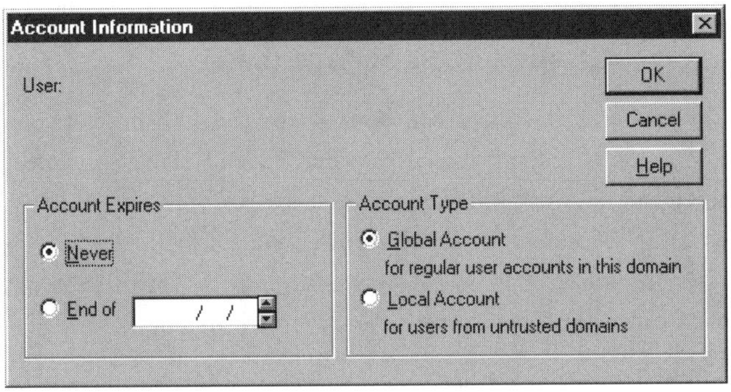

Figure 6.7 *Set an expiration date and the type of account for a user.*

for the account to expire. When an account expires, the account is disabled (not deleted); the user, therefore, cannot log on again unless you enable the account.

In the Type of Account area, you can choose to make the account either global or local. Global is the default setting and is the account for the normal user in his or her home domain. You might choose the local account type for a user from a domain that is not trusted, thus limiting access to your domain.

Dialin

Remote Access Service (RAS) is a service provided by NT that enables remote and mobile users to connect to the network over a modem, ISDN, or X.25. All services provided by the RAS are usually the same as services available to a LAN-connected user. Figure 6.8 shows the Dialin Information dialog box.

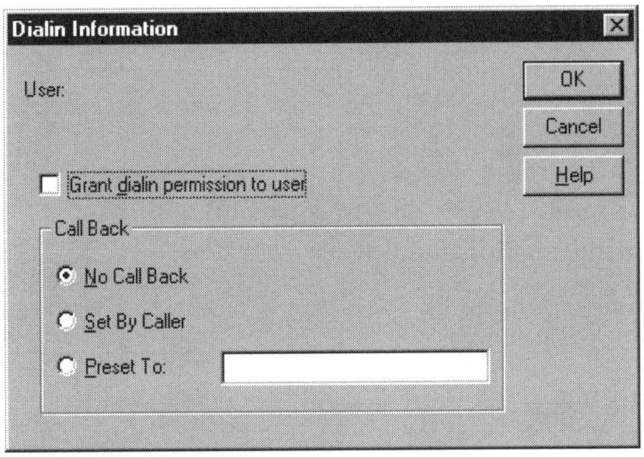

Figure 6.8 *Grant permission for users to dial in to the server using RAS.*

Remote Access Service (RAS)

Users that work away from the office can connect to the NT network and its re-sources using the Remote Access Service supplied by NT. RAS includes file and print services, messaging, and database access. RAS works with any client computer running Windows NT, Windows for Workgroups, MS-DOS, LAN Manager, or a PPP client. The user must have a 9600 or higher modem, X.25, or ISDN card. Ad-ditionally, the remote access software must be installed to the client.

You will also need a dedicated remote access server for best results and improved performance. You install the RAS program to control the remote access server; your server will need a multiport adapter or modems and analog telephone lines or other WAN connections. If you're planning to provide access to the network, the server will also need a separate network adapter card installed and connected.

NT Server's RAS feature permits up to 256 clients to dial into the network. Addi-tionally, you can configure RAS to provide access to all network resources or you can limit access to the RAS server only.

In addition to the LAN protocols—TCP/IP, IPX and NetBEUI—NT supports re-mote access protocols, including PPP (Point-to-Point Protocol), SLIP (Serial Line Internet Protocol), and Microsoft RAS Protocol. The LAN protocols are used to in-tegrate the RAS clients with the rest of the network; remote access protocols control the transmission of data over a WAN (wide area network). NT automatically picks up any LAN protocols installed to the network when you install the remote access service.

RAS also enables NT to provide services to the Internet. You could, therefore, con-figure an NT Server computer as an Internet Service Provider and offer dial-up In-ternet connections to a PPP client. The PPP client must use TCP/IP, IPX, or NetBEUI to access the RAS server; the NT RAS software needs no special configu-ration for non-Microsoft PPP clients.

Installing and configuring a remote access service is beyond the scope of this book; however, you can get more information about RAS from Windows NT Server doc-umentation and on-line help.

The Dialin button leads to the Dialin Information dialog box. Use this dialog box to set permission for remote users to connect to the network through dialup networking. You can also set call-back options in this dialog box.

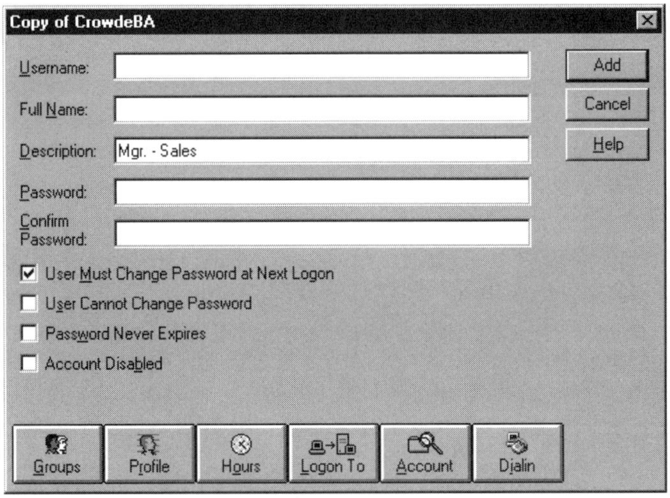

Figure 6.9 *Copy a user's account as a foundation for new users.*

Adding Multiple Users

If you have a lot of users to add, NT Server Directory Services provides a method by which you can copy an existing account, then just change the username, full name, password, and whatever else needs to be changed.

To copy a user account, select the user in the User Manager and choose User, Copy. The Copy of dialog box appears (see Figure 6.9). All properties are set like the original user; all you have to do is fill in the names and password.

Deleting Users

To delete any user, select that user in the User Manager pane and press the DELETE key. A confirmation dialog box appears; choose OK to delete the user. Select several users for deletion by holding the CTRL key as you click on each user name.

Remember, if you delete a user, you also delete the user's unique SID (security identification) number; if you ever add that user back to the domain, a new SID will be created. Thus, you will have to recreate all of the user's account information, as well.

Editing Users

You will probably need to modify some accounts as your network grows and needs change. You can edit any user account in the User Manager for Domains by dou-

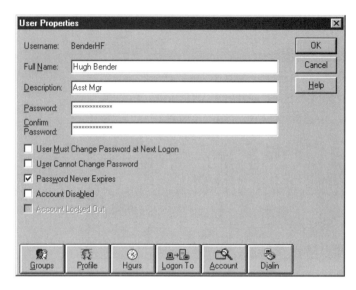

Figure 6.10 *Edit user properties, such as password, group membership, and profile issues.*

ble-clicking the user's name, which opens the User Properties dialog box, as shown in Figure 6.10.

In the User Properties dialog box, make any changes to options as described in the section, "Adding Users." Choose OK to close the User Properties dialog box and save the changes.

TIP: To edit several users at one time and apply the same properties—such as password restrictions—select the first user and hold the CTRL key as you select each subsequent user. Then choose User, Properties. All of the usernames appear in the User Properties dialog box; all modifications apply to those names listed.

You can also edit a user by selecting the user and choosing User, Rename to rename the username. You can edit various security policies for each user and each group, as described in the next section.

Understanding Groups

Groups are collections of users that have certain rights granted them. NT supplies built-in groups with rights already assigned to make administration of users easier. Instead of assigning individual rights to each user, you assign a user to a group with the rights you want that user to have. Group the users according to the network access their jobs require.

Edit and modify the rights to any built-in group to customize them for your users and network. Additionally, you can add groups to your network and set the rights you want from scratch. This section covers a description of NT's built-in groups, editing group properties, adding groups, and deleting groups. For information about assigning rights and permissions, see Chapter 7.

Note: You assign permissions to files and folders and these permissions control various users' access.

NT Server supplies eight built-in local groups and three built-in global groups to which you can assign users for quick rights management and control. In addition to specific rights, each group may or may not be granted certain abilities to perform tasks on the server and/or network. Rights include such actions as accessing the server or network, shutting down the system, backing up files and folders, changing the system time, and loading device drivers, as described previously in this chapter. Abilities include such tasks as adding a workstation to the domain, creating and managing user accounts and groups, assigning user rights, locking the server, formatting the server's hard disk, and so on. Abilities are automatic and cannot be assigned; only rights can be assigned.

Local and Global Groups Distinctions

Microsoft supplies two types of groups, local and global, for use with security and organization. A global group consists of user accounts from one domain—the domain in which the global group was created. Global means the group can be granted rights to use resources in multiple, global domains. Global groups can only be created on a domain controller; and can only contain individual user accounts, not other groups.

Local groups include user accounts and global groups from one or more domains, as long as the other domains are trusted. Local means the group can only be granted rights to use resources in only a single or local domain. A local group can contain users and global groups, but not other local groups.

To help you decide how to use local and global groups, consider these guidelines:

- Use global groups to simultaneously add many users to a local group in another domain. The local group's rights and permissions are automatically provided to the global groups that are added to it.

- Add global groups to local groups in the same domain or in trusting domains.

- Grant rights and permissions to local groups; use global groups as a method of arranging users you'll place in one or more local groups.

- In a single-domain NT Server network, global groups are basically irrelevant; however, if you plan to join a multiple-domain network, you'll need to use local and global groups.

- You must use the local group if your members need rights and permissions in one domain only.

- You must use a local group if you want a group that can contain other groups as well as users.

- You must use a global group if you want to group users of one domain into a single unit for use in other domains.

A member of a built-in local group has the rights to perform various tasks on the domain controllers, member server, and/or workstation in the domain. By default, every new domain user is a member of the Domain Users global group and therefore, a member of the Users built-in local group.

Local Groups

Following is a brief description of each group in NT Server; for more information about group rights and permissions, see Chapter 7.

The Administrators group grants full control access of the network to its members and is the only group that does, by default. Administrators can access workstations, files, and folders; manage and control users and groups; choose which resources to share, such as printers, CD-ROM drives, and so on; and so on. The Administrator has all rights and abilities on the NT Server.

The Server Operator group grants its members the rights and abilities needed to administer the primary and backup domain controllers: logging on locally to the server, shutting down the system, backing up and restoring files, locking and unlocking the server, sharing resources, and so on.

Members of the Account Operators group have the abilities to manage and create accounts for users and groups using the User Manager for Domains. An Account Operator cannot, however, modify the Administrators, Servers, Account Operators, Print Operators, or Backup Operators local groups or any local groups that are members of these local groups. Additionally, an Account Operator can log on locally to the server and shut down the system.

Print Operators can also log on to the server and shut the system down. The only ability granted a Print Operator is the ability to create, edit, delete, and manage printer shares.

Backup Operators have the control over the server they need to perform backup and restores. In addition to accessing the server from the network, the Backup Operators can shut down the system, back up files and folders, and restore files and folders. No abilities are granted the Backup Operator.

The Replicator group does not have actual users as members; instead, the only member of the Replicator group is an account used to log on the Replicator services of the primary domain controller and the backup domain controllers of the domain.

Users in the Users group have no rights on the server and no abilities either, unless you assign them. Finally, Guests have no rights or abilities on the server.

NT also includes some special groups you may see in a list, but you cannot modify the members of these groups: Everyone (anyone using the computer), Interactive (anyone using the computer locally), Network (all users connected over the network), System (the operating system), and Creator Owner (for permissions sake, the creator of a file or directory). The words directory and subdirectory mean the same thing as folder and subfolder—a convenient way of organizing and grouping files and other directories in a hierarchical file system.

Note: NT Workstation and member servers also include the Power Users group, which has rights to the local computer and shutdown rights, as well as the ability to use the User Manager for the specific computer and create groups, users, and shares.

Global Groups

In addition to the previously described groups, there are three global groups built in to a domain's primary and backup domain controllers: Domain Admins, Domain Users, and Domain Guests.

Domain Admins is a member of the Administrators local group; the built-in Administrator user account is a member of the Domain Admins global group. An Administrator can administer the domain, the primary and backup domain controllers, and all other computers running both NT Server and Workstation in the domain.

Domain Users is a member of the Users local group for the domain and of the Users local group for every NT Workstation and member server on the network. Domain Users have normal user access.

The Domain Guests group contains the domain's built-in Guest user account and the rights are limited. You could move any Domain Users to the Domain Guests group if you want to limit their rights and permissions.

Group Suggestions

To help you get started with assigning your users to groups, here are a few suggestions:

- At least two people should be members of the Administrators group. These people will be responsible for planning and maintaining the network security for the domain. You will want two members of the Administrator's group in case one gets sick, takes a day off, or goes on vacation; someone must be available to administer the server every day.

- If you're using only two members of the Administrators group, assign two or three members to the Server Operators group. This group can shut down servers, set the system time, lock servers, share directories and printers, and so on. Don't try to depend on only one or two people to manage the everyday workings of the server.

- Assign those people in the Personnel department, or managers responsible for hiring new employees, to the Account Operators group. They can create and edit domain accounts and put the accounts into the proper groups.

- Add at least two people to the Print Operators group to ensure printer problems will always be addressed quickly.

Managing Groups

You can change the description of any group at any time. NT makes it easy to edit a group's rights and to add or remove users to the group, whether the group is built-in or you create the group yourself. It's much easier to manage eight or so groups than it is to manage many, many users; therefore, work with group rights first, then simultaneously add and remove users to that group for ease of administration.

Keep in mind that you can add a user to more than one group; a user can, for example, be a member of both the Print Operators and Backup Operators groups. The user, then, has all the rights granted to both of the groups.

Editing Groups

You can edit groups to add or remove users, adjust rights to the group, view group members, and so on. To edit a group, follow these steps:

1. In the User Manager for Domains, double-click on the group you want to edit; alternatively, select the group, then choose User, Properties. The Local Group or Global Group Properties dialog box appears (see Figure 6.11).

Member Server Groups

Not all built-in local groups exist on both NT's domain controllers and NT's member servers (or NT Workstations, for that matter). When administering a member server, notice that several groups, as follows, are missing:

Domain Controllers Groups	Member Servers Groups
Administrators	Administrators
Backup Operators	Backup Operators
Server Operators	Power Users
Account Operators	Users
Print Operators	Guests
Users	Replicator
Guests	
Replicator	

This means an Account Operator, Print Operator, or Server Operator cannot perform his or her duties from the member server; these users can only perform their duties from the domain controller. Since the group dynamics are different for member servers, when you add an administrator user, add that user directory to the Domain Admins global group so he or she is also administrator on workstations and member servers.

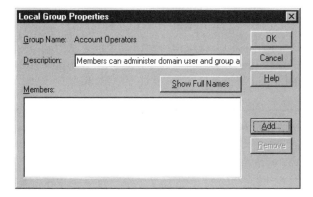

Figure 6.11 *View a list of members to a group, add new members, or edit the description of the group.*

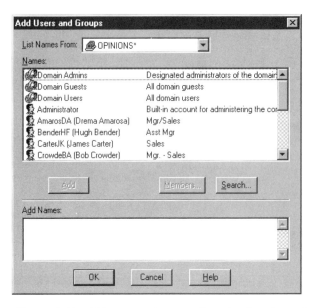

Figure 6.12 Add users and groups from the domain to the local group.

2. To edit the description, select the text in the Description text box and enter new text.

3. To remove a member, select the member and choose the Remove button; NT removes the user without warning or confirmation.

4. To add a member, choose the Add button; the Add Users and Groups dialog box appears, as shown in Figure 6.12.

5. In the List Names From drop-down list box, choose the server containing the names of the users and/or groups you want to add.

6. In the list of Names, select the name you want to add, then choose the Add button. The name appears in the Add Names list at the bottom of the dialog box; add all of the names you want to the list box.

Note: You can search for any member or group name by choosing the Search button. The Find Account dialog box appears. Enter the user or group name for which you're searching and choose the Search button.

---

7. To view the members of any group, select the group name in the Add Users and Groups dialog box, then select the Members button. A list of that group's members displays at the end of the users list of Names.

8. When you're done, choose OK to close the dialog box and return to the Local Group Properties dialog box. Choose OK to close the box and return to the User Manager.

Adding Groups

You might want to add new groups to your system for organizational and management purposes; for example, add a group for users who belong to a specific department or office, or for users who require only certain resources. When you add a group, you can assign users and rights to the group, edit the group, and otherwise manage the new group.

TIP: When naming a local group, you can use up to 256 characters in the name; for a global group, you can use up to 20 characters. A group name can contain any uppercase or lowercase characters except the following: " / \ [ ] : ; | + , * ? < >

Add a new local group so you can grant permissions to files, directories, and other resources, to the group and its members. Add a global group to organize users based on the type of work they do. Suppose you have a printer you want to limit access to. First create a local group that has permission to use the printer; next create a global group containing users who are allowed to use the printer. Add the global group to the local group, then control access to the printer by adding or removing members to the global group.

Note: You cannot rename a group after you create it.

Local Groups

You can create a new local group and add its members from scratch or you can copy any existing group and its members as a foundation for the new group. When you copy a new group, the permissions and rights of the original group are not copied to the new group, only the members are the same.

To add a group, follow these steps:

1. In the User Manager for Domains, choose one of the following: Select the group you want to copy in the User Manager for Domains Group list or Choose the User menu, New Local Group command. The New Local Group dialog box appears, as shown in Figure 6.13.

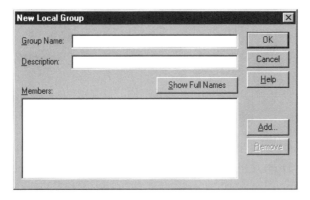

Figure 6.13 *Add users and groups from the domain to the local group.*

2. Enter the new group's name in the Group Name text box; this name must be unique.

3. In the Description text box, optionally enter a description of the group.

4. In the Members list box, you can add more members to the group by choosing the Add button. The Add Users and Groups dialog box appears (see Figure 6.14).

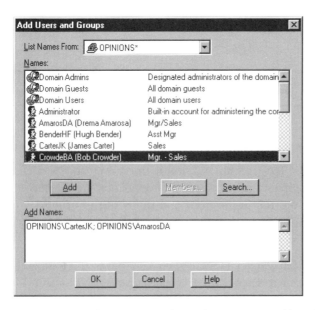

Figure 6.14 *Choose users and/or other groups to add to the new local group.*

> **TIP:** To display the full names in the Members list box, choose the Show Full Names button.

5. In the List Names From drop-down list box, choose the server or domain from which you want to choose groups and users.

6. Select the users and/or groups from the Names list to add to the new group. You can add one name at a time or several. To add names in the list that are adjacent to each other, hold the SHIFT key as you click on the first and last names you want to add; all names in between are also selected. To add names that are not adjacent to each other in the list, hold the CTRL key as you click on each name.

7. Choose the Add button. You can change servers and/or domains and add more names, if you want. Additionally, if you cannot locate the users or groups you want to add, choose the Search button to display the Find Account dialog box; enter the name of the user or group and choose the Search button. When NT locates the user or group, choose the Add button to attach that name to the list.

8. When you're done, choose OK in the Add Users and Groups dialog box to return to the New Local Group dialog box. Choose OK to close the dialog box and return to the User Manager. The new group is listed in the Manager.

Global Groups

Creating a global group is similar to creating a local group; you can either copy an existing group or start a new one. In the User Manager for Domains, choose User, New Global Group to start a new group; choose User, Copy to copy an existing group. The new Global Group dialog box appears, as shown in Figure 6.15.

Enter the Group Name and optionally, a Description. In the Not Members of list, choose the users to add, then select the Add button. Unfortunately, you can add only one user at a time instead of selecting multiple users in this dialog box. When you're done, choose OK to close the dialog box.

You can assign rights to the new group, as you would with an existing group. For more information, see Chapter 7.

Deleting and Editing Groups

You can delete and edit groups you create, just as you can delete and edit built-in groups. To delete a group, select the group in the User Manager for Domains

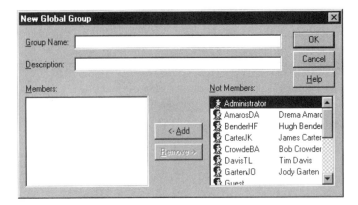

Figure 6.15 *Choose users and/or other groups to add to the new global group.*

Group list and choose User, Delete. NT warns you with a message dialog box that once you delete a group, you cannot restore access to resources without completely recreating the group and reassigning rights. Choose OK and confirm the deletion in another dialog box to erase the group from the list.

To edit a group's properties, select the group name and choose User, Properties. The Local Group Properties dialog box appears, in which you can edit the description of the group and add and remove members.

Macintosh Considerations

Macintosh users use the same accounts database on the Windows NT Server as PC users because of NT's Services for Macintosh. You can create accounts for your Macintosh users and the users log on to the server as a guest or as a user with a password. You can set up guest logons and specify which resources the guests have access to; a Macintosh user can access the resources without the use of a password.

Using NT's Services for Macintosh, you can also set up either cleartext or encrypted passwords for your Macintosh users, to guarantee security on the network from intruders. Cleartext passwords provides less security than encrypted and can be no more than eight characters long. Use cleartext passwords with Macintosh users using the standard AppleShare client software or System 7 file-sharing.

Encrypted passwords offer more security than cleartext becasue NT encodes the passwords and stores them so they cannot be stolen from the client computer. An encrypted password can be as long as 14 characters and can be offered to your users through Services for Macintosh.

Summary

This chapter covers the use and implementation of users and groups in a Windows NT Server domain controller. By using users and groups, you can control access to the server and the network. You also can grant others rights so that they can help you administer the network.

7 Managing Network Security Policies

Chapter 6 presented a discussion about various built-in groups supplied by Windows NT Server. Each group has specific rights and abilities assigned to it, enabling the members of that group access to the network and its resources. As administrator of the network, you can modify the rights and abilities to any group, assign rights to new groups, and designate which groups your users belong to.

In addition to user and group rights, you can set specific permissions for directories, files, and other resources, such as printers. Permissions designate access to the specific resource; for example, you might set a read-only permission to a file, a read and write permission to a directory (folder), or full control to a printer on the network.

TIP: In this chapter and others, I'll be using the words directory and subdirectory most of the time instead of folder and subfolder; however, both words mean the same thing: a convenient way of organizing and grouping files and other directories in a hierarchical file system.

This chapter covers the following:

- Understand the differences between rights, abilities, and permissions
- Manage the user rights policy
- Understand sharing resources
- Share and stop sharing resources
- Grant permissions for files, directories, and other resources

NT Server Rights and Abilities

Rights and abilities authorize users and groups to perform certain tasks, such as logging on to the server, managing security logs, adding users to the domain, and so on. NT's built-in system of security grants these rights and abilities to predetermined groups of users. The Administrators group, for instance, has full control over the network; a member of the Administrators group has all rights and abilities so he or she can perform all of the tasks necessary to administer the network. A member of the Print Operators group, on the other hand, has only the rights necessary to performing his or her job: logging on to the server, shutting down the system, and sharing and stopping the sharing of printers.

NT divides rights among the different groups to divide the workload. The Administrator could perform all of the tasks, as necessary; however, it's easier and more efficient to assign specific users to perform such tasks as managing printers, user accounts, and backup operations. It is up to you to assign the users of your network to the specific groups that match the rights and permissions you want them to have.

Rights and abilities apply to tasks the user can perform on the network. There are regular rights you can assign as well as advanced rights. For the most part, you'll work with the regular rights, since advanced rights deal with programmers writing applications running on NT. Some advanced rights are: create a pagefile, debug programs, increase quotas for objects, log on as a batch job, and so on. For more information about advanced rights, see Windows NT Server help.

Abilities are built-in devices or rights that enable users to perform tasks. You cannot assign abilities; NT assigns them so they are native to certain groups. For example, all users have the ability to create and manage their local group, that is the group of users that access their own machine.

Chapter 6 detailed the rights that you can grant users; remember the following guidelines dealing with rights:

Rights are granted and restricted on the domain level.

- Rights apply to group members on all primary and backup domain controllers in the domain.

- Rights assigned on Windows NT Workstation computers or NT Server member computers apply only to that single computer.

- You use the User Manager for Domains on a primary or backup domain controller to assign rights for the domain.

- You use User Manager on a member server or NT Workstation computer to assign rights to local groups and users.

Describing Rights and Abilities

Assign rights to a user or to a group. You will save time and effort by assigning rights to groups, however, then place the users in those groups. Abilities are built-in. You cannot assign abilities as you would rights; however, you can assign users to the groups with built-in abilities you want the user to have. Following is a more thorough description of available rights and abilities in NT; assign these rights by way of the User Manager for Domains, as described in Chapter 6.

Rights

Following is a description of the regular rights:

Log on locally: Enables a user to log on locally to the server computer. Groups granted this right by default include the Administrators, Server Operators, Account Operators, Print Operators, and Backup Operators groups.

Access this computer from the network: Enables the user to connect and use the server's resources over the network. Groups granted this right by default include the Administrators and Everyone groups.

Take ownership of files: Allows the user to take ownership of files and objects owned by other users; when a user has ownership of a file, he or she can read and edit the file, move the file, even delete the file from the drive. Groups granted this right by default include the Administrators group.

Manage auditing and security log: NT includes the Event Viewer program that can be set to monitor events such as unsuccessful logons and other breaches to security. The events that are monitored are recorded in a security log. This right enables the user to specify the type of events that are monitored as well as the type of resource events that will be audited. Additionally, the user can view and clear the security log in the Event Viewer if granted this right. Groups granted this right by default include the Administrators group.

Change the system time: Allows the user to set the time for the internal clock in the server computer. Groups granted this right by default include the Administrators and Server Operators groups.

Shut down the system: Enables the user to shut down the entire NT network from the server. Groups granted this right by default include the Administrators, Server Operators, Account Operators, Print Operators, and Backup Operators groups.

Force shutdown from a remote system: Allows the user to shut down the network from any workstation or remote access system. Groups granted this right by default include the Administrators and Server Operators groups.

Backup files and directories: Allows the user to create backups of the files and directories (folders) on the network. This right overrides any file and directory permissions set on individual computers or the server. Groups granted this right by default include the Administrators, Server Operators, and Backup Operators groups.

Restore files and directories: Enables the user to restore backed up files and directories. This right overrides any file and directory permissions, as well. Groups granted this right by default include the Administrators, Server Operators, and Backup Operators groups.

Load and unload device drivers: Users can load and unload device drivers to the server for operation of hardware. Groups granted this right by default include the Administrators group.

Add workstations to the domain: In addition to being a built-in ability for the Administrators and Account Operators groups, this is also a right that enables the user to add workstations to the domain. This right is granted to no one group in particular; however, members of the Administrators or Account Operators groups can assign this right to others.

Built-in Abilities

Following are descriptions of the built-in abilities and the groups to which they are granted:

Add workstation to domain: Users can add a workstation to the home domain, for instance when a new workstation is added to the network. Groups granted this ability by default include the Administrators and Account Operators groups.

Create and manage user accounts: Users can open the User Manager for Domains and create, delete, edit, and otherwise control user accounts for the domain. Groups granted this ability by default include the Administrators and Account Operators groups; however, members of the Account Operators group cannot modify the accounts of the Administrators, Domain Admins global group, or the Administrators, Servers, Account Operators, Print Operators, or Backup Operators local groups (or any global groups that are members of these local groups).

Create and manage global groups: Users can create and manage global groups in the User Manager for Domains. Again, the Administrators and Account Operators groups are granted this ability by default and the Account Operators group is limited in which groups it can manage (see previous paragraph).

Create and manage local groups: Users can create, edit, and manage local groups. The abilities are granted to the Administrators and Account Operators groups, by default, and the same limitations apply to the Account Operators groups as outlined in the previous paragraph. In addition, users have this ability; however, users cannot create local groups on the server if they do not have the ability to log on to the server or access to the User Manager for Domains tools.

Assign user rights: Users can assign user rights to any member of the domain. Groups granted this ability by default include the Administrators group.

Lock the server: Users can lock the server so no changes to configuration can be made. Groups granted this ability by default include the Administrators, Server Operators, and Everyone groups. Although the Everyone group has the ability to lock the server, only those who can log on to the server can actually lock it.

Override the lock of the server: Users can unlock the server if it has been locked. Groups granted this ability by default include the Administrators and Server Operators groups.

Format server's hard disk: Users can format the server's hard disk, thus erasing all data from that disk. Groups granted this ability by default include the Administrators group.

Create common groups: Users can create groups. Groups granted this ability by default include the Administrators and Server Operators groups.

Share and stop sharing directories: The ability to share and stop sharing directories means to designate any directories on the server as one that can be accessed by others on the network. Groups granted this ability by default include the Administrators and Server Operators groups. See the section "Sharing Resources," later in this chapter for more information.

Share and stop sharing printers: Sharing a printer designates that resource as one others on the network can access and use. Groups granted this ability by default include the Administrators, Server Operators, and Print Operators groups. See the section, "Sharing Resources," later in this chapter for more information.

Assigning Rights to Users and Groups

To assign or revoke rights, you use the User Manager for Domains on the primary domain controller. Following are the steps to assigning and revoking rights. For more information about users and groups, see Chapter 6. To assign or revoke user rights, follow these steps:

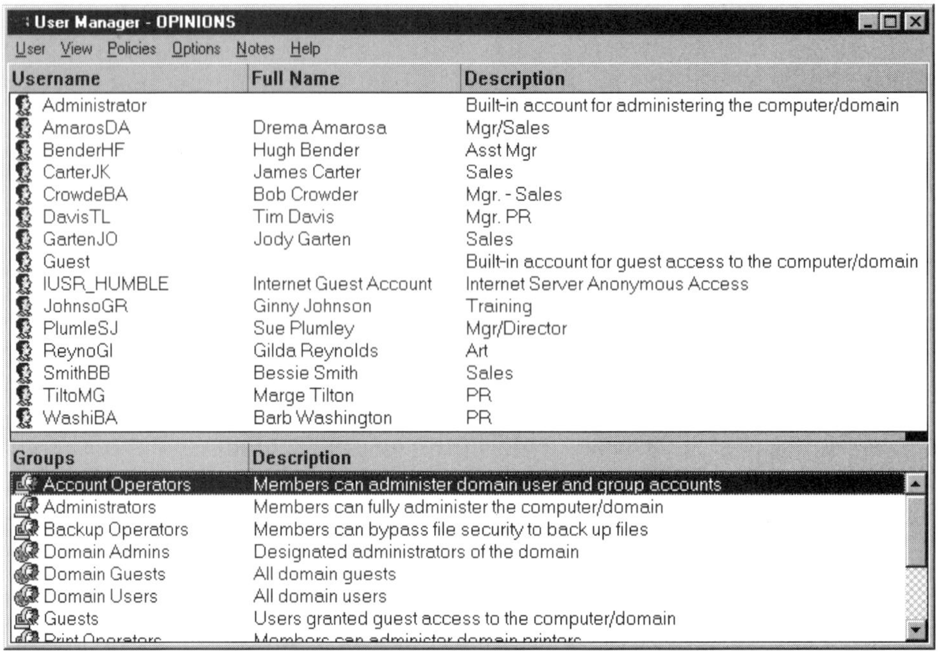

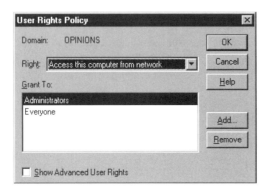

Figure 7.1 *Control users and groups for the entire domain in the User Manager for Domains.*

1. Open the User Manager for Domains by selecting the Start button, Programs, Administrative Tools, and User Manager for Domains. Figure 7.1 shows the User Manager for Domains tool.

2. Choose Policies, User Rights. The User Rights Policy dialog box appears (see Figure 7.2).

Figure 7.2 *Grant rights to groups in the User Rights Policy dialog box.*

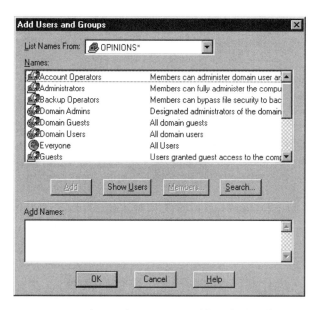

Figure 7.3 *Choose the names to add to the list for granting rights.*

3. In the Right drop-down list, choose the right you want to assign (refer to the list of rights and descriptions in the previous section). When you select a right, the group names to whom the right is assigned appear in the Grant To list box.

4. To add users or groups to the Grant To list, select the Add button. The Add Users and Groups dialog box appears, as shown in Figure 7.3.

5. In the List Names From drop-down list box, select the domain or server you want to work with. If an asterisk appears next to a domain or computer name, that indicates that the local groups of that domain or computer can be listed in the Names list box. Look at the end of the list to view those names.

6. Select a group from the Names list and choose the Add button. The domain name and group name appear in the Add Names list at the bottom of the dialog box. You can continue to add users and groups to the list without closing the dialog box in between.

7. You can also choose from the following:

   To display the users in the domain, choose the Show Users button. By default, only groups are displayed.

   To display the members of any group, choose the Members button.

To search for a group or member not listed, choose the Search button and enter the name in the Find User or Group text box and choose the Search button.

In the Add Names list box, you can type in account names (separate multiple names by semicolons).

Note: If you accidentally add a user or group and you want to remove it, you can either cancel the dialog box and start again or you can choose OK and remove the one name from the User Rights Policy dialog box by selecting the name and choosing the Remove button.

---

8. Choose OK to close the Add Users or Groups dialog box. The names appear in the Grant To list in the User Rights Policy dialog box. To remove any name in the dialog box, select the name and choose the Remove button.

9. You can choose OK to close the User Rights Policy dialog box and save the changes, or you can choose another right from the drop-down Right list and add or remove users and/or groups to that list.

Setting Account Policies

NT provides account policies that govern password restrictions. In NT, you set a general password and lockout policy in the Account Policy dialog box, then, if necessary, set user-specific policies in the User Properties dialog box as explained in Chapter 6. The account policy in NT governs password restrictions, length, and uniqueness, and account lockout for all users on the domain. You set the account policies for all users in the User Manager for Domains.

To open the Account Policy dialog box, in the User Manager for Domains choose the Policies menu, Account command. Figure 7.4 shows the Account Policy dialog box; Table 7.1 describes the options in the dialog box.

Setting Audit Policies

One final security policy you can set in the User Manager for Domains is the audit policies. Audit policies determine the tracking of certain user activities and the recording of those activities in a security log. You can then view the security log in a Windows NT Server utility called the Event Viewer; see Chapter 11 for information about using the Event Viewer. Note that the security log is limited in size (as defined in the Event Viewer), so be careful when selecting events to be logged.

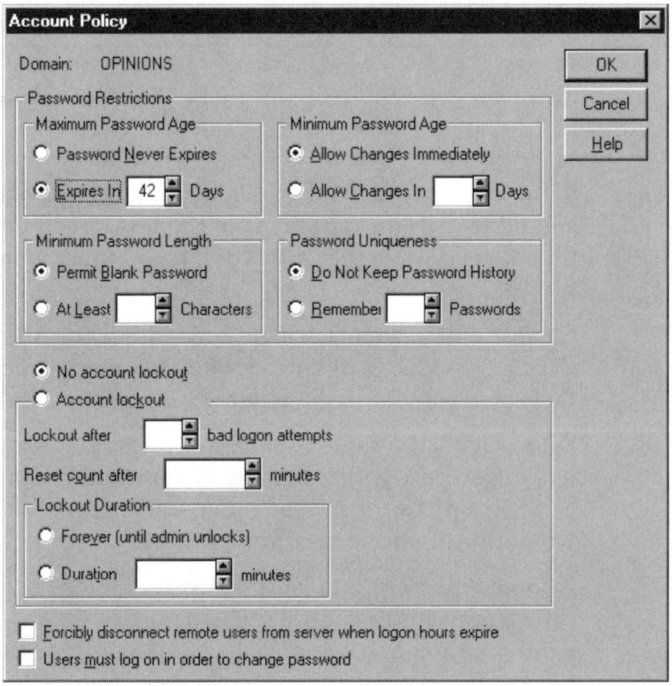

Figure 7.4 *Manage passwords and account lockouts in the Account Policy dialog box.*

To set auditing policies, choose Policies, Audit in the User Manager for Domains. The Audit Policy dialog box appears with the default option, Do Not Audit, selected. To activate the auditing of certain events, choose the Audit These Events option, then select the events you want to audit. When selecting each event, you can choose to log successful occurrences of the event and/or failed occurrences of the event. Figure 7.5 shows the Audit Policy dialog box and Table 7.2 describes the types of events.

Sharing Resources

NT Server enables you to designate resources you want to share across the network, including files, directories, and printers. NT also lets you restrict the use of resources to certain users and groups using permissions to limit access to files and directories.

Before you set the permissions on a file or directory, you must designate the directory as a shared directory. Users cannot access any file or directory on the server or other network computer unless it is shared. When you share a directory,

Table 7.1 Account Policy Options

OPTION	DESCRIPTION
PASSWORD RESTRICTIONS AREA	
Maximum Password Age	Choose either Password Never Expires or Expires In x Days and fill in the number of days in the text box to limit the time users can use their password; the number ranges from 1 to 999.
Minimum Password Age	Choose either Allow Changes Immediately or Allow Changes In x Days to govern when the users can change their own passwords; the number ranges from 1 to 999.
Minimum Password Length	Choose either Permit Blank Password or At Least x Characters to govern whether the user can press ENTER instead of using a password and the minimum length of the password; the numbers range from 1 to 14.
Password Uniqueness	Choose either Do Not Keep Password History or Remember x Passwords to control the users' use of the same password over and over again; you can choose from 1 to 24 passwords if you select the Remember option.
Account Lockout	Choose either No Account Lockout or Account Lockout.
ACCOUNT LOCKOUT AREA	
Lockout After x Bad Logon Attempts	If you choose the Account Lockout option, enter the number of failed logon attempts NT should accept before locking the account out; numbers range from 1 to 999.
Reset Count After x Minutes	Enter the number of minutes you want NT to wait before another logon attempt; the number ranges between 1 and 99999.
Lockout Duration	Choose either Forever or Duration x Minutes to indicate the lockout lasts until the administrator unlocks it in the user's User Properties dialog box or the length you want the lockout to remain in place; the number ranges from 1 to 99999.
Users Must Log on in Order to Change Password	Select to require a user to log on before the password can be changed (if this box is not checked, the users can change their expired passwords without notifying the administrator).

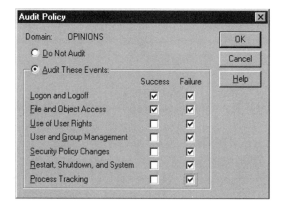

Figure 7.5 *Activate tracking of certain events for security purposes.*

all subdirectories and files in that directory are also shared. Then you set permissions to control access to the shared resources.

You designate shares with the NT Explorer, which looks and acts similarly to the File Manager in previous versions of Windows. Open the NT Explorer by

Table 7.2 Audit Policy Event Types

OPTION	DESCRIPTION
Logon and Logoff	Applies to a user logging on or off the server or making a network connection.
File and Object Access	Records when a user accesses a directory, file, or printer that is set for auditing.
Use of User Rights	Records any exercised user right other than logging on or off the network.
User and Group Management	Reports a user account that has been created, edited, deleted, renamed, disabled, or enabled or when a password has been set or changed.
Security Policy Changes	Documents any change to the User Rights or Audit policies.
Restart, Shutdown, and System	Records when a user shut down or restarted the server or some other event that affects the entire system.
Process Tracking	Provides tracking of events such as program activation, indirect access of an object, process exit, and so on.

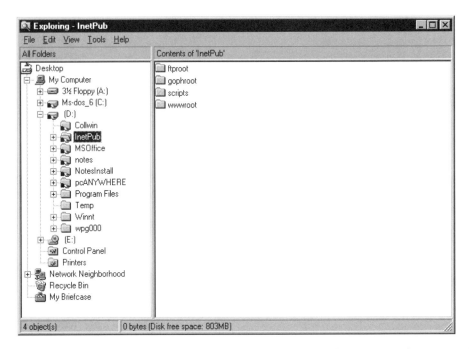

Figure 7.6 *The NT Explorer lets you manage the files and directories on the server and on other computers attached to the network.*

choosing Start, Programs, and Windows NT Explorer. Figure 7.6 shows the Explorer; the left window pane displays the hard drive plus folders on that drive, floppy drives, tape and/or CD drives, the Network Neighborhood, and other items on the Desktop. The right pane displays the folders and files of any element selected in the left pane.

Note: For more information about using the NT Explorer, see Chapter 11.

Sharing Resources Guidelines

When you share a directory on an NTFS volume, all files and directories within that directory become available to the network users. You can, however, place restrictions on any file or subdirectory to limit access with permissions (see the following section, "Granting Permissions").

Users can view shared drives from their Network Neighborhood (Windows NT Workstation, Windows NT Server, and Windows 95), in the Connect Network Drive dialog box (Windows for Workgroups), or from the command prompt (DOS workstations).

When sharing a directory, you choose a share name that represents it to the users; normally, it's easier to use the directory's given name as a share name. Since Windows NT enables the use of long file names, you can use up to 80 characters (including spaces) in the file names if your clients use only Windows NT and/or Windows 95 operating systems.

You can still use the long file names for files and directories, even if you do have DOS clients on the network. NT provides name mapping that assigns a file or directory a second name, in addition to the long file name, that follows the 8.3 convention. NT converts long file names using the following guidelines:

- Removes all spaces.

- Changes characters allowed in DOS names to an underscore (_).

- Truncates the name to its first six characters, adds a tilde (~) and a digit (1, 2, and so on).

- If the name has a period in it, NT uses the first three characters after the period as the extension in the DOS name.

Note: You can still use applications that do not support long file names in NT; however, if the application opens a file with a long file name, the long name is lost and only the short name remains.

Sharing NT Server Resources

To share the resources on the server, you use the NT Explorer to designate those shares. You must be logged onto the domain controller as a member of the Administrators or Server Operators group or have the right to create permanent shared objects to designate shared directories on the domain. The Explorer represents shared directories and files with an outstretched hand icon (refer to Figure 7.6). To share a directory, follow these steps:

1. In the Explorer, select the directory you want to share.

2. Choose File, Properties; the directory's Properties dialog box appears.

3. Choose the Sharing tab. To activate sharing, select the Shared As option and the sharing area becomes available (see Figure 7.7).

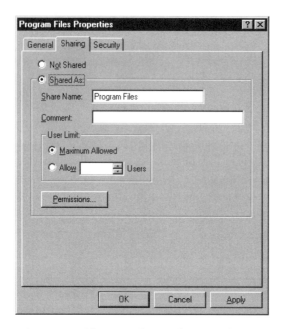

Figure 7.7 *Choose to share a directory, then set the options for the share.*

4. If you want to change the share name, enter a new name in the Share Name text box; users will identify the resource by its share name.

5. Optionally, enter text in the Comment text box; this text will be displayed for users to see.

6. You can set a limit to how many users can access the directory at one time. In the User Limit area, choose one of the following options:

> Maximum Allowed enables the highest possible number of users to access the directory at one time.

> Allow *x* Users enables you to set a limit as to how many users can access the directory at one time.

7. Click the Permissions button to view the list of users and groups that can access the directory. The Access Through Share Permissions dialog box appears (see Figure 7.8).

8. You can decide who has access to the directory:

> To add users and/or groups, choose the Add button. The Add Users and Groups dialog box appears (refer to Figure 7.3). Add users and/or groups, then choose OK to close the dialog box.

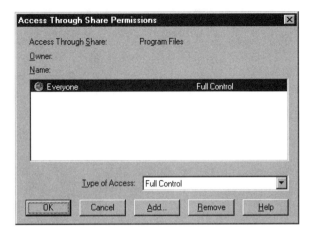

Figure 7.8 *By default, Everyone has permission to access the directory.*

To remove Everyone, or any other group or user, by selecting the name in the Name list and choosing the Remove button.

9. To set the access level for anyone on the list, select the name and choose the Type of Access drop-down box; you can select Full Control, No Access, Read, or Change.

10. Choose OK to close the dialog box and choose OK again to close the Properties dialog box.

Stopping Sharing

You can stop sharing a directory at any time from the NT Explorer. Select the directory and choose File, Properties; alternatively, you can right-click a directory and choose Sharing from the shortcut menu. Choose the Sharing tab of the Properties dialog box and select the Not Shared option. Choose OK to close the dialog box.

Printer Sharing and Permissions

Users logged on to a domain controller as a member of the Administrators, Domain Admin, Server Operators, or Print Operators can choose to share or stop sharing printers. A shared printer can be used by anyone on the network, unless specific permissions are applied. After you share a printer, you can set access permissions that govern the printer.

Designating Shares with the Server Manager

NT Server also supplies a Server Manager that you can use to designate and view shared drives. The Server Manager also enables you to manage directory replication, mange services, send messages to connected users, and more. For more information about the Server Manager, see Chapter 15.

You must be logged on as a member of the domain Administrators local group; you can designate shared directories using the Server Manager. Any member of the Administrators or Server Operators groups can also use the Server Manager to designate shared resources.

To open the Server Manager, choose Start, Program, Administrative Tools, and Server Manager. To set shares, select the server or other computer and choose Computer, Shared Directory. The Shared Directory dialog box displays only shared directories.

You can add a share by choosing the New Share button. In the New Shared dialog box, enter a share name, the path to the directory, any comment you want to add, and choose the User Limit (the same as you would in the Sharing tab of the Properties dialog box for any directory). Choose OK to close the dialog box or choose the Permissions button to set access permissions.

To stop sharing a directory, in the Shared Directory dialog box, select the directory and choose the Stop Sharing button. To close the dialog box, choose the Close (X) button. Click the Close button (X) in the title bar of the Server Manager to close the utility.

TIP: You also can share CD-ROM drives, floppy drives, tape backups, and other resources using the similar steps as you use to share directories; just locate the item in the Explorer and designate it as shared.

For more information about installing a printer to the network, print queues, and other printing issues, see Chapter 8.

Sharing a Printer

To share a printer, you use the Printers folder instead of the NT Explorer. Follow these steps:

Figure 7.9 *All network printers appear in the Printers dialog box.*

1. Choose Start, Settings, Printers. The Printers folder window appears (see Figure 7.9).

2. Select the printer you want to share and choose File, Sharing. The printer's Properties dialog box appears, as shown in Figure 7.10.

3. In the Sharing tab, choose the Shared option.

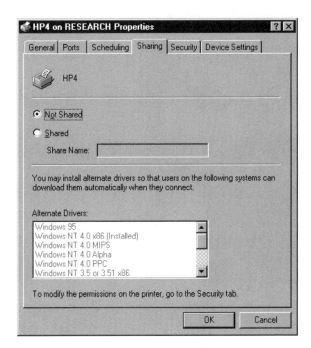

Figure 7.10 *The Sharing tab of the Properties dialog box appears, ready for you to modify.*

4. In the Share Name text box, accept the default name or enter a name for users to see when they access the printer.

5. If necessary, choose additional drivers to install for users to access from the network; you must have your NT Server CD to install new drivers.

6. Choose OK to close the dialog box.

Setting Printer Permissions

You can also set permissions on printers. Since printer permissions are similar to directory access permissions, I'll discuss those in this section rather than in the next.

To set permissions for a printer, follow these steps:

1. Open the printer's Properties dialog box by choosing Start, Settings, and Printers.

2. Choosing File, Sharing.

3. Choose the Security tab in the printer's Properties dialog box, as shown in Figure 7.11.

Figure 7.11 *Set printer permissions in the Security tab of the Properties dialog box.*

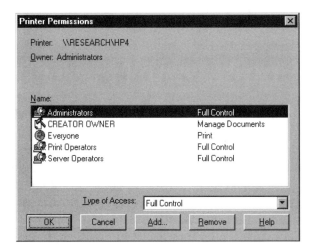

Figure 7.12 Set access permissions for users and/or groups.

4. Choose the Permissions button to display the Printer Permissions dialog box (see Figure 7.12).

5. To add groups and/or users, choose the Add button to display the Add Users and Groups dialog box. Select the names you want to add, then choose OK to close the dialog box. To remove any names from the list in the Printer Permissions dialog box, select the name and choose the Remove button.

6. Select the name in the list, then choose the access you want to apply from the Type of Access drop-down list. You can choose from the following permissions:

> No Access: User or group does not have permission to print or otherwise use the printer.
>
> Print: Grants permission to print to the printer.
>
> Manage Documents: Grants permission to open the print queue and rearrange printing order, delete or pause printing, and otherwise manage the printing of the documents in the queue.
>
> Full Control: Grants permission to print, manage print jobs in the queue, and to manage the printer.

7. Choose OK to close the Printer Permissions dialog box and choose OK again to close the printer's Properties dialog box.

Granting Permissions

When you designate a shared directory, all files and subdirectories it contains are also shared. You can limit access to the shared directory by setting access permissions, as described in the last section. Additionally, you can set file and directory permissions for each file or subdirectory you share. You set file and directory permissions in the NT Explorer. Some limits do apply depending on whether you use the NTFS or FAT file system.

Directory permissions can be granted to local groups, global groups, and individual users in the server's domain; global groups and individual users from trusted domains; and special groups: Everyone, System, Interactive, and Creator/Owner. Permissions apply to both users working on the local computer and users accessing the computer's resources over the network.

The following guidelines and rules apply to permissions:

- Permissions are cumulative. If a user is a member of several groups, each group's permissions apply.

- The No Access permission overrides all other permissions.

- Newly created subdirectories and files inherit permissions from the directory.

- The owner (or creator) of a file or directory controls access to that file or directory.

- Members of the Administrators group can take ownership of files and/or directories.

TIP: User rights take precedence over object permissions; for example, the Backup Operator has rights to get to your files, even read-only files.

File Systems and Sharing

NT's permissions are more effective when used on an NTFS than when used with the FAT file system. When using NTFS volumes, you can set not only directory permissions but also file permissions. NTFS permissions apply to users and groups, both locally and over the network.

Volumes that use the FAT file system are somewhat limited as far as permissions are concerned. You can protect files but only at the directory level, and only over the network. You first choose to share the directory, then you can protect it by specifying permissions that apply only to a directory. File-level permissions aren't available on FAT volumes.

Table 7.3 Standard Permissions

PERMISSION	DESCRIPTION
Read (R)	Allows display of a directory or file's contents, attributes, owner, and so on
Write (W)	Permits creation of subdirectories and files, changes to file's data and attributes, display of permissions and owner
Execute (X)	Allows display of attributes, permissions, and owner, changing to subdirectories, and running program files
Delete (D)	Enables deletion of a directory or file
Change Permissions (P)	Permits changes to the file's or directory's permissions
Take Ownership (O)	Allows changes to directory's or file's ownership

Directory and File Permissions Described

Directories inherit their permissions from their parent directories and files inherit their permissions from the directory in which they reside. The standard permissions that you can apply to a file or directory are described in Table 7.3.

Directory and file permissions consist of combinations of the standard permissions listed in Table 7.3. Table 7.4 describes the directory and file permissions. The standard permissions in the first set of parentheses refer to permissions for the directory itself and those in the second set of parentheses, the individual permissions that apply for new files subsequently created in the directory.

Setting Permissions

You set directory and file permissions in the NT Explorer. The procedures for setting permissions for files and directories are the same; only the permissions you choose change. To set directory and/or file permissions, follow these steps:

1. In the Explorer, select the directory or file.
2. Choose File, Properties; alternatively, right-click the file or directory and choose Properties from the shortcut menu. The folder's Properties dialog box appears.
3. Choose the Security tab (see Figure 7.13).
4. Choose the Permissions button; the Directory or File Permissions dialog box appears (see Figure 7.14).

Table 7.4 Directory and File Permissions

PERMISSION	DESCRIPTION
DIRECTORY PERMISSIONS	
No Access (none) (none)	Cannot access the directory in any way, not even to view directory, subdirectory, or file contents
List (RX) (not specified)	List subdirectories and files in the directory and change to a subdirectory; cannot access new files created in the directory
Read (RX) (RX)	Read file contents and run applications in the directory
Add (WX) (not specified)	Add files to the directory; cannot read or change the contents of current files
Add and Read (RWX) (RX)	Add files to directory and read current files; cannot change files
Change (RWXD) (RWXD)	Read and add files, change contents of current files
Full Control (all) (all)	Read and change files, add files, change permissions for the directory and its contents, and take ownership of the directory and its files
FILE PERMISSIONS	
No Access	Cannot access the file in any way
Read (RX)	Read file contents and run application files
Change (RWXD)	Read, change, and delete the file
Full Control (all) ship of the file	Read, change, delete, set permissions for, and take owner-

5. By default, directory permissions apply only to the directory and its files. You can, however, choose one of the following options in the Directory Permissions dialog box:

> Replace Permissions on Subdirectories. A check in the box applies the permissions to all subdirectories.

> Replace Permissions on Existing Files. Clear the check box to apply permissions to the directory only.

6. In the Name list box, a list of the groups and users who have permission to use the file or directory appears. Select a group or user and choose the permission you want to set from the Type of Access drop-down box.

7. You also can add or remove groups and users:

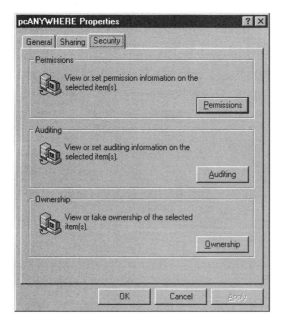

Figure 7.13 *Set permissions in the Properties dialog box.*

To add users or groups, choose the Add button to display the Add Users and Groups dialog box.

To remove names, select the name and choose the Remove button.

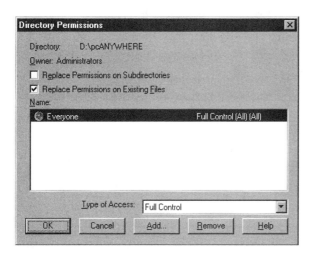

Figure 7.14 *The Directory Permissions dialog box provides two Replace options the File Permissions directory dialog box does not.*

8. Choose OK when you're done to close the dialog box; choose OK again to close the Properties dialog box.

Note: NT provides special directory access and special file access permissions you can set to customize permissions. In the Directory or File Permissions dialog box, select the user or group you want to customize permissions for, then choose the Type of Access drop-down list and from it select either Special Directory Access or Special File Access. In the Special Access dialog box, choose the permissions you want to apply and choose OK.

Taking Ownership

Members of the Administrators group control permissions set on files and directories; however, the user who created the files and/or directories is also the owner and can control permissions. This way, users can keep their files on the server private.

TIP: The Creator/Owner specialized group applies to the creator of a file or directory.

Members of the Administrators group generally create and own most files on the server because it is the administrator who installs applications and creates directories. Individual users often create only data files to store on the server and those are usually stored in the users home directories. The administrator can take ownership of a file or directory at any time by following these steps:

1. Open the directory's or file's Properties dialog box and choose the Security tab.
2. Choose the Ownership button. The Owner dialog box appears.
3. Choose the Take Ownership button and then close the dialog box.

Auditing Security Events

You can use the Directory and File Auditing feature to audit the use of a file or directory by users and groups. You view the results of the auditing in the Event Viewer. See Chapter 11 for information about viewing and auditing events.

Note: Before you can audit security events, you must activate the security log in the User Manager for Domains. Open the User Manager for Domains and choose

Policies, Audit. In the Audit Policy dialog box, choose to Audit These Events and choose Security Policy Changes. Choose OK to close the dialog box. For more information about the User Manager for Domains, see Chapter 6.

By default, auditing changes on a directory apply only to the directory and its files. The Directory Auditing dialog box offers two options not found in the Files Auditing dialog box. A check mark in the Replace auditing on Subdirectories check box applies auditing to all subdirectories; clearing the check box in front of Replace Auditing on Existing Files applies the auditing to the directory only. To audit events, follow these steps:

1. Open the directory's or file's Properties dialog box and choose the Security tab.

2. Choose the Auditing button to display the File or Directory Auditing dialog box (see Figure 7.15).

3. The currently audited groups and users appear in the Name list. You can add or remove groups and users to the list by doing the following:

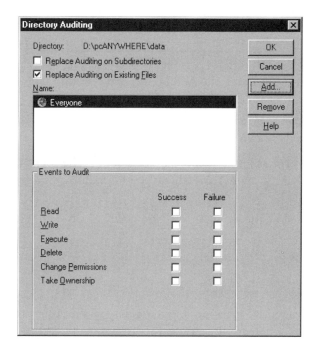

Figure 7.15 *Audit the use of directories and files.*

Macintosh Users and Permissions

Macintosh permissions differ from NT permissions in that the Macintosh permissions can only be set for folders, or directories, not files. NT, however, enforces file permissions; the Macintosh user won't see any indication in the Finder that these permissions exist. Following are the four types of Macintosh permissions on a folder:

- *See Files*: Enables a user to see what files are in a folder and read those files.

- *See Folders*: Enables a user to see folders contained in a folder.

- *Make Changes*: Enables a user to modify the contents of files in a folder, by renaming, moving, creating new files, and deleting existing files.

- *Cannot Move, Rename, or Delete*: Prohibits a user from moving, renaming, or deleting a folder.

These Macintosh permissions can be assigned to the owner or creator of a folder, a Macintosh group associated with the folder, or to everyone who has access to the server. Services for Macintosh translates Macintosh permissions to equivalent PC permissions and vice versa. So, NT's Read permission is translated to Macintosh's See Files, See Folders. NT's Write, Delete permission is translated to Macintosh's Make Changes.

Add names by choosing the Add button and selecting users and groups from the Add Users and Groups dialog box.

Remove names by selecting the user or group in the Name list and clicking the Remove button.

4. Select a group or user in the Name list, then choose the event you want to audit by selecting the appropriate check box for auditing Success or Failure of the event.

5. Choose OK to close the dialog box. Choose OK to close the Properties dialog box.

Summary

This chapter has presented information about rights you can assign to users and groups, abilities that are automatically assigned to groups, and permissions you can set on resources such as files, directories, and printers. By managing the security policies in NT Server, you can successfully protect your server's files and limited resources.

8 *Managing Printing*

Printing is one of the most important tasks on a network; if the users cannot print, the network is worthless. Users must be able to use network printers easily and efficiently with the applications they use both on the network and locally. It's the administrator's job to make it so, either by managing printing services him or herself or by delegating the responsibility. In this chapter, you will learn how to do the following:

- Plan and set up a print server
- Configure a printer
- Connect to a shared printer
- Control printing through a print queue

Understanding Print Services

NT Server can supply seamless printing services to your workstation computers, whether your workstations run Windows 95, NT, Windows for Workgroups, Macintosh, or other operating systems. There are two ways you can set up printing with NT; you can use local printers or network printers. Obviously, using network printers supplies more services to more clients than local printing. Local printing refers to one printer attached to a computer, whether server or workstation, so that the printer serves only that one computer.

Network printing refers to at least one printer, often more, attached to the network and available for use by any workstation on the network. NT enables you to manage network printers by arranging print job order, pausing and stopping printing, and otherwise controlling the jobs sent to the printers on the network.

There are certain terms, with which you're probably familiar, that NT uses to refer to printing and print services. Briefly, I'll describe some of them for you. A *print server* is the computer to which one or more printers are connected and on which the printer drivers are stored. The print server shares the printers with workstations on the network. A print server may be a computer running NT Server or it could be a hardware device that connects the printer to the network through a parallel or serial port on one side and a network cable on the other. Generally, I'll be talking about NT Server as a print server in this chapter.

A *print device* is the actual printer that produces output, usually called a printer. In NT, the *printer* is the software interface between the operating system and the print device. A single printer can send print jobs to multiple print devices; you control the printer by means of NT's Printer folder.

A *print job* is the data type that has been sent to the printer from an application on a workstation or server and a *print queue* is a list of jobs waiting to be printed. Finally, the print *spooler* receives, processes, and schedules the print jobs. The processing of spooling writes the contents of a print job to a file on disk; the spooled data remains in the server's memory until the job is sent to the printer, even if the power is lost to the printer.

Advantages of the NT Print Server

With NT, you can use one computer as a print server whether that computer is the domain controller, a member server, or a computer running NT Workstation. A server computer can function as a file server as well, depending on the number of clients and the traffic on your network.

Note: If your network is small—10 clients or less—you can use a computer running NT Workstation as a print server. NT Workstation is, however, limited to only 10 connections; therefore, a larger network will need to use a computer running NT Server instead. Additionally, NT Workstation does not support Macintosh services or Gateway services for NetWare, thus it is impractical if your network administers to those clients.

NT Server software is perfectly suited to use as a print server. Consider the following features NT offers:

- Using various methods—Network Neighborhood, Add Printer Wizard, Print Setup dialog box of Windows NT and Windows 95 clients—clients can browse the network for available printers.

- Clients can use network printers supplied by other operating systems, such as LAN Manager 2.x.

- Windows NT and Windows 95 clients do not need printer drivers installed to their workstations; installing the printer driver files to the print server is all that's required for these clients to use the network printer.

- An administrator can remotely administer the NT print server, printers, documents, and printer drivers.

NT also supports the use of network-interface printers, printers containing built-in network cards that are connected to the network by cable rather than requiring a parallel or serial connection. Although you can use the network-interface printer directly, it's better to connect through a print server because there is no print queue associated with a network-interface printer.

Note: Windows NT and Windows 95 clients can install and update printer drivers using drivers loaded to the NT print server. MS-DOS and Windows for Workgroups clients can also access Windows NT printers; however they must redirect the output ports to the appropriate *\\server\sharename*. Additionally, non–Windows NT clients must install the printer driver manually, then connect to the server.

Planning Your Printing

You may already have print devices if you're upgrading your network; you may even have the computer you want to use as a print server. If you need to purchase printers, however, or upgrade them, the following are just a few guidelines for choosing the equipment you need to work with NT. More importantly, however, you'll want to think about how to set up your NT printers for the most efficient use of your print devices. This section offers some options for setting up print servers.

Print Devices

NT supports most print devices: dot matrix, inkjet, and laser printers, as well as network-interface print devices and network-aware print devices connected to the network using AppleTalk or TCP/IP protocols. For an updated version of the Windows NT hardware compatibility list (HCL), see the Microsoft World Wide Web site at http://www.microsoft.com.

Note: When installing a network-interface print device, you install the DLC (data-link control) protocol, AppleTalk protocol, or the Microsoft TCP/IP Printing service from the Network icon in the Control Panel folder. See the sidebar, "Using NT's TCP/IP Printing Service," for more information.

When choosing the print devices to use with NT, or any network, consider the following: printer speed, graphics support, quality, and durability. Consider, too, which of the add-on features you'll need, such as double-sided printing, dual paper bins, and so on.

Print Servers

A computer that serves as a print server on NT can also be used as a file or database server or as a dedicated print server. The computer should have at least 16 MB RAM for a small number of print devices; more memory will be needed to manage a larger number of print devices or many large documents. Disk space required is minimal.

If you choose to use one server as both a file and print server, there are a few guidelines you should to be aware of. File operations always take first priority over printing transactions, although the impact printing has on file access and vice versa is insignificant. You will want to use a dedicated print server only if you'll have heavy traffic to multiple printers. The only other consideration with using one computer as a file and print server is security. A print server needs to be available to all users, but you might want to physically isolate a file server for security's sake.

Printer Drivers

As you already know, you must make sure any printer you attach to the network is compatible with NT Server 4 and you must also obtain updated printer drivers to use with NT 4. A printer driver is the software that enables applications to communicate with the print device. NT supplies a number of print drivers for various manufacturers, including Apple, Compaq, Digital, Epson, Hewlett Packard, IBM, Lexmark, NEC, Okidata, Panasonic, Sharp, Toshiba, Xerox, and many more.

Note: A printer driver includes three files that work to provide printing services: a printer graphics driver, a printer interface driver, and a characterization data file. Together, these files interpret the printer language, provides a user interface, and specifies certain characteristics and capabilities about the specific make of printer.

Access to Printers

You can set up the users' access to printers in various ways with NT. You can set up a single printer to a single print device, multiple printers to a single print device, or a single printer to multiple identical print devices. This final option enables the most flexibility.

Using multiple printers leading to one print device, you can schedule printing times for specific print devices; for example, postpone the printing of less important documents until nonwork hours. You also can set different priority levels to control printer access, assign different groups to each printer, and assign rights to the groups so that you prioritize documents by user instead of the actual document sent to the printer.

Another option to manage users' access to the print devices is a printing pool. A pool consists of multiple, identical print devices associated with one printer. The idle print device, then, receives the next document to be printed. When the document is printed, NT's Messenger Service (if active) notifies the client and identifies the printer port to which the document was printed.

All of the print devices in a printing pool are the same hardware model and they act as a single unit; therefore, all print settings apply to the entire pool. Ports, however, can be the same type or mixed: parallel, serial, and/or network. If one print device in the pool stops working for some reason—paper jam, runs out of paper, and so on—it holds the last document sent to it until someone fixes the problem; other documents sent to the pool continue to print from other devices.

Note: NT supports an unlimited number of serial and parallel ports; however, finding an available IRQ level may be difficult. The standard devices are assigned to IRQs as follows: LPT1 = IRQ7, LPT2 = IRQ5, COM1 = IRQ4, and COM2 = IRQ3. To see the current IRQ settings on your computer, run the Microsoft Diagnostics program by choosing Start, Programs, Administrative Tools, Windows NT Diagnostics. NT analyzes your hardware and displays the results on the various tabs in the Diagnostics window.

Creating Printers

After you attach the print devices, you must create a printer on the print server by choosing a port, printer manufacturer, model, and otherwise defining the printer. To create a printer on the domain controller, you must be a member of the Administrators, Server Operators, or Print Operators groups. To create a printer on a

---

Using NT's TCP/IP Printing Service

Clients on your network can print to most print devices attached to UNIX computers if you install the TCP/IP protocol and the Microsoft TCP/IP Printing service to the print server on the network.

Open the Control Panel and double-click the Network icon. Choose the Protocols tab, then select the Add button. From the list of protocols, choose the TCP/IP protocol and choose OK. Configure the protocol by selecting TCP/IP in the Protocols tab of the Network dialog box, then choosing the Properties button. Set the IP address, DNS, routing, and other options in the Microsoft TCP/IP Properties dialog box.

To install the Microsoft TCP/IP Printing service, open the Network icon from the Control Panel and choose the Services tab. Choose the Add button and select the service from the list. Choose OK to close the dialog box and OK again. You'll have to reboot the computer to complete the service and protocol additions.

When you install the Microsoft TCP/IP Printing service, you also install the LPD (line printer daemon) service which enables the print server to receive documents from line printer remote (LPR) utilities running on client systems, much like that on a UNIX system. The LPD services must be set to run automatically; in the Control Panel, choose the Services icon and change the startup options for the TCP/IP Print Server service.

---

member server or NT Workstation, you must be a member of the Administrators or Power Users groups; the Power Users group has rights and abilities on the NT Workstation or member server that are similar to a Server Operator's rights on the NT Server.

To create a printer, follow these steps:

1. Choose Start, Settings, Printers. The Printers window opens (see Figure 8.1).

2. Double-click the Add Printers icon. The first Printer wizard appears (see Figure 8.2).

3. Choose the My Computer option to install a new printer or choose the Network Printer Server option if you're attaching to a network printer. Choose the Next button. The port for local printer dialog box appears if you chose to install locally; the Connect to Printer dialog box appears if you chose to install a network printer.

Figure 8.1 *Installed printers and the Add Printer icon appear in the Printers folder window.*

4. In the port dialog box, choose the port you want to use for the local printer, as shown in Figure 8.3. If you're installing a network printer, select the print device. If you do not see the print device, double-click the network, server, or computer attached to the print device to display the printer.

5. Choose Next; a message may appear stating the server doesn't have an installed printer driver and asking if you want to install the driver; choose OK.

6. When installing a local printer, the next printer wizard dialog box that appears enables you to choose the manufacturer of the printer from the Manufacturer's list, then choose the model in the Printers list (see Figure 8.4).

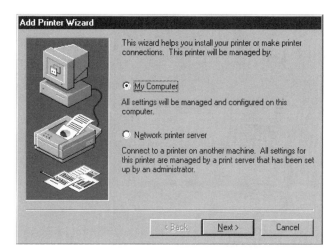

Figure 8.2 *The Printer wizard leads you step-by-step to installing a printer in NT.*

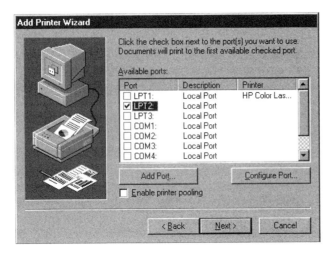

Figure 8.3 *Select the printer port for a local printer.*

7. Choose OK and insert the NT Server CD if prompted. NT copies the necessary printer drivers, then displays the specific printer's Properties dialog box. Figure 8.5 shows an HP Color LaserJet properties dialog box; however, the options in the dialog box change depending on the selected printer.

8. Choose the settings such as paper tray, font cartridges, paper size, and so on. When you select a setting in the upper window of the dialog box, the options in the lower portion of the dialog box change to related options.

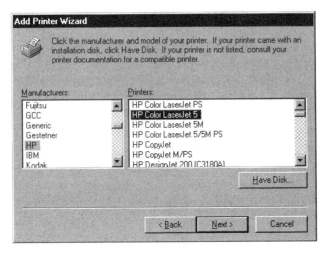

Figure 8.4 *Select the manufacturer of the printer to display available drivers for specific models.*

Figure 8.5 *Settings are specific to the selected printer.*

TIP: You can change the settings for the printer at any time by opening the Printer window, right-clicking the printer to display the shortcut menu, and selecting Document Defaults from the menu.

---

9. Choose OK to close the settings dialog box and the final wizard box appears stating that the printer installation was successful. Choose the Finish button. The printer appears in the Printers window.

TIP: You can set up additional printers for the same print device by using the same steps for creating a printer.

Configuring a Printer

When you configure the printer, you set up ports, separator pages, scheduling and priorities, spooling options, and so on. You can modify a printer's properties at any time by opening the Printers folder window and right-clicking the printer. From the shortcut menu, choose the Properties command; the printer's Properties dialog box appears. Various tabs within the dialog box control the settings and configuration, as described in the following sections. Depending on the type of print device you've installed, some of the options described here may or may not be available.

General Tab

The General tab of the Properties dialog box covers such information as the printer driver, separator page, print processor, and so on. Figure 8.6 shows the General tab and Table 8.1 describes the options in the dialog box.

Note: NT enables you to use any of its three built-in separator pages or you can create your own custom pages. You must enter the file name of the separator page in the General tab of the printer's Properties sheet to use it. SYSPRINT.SEP prints a page before each document and is compatible with PostScript; PCL.SEP switches the printer to PCL printing and prints a page before each document; and PSCRIPT.SEP switches the printer to PostScript printing without printing a separator page. To set up a custom separator page, rename and modify one of the supplied files.

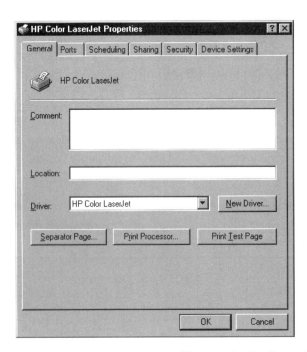

Figure 8.6 Enter comments and location in the General tab.

Table 8.1 General Tab Options

OPTIONS	DESCRIPTION
Comments	Enter any remarks you want the users to see when browsing the network printers.
Location	Enter the physical location of the print device.
Driver	Set or change the print device type (for example, from an HP LaserJet 4MP to an HP LaserJet 5P).
New Driver	Select this button to choose a new driver.
Separator Page	Print one or more separator pages at the beginning of each document.
Print Processor	Install or select a print processor.
Print Test Page	Click this button to print a test page to the printer.

Ports Tab

The Ports tab of the printer's Properties dialog box enables you to set a port, add or delete a port, and configure ports. Figure 8.7 shows the Ports tab. In the list of

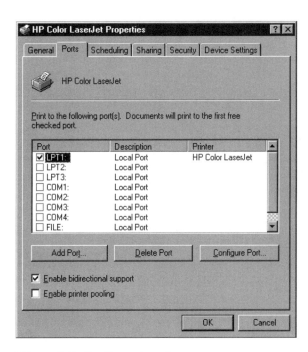

Figure 8.7 *Configure the printer ports.*

Ports, select a check box to select or deselect that port; a check mark in the check box means the port is selected.

Add a port by choosing the Add Port button. You can choose from such ports as digital network port, local port, and so on. Additionally, select any port in the list and choose the Delete Port button to delete that port. The Configure Port option enables you to modify settings for serial or parallel ports. Settings include baud rate, data bits, parity, stop bits, flow control, and so on. Be careful, when you adjust settings for a serial or parallel port, you affect not only the printer but the entire system.

Scheduling Tab

Figure 8.8 shows the Scheduling tab of the printer's Properties dialog box. You can choose when the printer will be available: Available Always or From and set certain times. Additionally, you can choose the document priority by moving the Priority slide bar from low to high. Using these scheduling options enables you to ease traffic to the print devices.

You can also choose spooling options in the Scheduling tab, as described in Table 8.2.

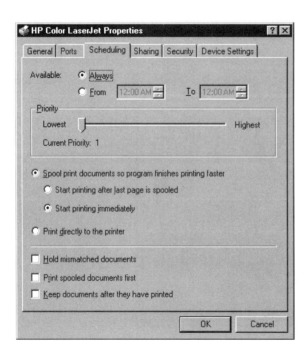

Figure 8.8 *Set scheduling and spooling options for the printer.*

Table 8.2 Spooling Options

OPTION	DESCRIPTION
Start Printing After Last Page is Spooled	Select this option to prevent delays caused by a fast print server.
Start Printing Immediately	Select to print pages as quickly as possible.
Print Directly to the Printer	Use this option to send documents directly to the printer instead of first writing them to the server's hard disk.
Hold Mismatched Documents	Select to have spooler hold documents that do not match the available form.
Print Spooled Documents First	Use to have the spooler print the documents in the order in which they finish spooling instead of the order in which they start spooling.
Keep Documents After They Have Printed	Select this option to keep documents in the print queue so users can resubmit a document for printing without going back to the original application.

TIP: Use the Print Spooled Documents First and Start Printing Immediately options together for more efficient printing.

Sharing Tab

You use the Sharing tab to designate printers as shared and to designate drivers for the clients to use. Choose Shared to share the printer, then enter a shared name (see Figure 8.9). For more information about sharing printers, see Chapter 7.

Note: Remember, when creating a share name for a printer, don't use long names containing spaces or special characters if your network has some clients who will not recognize those names, such as MS-DOS-based clients

Because different hardware platforms and operating systems require different printer drivers, you can designate drivers in the Sharing tab that clients can download when they connect to the print server. Select each version/hardware platform you want to add from the dialog box and follow any directions that may be displayed.

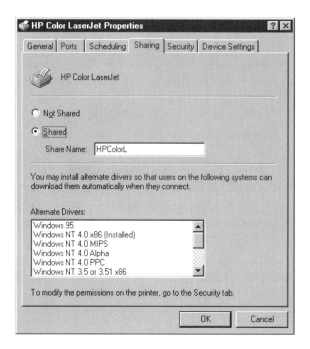

Figure 8.9 *You must designate a printer as shared before clients can see it on the network.*

Security Tab

Use the Security tab to assign permissions to users and groups who will use the printer, and to set auditing policies and ownership of the resource; by default, all shared printers are available to all network users. You must be the owner of the printer or have Full Control permission to change permissions on the printer.

The four types of permissions you can set to a network printer are: No Access, Print, Manager Documents, and Full Control. Permissions and the Security tab are covered completely in Chapter 7, if you need more information. Figure 8.10 shows the Security tab of the printer's Properties dialog box.

Device Settings

Device settings govern the physical configuration of the print device, including memory, paper trays, and so on. This is the same dialog box you see when you create a printer (see Figure 8.11).

Set printer memory, print forms (discussed in the next section), and font types in the Device Settings tab of the printer's Properties dialog box. Depending on your printer, your options may differ from those shown in the figure. After you

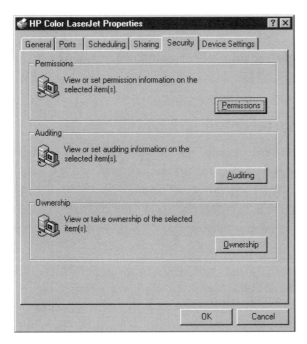

Figure 8.10 *Assign permissions to those users and groups using the printer.*

Figure 8.11 *Default settings work for most printers; however, you can change the print device's configuration if you need to.*

create and share a printer, the printer appears in the network printer browse list for clients to view and use.

Configuring Server Properties

Server properties govern port settings for all ports on the server, the creation of custom forms made available to all printers on the server, and spooling logging and notification. To open the Server Properties dialog box, select the printer in the Printers folder window, then choose File, Server Properties.

Forms Tab

A form defines the paper size and margin size of the paper that can be printed to the printer. You must have Full Control access to create forms. Figure 8.12 shows the Forms tab from which you can define a new form for the printer to use.

In the list of paper and envelope sizes, select a form to use as a base. Choose Create New Form and enter a new name in the Form Description For text box. Enter the paper size and printer area margins in the appropriate text boxes, then

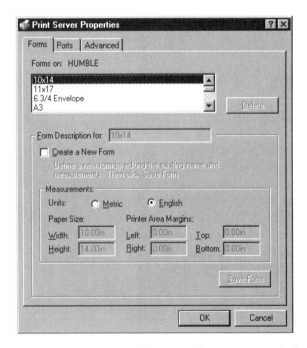

Figure 8.12 Create and save new forms to use with the printer.

choose Save Form. New forms are added to the print server's database and can then be accessed by the clients. After you create a from, specify its use with a specific print device in the printer's Properties Settings dialog box.

Ports Tab

Similar settings in the Ports tab appear in the Port tab of the printer's Properties dialog box. You can use the Ports tab of the Server Properties dialog box to add, delete, and configure ports as discussed previously. The only difference between the two Ports tabs is that you must use the printer's Properties Ports tab to increase or decrease the number of printers in a print pool and to change the port to which a printer is connected.

Advanced Tab

The Advanced tab of the Servers Properties dialog box enables you to set the spool folder location, enable spooler event logging, and to set notification options for printing. Figure 8.13 shows the Advanced folder.

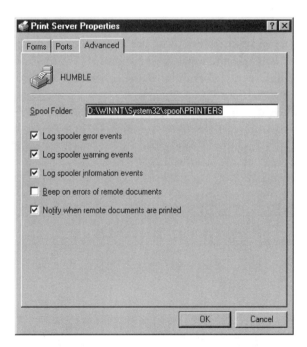

Figure 8.13 *Set spooling and notification options in the Advanced tab.*

Note: Important: If the spool folder is located on an NTFS drive, users must have the Change permission to print; see Chapter 4 for more information about granting users and groups permissions.

To log spooling events in the system log, choose any or all three of the logging options for spooling; you can log error events, warning events, and/or information events. To view the events, open the Event Viewer (Start, Programs, Administrative Tools, Event Viewer). Additionally, you can choose to have the print server beep when there is an error in remote printing. Finally, choose to notify the client when the document has finished printing.

Using the Print Queue

Members of the Administrators, Print Operators, and Server Operators groups (and anyone else who has Full Control access) can manage documents in the printer server's print queue by changing the printing order, pausing printing, purging the printer, and so on. The print queue for any printer enables you to control both the printer and the documents in the queue.

To open the print queue for any printer, open the Printers folder window and double-click the printer you want to view. The print queue opens, displaying all of the print jobs in the queue and their status (see Figure 8.14). Also displayed for each document are the following: document name, owner, pages, size, port, and the person or machine that submitted the document.

To control the printer, use the Printer menu. Choose the Pause Printing command to suspend all printing; select the command again to resume printing. Choose the Purge Print Documents command from the Printer menu to delete all jobs in the print queue.

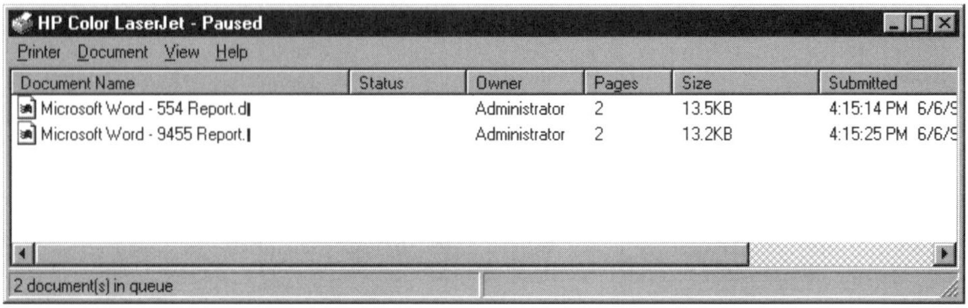

Figure 8.14 You can control the printing of documents in the print queue.

Control individual or multiple documents by first selecting the documents, then choosing any of the following commands on the Document menu: Pause to suspend printing of the selected document(s); Resume to continue printing; and Cancel to delete a selected document from the print queue. You also can choose Properties from the Document menu to view a selected document's properties.

Note: If you have Full Control access, you can manage the print server from any NT workstation or server on the network. Open the Network Neighborhood and select the printer. Change its properties or even create new printers. You can also manage document printing by rearranging the order of documents in the queue, deleting documents to be printed, and so on.

Clients can view printers and the progress of their documents at any time; however, clients cannot manage any documents other than their own unless they have Full Control or Manage Documents permission.

Font Management

Printing to any print device can be troublesome when it comes to fonts, especially when you're using different client operating systems. As you know, a print device can use any of three types of fonts: device fonts, screen fonts, and downloadable soft fonts. Any device fonts that reside in the print device or a font cartridge can be used with NT and NT clients. NT can also use screen fonts; you can install screen fonts using the Control Panel, Fonts option on the print server. Downloadable soft fonts, on the other hand, should be installed locally to the client computers; then clients can print to the NT print server.

NT software supplies True-Type fonts (the same font type as with previous versions of Windows). Since True-Type fonts are device-independent, the font you see on the screen can be duplicated in any print device. True-Type fonts are versatile, high-quality, and easy to use; if you can use True-Type fonts all the time, you should if only because documents using True-Type fonts are compatible with any print device, application, or system.

NT also supports raster, or bitmapped, fonts. Raster fonts are device-dependent; if a print device doesn't support them, they don't print. Vector fonts, such as those used as pen plotters, are also supported by NT.

Clients and Printing to NT

A variety of clients can print to an NT print server, including NT network and local clients; networking clients running Windows 95, Windows for Workgroups, and MS-DOS; and clients running UNIX, NetWare, and Macintosh. Each client requires specific protocols or redirectors to complete the print job. A *redirector* is a software module loaded onto the workstation that intercepts application requests for printer-sharing services and diverts them to the print server for action.

Windows NT and 95

Windows NT clients can use the following network protocols to send print jobs to the print server: TCP/IP, NetBEUI, NWLink, or AppleTalk. Additionally, you don't have to load the network's printer drivers onto an NT network client; the driver is automatically installed on the client's hard disk by the server when the client begins its print operation. The server can even supply earlier versions of print drivers for NT 3.51 clients.

Windows 95 clients use a redirector to send a print job and the redirector uses one of the following protocols: NetBEUI, NWLink, or TCP/IP.

DOS-Based Clients

Windows for Workgroups and other Windows 3.x clients support printing from DOS-based applications and Windows-based applications. They both use the 16-bit printer driver installed on the computer and send jobs to the NT print server by using an MS Network client redirector. Windows for Workgroups includes its own built-in redirector. The same protocols—NetBEUI, NWLink, and TCP/IP—are used by the redirectors.

MS-DOS clients also use a client redirector and the NetBEUI or TCP/IP protocol. If you have trouble printing from an MS-DOS-based application, that application may not allow for a network redirector to forward the job to the print server. You'll need to upgrade to a network-aware application to enable network printing.

Other Clients

NT supplies the TCP/IP Print Server (also know as LPD—line printer daemon) service to enable UNIX clients to print to the print server but this service may not always work for you. For example, in order to use NT's print services, the UNIX client must support Request for Comment (RFC) 1179—a distinctive specification that many systems do not comply with. If RFC 1179 is not supported, errors of all kinds—from severe to minor—are reported as the same error type.

To support NetWare clients, you must install the Microsoft File and Print Services for NetWare, an add-on product you can purchase. NetWare clients use

---

Macintosh Printing

Services for Macintosh is a special service you add using the Network icon in the Control Panel, Services tab. The services utility enables Macintosh clients to access files stored on the NT server and to use any printer connected to the computer running NT server.

After you set up the Services for Macintosh, the Print Server for Macintosh is integrated into NT Server's Print Manager. The print server then makes its printers available to Macintosh clients and it makes AppleTalk PostScript printers available to PC clients. Macintosh users can submit PostScript files and the NT print server translates the files so they can be printed to a non-PostScript printer.

Both Macintosh and PC print jobs sent to the print server are spooled, meaning they are sent to a spool file to wait until their turn to print; thus, the users can continue to work after submitting their print jobs without waiting for the print job to finish printing.

IPX/SPX-compatible protocol to print to the NT print server. Using the FPNW services, the NetWare client sees the NT printers as print queues.

Macintosh clients can send jobs over AppleTalk to the print server, which looks like any other AppleTalk device to the client. Services for Macintosh must be installed and configured in NT Server to communicate with the Macintosh client (see sidebar, "Macintosh Printing," for more information).

Summary

This chapter has covered setting up a print server, configuring printing services, and managing print jobs through the print server. You've learned how to plan your printing services, configure printers, connect shared printers, and to understand printing services in NT.

PART
IV

Preparing and Managing Workstations

9 *Workstation Requirements and Recommendations*

Whether you're upgrading from an existing network or you're starting from a few standalone computers, you can probably use some of the equipment you have for network client computers. Assess your current computers, their operating systems, software, and peripherals before deciding on upgrading or purchasing new equipment.

You don't want to waste anything you have; but you do want to make the most of your NT network. Each client operating system offers certain advantages and disadvantages when networking with NT; this chapter outlines the pros and cons of each operating system, and covers other issues you will need to consider. This chapter will focus on the following:

- Uses and features of various client operating systems
- Advantages and disadvantages of various client operating systems
- Hardware requirements for different operating systems
- Software and peripheral considerations for client computers

Features of Various Client Operating Systems

You may already be familiar with the various operating systems you can use on client computers with NT networking; however, this section covers each of the programs, in case you're not acquainted with them all. Following are the operating systems you can use on client computers:

NT Server 3.51 and 4.0
NT Workstation 3.51 and 4.0
Windows 95A and 95B
MS-DOS and Windows for Workgroups

MS-DOS and Windows 3.x
Macintosh

This section covers a few of the general features and uses for each operating system. The next section explains the advantages and disadvantages to using each client operating system on the NT network.

NT 3.51 and 4.0

The NT Server and NT Workstation operating systems offer the user all of the benefits of a 32-bit operating system, networking flexibility, a multitude of built-in accessories, and more. NT outperforms previous Windows versions by providing more speed, flexibility, and power for running applications and completing tasks. The following information applies to both versions of NT Server and NT Workstation.

Architecture

NT's architecture includes features that enable you to add hardware—such as video or sound cards, modems, memory, hard drives, and even processors—that extends the operating system's usefulness. Configuring that hardware is also made efficient by the use of the Wizard dialog box that guides you through the process. Figure 9.1 shows a computer running NT Workstation with the Install New Modem Wizard dialog box displaying.

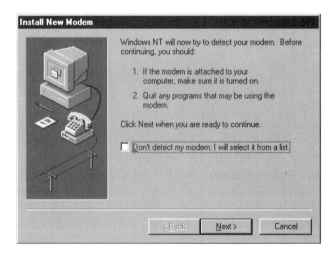

Figure 9.1 *Wizards help you install hardware, peripherals, programs, and so on to computers running NT.*

Also, NT was designed to run various applications, such as DOS-based, Windows, and even OS/2 applications. The operating system supports document creation and modification in these various programs as well as provides printer, graphics, upgrade, and information-sharing support for many applications designed to work with other operating systems.

NT is a reliable operating system, designed to isolate system problems so they cannot affect the other areas of the system; you'll see less crashes when using NT than you would from previous Windows versions.

NT's Features and Accessories

NT Server includes many features that make day-to-day work more efficient and enjoyable. As a workstation, NT provides multiple printer support, easy handling of files and folders, customization attributes, and a multitude of accessory programs you can take advantage of.

Printers are easy to use with an NT workstation because of Installation Wizards, drag-and-drop printing, print management and security features, and so on. After you use a Wizard to install a new printer (whether it's a local or network printer), you can track print jobs, pause or cancel jobs, set a default printer for all applications, place a printer shortcut on the desktop for quick printing, and monitor the use of a local printer. Figure 9.2 shows a local printer's Properties dialog box; a user can set up a local printer to suit the type of work he or she does most.

The NT Explorer makes file management on the client smooth and simple. If you're used to a previous version of Windows, NT's Explorer is similar to the File Manager. You can create folders, copy and move files, and otherwise organize and manage your disks and drives in the Explorer. Figure 9.3 shows the NT Explorer; drives and folders are listed on the left while files and subfolders are listed on the right. See Chapter 11 for more information.

NT also includes many accessory applications you can use to attach to the Internet, create word processing documents, send and receive e-mail over the network, view events on the computer that cause errors or problems, and so on. Other features that are handy to a user include the following:

- Multimedia support, such as various video and sound drivers, accessory programs for listening to a CD player and recording sounds, and more.

- A Find feature in which you can locate any file or folder on the computer, and on the network.

- The Briefcase enables you to transfer files from your work computer to a floppy disk, copy it to a different computer (such as a notebook or home computer), work on the files, then update the files back to your work computer.

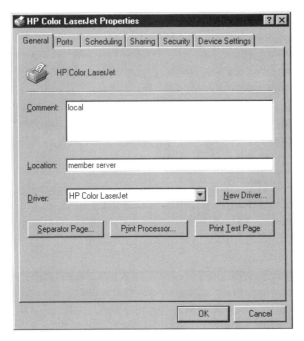

Figure 9.2 *Configure a Local printer using the printer's Properties dialog box.*

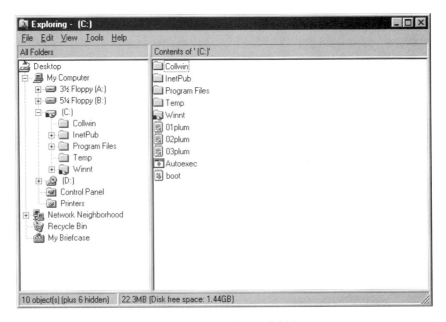

Figure 9.3 *Use the Explorer to manage files and folders.*

- A Command Prompt accessory provides a DOS window in which you can execute many of the DOS commands with which you're familiar and run DOS-based applications.

- Customization features provide you with the tools to change keyboard, desktop, font, date and time, mouse, and other settings to suit your particular working style.

- Dial-up networking support provides you with a connection to the network from your home or on the road.

All in all, you'll find NT is an expedient and reliable operating system to use for client computers on your NT network.

Version Differences: 3.51 and 4.0

Both NT 4.0 and 3.51 are 32-bit operating systems. Both support multiple processors, multitasking, can support large quantities of RAM, have Event logging, support remote access services, include both domain and workgroup-based administration features, incorporate features that support fault tolerance and RAID. Either version of the operating system supports NetWare, TCP/IP, NetBEUI, and Macintosh as well as security, user management, system monitoring, print services, server management, and the list goes on and on. Obviously, NT 4.0 was built on a very successful and stable NT 3.51.

What's the difference? NT 4.0 sports a whole new look and feel. Version 3.51 looks like the previous versions of Windows—3.1 and 3.11—with a Program Manager, File Manager, a basic network browser, and so on. Windows NT 4.0 is sleek with its Desktop and taskbar, Windows Explorer, Network Neighborhood, shortcuts, Internet Explorer, My Computer window, and more.

NT 4.0 includes programs that help you get your work done faster: a Find Files, Folders, or Computers dialog box, faster printing, a Quick View utility, and more. The taskbar offers more efficient switching between open applications; the Start menu offers quick and easy access to help, documents, programs, and more.

Customizing NT 4.0 is simpler than ever and the options offer a more useful interface with the program. Create shortcuts on the desktop for opening applications, documents, even for printing. Get to the Control Panel or Printers folder with one click of the mouse. Modify screen elements so they better suit your way of working; change colors, screen savers, fonts, and other elements on-screen to make your workstation your own.

NT 4.0 offers new applications, improved accessories, utilities for working from home or on a laptop easier, improved dial-up networking, and extra services.

Windows 95

Windows 95 is a full step or two above previous versions of Windows in that it offers the user more power and speed, expanded features, a more intuitive interface, improved printing and networking characteristics, and more.

Windows 95 enables users to install and run both 16-bit and 32-bit applications. Because of Windows 95 architecture, performance is improved with printing, file handling, and applications use; also, there's less chance of the applications failing in Windows 95. Windows 95 is compatible with previous Microsoft operating systems, in that you can use DOS and Windows 3.1 programs with the operating system.

Installation of the operating system and of drivers, hardware, applications, and so on, is smooth and simple thanks to Wizards that guide you through the process, detect hardware, and numerous device drivers included with Windows. As a user, you can take care of many tasks by yourself, without the help of the network administrator or other technicians.

Consider the following additional features of Windows 95 as a client operating system:

- Intuitive file and folder management is provided using either the My Computer window or the Windows 95 Explorer. Copy, delete, move, and create files and folders with the click of the mouse.

- Printing speed is increased because of the 32-bit print subsystem, meaning printing can take place in the background without causing delays in the current application and printing is actually faster than it was in previous versions of Windows.

- Accessory programs provide word processing, drawing, Internet access, multimedia support, and more.

- Support for mobile users enables easy configuration, more variety in hardware, power management for notebook computers, and so on.

- Customization options enable the user to change colors, screen savers, fonts, wallpapers, and other settings to make the application more comfortable and individual.

- Plug-and-Play architecture enables Windows to quickly detect hardware you add to the system and configure it automatically.

- An MS-DOS prompt supplies a DOS-like window in which you can use DOS commands and run DOS-based applications. Figure 9.4 shows the MS-DOS Prompt window in Windows 95 with the DIR command results.

Finally, improved network support of clients and protocols makes Windows 95 a perfect candidate for a network client operating system. You can connect a com-

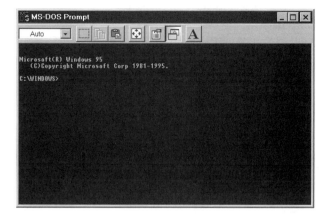

Figure 9.4 *Use the MS-DOS Prompt with commands or to run DOS-based applications.*

puter running Windows 95 to a NetWare network, NT network, the Internet, or a peer-to-peer Microsoft network effortlessly. Configuring printers, browsing the network resources, and so on are easier with Windows 95 than ever before in a Windows product. Figure 9.5 shows the Network dialog box from a Windows 95 client computer. You can add protocols, client services, and configure file and printer sharing; see Chapter 10 for more information.

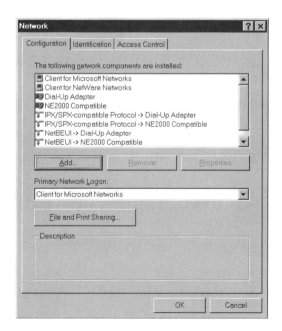

Figure 9.5 *Configure network components in Windows 95 similarly to Windows NT.*

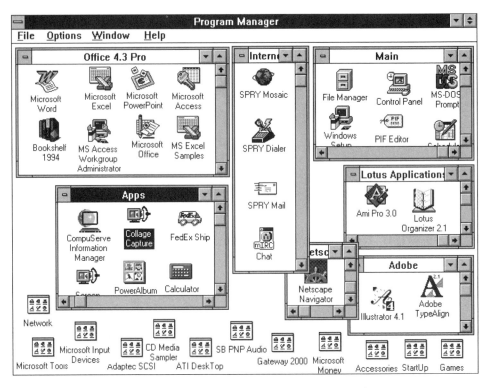

Figure 9.6 *Windows for Workgroups presents applications organized into program groups, or windows.*

MS-DOS and Windows for Workgroups

When a computer uses Windows for Workgroups, its operating system is actually DOS; Windows for Workgroups is simply the graphical interface used in conjunction with the operating system. Windows for Workgroups, or version 3.11, was Microsoft's answer to workgroup, or peer-to-peer, network. Using the familiar Program Manager, you can open applications, manage files, use Windows accessories to perform tasks, connect to a network, share data between applications, and so on. Figure 9.6 shows the Program Manager of a Windows for Workgroups client computer.

- Windows for Workgroups offers a user the following:
- An easy-to-use graphical interface
- A plethora of applications designed for Windows for Workgroups
- The capability of opening more than one program at a time and switching between applications

- A File Manager for management and organization of files and directories
- Accessory applications—such as a word processor, paint program, and calendar
- The True-Type font that prints just the way it looks on-screen and works with most printers
- The ability to use DOS applications from within Windows
- The ability to attach to a network and share resources over the network
- Object linking and embedding, as a way of sharing data between applications

MS-DOS and Windows 3.x

DOS computers can be used as clients on the NT network, but I recommend upgrading to a Windows application, if at all possible. DOS attachments to the network are primitive and offer more headaches than benefits. However, you might need to run a DOS workstation for a specific application or for another reason and only attach to that network periodically.

Note: DOS computers may also be running version 3.0 or 3.1 of Windows; when you attach a DOS computer to the NT network, the connection only works in DOS, not in Windows 3.0 or 3.1.

Macintosh

The Macintosh computer has long been a competitor of the PC and often the subject of heated debates. If you're a Macintosh user, you'll probably always use a Macintosh. That, if for no other reason, is good enough to use Macintosh clients on your NT network. But there are other reasons.

Macintosh is probably the best computer you can use for art programs, desktop publishing, image retrieval and manipulation, and other such uses. Applications for the Macintosh are numerous, and software is fully-developed, professional, and highly practical. You can buy powerful, full-featured Macintoshes, just as you can with a PC. Macintoshes include programs for file management, communications, accessories for printing and handling fonts, and applications for performing everyday tasks.

Generally, the Macintosh and PC worlds collide when it comes to sharing files; however, NT Server includes the Services for Macintosh which enables Mac users to attach to the NT network, share files with PC users, share printers, and so on. If you have Macintosh computers in your company, you can attach them very successfully to your NT network.

Networking Advantages and Disadvantages of Various Client Operating Systems

NT Server is a flexible network operating system; its open architecture enables it to communicate with various other network products and client operating systems. The major issue you will need to consider security. Various client operating systems present various levels of security. There are other factors that will weigh on your decision for operating systems. While you're reading this chapter and considering the possibilities, keep these questions in mind:

How much will it cost to upgrade and/or purchase new hardware and operating systems for each client?

How easy will the new operating system be to learn? How much training on the system will the users need?

What is the cost of upgrading the applications each client uses? What is the learning curve for the new software? Training costs?

How much time and frustration will it save your users to easily access the network and its resources?

Will learning a new or upgraded application be that difficult once the user is familiar with the new network and operating system?

How important are the files on the server? Is security really important in your organization?

Is it necessary for you to upgrade all of your client computers at the same time?

When setting up a client/server network with Windows NT Server 4.0, you can use a variety of operating systems on the client computers. Some work better than others; some will give you more headaches than others.

NT Server 3.51 and 4.0

Of all of the client operating systems you might use with an NT network, NT Server and Workstation are the best choices. NT Server software installed on a computer, as you know, can be configured as a primary or backup domain controller, or as a member server. You wouldn't want to use a domain controller as a workstation; the resources can be used to a greater benefit if you use domain controllers as authentication, file, print, Web, and other types of servers.

You can, however, use a member server as a workstation, or client computer. Naturally, if a member server also functions as a file, database, or another server that attracts a lot of network traffic, you will not want to use it as a workstation either. But, if you have a member server or two whose resources are seldom used by others on the network, you can safely double that computer's duties. Since a member server doesn't keep a database of user accounts or enable a user more access to the server than any other client computer, you can safely assign a computer running NT Server to any of your network users.

A computer running NT Server gains all of the benefits of the 32-bit operating system, security features of the NT network, plus other advantages, such as multiprocessing support, networking with a variety of protocols and services, fault tolerance, and so on. Figure 9.7 shows the Network Neighborhood window of NT Server installed to a member server.

The major disadvantage to running NT Server on a client computer is your hardware. NT Server software requires a powerful computer with enough memory to handle all of the operating system bells and whistles. The cost of upgrading or purchasing one computer that can run NT Server can be quite high; just consider the cost of upgrading *all* of your client computers. The next section covers required hardware for computers running NT Server.

NT Workstation 3.51 and 4.0

Similar to NT Server versions 3.51 and 4.0, NT Workstation provides many advantages when running the operating system on client computers. The difference between NT Server and NT Workstation, either version, is the use of the tools and utilities included with each program. NT Workstation provides user and group support, security features, system monitoring, and other utilities that administer the client computer, only. NT Server provides the same features, plus additional utilities, for administering multiple client computers on a network.

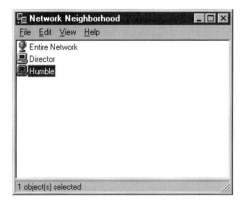

Figure 9.7 *Using the member server as a workstation, the user can view the server that is the primary domain controller.*

Figure 9.8 *NT Workstation is a perfect client for an NT network.*

You may, for example, create users with specific rights and assign permissions to your files and directories on NT Workstation; the only time that affects users is when they try to access the resources on that NT Workstation. Usually, you use the security features and other utilities on a client running NT Workstation when you're in a workgroup situation as opposed to a domain situation. Figure 9.8 illustrates the My Computer window and desktop of an NT Workstation 4.0 client computer; the interface is very much the same as NT Server.

Computers running the NT Workstation operating system work very well with the Windows NT network. Clients can take full advantage of the security features, such as user rights, sharing files and directories on the server, and permissions for resources; the 32-bit operating system and its speed and flexibility; various programs and applications included with the products, especially NT Workstation 4.0.

NT Workstation 4.0 provides complete protocol and client service support to the NT network. Installing and configuring for network use is similar to the task in NT Server. You browse the network using the Network Neighborhood, My Computer, or the Explorer and attaching to resources, such as printers is quick and easy.

Note: For information about version differences, refer to the previous sidebar, "Version Differences: 3.51 and 4.0." Many of the interface, customization, and application differences between NT Server versions also apply to NT Workstation versions.

Workgroup versus Domain

In a workgroup, all workstations are equal; each workstation shares its resources with the other computers in the workgroup. In a Microsoft workgroup, Windows NT, Windows 95, and even Windows for Workgroups can successfully participate, sharing files and resources within the group. You can even add Windows 3.x and MS-DOS computers into the mix as members of the workgroup.

Workgroups work well with a small group, as opposed to a large group of computers. Problems arise with workgroups, as they expand in members, with security, network traffic, file and resource management, and so on. With no one really in charge of a workgroup, individuals must monitor the resource use on their own computer; thus impairing the organization of the network.

NT Workstation enables you to set permissions and user rights, much the way NT Server does; however, these rights and permissions apply only to the computer on which you configure them. Therefore, the user of a computer running NT Workstation can easily monitor and control the use of his or her files and resources in a workgroup situation.

Often in workgroups, people use NT Workstation as a client/server of sorts. A computer running NT Workstation can serve as a file and/or print server to other workstations, enabling users and groups to access the computer, setting permissions on resources, such as files and printers, as well. One problem with using NT Workstation as a server in a workgroup situation is that you can attach no more than 10 computers to any service offered on the NT Workstation computer. Another problem is that NT Workstation doesn't offer all of the advanced utilities for administering a client/server network, much less for managing multiple workstations, servers, and multiple domains. Another problem is that users must remember a different password, and perhaps user name, for each NT Workstation computer to which they want access; as the system expands, users must remember more and more passwords and locations of resources.

The domain system, on the other hand, offers more security and less administration. Since all users in a domain are authenticated by the domain controller, they only need one password to gain access to all resources. Additionally, resources are easier to locate since only one or two servers, or specialized servers, provide what the users need. Multiple users (up to 26,000) can attach to one NT Server domain controller and access its resources; so NT Server is scalable, able to grow with the system and your business. Finally, NT Server offers advanced utilities and tools for managing multiple workstations and servers, as well as models for using multiple domains within the network.

Windows 95

Windows 95 clients on a Windows NT network is almost like using an NT Workstation computer on the network. The interface of Windows 95 is almost identical to Windows NT Workstation 4.0 and the architecture of the program is also similar. You can attach to the network using the Network Neighborhood, My Computer, or the Explorer, just as in NT Workstation. Configuring protocols and client services is similar, as well, and Windows 95 is also intuitive in that it uses Wizard dialog boxes to help you install modems, hardware, network services, and other utilities you may need.

A Windows 95 client can share its files and folders, and can access any of the shared resources on the network and server for which the user has permission and rights. Also, a Windows 95 client can take advantage of a network printer, just as an NT Workstation computer can. Figure 9.9 illustrates the Windows 95 Network Neighborhood, attached to the NT primary domain controller.

Other advantages to using Windows 95 clients include the flexibility of the program to run with other network operating systems, such as NetWare. So, if you used a different network before changing to NT, you may already have Windows 95 clients in place. If you are running a NetWare and NT network side-by-side, Windows 95 clients can take full advantage of both networks.

Also, there are many applications on the market that are Windows 95-compatible. If you already have Windows 95 computers and applications to run on those computers, you're better off using them as your clients on the NT network than upgrading to Windows NT Workstation. The cost will be less in training, upgrading hardware, purchasing new software, obtaining new drivers, and so on.

Figure 9.9 *The Windows 95 Network Neighborhood is similar to NT's.*

A disadvantage to using Windows 95 clients is, once again, in the hardware required to run the operating system. If you don't already have Windows 95 computers in place, you will have to upgrade computers running DOS and Windows 3.x to be compliant with Windows 95. See the next section for hardware requirements.

Note: Microsoft has released an upgrade of the Windows 95 operating system, called Windows 95B or OSR/2. This upgrade is only available pre-installed on new computers and offers improvements in the program's architecture and code to make it more compatible with new hardware. As a user, you will see a few differences in the interface—Windows 95B offers Internet Mail and Internet News, extra options in the Display dialog box, and other cosmetic changes—but the main difference is in how the program operates—more efficiently and effectively. Both operating systems work the same when it comes to attaching and configuring for network use, however.

MS-DOS and Windows for Workgroups

Probably the most likely computers in your current system run MS-DOS and Windows for Workgroups (version 3.11) with DOS as the primary operating system. Windows for Workgroups integrates very well into an NT network; however, when you're attached to the network using Windows for Workgroups, the connection is lost if you close Windows and work in DOS. You could, instead, shell out to DOS using the MS-DOS Prompt icon; as long as Windows is running, you're still attached to the network.

Windows for Workgroups is largely network-unaware. You will not see any of the NT features, such as security options, user and group membership, network browsing, and so on, but you can access the server to obtain files, directories, and printers for which you have permission and rights to access.

The major disadvantage of using Windows for Workgroups as a network client is the rudimentary networking features offered the user. However, if you are already running Windows for Workgroups on several computers and cannot immediately afford to upgrade, using the Windows for Workgroups client is the right choice for your network.

Note: You can also use NT Server's Network Client Administrator to create a TCP/IP client for use with Windows for Workgroups on the network. This client enables Windows for Workgroups to take better advantage of NT's security, resources, and 32-bit architecture. See Chapter 10 for more information.

MS-DOS and Windows 3.x

If your workstations run MS-DOS as the operating system and use Windows 3.0 or 3.1, I suggest you upgrade your hardware and operating system before continuing. You can create a DOS client to use with an NT network and access data across the network, but the headaches you will get from the process may not be worth it.

Note: Important: Even if your workstation computers have Windows 3.x installed, you cannot attach to the network through Windows or use Windows on the network when using an MS-DOS client.

NT supports MS-DOS clients by including support for TSR (terminate-and-stay-resident) programs, supplying a default PIF (program information file) that the DOS applications can use, and supplying updated printer drivers a DOS workstation can use to access the network printers. However, some DOS applications may not be able to print to the network printer, even with the correct driver; some applications still won't work with NT, even with a specially created PIF; and often, many applications, such as scanner drivers, disk maintenance software, and private printer drivers won't work with NT, even though you have application upgrades or NT-compatible device drivers.

Note: Chapter 10 describes how to create the MS-DOS client software from the NT Server Installation CD-ROM.

Using DOS, you can easily manage your files and directories, edit configuration files, manage devices, create and edit text, use commands to control the system, and make use of DOS-based applications.

Macintosh

The big advantage of using Macintosh clients is that you won't need any other hardware or software except your Macintosh operating system and NT Server to connect and use the clients on the network. If you already have Macintosh computers, Microsoft makes it easy and inexpensive for you to attach those computers to the network by including Windows NT Server Services for Macintosh.

NT's Services for Macintosh provides secured logon, easy-to-use graphical administration tools, printing to non-PostScript printers, multiple simultaneous client-connections, support for AppleTalk Phase 2, and more. The services enable the Macintosh client to share files and printers, all with simplified administration.

When using a Macintosh client on an NT network, you will see the following advantages:

- Shared files appear to PC users in the DOS 8.3 file-naming standard; those same files appear to the Mac user as if the files were created on the Macintosh computer.

- PC users can access any directories, or folders, designated as shared; if you indicate that same directory is Macintosh-accessible, Mac clients can also access the directory.

- Macintosh users aren't limited to the 8.3 file-naming standard; they can use long file names. The Macintosh limit is 31 characters, spaces included.

- Network security is enforced the same for Mac users as it is for PC users.

A few disadvantages include the following:

- Macintosh-accessible volumes must be on an NTFS partition; if your NT Server is formatted as FAT, the Mac clients can't use it.

- You may need to upgrade your Macintosh hardware, such as network adapter cards and routers, to make the connections work; consult NT Server's help and your hardware person for more information.

- You will need to learn how to administer the File Manager for Macintosh and the Print Manager for Macintosh.

Workstation Hardware

You will want to consider the client operating systems on your workstations so you can decide whether to upgrade hardware or stay with the status quo. If you upgrade workstations to Microsoft client software, you can take advantage of many services and features provided by NT Server. Microsoft client software includes MS-DOS, Windows for Workgroups 3.11, Windows 95, Windows NT 3.51 or 4.0 Server, and Windows NT 3.51 or 4.0 Workstation. NT even provides server services for Macintosh computers.

Following are some basic hardware requirements for each operating system; for more information about client computers, see Chapter 10.

Windows NT

Windows NT is a 32-bit, multitasking operating system that can operate on Intel processors and RISC processors. NT uses a graphical user interface, similar to Windows 95, and can run applications made for NT, Windows 95, Windows 3.1, and DOS. NT can even run some OS/2 16-bit character-based applications. Security in Windows NT machines is high and NT can support several file systems: FAT, HPFS, and NTFS.

You can use the following NT products as operating systems on client computers:

Windows NT 3.51 Workstation
Windows NT 3.51 Server
Windows NT 4.0 Server
Windows NT 4.0 Workstation

Computers running either NT Server 4.0 (used as a client or a member server) or NT Workstation 4.0 have a similar interface to that of the domain controller computer running NT Server. NT machines can control their own resources with their own User Manager by granting permissions to local files and directories. Figure 9.10 shows the User Manager on a member server running NT Server 4.0. The names listed in the User Manager window and the rights assigned to them apply only to this one computer, not to the entire domain.

Additionally, NT machines can connect easily to the server, and to each other, using the Network Neighborhood, Explorer, and/or the My Computer window. Loading protocols and services, configuring the workstations, and other procedures are nearly the same in NT Workstation computers as in NT Server computers.

To install Windows NT Server 4.0 to a client computer, you need the following hardware:

32-bit x86-based microprocessor (Intel 486 25mhz or higher)
16M RAM
125M hard disk space
VGA or higher resolution monitor
CD-ROM drive and 3.5-inch floppy drive or install from the network
Pointing device
Network adapter card

To install Windows NT Workstation 4.0 to a client computer, you need the following hardware:

32-bit x86-based microprocessor (Intel 486 25mhz or higher)
12–16M RAM
117M hard disk space
VGA or higher resolution monitor
CD-ROM drive and 3.5-inch floppy drive or install from the network
Pointing device
Network adapter card

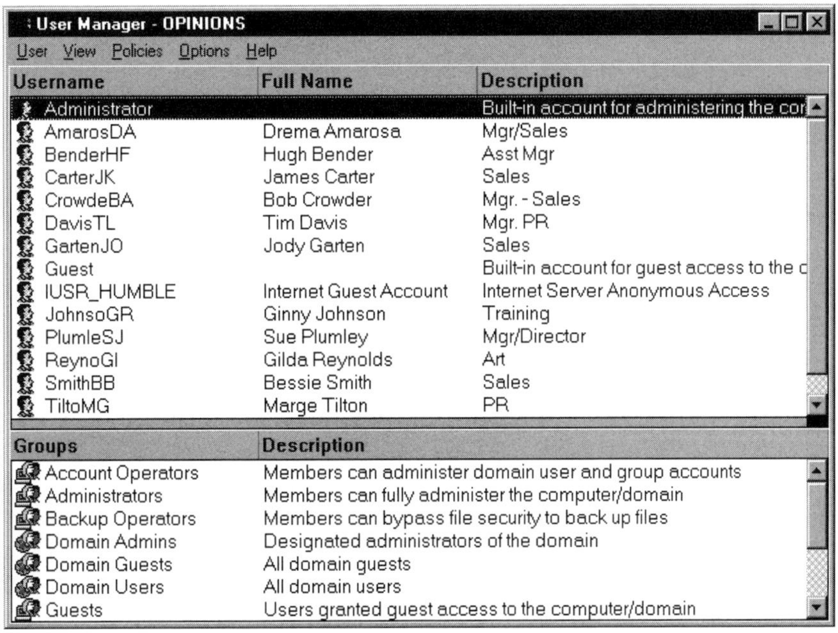

Figure 9.10 *An NT client computer can set rights for its own resources.*

To install Windows NT 3.51 to a client computer, you need the following hardware:

Intel x86 (386 25mhz or better for the 3.51 Workstation; 486 recommended for Server)
16M RAM, minimum
75M–100M hard disk space
VGA or higher resolution monitor
CD-ROM drive, disk drive, or network attachment to load the operating system
Mouse or other pointing device
Network adapter card

Windows 95

Windows 95, which has an interface similar to NT 4, also works well on an NT Server 4 network. Windows 95 offers a variety of protocols, the Network Neighborhood network browser, drive mapping, network printer installation and drivers, and much more. You'll also receive many of the benefits from NT Server when using 95, such as security features and the use of a Web browser for intranets.

To use Windows 95 on a workstation client, you need the following hardware:

386 25MHz or later processor
8M RAM
54M hard disk space
VGA or better resolution monitor
CD-ROM drive or a floppy 3.5-inch drive or install from the network
Mouse or other pointing device
Network adapter card

DOS-Based Clients

DOS-based clients include those machines running only MS-DOS, DOS and Windows 3.x, and DOS and Windows for Workgroups (version 3.11). I suggest you use MS-DOS 6.22 on any client computer as opposed to PC-DOS or an earlier version of MS-DOS. If you use client computers with an operating system other than Windows NT Server, NT Workstation, or Windows 95—such as MS-DOS and Windows for Workgroups—those computers can interact within the NT Server domain; however, they will not have the same logon security to protect their own resources from others on the network and they won't receive the maximum benefits of NT Server.

Windows for Workgroups 3.11 integrates well into the NT network, even though you lose many of the NT security features and benefits. Similarly, MS-DOS workstations can access NT networks, but you lose most of the NT innovations.

Note: The Windows NT Server CD includes a DOS client you can use to connect your DOS-based computers. It also includes a Windows for Workgroups client for TCP/IP. You can use Windows for Workgroups with your NetBEUI protocol without adding another software client to the workstation. See Chapter 10 for more information.

The hardware requirements for a DOS client include:

PC or compatible with at least 256K memory
A 3.5 or 5.25-inch floppy disk drive
4M of hard disk space
Network adapter card

The hardware requirements for a Windows for Workgroups client include:

MS-DOS version 5 or later
80386 processor or higher
640K conventional memory and 1024K extended memory
10M Free disk space
3.5-inch floppy drive
Display adapter that is supported by Windows
Mouse or other compatible pointing device
Network adapter card

Macintosh

When adding a Macintosh client to your NT network, the hardware requirements are minimal; however, you will need to add a couple of things to your server. You can use most any Macintosh computer as a client for the NT network, as long as it meets the following minimum requirements:

Capability to use AppleShare (the Apple networking software for the Macintosh)

Version 6.0.7 or later Macintosh operating system (including System 7 and higher)

LocalTalk, Ethernet, Token-Ring, or FDDI

For the NT Server to communicate with the Macintosh client, the following must be true of the NT Server computer:

2M extra hard disk space
The NTFS file system or partition to create directories for use by Macintosh
Services for Macintosh must be installed

Summary

In this chapter, you've learned about various operating systems you can use for client computers on the network, the advantages and disadvantages of each system, and the hardware requirements for using each operating system. Chapter 10 continues coverage of client computers by showing how to upgrade client software on your client computers.

10 *Installing and Upgrading Client Software*

Before connecting clients to your NT network, you need to install NT client software to each workstation. NT helps with this process by making various clients available to you through the NT server and the NT installation CD-ROM. After installing client software, you can connect the clients to the server. This chapter also shows how to connect to the server from the workstation and to the workstation from the server.

Naturally, you should make sure that each client computer has the appropriate hardware and operating system installed; see Chapter 9 for information about client computers and requirements.

Specifically, this chapter shows how to do the following:

- Create client software
- Install client software to MS-DOS and Windows for Workgroups
- Configure network components in Windows NT Workstation computers
- Configure network components in Windows 95 computers
- Connect clients to the NT server

Client Software Overview

NT provides a method by which you can create startup disks or installation disks for installing various clients. An installation startup disk enables you to start a client computer and connect to the NT server. From an installation directory created on the server then, you can install the client software. You could, alternatively, create a network installation disk set that contains all of the files needed to install the client software. Use the Network Client Administrator tool to create the client software.

Note: Remember that your Windows NT Server software license requires you to purchase a valid software license prior to installing additional copies of the Server software or any client software.

Using NT's Network Client Administrator, you can create a network installation startup disk for Windows for Workgroups 3.11 (TCP/IP version) and/or for a Network Client version 3.0 for MS-DOS. Users can attach to the NT server and access resources using this client software.

Windows NT Server versions 3.5, 3.51, and 4.0; Windows NT Workstation versions 3.5, 3.51, and 4.0; and Windows 95 computers can connect to the NT server without special client software, if you install the appropriate protocol—NetBEUI, IPX/SPX, or TCP/IP. Windows for Workgroups computers also can connect to the NT server using NetBEUI, if you're not set up to run TCP/IP.

If you prefer, you can create a set of installation disks for the following clients, instead of using the startup installation disks:

Network Client version 3.0 for MS-DOS

LAN Manager 2.2c for MS-DOS clients

LAN Manager 2.2c for MS OS/2 clients

Remote Access Service client 1.1 for MS-DOS

TCP/IP-32 for Windows for Workgroups 3.11

Starting the Network Client Administrator

Before you can create the client software, you must create a directory on the root of the NT server to hold the client software. You can do this in the NT Explorer; choose Start, Programs, Windows NT Explorer. Click on your hard drive icon, then choose File, New, Folder. The new folder appears in the right pane, ready for you to enter a new name. Type **CLIENTS** and press ENTER.

Make sure you designate the directory as shared by selecting the folder and choosing File, Sharing. Click the Shared As option and choose OK.

To start the Network Client Administrator, choose Start, Programs, Administrative Tools, and Network Client Administrator. The dialog box shown in Figure 10.1 appears.

The options in the dialog box are:

- *Make Network Installation Startup Disk*: Create a startup disk you can use to install the MS-DOS client software or the Windows for Workgroups TCP/IP client software.

Figure 10.1 *Create client software using the Network Client Administrator.*

- *Make Installation Disk Set*: Create a set of disks you can use to install the client software to the workstation before connecting to the network.
- *Copy Client-Based Network Administrative Tools*: You can copy the User Manager for Domains, Server Manager, and the Event Viewer to a computer running NT Workstation or Windows 95 for remote access to the server from a workstation. For more information, see your Windows NT on-line help or documentation.

Note: You can use NT Server's Network Client Administrator to create a TCP/IP/IP client for use with Windows for Workgroups on the network. This client enables Windows for Workgroups to take better advantage of NT's security, resources, and 32-bit architecture.

- *View Remoteboot Client Information*: If you're using NT's remoteboot service, you can view the computers attached with this option. The remoteboot service is a way of starting MS-DOS and Windows workstations over the network using software on the server, rather than on the client. For more information, see NT on-line help or NT documentation.

Copying the Installation Files

Before you can create the clients, you will need to copy files to your hard disk from the NT CD-ROM. You can create subdirectories in the CLIENTS directory and copy the files yourself from the NT CD-ROM disk or you can let the Network Client Administrator do it for you. The difference is that if you let the Network Client Administrator copy the files for you, it copies all of the files for all clients, the network administrator tools, and the remoteboot files to the server; you may not want or need all of these files on the server. You can copy the files

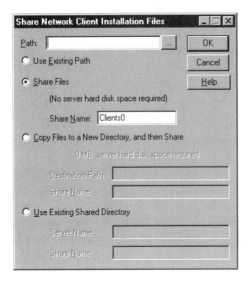

Figure 10.2 *Choose how to copy the files to the server's hard drive.*

yourself so you will have only the client files you need and thus save space on your hard drive (see the sidebar).

To let the Network Client Administrator copy the files for you, you use the Share Network Client Installation Files dialog box. When you choose either of the first two options in the Network Client Administrator dialog box—Make Network Installation Startup Disk or Make Installation Disk Set—and choose Continue, the Share Network Client Installation Files dialog box appears (see Figure 10.2).

In the Share Network Client Installation Files dialog box, the default path is to the CD-ROM drive; this is the source of the files you want to copy. You can choose the browse (...) button to view a network drive, if you've copied the NT distribution files to the network. Next, choose from one of the following options:

- *Use Existing Path*: Choose this option if you previously copied the NT distribution files to the hard drive and that path displays in the Path text box.

- *Share Files*: Choose this option to use the files directly from the CD. Enter a name for the share. I don't recommend this method because you will need to keep the CD in the drive until all clients have been installed; plus, I like to keep the CD as a backup of the files, just in case.

- *Copy Files to New Directory and Share*: This option copies the files (all client, remoteboot, and administration tools files) to the CLIENTS directory for you. Enter the destination path and the share name you want to use.

- *Use Existing Shared Directory*: If you copied files from the CD to selected directories within the CLIENTS directory, use this option.

After you copy the files, you're ready to create the client, as described in the following sections.

Creating the DOS Client

You can create the client software (Microsoft Network Client version 3.0 for MS-DOS) for an MS-DOS computer by creating installation disks or by using a startup disk. The method you choose depends on how many DOS workstations you need to configure. If you only have one or two DOS clients, create the installation disks and save the server disk space for other things. However, if you have several DOS clients, you will save time and effort by creating the startup disk and letting the clients attach to the server to copy the installation files.

Creating a Startup Disk

Using the startup disk to install the client is quick and easy. You will need one floppy disk, high-density and formatted as a system disk. Format the system disk

---

Copying Installation Files to the Server

If you want to copy the files for specific clients to the NT server instead of letting the Network Client Administrator do a blind copy of all of the files, you can easily do so using the NT Explorer; for more information about using the NT Explorer, see Chapter 11. Within the CLIENTS directory you created on the server, create any or all of the following subdirectories: MSCLIENT, Windows for Workgroups, LANMAN, LANMAN.OS2. Or if you want to copy the client-based administration tools to the server, create these subdirectories in the CLIENTS directory: WINNT.SRV or WIN95.SRV.

From the Windows NT CD-ROM, open any of the following directories and copy the NETSETUP or DISKS folder to the appropriate directory on the NT server:

Client	Directory	Space Required
MS-DOS Client	MSCLIENT	4M
Windows for Workgroups	TCP32WFW	25M
LAN Manager for DOS	LANMAN	3.5M
LAN Manager for OS/2	LANMAN.OS2	3.5M
Administration Tools for NT	SRVTOOLS\WINNT	11M
Administration Tools for 95	SRVTOOLS\WIN95	25M

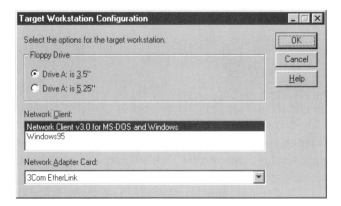

Figure 10.3 *Choose options for the floppy disk, client, and adapter card.*

on a DOS workstation as opposed to within Windows NT or 95 or even Windows for Workgroups.

When the client uses the network installation startup disk, the user boots the computer with the disk inserted in the drive. The disk directs the computer to connect to the server that contains the installation files and the disk initiates the installation process. The user enters the password, follows directions to complete installation, and the client software does the rest.

You must create one installation startup disk per workstation, since you use a unique computer name and username when creating the startup disk.

To create the startup disk, follow these steps:

1. Start the Network Client Administrator tool and choose Make Network Installation Startup Disk. The share Network Client Installation Files dialog box appears (refer to Figure 10.2).

2. Choose the method you want to use to copy the files and choose OK. The Target Workstation Configuration dialog box appears (see Figure 10.3).

3. Choose the size of the floppy disk drive of the client computer, choose the MS-DOS client, and select the network adapter card installed to the client.

Note: Make sure you select the correct NIC driver when creating the installation startup disks. The client software doesn't automatically detect the network interface card, so you must already have selected it.

---

4. Choose OK. The Network Startup Disk Configuration dialog box appears (see Figure 10.4).

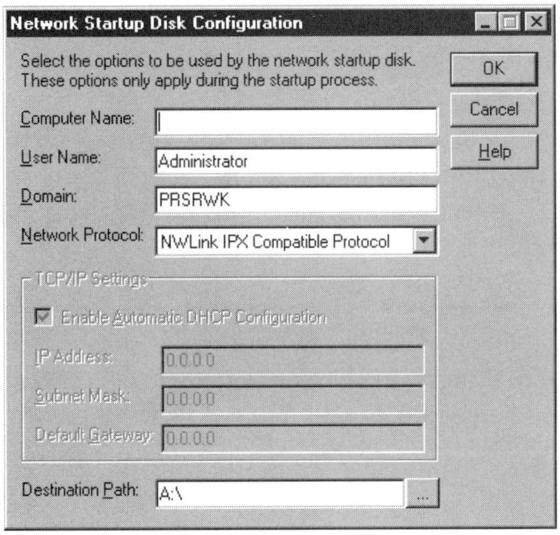

Figure 10.4 *Configure the client name, domain, and computer name.*

5. Enter a unique name for the computer, the user's name as it appears on the server, and the domain name. The only protocols listed in the box are those installed to the server that can support an installation over the network.

Note: If you're using TCP/IP and have installed and configured the DHCP server, choose the DHCP server to automatically configure the addresses; or you can enter the IP Address, Subnet Mask, and Default Gateway yourself. For more information about TCP/IP, see Appendix C.

---

6. In the Destination Path, enter the drive letter of the floppy disk to which you'll copy the client startup files and choose OK. The Network Client Administrator message dialog box appears, telling you to insert a disk and choose OK (see Figure 10.5).

Figure 10.5 *Insert a formatted, high-density disk in the floppy drive.*

7. Choose OK to confirm. The tool begins copying files, then displays a message box telling the files have been copied; choose OK.

You can use the startup disk to install the MS-DOS client to any workstation using the DOS operating system. The workstation can also use Windows 3.1 or Windows 3.11; however, the DOS client only enables you to connect to the network through DOS (see the section "Installing the DOS Client" later in this chapter).

Note: When you close the Network Client Administrator tool, it displays a dialog box reminding you of a few things you should check before installing the client; make note of any items you'll need to check. Choose OK to close the box.

Creating an Installation Disk Set

You can, alternatively, create a set of installation disks for installing the client to an MS-DOS workstation. The disk set consists of two disks and guides the user to install and configure the client, as described later in this chapter. After the user installs the client, he or she can then connect to the NT server and the network. You can use the installation disk set to install multiple client computers, as opposed to the startup installation disks which are created for a specific client computer. You will need two high-density, formatted disks to create the DOS installation disk set.

To create a set of installation disks, follow these steps:

1. Start the Network Client Administrator tool and choose Make Installation Disk Set. The Share Network Client Installation Files dialog box appears (refer to Figure 10.2).

2. Choose the method you want to use to copy the files and choose OK. The Make Installation Disk Set dialog box appears (see Figure 10.6).

Figure 10.6 *Choose options for the installation disk set.*

3. Choose the Network Client for DOS and Windows client.

4. Choose the Destination Drive: A or B and optionally, you can choose to Format the disks, if you haven't already formatted them.

5. Insert the first disk and choose OK. The tool copies the files. Insert the second disk when prompted. When the Network Client Administrative tool is finished, you're ready to install the client software to the client computers.

Installing the DOS Client

Whether you're installing the DOS client by using a startup installation disk or with installation disks, the software uses the same Setup program. The difference between the two is in the information you or the user must enter.

Using Installation Disks

To install the DOS client using an installation disk, start the computer, then insert the disk. Type **A:** and press ENTER. Type **setup** and press ENTER. The client software examines the network configuration and confirms the directory of the Network Client files. You will be prompted to choose a directory for the Network Client; the default is \NET. You can accept the default or enter a new directory. Next, the software copies the files to the hard disk.

During setup, you must enter and/or confirm setup options and configuration of the hardware. You will be asked to confirm or enter new names for the user, computer, and workgroup or domain. The username should remain the same as you entered on the installation disk when creating it, otherwise you could have trouble logging into the network.

Choose to Run Network Client if you want the network to start each time the user starts the computer. Choose Logon Validation for the user to enter a password and username each time the computer starts.

Next, you must choose between the basic and the full redirector. A redirector intercepts application requests for file- and print-sharing services and diverts them to the file server for action. The basic redirector provides all standard network configurations, such as connecting, disconnecting, and browsing the server. The basic redirector uses less memory and disk space. The full redirector, on the other hand, enables the user to log on to Windows NT and get more use from the server and resources. Unless the client computer is short on memory and/or disk space, use the full redirector.

You should also check the adapter and protocol configuration. You can choose the adapter, then the Settings option to set the interrupt and I/O port for the adapter or to add or remove an adapter. Choose the Protocol option to add or change the protocol; depending on your system, you can choose NetBEUI, IPX or TCP/IP.

The software finishes copying and configuring the network drive. Remove the floppy disk and reboot the computer. You can change configuration at any time by changing to the client directory (NET) and typing **Setup**. You will need at least 429K of conventional memory to run the Setup program at any time.

Using the Startup Disk

The MS-DOS client is easy to install using the startup disk created with the Network Client Administrator. With the computer off, insert the diskette and start the computer or reboot. The startup disk initializes, loads the NWLink protocol, and starts the NET commands needed to access the server.

The user enters his or her name, or presses ENTER to accept the default name, and enters the passwords for the workstation and the domain. After connecting, the client software copies files to the NET directory on the client and continues to set up the client. Using the same Setup program as described in the previous section, you can change user, domain, or computer names; configure adapters and protocols; and otherwise change options in the Setup program.

You also can start the Setup program on the client by changing to the NET, or other client directory you specified, and typing `setup` and pressing ENTER.

Attaching to the Network

When the DOS client computer boots, the user enters his or her name (or presses ENTER to confirm the listed name) and enters the password. The first time the user logs on, he or she will have to enter a password for the client, then confirm it; this password should be the same as the user's password for the network, for ease and efficiency. Then the user enters the password for the network. After the first login, the user enters only one password.

To attach to the network, the user types **net** at the DOS prompt and the Disk Connections dialog box appears; you could add the net command to the computer's AUTOEXEC.BAT if you want to automatically execute the file. The user can use the following commands, pressing the TAB key or using the ALT+bold-faced key to select the command, in the dialog box to connect and browse the network:

Drive: Enter the drive letter to represent the connection (mapping the drive).

Path: Enter the path to the network using the double slash and server name.

Connect: Choose to connect to the path specified using the drive letter specified.

Browse: View available resources on the network drive.

Disconnect: Disconnect from the network.

Note: The Net command is very similar to the Net command (located in the AUTOEXEC.BAT) used in the Windows for Workgroups network client.

Creating a Windows for Workgroups Client

You can attach a Windows for Workgroups computer to the NT Server as a member of a workgroup, using the NetBEUI protocol and a normal network connection. Alternatively, you can create a client for the Windows for Workgroups client to use if you're already using the TCP/IP protocol on your NT network.

Creating the Client Disks

You can create only installation disks for installing the TCP/IP-32 Windows for Workgroups client. You will need one high-density, formatted floppy disk for the installation disk. The process is similar to creating an installation disk for the MS-DOS client; refer to that previous section for more information.

To create the TCP/IP-32 Windows for Workgroups client, follow these steps:

1. Start the Network Client Administrator tool and choose Make Installation Disk Set. The share Network Client Installation Files dialog box appears (refer to Figure 10.2).

2. Choose the method you want to use to copy the files and choose OK. The Make Installation Disk Set dialog box appears (refer to Figure 10.6).

3. Choose the TCP/IP 32 for Windows for Workgroups 3.11 client.

4. Choose the Destination Drive: A or B and optionally, you can choose to Format the disk, if you haven't already formatted it.

5. Insert the disk and choose OK. The tool copies the files. Insert the second disk when prompted. When the Network Client Administrative tool is finished, you're ready to install the client software to the client computers.

Installing the Client to Windows for Workgroups

Install the client for Windows for Workgroups from the Network Setup dialog box in the Windows program on the client. The procedure is the same, whether you're

---

Previously NetWare Clients

Unlike a Windows NT or Windows 95 client in which two client services may be installed at the same time, you should remove all NetWare client software from the Windows for Workgroups workstation before installing the NT client. In addition to removing the DOS files that load the VLMs or IPX—such as STARTNET.BAT and related files—you should also remove references to the NetWare client in the WIN.INI and SYSTEM.INI files.

In the WIN.INI file, remove nwpopup.exe from the load=nwpopup.exe in the [windows] section. In the SYSTEM.INI file, remove the following:

Section	*Statement:*	*Change Statement to Read:*
[boot]	network.drv=netware.drv	network.drv=
[boot.description]	network.drv=Novell NetWare (v4.0)	network.drv=No Network Installed
[386Enh]	network=*vnetbios,vipx.386, vnetware.386	network=*dosnet,*vnetbios
[386Enh]	TimerCriticalSection=1000	(remove statement)
	ReflectDOSSln2A=TRUE	(remove statement)
	OverlappedIO-OFF	(remove statement)
	UniqueDOSPSP=TRUE	(remove statement)
	PSPIncrement=5	(remove statement)
[Network]	winnet=Novell/000400000	winnet=nonet

---

using the installation disks you created for the TCP/IP-32 client or whether you're going to use the Microsoft Networks connection; naturally, there's more setup to the TCP/IP-32 option.

Note: To prevent trouble with Microsoft's TCP/IP-32 and connecting to the network, you should remove any previously installed, third-party TCP/IP protocols from the workstation before installing the NT client.

Note: Windows for Workgroups includes a redirector, a module that loads into the workstation upon starting Windows that intercepts application requests for file-

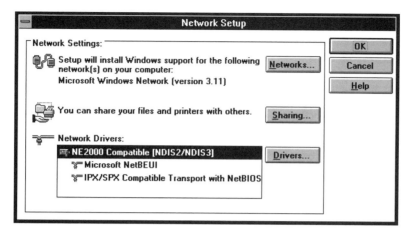

Figure 10.7 *Use the Network Setup dialog box to choose network options, sharing choices, and drivers for the client.*

and printer-sharing services and diverts those requests to the file server for action. You can install the redirector using Windows Setup if it wasn't installed on initial setup; the redirector wasn't installed if you chose No Network installed when you originally installed Windows for Workgroups.

To install the client, follow these steps:

1. In the Program Manager Network group, double-click the Network icon. The Network Setup dialog box appears (see Figure 10.7).

2. Choose the Networks button; the Networks dialog box appears (see Figure 10.8).

3. Choose the option Install Microsoft Windows Network. You can, alternatively, choose to support another network in addition to the MS Windows network.

4. Choose OK; Windows returns to the Network Setup dialog box.

5. Optionally, choose the Sharing button to indicate whether to share files and/or printers with the rest of the network; choose OK to return to the Network Setup dialog box.

6. Choose the Drivers button. The Network Drivers dialog box appears (see Figure 10.9).

7. Choose the Add Adapter button to install a different or additional adapter. Confirm the I/O port settings and choose OK. If you're adding a new

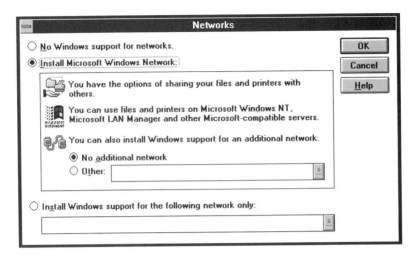

Figure 10.8 *Choose to install the Microsoft Windows Network.*

adapter, you may be prompted for one of the Windows for Workgroups installation disks. Insert the disk and choose OK.

8. In the Network Drivers dialog box, choose the Add Protocol button. From the list, select the NetBEUI or the MS TCP/IP-32 3.11b protocol and choose OK.

If you choose to install the TCP/IP-32 protocol, the Install Driver dialog box appears. Enter the letter for the disk drive containing the Windows

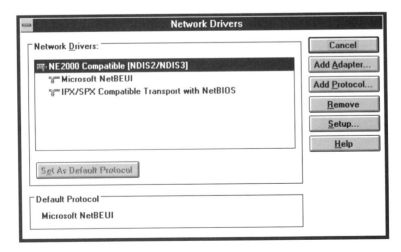

Figure 10.9 *Install additional adapters and/or protocols to the client.*

for Workgroups client and press ENTER. The software copies the appropriate files to the hard drive.

If you're installing the NetBEUI or other protocol, you may be
prompted for one of the Windows for Workgroups installation disks. Insert
the disk and choose OK.

TIP: If you are prompted to replace any files while the software is installing,
choose Yes to replace older files with the newer versions.

---

9. Windows returns to the Network Drivers dialog box. Choose Close to return to the Program Manager.

10. If you installed NetBEUI, remove the disk from the floppy drive and
restart the computer.

If you installed the TCP/IP-32 client for Windows for Workgroups, you have a
few more steps to complete the installation. The MS Windows Network Names
dialog box appears; enter the username, workgroup name, and so on. Additionally,
you will be prompted to enter configuration information for the TCP/IP protocol,
such as the default gateway, WINS server, IP address, Subnet mask, and so on. Remove the disk and restart the computer.

Accessing the Network

You can use the File Manager (from the Main Group in the Program Manager) to
connect to the network drive and map drives for your connections. Open the File
Manager and choose Disk, Connect Network drive. The Connect Network Drive
dialog box appears.

In the Drive drop-down list box, select the drive letter to represent this connection. Enter the path in the Path text box or select the path from the Show
Shared Directories On list box. Double-click any item in the Show Shared Directories list to expand their contents. In Figure 10.10, you see the Opinion domain
(along with other Windows for Workgroups computers attached under Workgroup) with two servers: Humble and Prsrwk (a print server/workstation). The
Humble server has been selected and in the shared Directories area of the dialog
box, you see the directories on the server to which the client has access.

After mapping a drive, the Windows for Workgroups client can open the
mapped drive or folder and access its contents. You can map as many drives to the
server as you like. Also, choose the Reconnect at Startup check box to automatically reconnect the mapped drives whenever you start Windows.

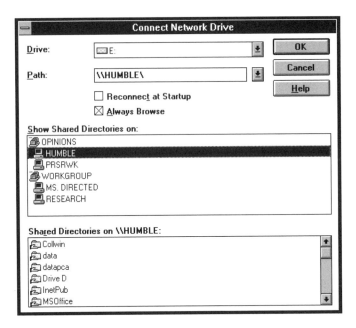

Figure 10.10 *Connect to the NT server in the Connect Network Drive dialog box.*

Using Windows 95 Clients

If you have Windows 95 installed to workstations, you do not need to install a client to make the program work with the NT server; all you need to do is configure the network settings, as explained in the following section.

If you do not have Windows 95 installed on a workstation, but have purchased an additional license for each workstation on which you want to use the software, you can create an installation startup disk using the Network Client Administrator that enables you to install Windows 95 from the Windows NT Server 4.0 Installation CD-ROM. Microsoft requires that you have a license for each installation of Windows 95 that you perform. Using the startup installation disk to install Windows 95 from NT's distribution files configures the client to view and access the NT server.

Creating the Windows 95 Client Installation Startup Disk

The NT Server software includes a client service for the installation of Windows 95. You create an installation startup disk that boots the workstation, then accesses the server. The files necessary to install Windows 95 reside on the NT CD-ROM or on the server itself, if you've copied them. You will need one high-density floppy disk that's formatted as a system disk.

Note: See Chapter 9 for hardware requirements for using Windows 95 on a client computer.

To create the installation startup disk to install Windows 95, follow these steps:

1. In the Network Client Administrator dialog box (Start, Programs, Administrative Tools, Network Client Administrator), choose Make Network Installation Startup Disk and choose Continue.

2. In the Share Network Client Installation Files dialog box, choose the source for the NT distribution files. Choose OK.

3. In the Target Workstation Configuration dialog box, choose Win 95 from the Network Client list box. Make sure you also select the appropriate adapter card for the client to which you're installing.

4. A message dialog box appears, stating you must purchase a license before you can install and use Windows 95. Choose Yes if you've purchased a license for the software.

5. The Network Client Administrator copies the necessary files to the startup disk and notifies you when it's done.

When you're ready to install Windows 95, insert the installation startup disk in the client's floppy drive and reboot the computer. Follow directions on-screen to enter the username and password. The disk connects to the server and initiates the Windows 95 Setup program. After checking the system for errors and running Scandisk, the program copies files to your hard drive and begins the Windows 95 Setup.

Follow directions on-screen to install the operating system. The disk and NT pretty much configure the workstation for you; however, if you need to configure any of the network components after the installation, see the next section.

Configuring Windows 95 Network Components

When configuring Windows 95 networking components, you will be prompted for the Windows 95 CD-ROM disk. Insert the disk when prompted so Windows can copy the necessary files. To configure the network in Windows 95, follow these steps:

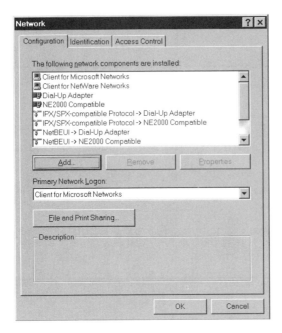

Figure 10.11 *Use the Network dialog box to add, remove, and configure adapters, protocols, and so on.*

1. Choose Start, Settings, Control Panel. In the Control Panel, double-click the Network icon to open the Network dialog box, as shown in Figure 10.11.

2. In the Configuration tab, you can choose Add to add a client, service, protocol, or adapter to the network configuration (see Figure 10.12).

3. Choose Client and select the Add button. The Select Network Client dialog box appears. Choose Microsoft in the Manufacturers list and choose

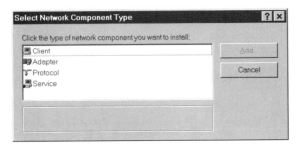

Figure 10.12 *Select the network component you want to install.*

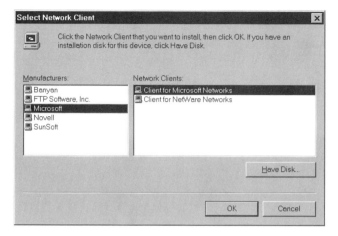

Figure 10.13 *Install the Microsoft client if it's not already installed to the Network dialog box.*

Client for Microsoft Networks in the Network Client list (see Figure 10.13).

4. Choose OK to return to the Select Network Component Type dialog box.

5. To add an adapter, select Adapter in the list and choose the Add button. Windows displays a list of Manufacturers and the adapters they make, as shown in Figure 10.14. Select the manufacturer and the adapter type, and choose OK to return to the Select Network Component Type dialog box.

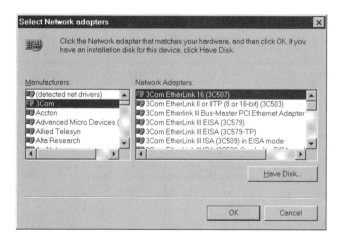

Figure 10.14 *Choose the driver for your make and model of network adapter card.*

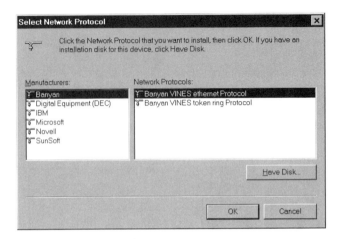

Figure 10.15 *Install the protocol you need to attach to the network.*

> **Note:** If you do not see the appropriate driver listed in the Select Network Adapters dialog box, contact the manufacturer of the adapter card for an updated driver that works with Windows NT 4.0. You can use the Have Disk button to copy that driver from a floppy or CD to the hard drive.

6. Select Protocol and choose the Add button. The Select Network Protocol dialog box appears (see Figure 10.15).

7. Choose Microsoft in the Manufacturers list, then choose NetBEUI or TCP/IP. Choose OK to close the dialog box and return to the Select Network Component Type dialog box.

> **TIP:** Microsoft's protocol is the most efficient and easiest to use of all those listed; however, you may want to choose a different protocol or even use one from a disk.

8. Select Services and choose the Add button. In the Select Network Service dialog box, select Microsoft from the Manufacturer list and choose File and Printer Sharing for Microsoft Networks, as shown in Figure 10.16.

9. Choose OK to return to the Select Network Component Type dialog box; choose OK to return to the Network dialog box.

10. To configure a service, adapter, or protocol, select the component in the Configuration tab and choose the Properties button.

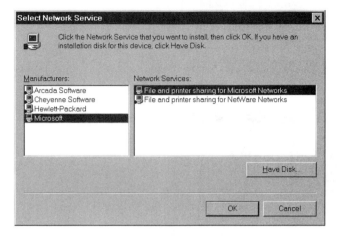

Figure 10.16 *The file- and printer-sharing network services enables the client to attach and exchange files with the NT server.*

Client properties configuration includes logon validation, the domain name, and logon options (see Figure 10.17). Choose to log on to a Windows NT domain; when the client computer starts up, the user is prompted for the domain password, username, and domain name. In the Network Logon Options area of the dialog box, you can choose the op-

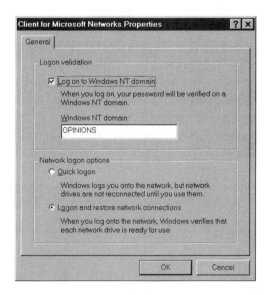

Figure 10.17 *Enter the domain name to enable the client to attach to the domain controller server.*

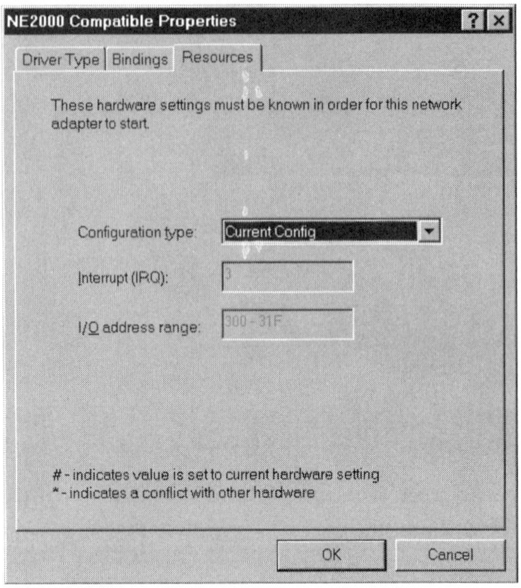

Figure 10.18 *The Resource tab lists the IRQ and I/O address configuration.*

tion that's best for the user: Quick Logon or Logon and Restore Network Connections.

Adapter properties include driver type, bindings, and resources. Figure 10.18 shows an adapter card's Properties dialog box. The Driver Type tab enables you to use a 32-bit or 16-bit driver. Generally, you will want to use the one Windows chooses by default; hopefully, that will be the 32-bit driver for best network performance.

The Bindings tab shows the bindings that are enabled between your card and the protocols; the protocol you're using for the NT Server must be enabled in this tab of the Properties dialog box.

Finally, the Resources tab shows the Interrupt (IRQ) and the I/O address range for which the card is set. Use the Resource tab to discover a conflict in settings; if you see an asterisk (*) beside the IRQ or I/O numbers, there's a hardware conflict present. IRQ (interrupt request) signals the processor that its attention is required; the I/O address range stands for input/output and identifies the transfer of data between the computer and its peripheral devices. For more information, see Chapter 3.

To change the values, choose Basic Configuration from the Configuration Type drop-down list, then enter the new values for Interrupt and IRQ.

Some adapter card types also display a Protocol properties tab, which includes bindings and property values for the card.

11. You can also set any of the following in the Configuration tab of the Network dialog box:

    Remove any component in the list by selecting the component and choosing the Remove button.

    If the client attaches to multiple networks, you can select the Primary Network Logon for the client. Select the network to log on to first from the drop-down list.

    Choose file- and printer-sharing options by selecting the File and Print Sharing button.

12. Use the Identification tab of the Network dialog box to assign the computer name and the workgroup name. In the Workgroup text box, enter the domain name of the NT network. A description is optional. Figure 10.19 shows the Identification tab of the Network dialog box.

13. Use the Access Control tab for controlling access to the files and printers on the client computer. These settings are normally used when the client is in a peer-to-peer network; if you're using the client for an NT client/server network, you don't need to set these options.

14. Choose OK to close the Network dialog box and a message appears to restart the computer for the setting to take effect. Choose Yes.

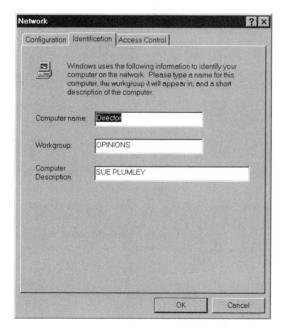

Figure 10.19 *Identify the computer to the network.*

Connecting to the Network

You can attach the Windows 95 client to the NT network after configuring the network settings. When a user logs on to the network, he or she must use a user-name and password that can be authenticated in the specified domain.

To connect to the network, the user double-clicks the Network Neighbor-hood icon on the desktop. The NT server appears in the dialog box, as shown in Figure 10.20. Double-clicking the server displays available resources the client can use.

The user can also access the server through the Windows 95 Explorer. In the Explorer, the user double-clicks the Network Neighborhood, then double-clicks the server to display the directories and printers to which he or she has access (see Figure 10.21).

Note: In the Explorer, you can use the Tools command to map a network drive for quick and easy access. Choose Tools Map Network Drive. In the Map Network Drive dialog box, choose the Drive letter to represent the mapped drive, then enter the path in the Path text box. Choose to Reconnect at Login if you want the drive to be mapped every time you log in to the network. Choose OK.

For more information about Windows 95, see the program's on-line help or documentation.

Using Windows NT Workstation Clients

In addition to taking full advantage of NT security and auditing features, the NT client enables you to use certain administrative tools for remote management of the server (see sidebar). One problem you will find with using the NT clients is that you may need to upgrade your workstations to run the NT software. After all, the NT Workstation software requires a 486 or higher processor, VGA moni-tor, 16-M RAM, and at least 123M disk space for the operating system. For more information about hardware requirements, see Chapter 9.

Note: Using computers running Windows NT Server software is nearly the same as using NT Workstation clients; the only difference is that NT Server has the ca-pability of performing more complex tasks. Changing network settings and con-necting are the same.

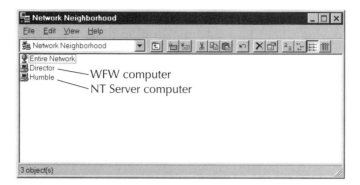

Figure 10.20 *Use the Network Neighborhood to view the NT server.*

Configuring the Network

NT workstations are ready to connect to an NT server without installation of a special client. Make sure you designate the same protocol, however, that you use on the NT server. You can install and configure adapter cards and protocols in the Network dialog box.

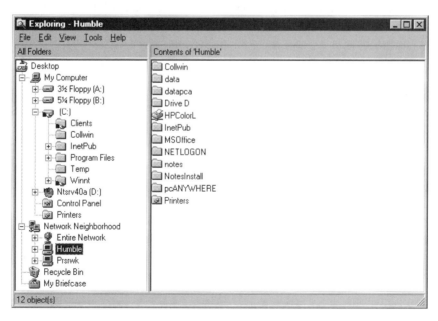

Figure 10.21 *Double-click the server in the left window pane to display available folders and printers in the right pane.*

Copying Client-Based Administration Tools

You may have need to administer the network from a computer other than the primary or backup domain controller. You can copy certain network administration tools to an NT Workstation computer or to a Windows 95 computer using the Network Client Administrator tool. Notice that you have more choices and more control over the network if you install the client-based network administration tools to a computer running NT Workstation. You must be a member of the Administrators group to copy the necessary files. Windows NT Workstation tools include the following, among others:

DHCP Manager: (dynamic host configuration protocol) When you configure a DHCP server, you enable that computer to automatically assign IP addresses to any client that requests it. Naturally, your network must use TCP/IP. For more information, see Appendix C.

Remote Access Admin: A tool for administering RAS (remote access service) used to connect remote and/or mobile users to a corporate network.

Remoteboot Manager: A tool that manages the Remoteboot service, which can start MS-DOS, Microsoft Windows 3.1, and Microsoft Windows 95 clients over the network.

Server Manager: A utility that administers the computers running Windows NT Server by connecting the servers, domains, workgroups, and domain controllers.

User Manager for Domains: A tool for adding, removing, and configuring users of a network.

Event Viewer: A utility that enables you to view events—system errors, application errors, and breaches in security—that occur on the network.

Windows 95 administration tools include only the Event Viewer, Server Manager, and User Manager for Domains.

To copy the administration tools, create the CLIENTS\WINNT.SRV or CLIENTS\WIN95 .SRV directory on the root of the NT Server computer and designate the folder as shared. Copy the files for the NT administration tools from the NT CD: \SRVTOOLS\WINNT and for the Windows 95 administration tools from the \SRVTOOLS\WIN95 directory on the CD.

Alternatively, in the Network Client Administration tool, choose the option Copy Client-Based Network Administrative Tools and choose OK. Choose the appropriate option in the Share Network Client Installation Files dialog box and the tool copies the files for you to the CLIENTS directory. After the files are copied and the directory is designated as shared, clients can access the directory and install the tools to their Windows NT Workstation or Windows 95 computers.

Note: Notice that configuring the network in an NT Workstation computer is similar to configuring the network in an NT Server computer. See Chapter 5 for information about the Network dialog box in the NT Server.

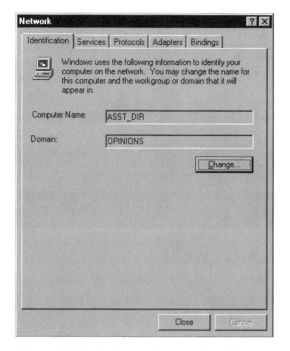

Figure 10.22 *Make sure the network configuration is correct before attaching to the network.*

To open the Network dialog box, choose Start, Settings, and Control Panel. Double-click the Network icon. Figure 10.22 shows the NT Workstation Network dialog box. The Identification tab lists the computer's name and the domain or workgroup name. You can change a name by choosing the Change button and entering the appropriate name.

Choose the Protocols tab to view installed protocols and add or remove protocols. In Figure 10.23, you see the list of Protocols already added to the computer; to add a protocol, choose the Add button and select the protocol from the list. To remove a protocol, select it in the Network Protocols list and choose the Remove button.

To view the properties of any protocol, select it and choose the Properties button. Similar to the Protocol Properties in Windows 95, NT protocol properties present frame types for IPX/SPX, for example, as shown in Figure 10.24. Additionally, the TCP/IP properties enable you to set the IP address, Subnet Mask, Default Gateway, DNS, and other options for the protocol.

Note: The Services tab enables you to install such services as TCP/IP services, remote access service, Client service for NetWare, and so on.

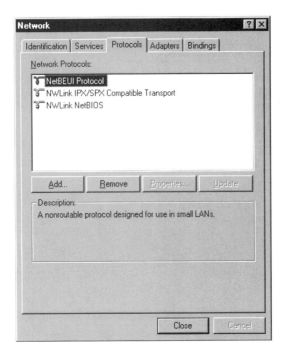

Figure 10.23 Add, remove, and/or configure protocols for the network.

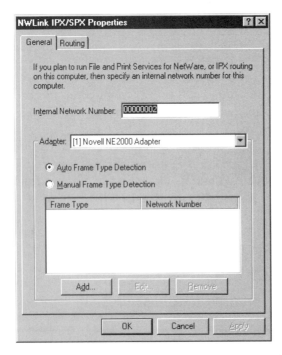

Figure 10.24 You can configure IPX/SPX protocol properties and TCP/IP properties in the Network dialog box.

262

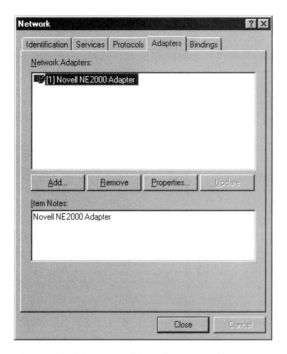

Figure 10.25 *View, add, and remove adapters in the Adapters tab of the Network dialog box.*

The Adapters tab enables you to add or remove an adapter card, update drivers, and review properties of any adapter. Figure 10.25 shows the Adapters tab of the Network dialog box. To view or change an adapter's properties, select the adapter in the Network Adapters list and choose the Properties button.

Figure 10.26 shows the selected adapter's Properties dialog box; change the IRQ or I/O port addresses for any adapter card by selecting the adapter and choosing the Properties button.

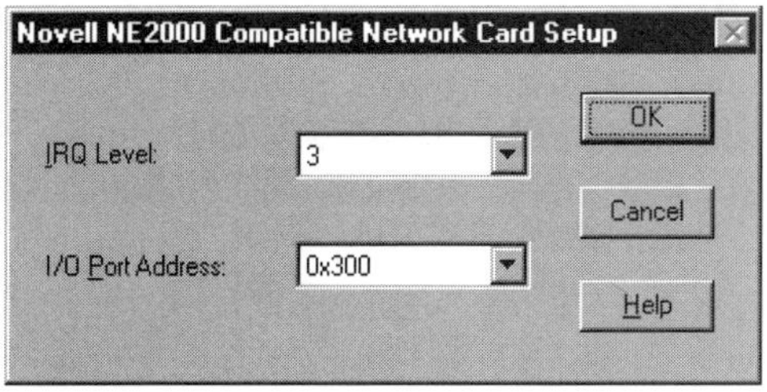

Figure 10.26 *Configure the IRQ for an adapter to make sure the client can use the adapter card.*

Note: The bindings tab displays all services and their bindings to protocols and adapters. You can enable or disable bindings in this tab.

When you're finished configuring the network in the client, choose OK to close the Network dialog box. You must restart the computer for the changes to take effect.

Connecting to the Network

When a user first starts the NT workstation, he or she must log in with a username and password that can be authenticated on the designated domain. To connect to the server, the user must open the Network Neighborhood from the desktop by double-clicking it.

Figure 10.27 shows the Network Neighborhood with the NT domain controller—Humble—displayed. Additionally, a second server—PRSRWK, a print server—displays in the window. The client computer can attach to either of the computers and access any resources for which he or she has permissions and rights by double-clicking the computer.

The NT client can also use the NT Explorer to open the Network Neighborhood and view the server and available resources by double-clicking the Network Neighborhood in the left pane of the Explorer Window. By double-clicking the server, the client can access any folders, files, or printers to which he or she has rights (see Figure 10.28).

Note: For more information about Windows NT Workstation, see the program's on-line help or documentation.

Macintosh Client Considerations

Before you can attach a Macintosh client to your NT network, you must first set up Services for Macintosh on the NT Server. When you set up these services, the AppleTalk Protocol, which can be configured through the Network icon in NT's Control Panel just like other protocols, is automatically added. Also, the File Server for Macintosh and Print Server for Macintosh start automatically. File Server for Macintosh enables you to designate a directory as Macintosh-accessible and mange permissions for Macintosh clients. The Print Server for Macintosh en-

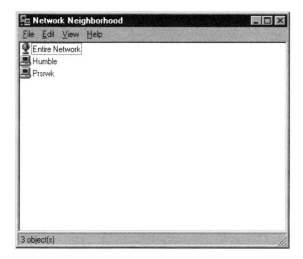

Figure 10.27 *Connect to the NT server and access its resources.*

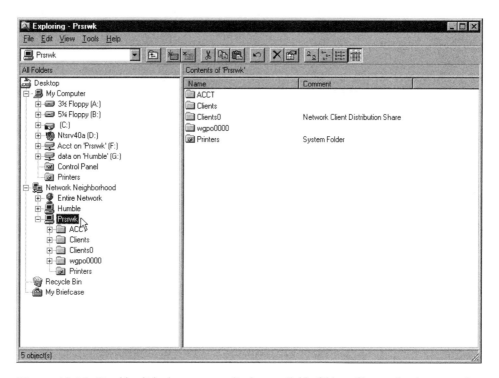

Figure 10.28 *Double-click the server to display available folders, files, and printers on the network.*

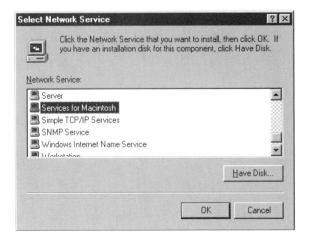

Figure 10.29 *Install the Services for Macintosh network service to the NT Server.*

ables all network users to send print jobs to the Windows NT Server so that the print services work in the background; users can continue to work after they send their print jobs.

Setting Up Services for Macintosh

You can set up the Services for Macintosh from the Control Panel on the NT Server; choose Start, Settings, Control Panel, then double-click the Network icon. In the Services tab, click the Add button; the Select Network Service dialog box appears. Figure 10.29 shows the Network Service list with Services for Macintosh selected. Choose OK.

You will be prompted for the NT CD-ROM; insert the CD into the drive and choose OK. NT copies the files it needs. To configure the protocol and other components, such as routing and zone, you must first reboot the server, then use the Services for Macintosh icon that will be added to the Control Panel.

Configuring Services for Macintosh

You can configure the zone in which printer will appear to the Macintosh clients; available printers appear in the Macintosh Chooser. You can also choose routing settings in the Microsoft AppleTalk Protocol Properties dialog box, as shown in Figure 10.30.

You enable routing if you want to use the NT Server as a router—a connecting device that can send data packets to the appropriate LAN segment among

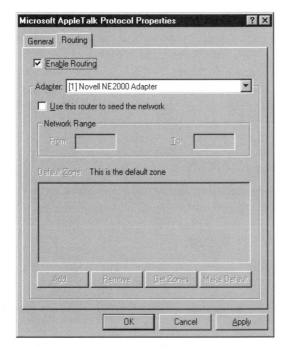

Figure 10.30 *Configure the zone and routing.*

many segments. If you bind the protocol to multiple network cards within the NT Server, Macintoshes on various segments of the network can see the NT Server and their data can be transferred through the server. If you do not enable routing, only those Macintoshes on the default network can see the NT Server.

Note: Routing and seeding the network for Macintosh services are beyond the scope of this book. For more information, see the NT Server documentation about Macintosh Services.

Stopping Macintosh Services

You can remove the Services for Macintosh from the Network dialog box, but you also must stop the services in the Devices dialog box. First in the Control Panel, double-click the Devices icon. In the Devices list, select the AppleTalk Protocol and click the Stop button. When asked to confirm the action, choose Yes. When the service is stopped, choose Close.

Next, open the Network dialog box and choose the Services tab. In the Network Services list, select Services for Macintosh and choose the Remove button. The Warning dialog box appears, confirming the removal of the services; choose Yes to continue. Close the Network dialog box by choosing Close; it may take a few moments for NT to restore the bindings and complete configuration. The Network Settings Change dialog box appears stating you must restart the computer. Choose Yes.

Authentication and the Macintosh

You might want to use Microsoft authentication to provide a more secure logon session for the NT Server. Microsoft authentication encrypts the password and requires users to specify a domain when they want to change their passwords.

To access the authentication files, follow these steps:

1. From the Apple menu, select the Chooser. The Chooser dialog box appears.
2. Choose the AppleShare icon, then select the AppleTalk Zone in which the NT Server computer resides.
3. Choose OK. A sign-in dialog box appears asking you if you're a guest or registered user.
4. Choose Registered User and enter the username in the Name text box. Notice the password is defined as cleartext.
5. Choose OK. If the Server dialog box appears, select the Microsoft volume you want to use and choose OK. Close the Chooser dialog box.

After you have the authentication files, you must install them. To install the authentication files to the Macintosh client, follow these steps:

1. From the desktop, double-click the Microsoft UAM Volume. The Microsoft UAM Volume window appears.
2. Move the AppleShare folder to the System Folder on the hard disk by dragging it. Do not overwrite the UAM Volume if warned that one already exists in the System Folder; there may be multiple UAMs already resident.

When the user attaches to the NT Server, the same authentication dialog box appears. Depending on the Macintosh system and setup, the authentication may ask whether the user is a guest or registered user; authentication will request the user's name and the password may be Microsoft Encryption or cleartext.

Summary

In this chapter, you've learned how to create client software for a variety of clients and seen how to connect to the network from MS-DOS, Windows for Workgroups, Windows 95, and Windows NT Workstation/Server. Now that your clients are ready to connect to the network, you need to learn more about applications that you can use with NT—installing, using, and managing.

PART

V

Application Management

11 *Using NT Server's Applications to Manage the Network*

Part of administering a network includes managing files and directories, troubleshooting errors and other network problems, setting up e-mail, and so on. NT Server offers several applications and administrative tools you can use to perform daily managerial tasks on the server and over the network. You've already learned to use the User Manager for Domains and the Network Client Administrator to manage users and client computers. In this chapter, you will learn to use other applications packaged with NT Server to perform common tasks on the server:

- Use the Windows NT Explorer to copy, delete, rename, and otherwise manage files and folders on the server and over the network.
- The Event Viewer enables you to identify security breaches, system errors, and application troubles.
- Set up a post office and enable your users to send e-mail with Windows Messaging.
- The MS-DOS Command Prompt supplies a DOS-based window in which you can enter commands, install DOS applications, and run DOS applications.
- Use the Microsoft Internet Information Server to provide intranet and/or Internet services to your users.

Windows NT Explorer

The NT Explorer is an application you can use to manage and organize files and folders on the server and network. With the Explorer, you can move and copy files and folders, delete and rename files and folders, create and view files and folders, start applications, create shortcuts, map network drives, and sort and find files or folders. You can perform any of these tasks on files and folders located on the server, on another server in the domain, or on any workstation in the network.

TIP: Notice that the Explorer uses the term "folder" in place of "directory" and "subfolder" in place of "subdirectory."

Starting and Exiting the NT Explorer

If you're familiar with the Windows 3.x File Manager or the Windows 95 Explorer, notice that the NT Explorer is extremely similar in the way it looks and in the tasks you can perform. You can start the Explorer by choosing Start, Programs, and Windows NT Explorer. You will also find the command Explore on the File menu of many windows, such as the My Computer window and the Network Neighborhood window. When you select a drive, folder, or file in one of these windows, you can choose to Explore it, which results in viewing the file and folder in the NT Explorer.

Figure 11.1 shows the NT Explorer in a window. The left pane contains icons representing the server's hard drives, floppy drives, CD-ROM and/or tape drives, folders, the Network Neighborhood, and other folders. The right pane of the window represents the contents of any selected item in the left pane; for example, if you click the hard drive (C) in the left pane, the right pane displays the folders and files in the root directory of C. A plus sign in front of a drive or folder in the left pane indicates that drive or folder contains subfolders.

Note: To open a drive or folder in the left pane, click that item one time; its contents appear in the right pane. To open a folder or file in the right pane, double-click the item. When you open a folder, the contents (files and/or subfolders) display in the right pane. When you open a file, the application associated with that file opens with the file, ready to view or edit.

To exit the NT Explorer, do one of the following:

- Choose File, Close.
- Click the Close button (X) in the title bar.
- Choose the Control menu, then click Close.
- Press ALT+F4.

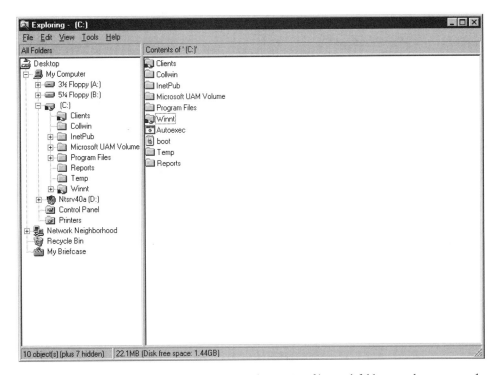

Figure 11.1 Use the Explorer to manage and organize files and folders on the server and over the network.

Viewing Files and Folders

You can view files and folders as icons with the file or folder name (refer to Figure 11.1) or you can view details about the files and folders, and sort the files to make locating specific data easier. File management is more efficient when you can quickly and easily identify the files you're viewing.

To change views in the Explorer, follow these steps:

1. Choose View, Details; alternatively, you can click the Details button on the Explorer's toolbar. Figure 11.2 shows the detail view of the Reports folder in the Explorer.

TIP: To display a toolbar that supplies buttons representing shortcuts to common commands, choose View, Toolbar. You can choose View, Toolbar again to hide the toolbar; you can also choose View, Status Bar to hide or display the status bar at the bottom of the NT Explorer window.

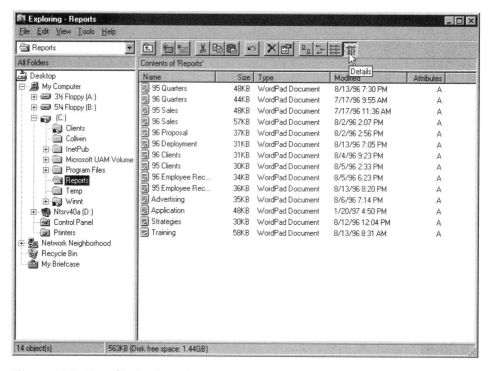

Figure 11.2 *View file details, such as type, size, and attributes for better file management.*

2. You can sort the files in the right window pane to help you locate a specific file. To sort files, choose View, then select one of the following:

By Name: Sorts files numerically first, then alphabetically by name.

By Type: Arranges the files alphabetically by file type.

By Size: Sorts the files by size; smallest files are at the top of the list and larger files are at the bottom, by default.

By Date: Arranges the files by the date they were created or last modified.

To change the order of the sort, click the gray heading button above the files in the right pane: Name, Size, Type, or Modified.

TIP: By default, NT doesn't display all files, such as hidden files, system files, device drivers, and so on. You can choose to display these file types, and others, by choosing View, Options. In the Options dialog box, choose the View tab and click Show All Files. Choose OK to close the dialog box.

Creating and Managing Files and Folders

You can create, delete, rename, copy, and move files and folders within the NT Explorer. You might, for example, want to create folders for specific file types, for use by certain groups of people, or to share files with everyone on the network. You can also copy a file or folder to another disk drive or to another folder for storage.

TIP: As previously mentioned, you can share a folder by right-clicking it in the Explorer and choosing Sharing. For more information, see Chapter 7.

Creating and Renaming Folders

To create a folder, first select the folder you want to be the parent folder; for example, if you want the folder to be located on the C-drive, select the C-drive. Then, choose File, New, Folder. The new folder appears in the right pane with its name—New Folder—selected and a box around the name (see Figure 11.3). Type a new name in the box and press ENTER.

TIP: You can rename a folder, or a file for that matter, at any time by selecting it and choosing File, Rename. Alternatively, you can select the file or folder, then click the name to display the box around the name in which you can type; be careful, though, if you click the second click too quickly, you will open the file instead of rename it.

Creating a File

You may find you need to create a file quickly while in the Explorer. Rather than exiting the Explorer and opening an application, you can simply create the file using the File menu. The file appears in the folder without first opening the application. You can create many files without opening their associated applications, as shown in Figure 11.4.

Select the folder you want to save the file to. Choose File, New, then choose the file type: Bitmap Image (Paint document), New Rich Text Document or New WordPad Document (Microsoft Word for Windows), New Text Document (NotePad), or New Wave Sound. To open any of the files and the associated application, double-click the file in the right pane of the Explorer window.

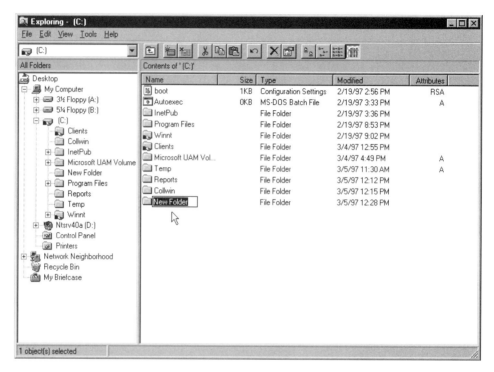

Figure 11.3 *Create and name the new folder.*

Moving Files and Folders

You can move or copy a folder by selecting the folder and choosing Edit, Cut, or Copy. Select the drive or folder you want to move to and choose Edit, Paste. Alternatively, you can click and drag the folder to a new position. The same principles apply to copying or moving files.

If you try to copy or move a file to a drive or directory containing a file or folder with the same name, NT will confirm the overwrite procedure before it proceeds.

Note: You can view the Properties of any file or folder by selecting the item and choosing File, Properties. The Properties dialog box lists information about the item such as type, location, size, and so on. Additionally, you can use the Properties dialog box to apply read-only, hidden, and other attributes and to set permissions, ownership, and auditing options. See Chapter 7 for more information.

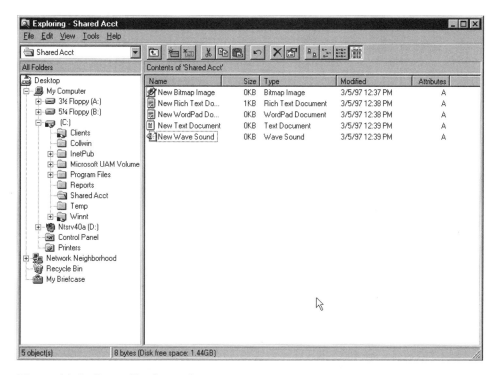

Figure 11.4 *Create files for use later.*

Finding Files and Folders

You can find files, folders, and computers in the NT Explorer, just as you can by choosing Start, Find. The two Find commands produce the exact same dialog box and results. To find a file or folder, follow these steps:

1. Choose Tools, Find, Files or Folders. The Find dialog box appears, as shown in Figure 11.5.

2. In the Name & Location tab, enter the name of the file in the Named text box; you can use wildcards to help your search. For example, type ***.doc** to find all files with a DOC extension; type **report??** to find all documents beginning with report and ending in any other two characters—such as report01, reportsp, and so on.

3. In the Look In text box, choose the drive to search. Use the Browse button to select a specific folder or you can type a folder name into the Look In text box—as in C:\Reports.

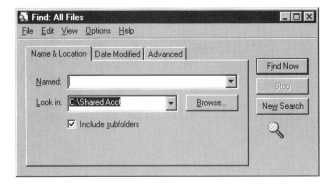

Figure 11.5 *Find files and folders on the server or attached disk drive.*

TIP: Make sure you check the Include Subfolders check box to look in all subfolders of the selected drive and/or folder.

---

4. Optionally, you can narrow the search by using the Date Modified tab in the Find dialog box. The Date Modified tab enables you to find all files created or modified at certain times, as shown in Figure 11.6. Choose the Find All Files Created or Modified option, then select one of the following options:

   Between: Enter the dates in the text boxes; you might search, for example, between 1/1/97 and 3/10/97.

   During the Previous x months: Enter or select the number of months, such as in the last 2 months.

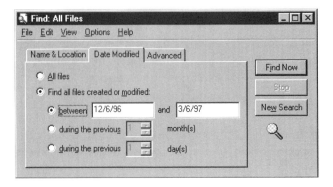

Figure 11.6 *Search for a file created or modified within a certain time period.*

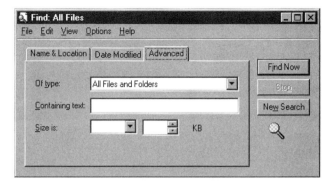

Figure 11.7 *Narrow the search by specifying size, type, or text within the file.*

> *During the Previous x days:* Enter or select the number of days, as in the last 10 days, for example.

5. You can also use the Advanced tab in conjunction with the Name & Location and the Date Modified tabs to narrow the search. Figure 11.7 shows the Advanced tab. Enter a value or text in any or all of the following text boxes in the Advanced tab:

> *Of Type drop-down list:* Choose the type of file for which you are searching, such as an Application, Bitmap, Configuration, Device driver, or other file type.

> *Containing Text text box:* Enter a word or phrase that would appear in the text of the file itself.

> *Size Is:* Choose At Least or At Most in the first list box, then enter the size, in KB, for the file.

6. Now. The Find dialog box expands to list all files found, as shown in Figure 11.8.

7. In the Find dialog box, you can also do the following:

> Stop a search by clicking the Stop button.

> Open any file in the Find dialog box by double-clicking it.

> Choose New Search to clear the search criteria and begin a new search.

8. Click the Close button when you're done with the search.

Finding Computers

You can also use the Find command, either in the Explorer or from the Start menu, to locate other computers on the network. In the Explorer, choose Tools,

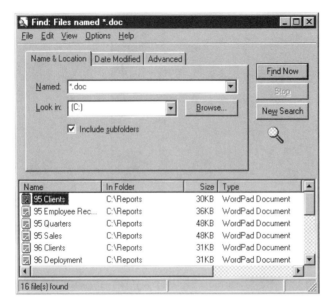

Figure 11.8. *Scroll through the files to locate the one you want.*

Find, Computer. The Find Computer dialog box appears. Enter the Computer's name in the Named text box and click the Find Now button. The results appear in the expanded dialog box, as shown in Figure 11.9.

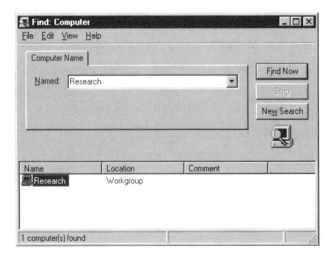

Figure 11.9 *Locate computers on the network.*

To view the resources on the found computer, double-click its name in the Find dialog box and a window opens, displaying folders, files, and printers available on the found computer.

Mapping Drives

Another important feature of the NT Explorer is the capability of mapping drives. When you map a drive, you're assigning a drive letter to a directory path on the network. A mapped drive enables the user to access the directory path quickly and efficiently. Drive mapping is particularly useful for network users to quickly access a folder on the server, or for the administrator to quickly access a print queue, specific folder, or drive on a member server or other computer on the network.

As an example, say a member server on the network contains accounting files you often access. Instead of opening the Network Neighborhood, double-clicking the server, and double-clicking the folder to access the files you need, map the directory path so you only double-click one item to get to that folder.

Figure 11.10 shows the mapped drive in the Explorer. Selected in the left pane is the Acct on Prsrwk (F) drive mapping. You see in the right pane, the folders available from the mapped drive. Also in the figure, notice the Network Neighborhood and the Prsrwk server opened so you can see the ACCT folder and its con-

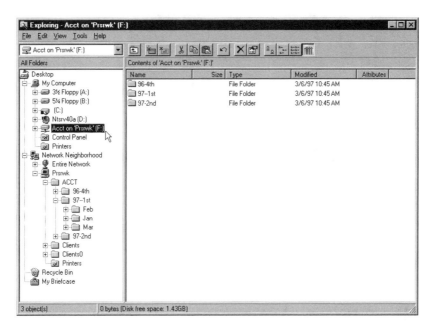

Figure 11.10 *Map drives for quick access to folders on another computer.*

tents. Selecting the mapped drive is faster and easier than opening the server and opening the folders you need.

To map a drive, follow these steps:

1. In the Explorer, choose Tools, Map Network Drive. The Map Network Drive appears with the domain and available servers in the Shared Directories dialog box.

2. In the Shared Directories list box, double-click the server or other computer to which you want to map. A list of shared folders appears, as shown in Figure 11.11.

3. Select the folder and the path appears in the Path text box; alternatively, you can enter the path, preceding the computer's name with two back slashes, as in \\HUMBLE, then entering the directory name.

4. If you want to log in to the computer using a different user account, enter the username in the Connect As text box.

5. Check the Reconnect at Logon check box to automatically connect the mapped drive each time you log in to the computer.

6. Choose OK to close the dialog box. The mapped drive appears in the Explorer.

Figure 11.11 *Use the Map Network Drive dialog box to locate the computer and folder you want to map to.*

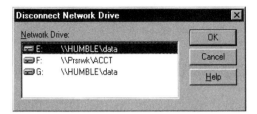

Figure 11.12 *Disconnect a mapped drive.*

To disconnect a mapped drive you no longer need, choose Tools, Disconnect Network Drive. The Disconnect Network Drive dialog box appears, as shown in Figure 11.12. Select the drive you want to disconnect and choose OK.

TIP: If you need help using the NT Explorer, choose Help, Help Topics in the Explorer at any time.

Other NT Applications and Accessories

NT includes many applications and accessories that you can use in your day-to-day work. In this chapter, I'm only covering in detail those applications you can use with the network; however, here's a brief description of other NT applications and tools you might want to try.

The Recycle Bin is one tool you'll use over and over. It's important to remember that when you delete a file or folder from the hard drive, it's not deleted until you empty the Recycle Bin. So you're not making extra disk space by deleting files in the Explorer or My Computer window. However, when you delete a file or folder from a floppy disk drive, that item is deleted without first going to the Recycle Bin. To empty the Recycle Bin, right-click the Bin on the desktop or in the Explorer, and choose Empty Recycle Bin; choose Yes in the Confirmation dialog box. You also can open the Recycle Bin to view the contents and even choose to restore deleted items in the Bin (open the Bin, select the file(s) you want to keep, and choose File, Restore).

Some Accessories included in NT may or may not be useful to you. To open any Accessory application, choose Start, Programs, Accessories and choose the program from the cascading menu. Here's a brief description of some you may find a use for:

WordPad: A unsophisticated word processor that saves files in a Word for Windows (DOC) format.

NotePad: A text editor, handy for editing or creating configuration files.

(continues)

Other NT Applications and Accessories (*Continued*)

Paint: A program for editing graphic files.

Hyperterminal: A primitive terminal program for contacting bulletin boards and online services.

Chat: A simple program you can use to hold on-line discussions with others on the network using the Chat program.

Another application you will likely use is the Command Prompt (Start, Programs, Command Prompt). The Command Prompt displays a DOS-like window from which you can install and run DOS-based programs. You also can use many familiar DOS commands to view directories, copy and move files, get help, perform network procedures, and so on. For more information about the Command Prompt, see Chapter 12.

Additionally, NT includes several Administrative Tools you might use in your administration of the network. Many of those tools are described throughout this book, including the User Manager for Domains, Windows NT Diagnostics, Event Viewer, Network Client Administrator, and so on.

You may find a use for some of the other tools, such as the Performance Monitor or License Manager. For more information, use the Help feature in NT or your NT documentation.

Finally, NT includes some Administrative Wizards that guide you to performing certain tasks in NT: adding user accounts, managing groups, managing permissions, adding a printer, adding programs, installing a modem, using the Network Client Administrator, and checking application licensing. Choose Start, Programs, Administrative Tools, then choose Administrative Wizards. In the Administrative Wizards dialog box, you can select the task you need and let the Wizard guide you through, step-by-step.

Event Viewer

The Event Viewer is an NT utility for viewing logs about significant occurrences on the network or on the server that require the user to be notified. Some events may display a message on-screen at the time of the event; whereas events that do not require immediate attention simply record in the event log for later viewing.

Note: The Event logging service starts automatically each time you start your computer. To record security events, however, you must enable event auditing. In the User Manager for Domains, choose Policies, Audit; in the Audit Policy dialog box, choose Audit These Events. Then select the events you want to record in the audit log. See Chapter 7 for more information.

You can record and then view logs about application, system, and security events. Application events include any incidents recorded by applications on the computer, such as a file or application error. System events record incidents involving system components, such as device drivers. Security events track possible security breaches to the system, such as unsuccessful attempts to log on to the server.

Starting the Event Viewer

To open the Event Viewer and view the events on the system, choose Start, Programs, Administrative Tools, and Event Viewer. Figure 11.13 shows the Event Viewer screen. Each event is recorded by Date, Time, Source, and other information, as follows:

Date	Time	Source	Category	Event	User	Computer
2/24/97	1:12:36 PM	NE2000	None	5003	N/A	PRINT SERVER
2/22/97	10:01:57 AM	RemoteAccess	None	20085	N/A	PRINT SERVER
2/22/97	10:01:57 AM	RemoteAccess	None	20086	N/A	PRINT SERVER
2/22/97	10:00:59 AM	NE2000	None	5003	N/A	PRINT SERVER
2/22/97	10:00:51 AM	EventLog	None	6005	N/A	PRINT SERVER
2/22/97	10:00:59 AM	Service Control Mar	None	7000	N/A	PRINT SERVER
2/21/97	8:03:23 AM	RemoteAccess	None	20085	N/A	PRINT SERVER
2/21/97	8:03:22 AM	RemoteAccess	None	20086	N/A	PRINT SERVER
2/21/97	8:02:22 AM	NE2000	None	5003	N/A	PRINT SERVER
2/21/97	8:02:14 AM	EventLog	None	6005	N/A	PRINT SERVER
2/21/97	8:02:22 AM	Service Control Mar	None	7000	N/A	PRINT SERVER
2/20/97	8:51:56 AM	RemoteAccess	None	20085	N/A	PRINT SERVER
2/20/97	8:51:56 AM	RemoteAccess	None	20086	N/A	PRINT SERVER
2/20/97	8:51:16 AM	EventLog	None	6005	N/A	PRINT SERVER
2/20/97	8:51:23 AM	Service Control Mar	None	7000	N/A	PRINT SERVER
2/20/97	8:51:23 AM	NE2000	None	5003	N/A	PRINT SERVER
2/19/97	9:01:20 PM	RemoteAccess	None	20085	N/A	PRINT SERVER
2/19/97	9:01:20 PM	RemoteAccess	None	20086	N/A	PRINT SERVER
2/19/97	9:00:48 PM	Service Control Mar	None	7000	N/A	PRINT SERVER
2/19/97	9:00:46 PM	EventLog	None	6005	N/A	PRINT SERVER
2/19/97	9:00:48 PM	NE2000	None	5003	N/A	PRINT SERVER

Figure 11.13 Events are listed by date; most recent events appear at the top of the list.

Date/Time: The date and time of the occurrence.

Source: The application or system component that recorded the event.

Category: Some events are defined by the source, such as Logon or Logoff, Policy Change, and so on; other events are not categorized.

Event: A number assigned to the event; use this number to identify an event to a technical-support representative.

User: Lists the user of the computer at the time, if applicable to the event.

Computer: Lists the name of the computer on which the event occurred.

The event log shown in the figure is the System log. You can change the log you view by selecting Log, then System, Security, or Application. Unless you've turned on the Audit policies in the User Manager, you won't see any security events. Application events appear only if there is a problem with an application and that application records the problem or error.

By default, the Event Viewer displays events that occurred on the current computer, whether a domain controller server, member server, or workstation. You can, however, choose to view any other computer's events by selecting Log, Select Computer. The Select Computer dialog box appears with the domain and available computers listed, as shown in Figure 11.14.

Select the computer and choose OK. Events relating to that computer appear in the Event Viewer. Figure 11.15 shows the Event Viewer with a Security event displayed for the domain controller on the network.

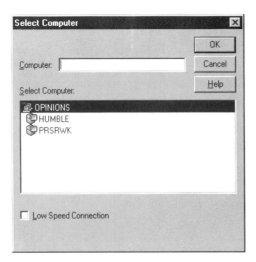

Figure 11.14 *Select the computer you want to view events for in the Select Computer dialog box.*

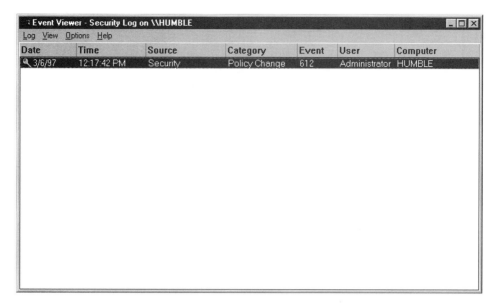

Figure 11.15 *View various events on any computer in the domain.*

Viewing Specific Events

You can view more details of any of the events in the log. Before choosing an event to view, you should know the symbols representing each event:

Information: Information is represented by a blue circle with an i in it. Information records successful operations within the computer.

Warning: A warning is represented by a yellow circle with an exclamation point inside and indicates an event that may later cause a problem, such as low disk space.

Error: Errors are represented by red stop signs; these are significant problems or faults with the system.

To view details about any event, double-click the event in the Event Viewer. Figure 11.16 shows the Event Detail dialog box for a Serial error in the System Log.

In addition to displaying the date, time, user, computer, event ID, source, type, and category, the Event Detail dialog box displays a text description of the event and binary data about the event. Use the text description to troubleshoot the problem. Click the Close button to close the dialog box; alternatively, click Previous or Next to view more events.

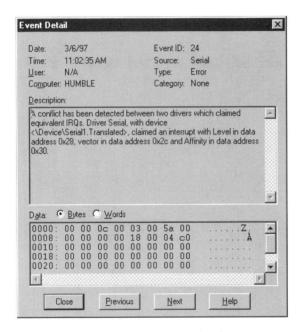

Figure 11.16 *Viewing an event's details may give you an idea of how to solve a problem or error.*

Setting Options for the Event Viewer

You can set various options for filtering out certain events, so you only view those events you want to view at any one time. When you record logs on multiple events—such as successful and unsuccessful security auditing—the event logs can become large and unwieldy. Set options for limiting the size of the event logs to prevent using too much disk space.

Filtering Events

To filter events for easier viewing, follow these steps:

1. Choose View, Filter Events. The Filter dialog box appears, as shown in Figure 11.17.

2. To limit the events you view by date, enter the dates and optionally, the times, in the Events On text boxes. You can enter the first date in the View From area and the second date in the View Through area. The Viewer will display all events that occurred between those dates.

3. You can also set the types of events you want to display in the Types area of the dialog box. Check the events you want to view. Note the Success Audit

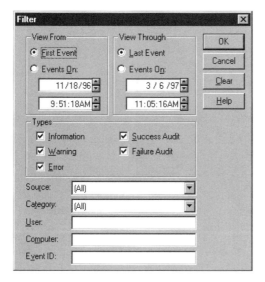

Figure 11.17 *Choose the events you want to view so you can more easily find specific events.*

and Failure Audit are the options you set in the User Manager for Domains, Audit Policies dialog box.

4. Finally, you can specify events by viewing one Source, Category, User, Computer, and/or Event ID by entering the parameters in the appropriate text boxes.

5. Choose OK to accept the changes and close the dialog box.

To turn off the filter and view all events at any time, choose View, All Events.

TIP: To search for specific events, choose View, Find. In the Find dialog box, choose the types of events and then the Source, Category, Event ID, User, Computer, and/or Description of the event. Choose Find Next to highlight the next event that fits the criteria.

Limiting Log Size

By default, NT limits the size of any one log to 512KB. Additionally, NT sets the default to overwrite any logged events older than seven days with new ones when the 512K of space is filled. You can, however, change these settings to better suit yourself.

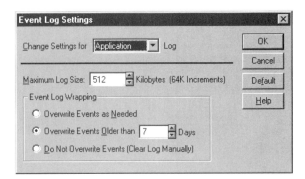

Figure 11.18 *Set the size of the log and choose log wrapping.*

To limit log size, choose Log, Log Settings. The Event Log Settings dialog box appears (see Figure 11.18. Choose the log you want to configure settings for from the Change Settings drop-down list box; you can choose the Application, System, or Security logs. Next, enter the maximum log size.

In Event Log Wrapping, indicate what you want NT to do when the log is full by selecting one of the following options:

Overwrite Events as Needed: Guarantees all new events will be logged by overwriting the oldest events first.

Overwrite Events Older than x Days: Retains the log for the indicated number of days, then overwrites events.

Do Not Overwrite Events (Clear Log Manually): Retains all events. When the log is full, you must clear events manually by selecting Log, Clear All Events. If you don't clear the log, new events are not recorded.

To switch back to the default settings at any time, choose the Default button.

TIP: You may want to save logs on a weekly basis in case you need to refer back to them at any time. To save a log, choose Log, Save As. Choose a location and assign a name for the log and click the Save button in the Save As dialog box. Open a saved log at any time by choosing Log, Open.

E-Mail and Windows Messaging

NT includes Windows Messaging e-mail through which you can send and receive e-mail using a Microsoft Mail post office or over the Internet. Windows messaging supports both Microsoft Mail, which enables e-mail exchange over the network, and Internet Mail, which enables e-mail exchange over the Internet. Microsoft Mail also supports e-mail through various versions of Windows, including Windows NT 3.51, Windows for Workgroups, and Windows 95, through a common post office you set up on the server. Internet Mail requires that the mail server be supported by a Dial-Up Networking dial-in server. This section discusses Windows Messaging as it applies to the network; for more information about Internet Mail, see NT Help.

Note: Internet Mail provides support for MIME mappings to file name extensions, thus automating transfer of MIME attachments.

Setting Up a Post Office

You'll need to set up a Microsoft Mail post office on one server computer that is available to all computers in the domain that want to use e-mail. You can locate the post office on the server's hard disk (C: for example), the Wizard creates a folder on the hard disk for the post office. To set up a post office, follow these steps:

1. Choose Start, Settings, and the Control Panel; double-click the Microsoft Mail Postoffice icon to open the Microsoft Workgroup Postoffice Admin Wizard.

2. Choose Create a New Workgroup Postoffice option and choose Next.

3. In the next Wizard dialog box, enter the folder's path and name in the Postoffice Location text box (see Figure 11.19); alternatively, click Browse to locate the folder that will hold the post office. Click the Next button.

4. Confirm the location and post office name in the next Wizard dialog box; the Wizard names the post office folder wgpo0000. Click Next.

5. The Enter Your Administrator Account Details dialog box appears. Enter the details, as shown in Figure 11.20, and choose OK. For the Mailbox text box, consider using the user's username as listed in the User Manager for Domains; this will make managing the post office easier and means all mail boxes adhere to a standard naming convention.

6. A Mail message dialog box appears, telling you you will need to share the directory. Choose OK and the dialog box closes.

To create mail boxes for the other users on the network, double-click the Microsoft Mail Postoffice icon in the Control Panel. Choose Administer an Existing

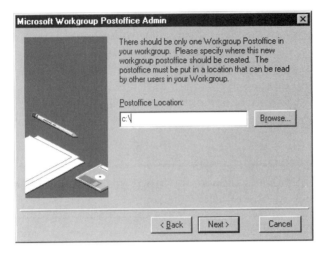

Figure 11.19 *Enter the drive that will contain the post office.*

Workgroup Postoffice and click Next when the Wizard dialog box appears. The Postoffice location appears in the next Wizard dialog box; click Next. In the third Wizard dialog box, enter your mailbox name and your password, as shown in Figure 11.21. Then choose Next.

The Postoffice Manager dialog box appears with your name only in the list of users. Click the Add User button to display the Add User dialog box (see Figure 11.22). Enter names and the other requested information, then choose OK. Add as many users as necessary; you can always open the Microsoft Mail Postoffice and add and edit users. Choose Close when you're done.

After you've added the users to the Postoffice, open the NT Explorer and select the post office folder (wgpo0000). Right-click the folder and choose

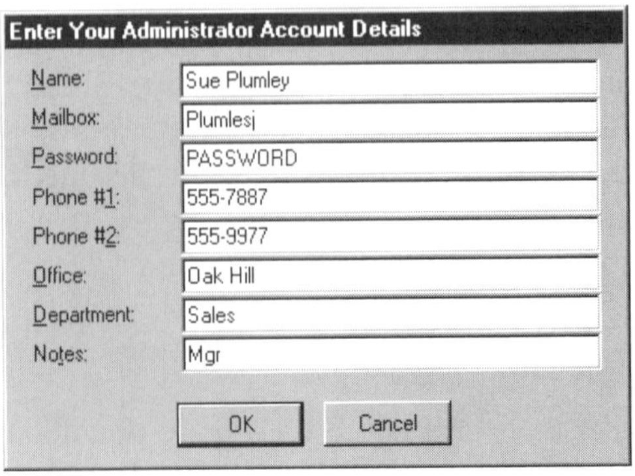

Figure 11.20 *Enter the requested information.*

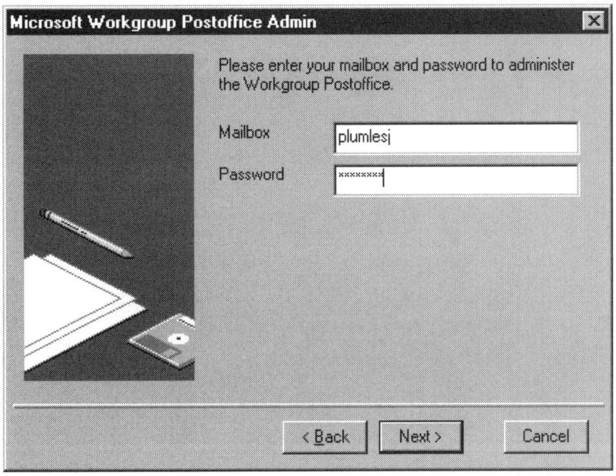

Figure 11.21 *Enter your mailbox name and password.*

Sharing, then indicate the folder as shared. Choose OK to close the Properties dialog box.

Setting Up Windows Messaging

You can set up Windows Messaging on any client computer after the post office is created and the users' mail box is added as previously described. Windows NT and Windows 95 Windows Messaging are very similar in their setup. For help setting up a Windows for Workgroups computer, see Windows for Workgroups help or documentation.

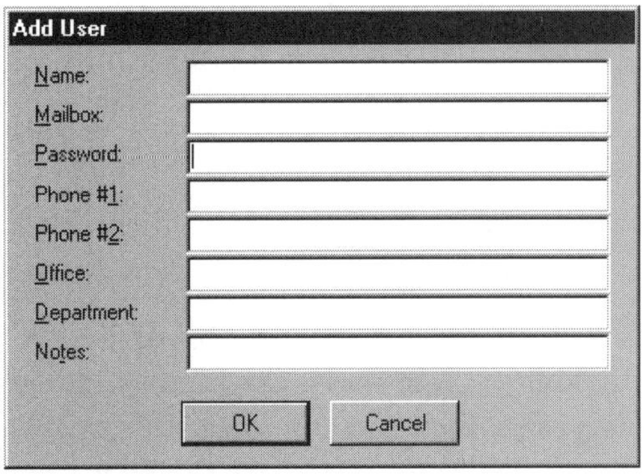

Figure 11.22 *Add the names and other details of those who will use the post office.*

Figure 11.23 *Let the Wizard help you set up Windows Messaging.*

To set up Windows Messaging, double-click the Inbox on the desktop; alternatively, choose Start, Programs, and Windows Messaging. The Windows Messaging Setup Wizard dialog box appears, as shown in Figure 11.23. If you've installed various other information services, such as Internet Mail or Microsoft Exchange, those services appear in this dialog box along with Microsoft Mail. You can check all of the services or just Microsoft Mail.

Choose the Next button to display the next Wizard dialog box. Confirm the post office location and click Next. In the next dialog box, choose your name from the list of users and click Next. Enter your password, as shown in Figure 11.24, and click Next.

The Wizard displays a default path to your personal address book. Accept the default and choose Next. The Wizard then displays the default path to your personal folders; you can accept the default or change the path, if you want. Choose Next. Click the Finish button in the last Wizard dialog box to complete the set up of Windows Messaging.

Using E-Mail

After setting up Windows Messaging, NT opens the Inbox. You also can open the Inbox by double-clicking the Inbox icon on the desktop or by choosing Start, Programs, Windows Messaging. Figure 11.25 shows the Inbox window.

The left pane contains folders in which you can store your mail messages; the right pane displays e-mail messages you've received. Use the View menu to display

Figure 11.24 *Verify your username and mail box; then enter your password.*

or hide items in the Inbox window; for example, choose View and then Folders, Toolbar, and/or Status Bar to display or hide these items.

Sending Mail

To send an e-mail message, choose Compose, New Message. The New Message window appears, as shown in Figure 11.26. In the To text box, enter the name of the recipient of the mail; the name must match the name entered by the adminis-

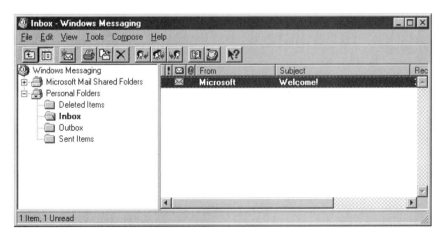

Figure 11.25 *The inbox enables you to send and receive e-mail over the network.*

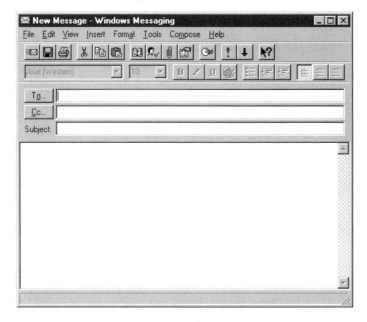

Figure 11.26 *Send messages to others over the network.*

trator. If you're unsure of the name to enter, click the TO box and the address book appears; select the name you want to send the message to.

If you want to send a carbon copy of the message to someone, enter that person's name in the CC box; alternatively, click the CC button and choose the name from the address book. Enter a topic in the Subject text box, then enter the message in the message area.

You can also do the following things in the New Message dialog box:

- Format the text in the message area by using the Format menu and/or Formatting toolbar.
- Print the message by choosing File, Print.
- Insert a file (such as a document or spreadsheet) by choosing Insert, File and selecting the file to attach to the message.
- Get help by choosing the Help menu.

To send the message, choose File, Send or click the Send button in the Toolbar.

Receiving Mail

When you attach to the server from your workstation and open the Inbox, your e-mail messages will be delivered to your Inbox and appear in the right pane of

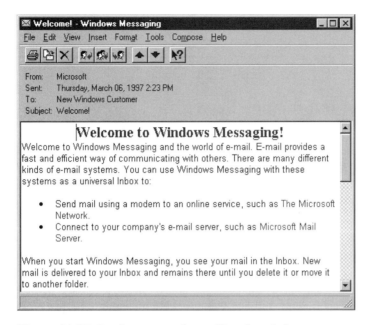

Figure 11.27 *Read a message by scrolling the window.*

the window. To open a message, double-click it in the right pane. Figure 11.27 shows the Microsoft Welcome message opened for reading.

After you finish reading the message, you can do any of the following things:

• Close the message by choosing File, Close.

• Save the message to a file by choosing File, Save As and assigning a name and location for the file.

• Print the message by choosing File, Print.

• Delete the message by choosing File, Delete.

• Move the message to another folder by choosing File, Move and selecting the folder in the Move dialog box.

• Reply to the message by choosing Compose, Reply to Sender; reply to the sender and to anyone who received a carbon copy by choosing Compose, Reply to All.

• Forward the message to another party by choosing Compose, Forward.

Note: There are many more options to using Windows Messaging. You can customize the Inbox and/or your messages, add services, change your password, view a session log, and much more. For more information about using Windows Messaging, see the Help feature in the Inbox.

Microsoft Internet Information Server

Windows NT Server includes several additional applications you can use to create an intranet on your network or to create a presence on the World Wide Web over the Internet. An intranet is a private corporate web site that uses Internet software and TCP/IP protocol to supply only users of the network with web pages, documents, and other distributed information. An intranet doesn't have to include a connection to the Internet, but it can.

NT ships with the Microsoft Internet Information Server, an application you can use to manage and administer a Web server. The Internet Information Server (IIS) enables you to transmit information in HTML using HTTP over a TCP/IP network. HTML (hypertext markup language) is the language with which Web documents are formatted; HTML defines the appearance and placement of fonts, graphics, text, links to other sites, and other such elements in a Web document. HTTP (hypertext transfer protocol) is the protocol used to manage the links between one hypertext document and another.

Note: Microsoft's IIS also includes ftp and Gopher services for transferring files and publishing information archives. Additionally, NT Server contains Front Page, a comprehensive Web publishing package that enables you to edit, design, distribute, and browse Web pages. Clients can then use the Internet Explorer to access these Web pages, whether on an intranet or the Internet. The Internet Explorer is built-in to Windows NT and Windows 95, and a version of the Explorer is also available from Microsoft's Web site for Windows for Workgroup clients.

Using NT Server with Microsoft's Internet Information Server provides a powerful tool for distributing and sharing data over your network. IIS services completely integrate with NT's user accounts and file permissions. Tools and utilities you use with IIS are similar in look and feel to NT's; so learning to manage and use the IIS services is simple if you already know how NT works.

You can install the Internet Information Server at the same time you install NT or later, as a service. Installing the IIS also installs the Internet Service Manager that you use to view and edit servers and services. To install the IIS service, open the Control Panel and double-click the Network icon. Choose the Services

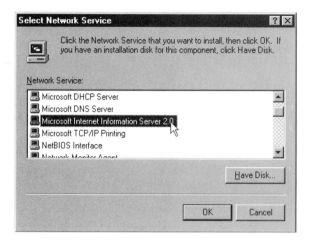

Figure 11.28 *Install the IIS as a network service.*

tab, then choose Add. In the Select Network Service dialog box, choose the Microsoft Internet Information Server, as shown in Figure 11.28.

Choose OK. NT will prompt you to insert the NT Server installation CD–ROM and will copy the necessary files needed for the IIS service. After installation, you can find the Internet Service Manager plus product documentation by choosing Start, Programs, Microsoft Internet Service.

Note: For more information about building an intranet, see *Building Your Intranet with Windows NT 4.0* by Stephen Thomas and Sue Plumley (John Wiley & Sons, Inc., 1997).

Summary

In this chapter, you've learned to use several NT applications and accessories to help manage and expand your network. You can manage files and folders with the NT Explorer, view system and application errors as well as security breaches with the Event Viewer, set up e-mail for your users and even publish Web pages for use on the Internet or your own private intranet. In the next chapter, you learn to install and use applications within the NT network.

12 *Installing and Using Applications*

You've seen how many of NT Server's built-in applications and accessories can help you manage and organize files and folders on the network, troubleshoot errors and problems on the network, and expand your network's possibilities. There are also many applications available to use with NT Server and with your network. You may, for example, want to use any of the suites of applications available, such as Lotus SmartSuite, Microsoft Office, or Corel's Perfect Office. You will likely need an accounting program of some type, perhaps vertical applications created specifically for your business, and maybe even some DOS-based applications to run on the network. This chapter describes some of the possible application types and brands you can use and suggests some effective ways to implement the applications to your network. This chapter covers the following:

- Installation instructions for DOS-based and Windows 3.x applications
- Installation instructions for Windows 95 and NT applications
- Advice about when to install to the server or to the workstations
- Tips for using applications
- Directions on how to remove applications

Basic Application Issues

One of the largest parts of using a network is using applications. You might use commercial applications such as Word, Excel, and Microsoft Office or Lotus' 1-2-3, Word Pro, or SmartSuite. You probably do use an accounting program of some type—Peach Tree, MAS90, QuickBooks/QuickPay, for example. And many businesses use vertical applications created specifically for their business, such as real estate marketing, printing estimation, or medical records programs.

No matter which applications you use, there are some issues that apply to the network and the applications you plan to use. Make sure, for example, that you plan your application installation and use just as you planned your implementation of the network. Consider whether each program should be installed to the server or individual workstations, think about the versions of applications you're using and whether to upgrade, and don't forget to plan the file and directory structures for storing the files that are produced from each application (see Chapter 2 for more information).

Note: Important: If you plan to install an application to the network for use by clients or for installation by clients, make sure you share the directory in which the application's files are stored.

Server versus Workstation Installations

Your first concern for most of your applications is to decide whether those programs will be installed to the server or to the individual workstations. There are several issues that can direct your decision; following are just a few questions to consider.

What is the specific licensing for the product? Some products keep track of how many people are using the application at one time, as do some Lotus applications for example. If this is the case, you will need to install the application on the server so that the application can track the users.

What does the software require? Some applications specifically state they are for network use or are not for network use, while other programs can be used either way. If you configure an application for multiuser operations, the application needs to know how many people are using the files so it can update files, lock records, perform file purges, or compress data.

Microsoft Access is a database application that you can install to a standalone computer or to a network for multiuser operation, for example. Also, accounting programs are often made to go on the server as opposed to a workstation. These applications tear down a file and rebuild it periodically, so they must know when the files are free to perform these tasks.

How much control do you want over the application? If you want all applications to look exactly the same on each workstation, then you can install the application to the server and control the settings for colors, fonts, setup, and other configuration options within the program. You might want to control the look of an application if you're training users, for example, and you want to direct them to perform the exact same tasks without individualized attention. Another example for maintaining control over an application's appearance and configuration is if your users travel between workstations and you want them to have the same exact setup no matter which computer they use. In cases such as these, you install the application, whether a word processor, spreadsheet, or other program, to the server.

What are your administration duties? Installing applications to the server means your administration is easier because all options are the same. Each application is consistent to all users. On the other hand, administration may be easier if you let the user control how the application looks. You don't have to set initial configuration settings or worry about what each user is doing within an application.

How fast do you want the program to load and access data? Any application installed to the server and accessed by more than one person will take a bit longer to load and use. Screen redraw will be slower over the network as will document formatting, inserting graphics, searching for topics or items, and any other procedure you perform in the program. Installing an application to the workstations, on the other hand, means accelerated response time and more efficient use of the program.

In conjunction with speed of running an application over the network, consider the network traffic of using applications installed to the server. More traffic results from multiple users accessing the application as well as the files, printer, and other resources.

Consider too, the slowed pace of the traffic if you're using an ISDN line or loading applications over a WAN. The traffic over a remote connection is definitely slower than over a direct connection; add to that the loading of large applications and your network could come to a complete halt. If you're using a network between two or more sites and attaching the network via frame relay or ISDN, think about installing the applications either to the workstation or to a server on the same side as the majority of users, so the application files don't have to travel long distances to get to the workstations.

How important is constant productivity? If you have 20 people on your network, and each of them is using an application that is installed to the network, productivity stops if the server goes down. Users who have applications installed to their workstations, however, can continue to work even if there is a network problem. You may, then, want to install some applications to the network and others to the workstations, to prepare for a server crash.

Note: You should store most, if not all, working files on the network, so the users can share them and backup of the files is easier and more efficient.

Compatibility

The Windows NT Server and Workstation operating systems are compatible with a variety of applications, including DOS-based programs, Windows 3.x applications, and Windows 95 versions of programs. There is also a new generation of Windows NT-specific applications being developed for use both on a workstation and over a server. NT's architecture enables the operating system to support both 16-bit and 32-bit applications; separate internal subsystems support each type of application.

Note: Windows NT 4.0 can also run 16-bit OS/2 applications and POSIX-based applications. See the NT documentation for more information.

Note too, that applications not designed specifically for NT sometimes use device drivers that NT will block from being installed with the application because of the way the drivers communicate with the computer hardware. If you have trouble installing an application or have driver problems, contact the manufacturer of the application for an NT-compatible driver or for an upgrade of the application.

DOS Applications

DOS applications are character-based (as opposed to a graphical interface like Windows) and 16-bit. The only way you can run DOS applications in Windows NT is by using the Windows Command Prompt. Even with NT's Command Prompt, be warned that some DOS-based applications will cause problems and some may not run at all. The only way you can know for sure is to try the program for a while to see.

NT does emulate expanded memory for DOS applications that require it. If you're using a x86 computer, you can run the DOS-based application either in a window or in full-screen mode; however, applications that use graphics will run in full-screen mode.

I suggest you place DOS-based applications on workstations as opposed to the server. If you have a DOS-based client you can use, that would be perfect. DOS-based applications often cause lock ups and other problems on an NT or Windows 95 computer, as well as printing problems and file-sharing errors.

Windows 3.x Applications

Windows 3.x applications are also 16-bit applications (also known as Win16). NT provides support for these applications similar to the enhanced-mode environment in Windows 3.x. Notice, however, problems with system crashes as well as application crashes when using Windows 3.x applications under NT; see the section, "Running Windows 3.x Applications," later in this chapter for information about memory space.

Windows 95 Applications

Windows 95 programs are 32-bit applications built specifically for Windows 95. Many Windows 95 programs will run on Windows NT without incident. Since Windows 95 is so popular, there are many many applications from which to choose.

Windows NT Applications

Windows NT 3.51 and 4.0 are 32-bit applications built especially for NT. Note, however, that you should purchase the appropriate version of software for NT 4.0. Windows NT 3.51 has an interface similar to Windows 3.x, even though the system is 32-bit; the NT 4.0 interface is more like Windows 95. Naturally, NT applications work the best with NT Server and Workstation; however, vendors are just now beginning to manufacture applications specifically for use with NT.

General Installation of Applications

The processes for installing programs is almost always the same for a particular platform: DOS, Windows 3.x, Windows 95, or Windows NT. Most applications come with a setup or installation program that makes it easy to install and configure an application for use on a PC. Here are a few general basics to remember:

- You should always read the documentation that comes with the application, especially the installation instructions.
- You will likely use an INSTALL or SETUP program, generally with an extension of EXE, COM, CMD, or BAT often located on the root directory of the floppy disk or CD-ROM.
- Applications on CD-ROMs install much quicker and easier than those on floppy diskette; but installing from the network to workstations and/or servers is the fastest method of installation.
- Usually, there is a README.TXT or READ.ME or SETUP.TXT file on the disk with the program files; use the Notepad or WordPad to read the file to see if there are any special instructions before you install it.

Installing from a CD-ROM or a diskette means you must install the application to one computer at a time. Some CD-ROMs come with the AutoRun feature so that the first time you insert the CD, it automatically launches an application or utility on the CD. Often, you can simply click a button in the CD's window that will install or set up the application.

Installing from the network means you can let each workstation install its own software quickly and with the least amount of administrative duties for you. The way you install an application and the number of times you install it depend on the installation instructions and licensing of the software; be sure to check the documentation before you install.

Many applications enable you to copy the program files to the server; then users can install the program from the server to their workstation computers. Network installation is by far the easiest method since you only copy the files once and the users do the rest of the work. Microsoft Office, Lotus SmartSuite, and many other applications allow this type of installation; check in the application's documentation index under Network or Network Installation for more information.

You can purchase commercial applications, such as Microsoft Office, in which case you will receive a CD-ROM or a number of floppy disks from which you can install the application. You also may download a program, such as shareware or beta copies, from the Internet or a commercial bulletin board service. This type of program usually comes to you as one compressed file that contains all of the files needed to install and run the application.

If you plan to use a compressed or self-extracting file, you need to decompress the file before you can use it. If the file was compressed with a utility such as PKWare's PKZIP, you need a copy of that utility to unzip or decompress the file. If the file is a self-extracting file, you simply copy the file into a directory you've made for it, then execute the file. In DOS, you type the file name and press Enter; in Windows, you can double-click the file name in the NT Explorer. When the file extracts, it releases all of the files you need to run the setup or install program.

Note: Important: If you use a self-extracting file, make sure you place it in its own directory or folder before you extract it; you don't want all of the files straying all over your root directory, for instance.

TIP: Install and test new software before enabling everyone on the network to use it. This includes upgrades. This gives you an idea of potential software and/or hardware problems and enables you to develop documentation, such as training material, guidelines for use, instructions for file storage, and so on. If you don't test first, you could have a server failure or other network problem that severely impacts prodcutivity and perhaps will put your data at risk.

Installing and Using DOS-Based Applications

DOS-based applications are probably the most difficult to work with in a Windows environment, whether you're using Windows 95 or Windows NT. DOS applications tend to lock up when run in a Command Prompt window (which is the only way to use them in NT unless you've created a dual boot), and often cause printing and graphics problems, as well as system and application errors. Luckily, NT includes some features and utilities that enable you to better control DOS-based programs; so if you must run DOS applications within NT, perhaps it will be an equable experience.

Note: A dual boot is an installation plan in which you divide a server's drive into two partitions. In the first, primary partition, you install DOS. To the second partiton, you install NT. You can format the second partition to NTFS or FAT, as long as the first partition remains formatted FAT and retains DOS as its operating system. After the NT installation, the computer boots and the boot loader screen enables you to choose between the two operating systems. If you choose the DOS partition, you can run it just as you would any DOS drive—add DOS applications, Windows 3.x and related applications, and so on. To get to the NT partition, you must reboot the computer and choose NT from the boot loader options.

Installing DOS Applications to NT Computers

You can install most DOS applications to NT via the Command Prompt window, similarly to installing a DOS-based application to a DOS operating system. This section runs through a simple installation of WordPerfect 6.0 for DOS on an NT member server. To install a DOS application, follow these steps:

1. Close all other programs on the NT computer. Choose Start, Programs, Command Prompt. The Command Prompt window appears, as shown in Figure 12.1.

2. Insert the floppy disk or the CD and per the application's documentation, type the installation command, such as **a:install** or **d:setup**. Press ENTER.

3. The Installation screen appears in the DOS window (see Figure 12.2).

4. Follow the directions on-screen. If you have any questions about the installation of the program, consult the application's documentation. It's often easiest and useful to accept the default options.

Figure 12.1 Start with a Command Prompt window.

5. When installation is complete, try opening the program according to the application's documentation to test the installation. If you have any trouble with the application, check the troubleshooting section of the application's documentation. You may also be able to modify an application's PIF files, as described in the next section, to alleviate problems.

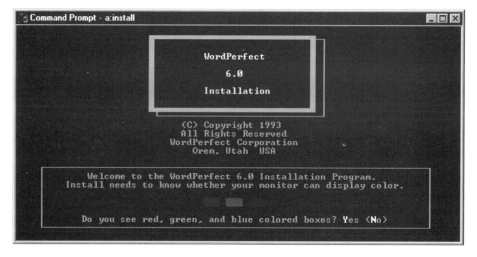

Figure 12.2 The installation screen appears in the Command Prompt window as it would if you were installing the application to DOS.

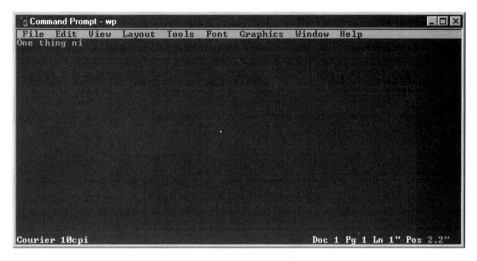

Figure 12.3 *Run DOS applications in the Command Prompt window.*

Note: Important: If you have trouble installing an application—such as WordPerfect 6.0 for DOS—because the program needs addtional file handles (files=30, for example), open the Config.NT using Notepad. Scroll to the bottom of the file and enter the appropriate number of files, 30 to 50 is a reasonable value. Save the Notepad file and close the program. You don't need to restart the computer to continue the installation.

Figure 12.3 shows the WordPerfect program open in a Command Prompt window. You use the application as you normally would when it's installed to a DOS operating system. Exit the program as you normally would before you close the Command Prompt window. For more information about the Command Prompt window, see the sidebar, "Using the Command Prompt."

Program Information Files (PIFs) for DOS Programs

DOS-based applications use program information files (PIFs) to provide information to NT about how best to run the application. When you start a DOS application, NT searches for the application's PIF. If NT can't find the PIF, it uses its default.pif file that contains settings that work with most DOS-based applications.

If you need to create or modify a PIF, right-click the application file in the Windows NT Explorer and choose Properties. The PIF's Properties dialog box appears, as shown in Figure 12.4.

Creating a Shortcut for 16-bit Applications

You can create a shortcut for a DOS application and/or for a Windows 3.x application. The shortcut enables you to quickly launch the application from the NT Desktop. To automatically create a shortcut, follow these steps:

1. Open the Windows NT Explorer and restore the window so you can see the Windows desktop on the same screen.

2. Open the folder containing the DOS or Windows 3.x application.

3. Locate the application file. (Generally the application file has an EXE, CMD, BAT, or COM extension; show extensions by choosing View, Options and deselect the Hide File Extensions For Known File Types check box. Choose OK.)

4. Drag the extension to the desktop. Windows creates a shortcut.

To open the application, double-click the shortcut.

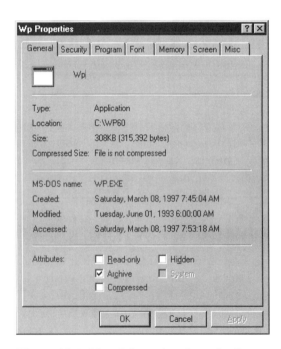

Figure 12.4 *View information about the Program Information Files for a DOS-based application.*

The tabs in the PIF's Properties dialog box govern the following configurations:

- *General tab*: Contains information about the PIF, such as type of file, location, size, DOS name, creation date, and attributes applied to the file.

- *Security tab*: Contains the Permissions, Auditing, and Ownership buttons that enable you to set permissions on the file as you would any NT file.

- *Program*: Enables you to name the file and edit configuration settings, as described later in this section.

- *Font*: Includes font types, sizes, and a preview of the fonts you can choose for the program.

- *Memory*: Enables you to set conventional, expanded, extended, and protected-mode memory for the program.

- *Screen*: Includes options for displaying the program on-screen and in a window.

- *Misc*: Enables you to set options about shortcut keys, mouse use, foreground and background use, and termination of the DOS program.

The Program tab contains some very specific and critical options you can edit or create for any PIF, thus editing the way the DOS-based program runs. Figure 12.5 shows the Program tab. The first text box in the tab contains the name of the

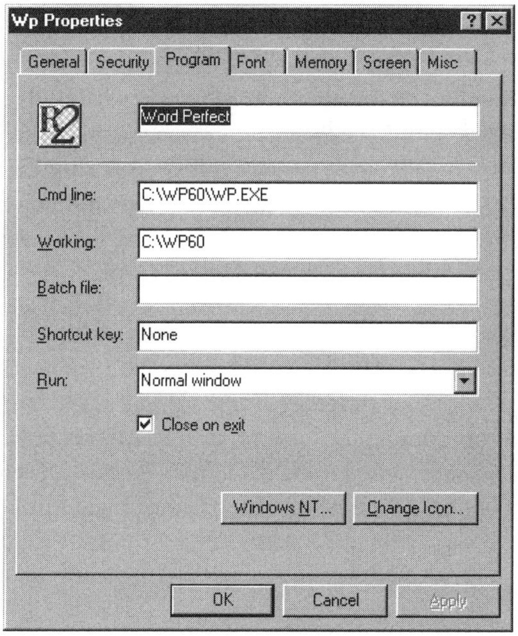

Figure 12.5 Name the PIF or edit its properties.

program; if no name is displayed, you can enter a name in the text box. The Program tab includes the following information you can edit:

- *Name text box:* The name of the program appears in the first text box in the Program tab; you can change the name of the program if you want, but do not put an extension other than PIF on the file name.

- *Cmd Line:* Enter the path and the command to start the program; you may need to include the drive, folder, and file name extension as well as any parameters or switches needed to complete the command.

- *Working:* Enter the name of the folder the program loads from. This also specifies the directory in which to save files.

- *Batch File:* Enter the name of a batch file that should run each time the program is started. Include a drive, directory, and any parameters needed to run the command.

- **S**hortcut Key: Enter a shortcut key you want to use to start the program; if the shortcut key conflicts with a shortcut used to access a Windows-based program, the DOS shortcut key will not work. The shortcut key must include Ctrl or Alt and can include both; an example of a shortcut key might be Ctrl+F6 or Ctrl+Alt+R.

- *Run:* Choose how you want the window to be displayed when you start the window: normal, minimized, or maximized. Some DOS-based applications will not take up the whole screen when maximized.

- *Close On Exit:* Check the box to close the application automatically when you exit the Command Prompt window.

- *Windows NT button:* Choose whether to set the program up to have exclusive use of the computer in DOS-mode or to enable Windows-based applications to run at the same time.

- *Change Icon:* Enables you to choose a different icon to represent the program.

You can use multiple PIFs for one application; use multiple PIFs when you run the application under various and different circumstances. You might, for instance, specify an amount of expanded memory to use with large files. You can choose the Memory tab in the PIF's Properties dialog box to specify memory; however, NT sets the memory and environment automatically. Unless you have specific needs of conventional, expanded, or extended memory, leave the defaults in place.

TSRs (Terminate-and-Stay-Resident) DOS Programs

A TSR (terminate-and-stay-resident) program is a DOS program that stays loaded into memory, even when it's not actually running; the program can then be in-

---

AUTOEXEC and CONFIG Files

People often ask where are the AUTOEXEC.BAT and the CONFIG.SYS in the Windows NT system. Briefly, here's what happens to them. NT uses the AUTOEXEC.BAT to define path and environment variables at system startup. You set environment variables in the Control Panel, System option, Environment tab and place those configurations into the Registry; thus, NT ignores the CONFIG.SYS unless a DOS-based or Windows 3.x application requires it.

NT uses the AUTOEXEC.NT and CONFIG.NT files to configure environment for DOS and Windows 3.x applications instead of the AUTOEXEC.BAT and CONFIG.SYS. Each MS-DOS application you start in a Command Prompt window reads these two files and performs any commands in them. You can edit either of these files as you would the AUTOEXEC.BAT and the CONFIG.SYS. The files are located in the \SYSTEM32 directory.

Use the Notepad to edit these files by opening the Run dialog box (Start, Run) and typing Notepad and the name of the file. Press ENTER. Make any changes you want to the NT file, then choose File, Save. Choose File, Exit.

When modifying the CONFIG.NT file, you can use several NT commands (see the On-line Command Reference in Help for more information), including COUNTRY, DEVICE, DOS, DOSONLY, ECHOCONFIG, FILES, INSTALL, LOADHIGH, and so on. If you use any commands that NT doesn't recognize, NT ignores the command. To modify the AUTOEXEC.NT, you can use similar commands. Again, see the On-line Command Reference in NT for more information.

---

voked quickly to perform a specific task. Some popular TSRs include calendars, appointment schedulers, calculators, and so on, invoked from a DOS-based word processor or spreadsheet, for example. A TSR occupies conventional memory space or memory accessible by DOS in real mode (normally the first 640K. Real mode is the only operating mode supported by DOS; it doesn't offer any advanced hardware features for memory management or multitasking.

NT does support many DOS-based TSR programs; however, the TSR runs only in the Command Prompt window in which it was opened and can only be used within that window. Make sure you start a TSR only in a Command Prompt window as opposed to adding the command to your AUTOEXEC.NT or CONFIG.NT files; when you add the TSR to your configuration file, a copy of the TSR opens each time you start any application that runs those configuration files. You may end up with several copies of the TSR running, thus wasting valuable memory. So make sure that if one of your DOS applications requires a TSR to work, you first start the TSR in the Command Prompt window, then start the DOS application in that same window.

Using DOS Applications

Considering the information you've read concerning DOS-based applications, you will want to be careful of the method you choose to run DOS applications in NT. You can probably run a DOS application from the Command Prompt safely, if it has few environmental requirements, such as specific amounts of extended or expanded memory available. When you run a DOS application from the command line, settings in the CONFIG.NT and AUTOEXEC.NT are used to initialize the DOS environment. If there isn't a PIF installed for the DOS application, NT uses the _DEFAULT.PIF, which points to the AUTOEXEC.NT and CONFIG.NT; so if necessary, create a new PIF and modify it to best suit the application before running the program.

TIP: Press ALT+ENTER to toggle an open DOS application between full-screen and window modes.

After you open the application, use it as you normally would in any DOS operating system.

Using the Command Prompt Window

You can open the Command Prompt window in NT and run DOS programs as well as execute DOS commands, such as DIR, COPY, MOVE, MD, CD, and so on, and for administering network commands. Since the DOS in the Command Prompt window is Windows NT Version 4.0 DOS as opposed to DOS 6.0 or 6.22, some of the commands you may be used to won't work in the Command Prompt window.

To open the Command Prompt window, choose Start, Programs, Command Prompt. To exit the Command Prompt window, type **exit** at the prompt and press ENTER. Alternatively, you can click the Close button in the window's title bar. If you have an open DOS program in the Command Prompt window, you should close the application before closing the window.

You can open more than one Command Prompt window at a time; you might run a program in one window, use another to issue commands, and use yet another to configure network resources, for example.

(continues)

Customizing the Window You can modify the current Command Prompt window by clicking the Control menu button of the open window and selecting Properties. You can change the following options:

Options tab: Change the cursor size to small, medium, or large; choose either to view the screen as a window or full-sized, and set a buffer size for recording the command history of the current screen.

Font tab: Select the font size and font, or typeface.

Layout tab: Choose the screen size, window size, and window position.

Colors tab: Select various colors for the screen text, background, popup text, and so on.

If you find the screen looks distorted or fonts are hard to read with some applications or just when using the command prompt, choose to view full-screen. Often the DOS window looks more like what you're used to in full-screen.

Starting Programs To use applications at the command prompt, you will most likely need to change directories to the program's directory before you enter the command to start the program. For example, type **cd\wp60** and press ENTER to change directories; then type **wp** and press ENTER to start the program.

Copying and Pasting You can copy and paste data between applications running in Command Prompt windows and Windows applications using the Windows Clipboard. Use the Control menu, Edit, Mark command to select text for copying. When the text is selected, choose Control menu, Edit, Copy. Then you can change windows, documents, or otherwise position the cursor; choose Control menu, Edit, Paste to paste the items on the Clipboard.

Using Commands Many of the commands you're used to with DOS are available in the Command Prompt window. You can use parameters and switches to further define the commands. A parameter is additional information that defines the item—files, directory, and so on—you want the operating system to act upon. For example, in the command `copy` `report01.doc a:\quarters`, `copy` is the command and `report01.doc` and `a:\quarters` are the parameters.

In addition to parameters, you can use switches to modify how the command performs a task. Say you're using the `dir` command to list the directory of the root. Using the switch `/w` lists the directory wide and in columns; using the switch `/s` lists the directories and all subdirectories. The command could be written `dir /w`, `dir /s`, or `dir /w /s`.

Removing DOS Applications

DOS-based applications considerably change your AUTOEXEC.BAT and CONFIG.SYS upon installation. Check these configuration files and remove any references to the DOS program and/or its directories.

Before deleting any directories containing the files you want to remove, rename the directory and leave it on the system for a few days. Check to make sure the system will restart and that other applications work without that directory. When you're sure everything is in working order, you can delete the directory.

Installing and Using Windows 3.x Applications

You can use Windows 3.x applications in a computer running NT Server or Workstation because NT includes the CONFIG.NT and AUTOEXEC.NT files that help configure the applications. Notice that there are often problems with Windows 3.x applications in that they often lock up or even crash the system. If at all possible, I suggest you upgrade the application you're using to a Windows 95 or Windows NT version for the best results and less headaches.

Installing Windows 3.x Applications

You install a Windows 3.x application to an NT computer using the Run dialog box. Choose Start, Run. The Run dialog box appears (see Figure 12.6).

In the Open text box, enter the drive letter and the name of the installation or setup program. If necessary, enter the drive letter, then click the Browse button to locate the installation file (see Figure 12.7). Select the file and choose the Open button to return to the Run dialog box.

After entering the command line, click OK in the Run dialog box. Windows begins to install the program, as shown in Figure 12.8. Follow directions on-screen, changing disks if prompted, and answering any questions or prompts.

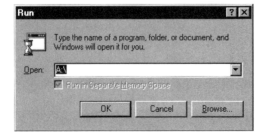

Figure 12.6 *Use the Run dialog box to install a Windows 3.x application.*

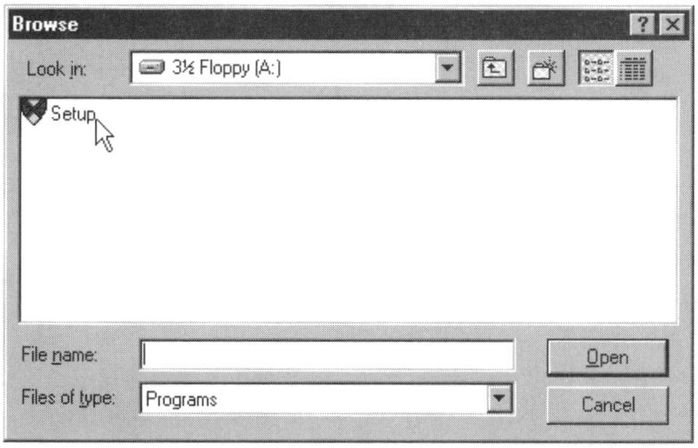

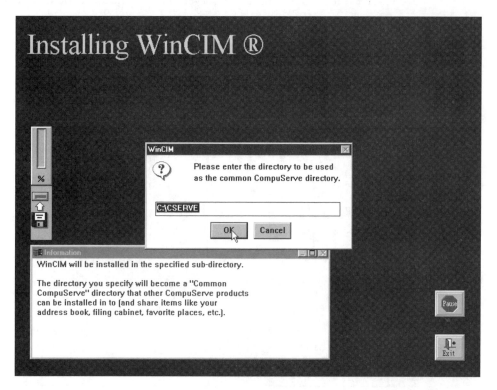

Figure 12.7 *Browse for the setup or install file.*

When installation is complete, Windows may ask about the program group in which you want to place the files; accept the defaults. Next, Windows displays the icons representing the program files in a window, as shown in Figure 12.9.

Figure 12.8 *Install the program as you would in Windows 3.x.*

Figure 12.9 *The program icons appear in a window.*

The application is also added to the Programs menu, usually with its own menu leading to various program files related to the application, such as Read Me files, the executable files, setup files, and others. You can use the Programs menu to start the application or you can create a shortcut on the desktop for the application, as described earlier in this chapter.

Figure 12.10 shows the CompuServe Information Manager for Windows 3.x loaded onto an NT member server. The application looks and works the same as it does in Windows 3.11.

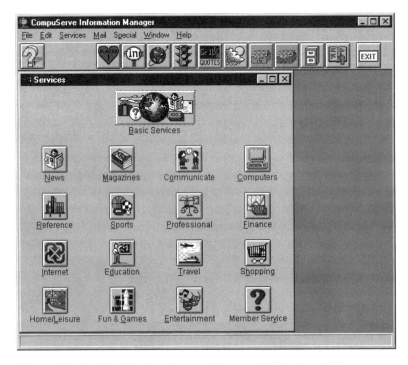

Figure 12.10. *Use Windows 3.x applications in Windows NT.*

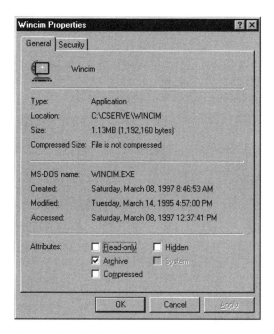

Figure 12.11 *The General tab of the Properties dialog box describes the application by type, location, size, and other factors.*

Configuring Windows 3.x Applications

You can modify the properties sheets for a Windows 3.x application. In the Explorer, locate the application file by opening the application's directory. Right-click the application and choose Properties. Figure 12.11 shows the Wincim Properties dialog box.

The Properties dialog box contains the General and Security tabs, similar to tabs of the same name in the DOS application's Properties dialog box. The General tab contains a set of information that describes the application and a set of attributes you can set for the application. The Security tab enables you to control access via permissions, auditing, and ownership; see Chapter 7 for more information.

Some applications may include a Shortcut tab, which includes the Target text box, that indicates the file launched when the shortcut is selected and the Start In text box, meaning the working directory of the application. Other options in the application's Properties dialog box include the Run text box in which you choose the type of window to run the application in and the Shortcut Key text box, in which you optionally enter a shortcut key for starting the program.

Running Windows 3.x Applications

You may discover a problem when several Windows 3.x applications are running at one time within NT. If NT crashes often, it is likely that the Windows 3.x application hung the system or otherwise caused the crash. All Windows 3.x applications run in a shared memory space, a virtual DOS machine. One application crashing can result in all Windows 3.x applications locking up and even other applications, as well as the operating system, crashing.

You can avoid this problem by running a Windows 3.x-based application in its own memory space. Running several Windows 3.x-based programs, each in its own memory space, will use more NT memory and may slow the system.

To run a Windows 3.x application in its own space, choose Start, Run, then enter the path and the name of the application you want to run. In the Run dialog box, select the Run in Separate Memory Space check box. Figure 12.12 shows the Run dialog box with the path to the Wincim program and the Run in Separate Memory Space option selected.

Removing Windows 3.x Applications

Windows 3.x applications considerably change your AUTOEXEC.BAT, CONFIG.SYS, as well as your SYSTEM.INI and WIN.INI. The AUTOEXEC.BAT and CONFIG.SYS files appear in your root directory; the SYSTEM.INI and WIN.INI files are generally located in the \WINNT directory. Additionally, these applications sometimes install older versions of critical common library files to the System subdirectory of the main Windows directory.

When you want to remove a Windows 3.x application from an NT computer, check the SYSTEM.INI and WIN.INI. Search for any occurrence of the application or its installation directory. Check first to see if any other application is using the application's directory and if not, delete references in the INI files. If another application may be using the directory, it would not be wise to delete it, even

Figure 12.12 *Use separate memory spaces for each Windows 3.x application you run.*

though many of these INI files are not used by NT other than to support DOS and Windows 3.x programs. INI files supply initialization information to Windows 3.x and to applications that run in Windows. The INI files in NT are maintained to provide compatibility with Win16 applications. Instead of INI files, NT uses the Registry to record most program configuration changes.

Before deleting any directories containing the files you want to remove, rename the directory first and leave it on the system for a few days. Check to make sure the system will restart and that other applications work without that directory. When you're sure everything is in working order, you can delete the directory.

Installing and Using Windows 32-Bit Applications

Windows 32-bit (or Win32) refers to Windows 95 and its upgrades, Windows NT 3.51 Server and Workstation, and Windows NT 4.0 Server and Workstation. There are more applications available now for Windows 95 than for Windows NT; however, NT-specific applications are becoming more and more popular.

Note: Important: While you're waiting for more NT 4.0 applications to be released, you can rest assured that Microsoft has a plan you can take advantage of now. Before Microsoft will lend its official Windows 95 logo to an application, that application must also be able to run on Windows NT. With the great popularity of Windows 95, that coveted logo means a lot to any software developer; so there are more applications out there than you may have realized.

Installing Applications

Installing Windows 95 and Windows NT applications is fairly automatic. Most 32-bit applications come on CDs these days; however, you may find some on diskette. You can install an application using the AutoRun feature, the Run dialog box, or the Add/Remove Programs icon in the Control Panel.

AutoRun

If you're using a CD, often the AutoRun feature opens the CD when you insert it, as shown in Figure 12.13. AutoRun is an automatic utility that opens a CD when you first insert it to your computer. Usually, a Welcome screen appears with several options; one option is generally to start the installation process.

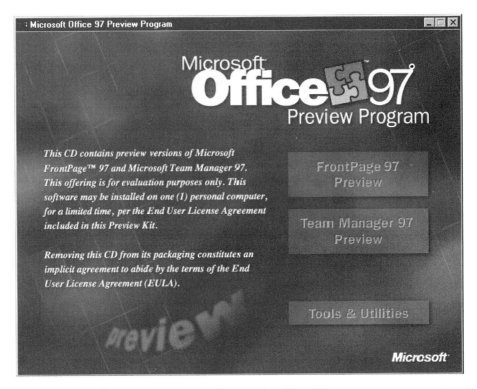

Figure 12.13 *If the AutoRun feature displays the CD's Welcome screen, you may be able to start the installation process from there.*

Run Dialog Box

To begin installation of an application using the Run dialog box, choose Start, Run and enter the disk drive in the Open text box. Use the Browse dialog box to find the Setup or Install file, as shown in Figure 12.14. Select the file and choose Open; then choose OK in the Run dialog box to begin installation of the program.

The Setup program generally will copy files to your hard disk, look for previous versions of the application, then display a welcome screen (see Figure 12.15). Follow the directions on-screen, referring to the application's documentation, if you have questions. When the installation is complete, NT places a new menu on the Programs menu for the new application.

Add/Remove Programs

NT also includes a Wizard for helping you install programs; the Add/Remove Programs icon is located in the Control Panel (choose Start, Settings, Control Panel).

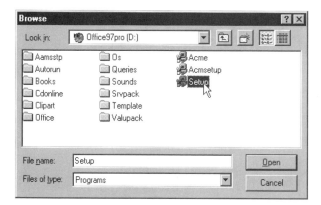

Figure 12.14 *Use the Browse dialog box to locate the setup file.*

Double-click the icon to display the Add/Remove Programs Properties dialog box. Choose the Install button to display first Wizard dialog box, as shown in Figure 12.16.

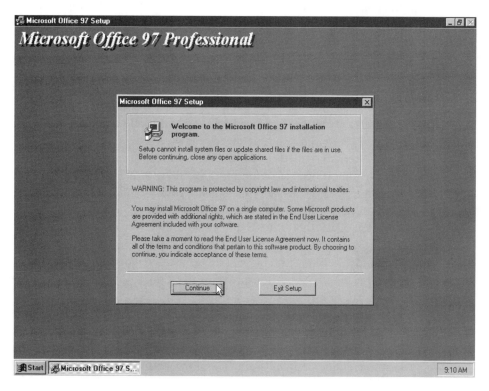

Figure 12.15 *Follow the installation program's directions.*

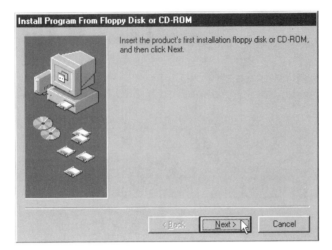

Figure 12.16 *Use the Add a Program Wizard to install new programs.*

Follow the directions in each Wizard dialog box, clicking Next to continue from box to box. When the Wizard is done, the application is installed to your computer.

Network Installation

Installing an application from the network is similar to installing from a floppy or CD disk drive. In the Run dialog box, for example, instead of entering A:, B:, or D:, enter the network drive, such as \\HUMBLE\MSOFFICE. You can also browse to locate the setup file on the network.

An alternative method of installation from the network is to open the Network Neighborhood, My Computer window, or NT Explorer, then open the network drive. Locate the appropriate folder and install or setup file, then double-click the file to start the installation process.

Figure 12.17 shows the Explorer with the Network Neighborhood opened in the left pane of the window. On the Humble server, I've selected the NotesInstall folder and the Notes subfolder. Notice in the right pane of the window, I've selected the Install application program. By double-clicking the Install icon, I start the installation process to the member server. For more information about Notes and other groupware applications, see Chapter 13.

After you install a product to the NT computer, you can open it on that computer or share it over the network. Figure 12.18 shows Microsoft Excel from the Microsoft Office 97 installation. This application is listed as Windows 95 and Windows NT compatible in the application's documentation.

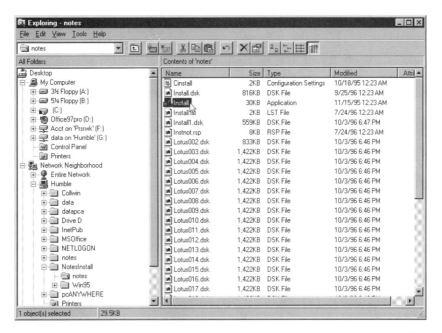

Figure 12.17 *Install an application from the network for fast and easy installation.*

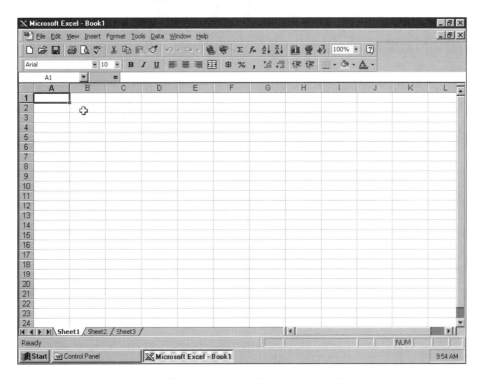

Figure 12.18 *Microsoft's Office 97 was built for use with NT.*

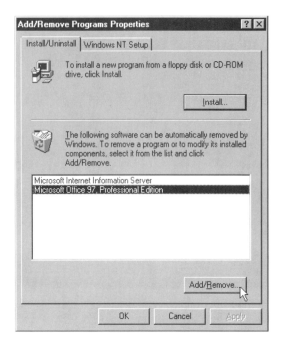

Figure 12.19 *Choose the Install/Uninstall tab of the Properties dialog box.*

Uninstalling Applications

Most Windows 95 and Windows NT applications include built-in support of uninstalling the applications. The uninstall program that comes with the application restores the system's registry and removes all references to the application when you uninstall.

To uninstall an application automatically, follow these steps:

1. Open the Control Panel and double-click the Add/Remove Programs icon. The Add/Remove Programs Properties dialog box appears, as shown in Figure 12.19.

2. In the Install/Uninstall tab, select the application you want to remove from the list. Click the Add/Remove button. You may be prompted to insert the application's CD; do so and click OK.

3. If the program doesn't prompt for a CD, Windows uninstalls the program automatically, removing all configuration files, directories, program files, and so on.

   If the uninstall program uses the CD's setup program to remove components, you will see a screen similar to the one in Figure 12.20.

4. Follow any directions on-screen to complete the process.

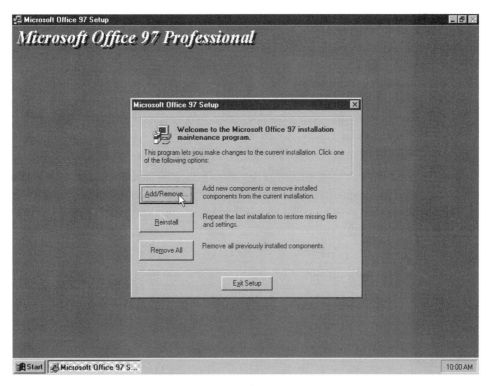

Figure 12.20 *Use the application's Setup program to remove the application.*

To uninstall an application manually, say if the software doesn't include an uninstall option, open the Explorer and delete all program files and directories associated with the program. To complete the removal of the application, you may need to remove all references to it from the Registry; however, editing the Registry is tricky and I wouldn't suggest it unless you completely understand how the Registry works. If you leave references to the application in the Registry, it shouldn't cause you any trouble, but it may cause minor inconveniences such as prompting for a file, dll, or other component periodically.

Information about Commercial Applications

You probably will want to use some of the more popular commercial applications, either on the server or installed to individual workstations. This section offers a little information about some of those applications. You can also contact the vendor or manufacturer, or visit the manufacturer's Web site on the Internet to find out more about any program or suite of programs.

(continues)

Information about Commercial Applications (*Continued*)

A suite is a group of related applications packaged and sold together by one manufacturer. Microsoft Office, Lotus SmartSuite, and Perfect Office are three prime examples of suites for business use. A suite usually contains a word processor, spreadsheet program, database application, and presentation program; often a scheduling and/or e-mail program is included. For more information about scheduling programs and e-mail applications, see Chapter 13.

Most suite applications work well together to enable you to share documents and data between the individual programs and with other Windows applications. Using various tools included with the program and with Windows NT, you can easily switch between applications, copy and paste between applications, share and link files and data between the applications.

Additionally, many suite applications include templates and style sheets that make creating documents, spreadsheets, or databases quick and easy. Many include spelling and grammar checkers, data tracking, automatic table and merge features, automated formulas, Internet features, charting, mapping, animation, and more.

Office includes all of the previously mentioned features plus more. The Office programs are Word (word processor), Excel (spreadsheet), Access (database), Outlook (scheduling), PowerPoint (presentation), and Binder (organizational). You can install all applications or only those you select. Being a Microsoft product, Office works particularly well with NT.

You can make Office available on your network for clients to install locally or save disk space by running a shared version over the network, as long as you have the license to install Microsoft Office on more than one client computer.

To install Office over the network, create a set of folders that holds the Office software and designate it as shared. The users then access the folder and install Office by running the Setup program. You will need 320M of disk space in order to create the installation folders on the server. For complete instructions to copying Microsoft Office to the network and setting it up to install to clients, see the file Netwrk8.txt on the Office 97 CD. If you're using a different version of Office, refer to the documentation.

Lotus SmartSuite also includes many of the features and advantages of a suite of applications. The SmartSuite programs include Word Pro (word processor), 1-2-3 (spreadsheet), Approach (database), Freelance Graphics (presentation), and Organizer (scheduler).

(continues)

As with most suites, you can install SmartSuite to a network server, as long as you have the licensing for multiple users. You also can enable users to install SmartSuite from the network as opposed to installing from the CD or disks. Lotus SmartSuite also uses shared directories and files that enable multiple users to use the applications, just as Office does.

One final bonus with using SmartSuite is that Lotus also makes the groupware products: Notes and Domino. Using SmartSuite applications in conjunction with Notes makes a powerful application for your business. For more information about Notes and Domino, see Chapter 13.

Other commercial applications you may need include the following:

Accounting programs: PeachTree, QuickBooks, TurboTax, ACT!

Databases for handling large amounts of data: FileMaker Pro, dBASE, Oracle

Art packages: CorelDRAW!, Adobe Illustrator, Adobe Photoshop, Visio

Utilities: Norton Utilities, Norton Navigator, FirstAid95

Desktop Publishing: Adobe PageMaker, FrameMaker, Micrografx Designer

Project Schedulers: Microsoft Project, FastTrack Schedule, SureTrak, Inspiration

Business Management: Timeslips, EstimatorPlus, TimeClock, ManagePro, B-Plan

Virus programs: Novi, Norton Anti-Virus

The best approach to buying applications for your business is to ask around, do some research, then figure out what works best for you and your users. You want a program that's easy to use and administer; but does the job quickly and efficiently.

Summary

In this chapter, you've learned many ways to install and use various applications, how to use DOS and Windows 3.x programs, as well as to install and use Windows 95 and NT applications. Choosing the right application and installation process takes planning and consideration. This chapter has given you some basic information to start you on your way. Chapter 13 covers groupware and communications applications.

13 *Using Groupware with NT*

M ore and more businesses are using groupware—application(s) that enable network users to e-mail, manage multiuser documents, conference, and schedule—within their companies so employees can collaborate on projects, and communicate with co-workers, and to facilitate workflow. The use of groupware over a network can change the way people within the company work by supporting the creation, flow, and tracking of information within the group.

Some of the popular groupware products covered in this chapter include Lotus Notes and Domino, Microsoft Outlook, cc:Mail, Organizer, and the Internet Explorer. Additionally, this chapter covers the following:

- Introduction to groupware
- E-mail, document management, conferencing, scheduling, and workflow
- Understanding the Internet Information Server
- Using the Internet Explorer
- Configuring the Internet Explorer
- Understanding FrontPage

Introduction to Groupware

Groupware is based on five basic technologies: multimedia document management, e-mail, conferencing, scheduling, and workflow. Various groupware products include one or more of these technologies. The more technologies included in the application, the more useful it will be in allowing your users to collaborate on projects; however, some offices will benefit greatly from just one or two of the technologies that are the foundation of groupware products.

Document Management

Document management describes the compilation of multiple documents organized into related topics so the documents can easily be located and utilized by the users of the network. Users can access documents, contribute new documents, sort, copy, save, and search the documents in the database. The word "database" here refers to the collection of documents; in Notes, for example, various databases store documents that are related to the same or similar topics.

The documents within the document management system can be made available to all network users or to only certain groups or individual users. Thus, members of small workgroups can access the documents they need, such as a budget analysis, to complete their work, while users of the entire network can access other documents, like reimbursement forms and time sheets, as needed. Most document management systems include reliable security features that make it easy for an administrator to designate user access.

The documents within the database may be created by the administrator of the network, IS managers, department heads, and other people who need to distribute data to multiple users. Network users can also contribute to the store of documents, enabling further sharing of information between individuals and the group.

Documents stored in the system can include text, images, graphics, even voice and video clips. Documents using multimedia technology are generally more interesting and therefore more widely utilized. Depending on the network protocols, cabling, and the groupware application, documents extensive in multimedia files take little or no more time to transfer, open, and view than plain text documents.

Documents are made available to users through a server which stores the collections of documents in databases. A computer running NT Server is an excellent choice for a groupware server because NT is fast, secure, enables application error logging, and otherwise fits most groupware requirements for efficient and effective use of the application. Once installed and configured on the NT Server, the groupware application stores documents, then indexes and retrieves them through various methods of identification, such as title, subject, author, text strings, and so on.

Suppose your company performs computer hardware and software training. You could create and store multiple training documents on the server and make those documents available to everyone in your company. Schedules of classes, descriptions of courses, biographies of the instructors, evaluation forms, course outlines and summaries, and more, would be available to everyone on the network. Furthermore, each instructor can create his or her own documents to add to the document database, so that everyone benefits from the experiences and research of the others.

You may store the documents in one database or organize them into several. Place registration and evaluation forms in one database, for instance; and store class descriptions in another. Or, store descriptions of each class type—such as Hardware Troubleshooting, Beginning Windows NT, Networking with NT, and so on—in databases titled Beginner, Intermediate, and Advanced or Client and Server, for example. The organization of the document databases depends on your needs and the needs of your users. The important fact to remember is that everyone on the network (with permission) can access and contribute to the document database, making the sharing of information easy, efficient, and beneficial to all.

E-mail

E-mail is one of the most popular collaborative tools used in business today. Using e-mail, your users can relate ideas, questions, motivation, inspiration, opinions, goals, and more to each other over your network and/or over the Internet. Users can send memos, notes, files, images, charts, and any other electronic item you can think of via e-mail. E-mail is a connection users can make without the time investment of a phone call or office visit. Also, users can answer a message when it's convenient, which is often more quickly than returning a phone call. E-mail may be the only groupware you need to establish a cooperative base for your company.

E-mail applications are perfect for client/server technology. Individual users use an e-mail application on the workstation to send and receive mail to a central post office, generally located on one server that collects the mail for the entire company. Depending on the size of the company, however, you may need to establish a post office for each domain, office, building, or other entity. E-mail is also the perfect compliment to the other groupware technologies—document management, scheduling, conferencing, and workflow—because e-mail facilitates collaboration via communication.

Your users may apply e-mail within the office to set meetings, ask questions, confirm project ideas, and so on; mobile users may want to communicate with colleagues back at the office via e-mail. Since e-mail is also handy for sending files, your users can electronically transfer files over the network, making collaboration easier and quicker than walking the files over on disk or explaining where on the server a colleague may find a file.

E-mail over the Internet opens new routes to business contacts. Your users can contact customers and vendors, research new products and services, order tools and software upgrades, and keep up on the latest information and news relating to your business. E-mailing between businesses, cities, and even countries can expand your company's reach and resources.

Whether you use it in a local network or over the Internet, e-mail can save time and effort in the office, speed communications, facilitate the sharing of information and files, and make interaction convenient.

Conferencing

Conferencing refers to electronic meetings in which users can post messages, questions, ideas, and so on, and read replies to their messages from other members of the group. There are two types of conferencing—real-time and anytime—that are supported by various groupware applications. Real-time conferences enable groups to collaborate on a project together, at the same time. Anytime conferences enable people to participate in a group discussion when and where it's convenient for them.

Conferencing can be useful over long distances—say between offices, buildings, cities, countries—and even within one room. Use conferencing software within one room, for instance, when you want to brainstorm ideas and discuss topics giving everyone a chance to communicate his or her thoughts completely, without interruption. In this type of meeting, only one person can display his or her comment at a time; each must wait on his or her turn to "speak," thus guaranteeing everyone the chance to have a say.

Over along distance, conferencing enables many people to meet and share ideas where otherwise, a meeting may not have been possible. Conference with colleagues, customers, manufacturers, sales or public relations people, publishers, or anyone else with whom you need to meet. All of those involved can type their thoughts, questions, comments, and ideas and read the responses of their peers.

Scheduling

Scheduling refers to recording meetings, sharing calendars, keeping ongoing to-do lists, and other methods of organizing your work day. A scheduling program enables an individual to list appointments, pencil-in meetings, and organize the work day, week, month, and more. You can set alarms to notify you of an upcoming appointment, reschedule easily, and often create an invitation to notify others of meetings.

In an office of busy people, a group scheduling application allows each person to see the others' calendars and, in many cases, update others' calendars when necessary. Assistants can keep their boss' schedule up-to-date; partners can pencil in appointments for each other; group meetings can be scheduled after checking everyone's calendar for availability.

Sharing calendars over the network is especially effective for lawyers, doctors, sales people, or realtors, for example, or any group of people whose schedule affects others in the office. Suppose one partner needs to consult the other's schedule before making an appointment integral to both partners; she could pencil in the appointment with a question about the date and, when the other partner returned to the office, he would see the calendar and respond to the proposed meeting. Organization, time management, and efficiency all improve with the help of a scheduling program on the network.

Workflow

Workflow is the act of routing work from one program and/or computer to another in a client/server environment. When using workflow applications, you define the operation at each stop, the value added at any stop, and what needs to be done at the next stop.

You can equate workflow with the paper trail in an office, for example. The front office starts the process of running a job through the entire shop by listing the customer's name and address, the order number, product requirements, due date, quantities, and so on. Then, this job form goes to the order department, that sends an order to the warehouse and an order form to the billing department. The warehouse fills the order and passes its form onto the truck driver; meanwhile, the billing department double-checks with the warehouse, then enters the form into the system for billing. And so goes the paper trail throughout the office.

The paper trail was created through a workflow model, similarly to the way an electronic workflow can be handled. Using a network application and electronic forms to complete these various steps throughout the process means a more orderly and efficient process, more accurate records, less likelihood of lost paper work, and better documentation of the process. Workflow applications help route information to people who need to supervise, manipulate, or act on it. Each workflow application provides some or all of the following:

- Status reports of work-in-progress
- Notifications of actions required
- Help on how to proceed at each step
- Routing from one person or stop to the next
- Rules that define what needs to be done and by whom
- Definition of roles of those involved with the process

SQL Databases

SQL (structured query language—SQL is pronounced "sequel") is a query language used to create, modify, and access data organized in tables in relational database management systems. Many databases implement SQL queries behind the scenes, enabling communication with database servers in systems with client/server architecture. Often, SQL databases are considered part of a successful network because they enable the sharing of information and data; however, SQL databases are not technically considered a groupware product.

A relational database is a database model in which the data always appears in two-diminsional tables, presented in rows and columns. The rows represent records, or collections of information about a specific topic, and the columns represent fields, or items that make up each record. A relational database may contain names, addresses, phone numbers, and other information, for example, about your clients or vendors. Some popular SQL databses include Oracle7, Sybase, IBM DB2, and Microsoft SQL Server.

SQL databases are not considered in the groupware range of applications. Relational databases deal with highly structured data that's accessed using SQL; whereas groupware products deal with highly unstructured data. Databases contain tables of data; groupware documents may contain text, images, mail, faxes, and/or bulletin boards. The end user of a database can receive data, in table form, about any information within the database; however, the end user doesn't normally create and contribute data to the database. The end user of groupware, however, can create documents of various kinds to add to the whole, contributing information that others can use and benefit from.

Often, workflow applications coordinate other applications to complete the tasks; working with e-mail, databases, and other programs means a more powerful and effective result.

Groupware Applications

There are many commercial groupware applications that can perform one or more of the five basic technologies: document management, e-mail, scheduling, conferencing, and/or workflow. You might find that one or two groupware programs are all you need to complete your network or perhaps you will need more than that to make collaboration between users effective and efficient. With their growing popularity, groupware applications are becoming more inclusive of basic collaborative technologies.

Microsoft Products

Microsoft has created several groupware products you can use with NT, each with its own functions and advantages. Some products offer more of the groupware technologies than others; however, you may want to combine two or more products for use on your server. Following are a few of the more popular groupware products made by Microsoft.

Microsoft Exchange

Microsoft includes an e-mail program with NT—Windows Messaging—that you can use for e-mail within your network and through the Internet (see Chapter 11 for more information). Windows Messaging is a small part of the larger Microsoft Exchange Server, an add-on product that Microsoft bills as an e-mail server with integrated groupware.

Microsoft Exchange is a client/server-based e-mail, fax, and voice mail application that is built to work with NT Server. There are many advantages to using Exchange. One advantage is that it's a Microsoft program so it's completely compatible with NT; also, it's easier to learn each successive Microsoft program because of similar interfaces, toolbars, and features particular to all Microsoft applications. Finally, Microsoft Exchange works well with NT Server and enables you to take advantage of NT's security features.

Exchange uses public folders to which users can post messages. These folders are displayed in a hierarchical configuration so users can see how the messages relate to each other. Therefore, tracing the initial message and all replies to it is easy and efficient. Exchange also includes the following:

- Each client has a universal inbox in which he/she can collect, filter, sort, and reply to messages.
- Internet mail fully supports simple mail transfer protocol (SMTP) and multipurpose Internet mail extensions (MIME). SMTP is used to get and set status information about a host on a TCP/IP network. MIME is a standard utility for specifying the format of messages; MIME enables the exchange of objects, character sets, and multimedia between different computer systems.
- 1500 concurrent users are supported on a Pentium 133 with 64M RAM and even more users on larger computers.

- Exchange enables communication over network links at speeds from 9600bps dial-up to 11Mbs FDDI fiber networks.

- Integrates with NT and BackOffice for expanded networking services.

- Supports workflow with inbox and out-of-office assistants that can automate e-mail.

Microsoft Outlook

Microsoft Outlook is a scheduling/e-mail program that ships with Microsoft Office 97. Although not a full-fledged groupware application, it is a capable scheduling and e-mail application which provides the following:

- Various e-mail features and tools, including mail management and storage, address book, text formatting and spell checking, file attachment utilities, and so on

- Calendar and scheduling features, such as appointments and events planning, automatic invitations to meetings and appointments, and a contact list for addressing and scheduling

- Task list tool for managing tasks, or to-do lists

- Journal for recording phone calls, meetings, and other important events during your work day

- Full and useful integration of the various utilities—e-mail, journal, task list, and calendar

- Internet services

Figure 13.1 shows the Outlook Inbox. You can open and read mail, reply or forward mail, save, delete, archive, sort, and otherwise manipulate mail messages in the Inbox. Using the Outlook bar, located down the left side of the window, you can choose whether to work in the Inbox, Calendar, Contacts, Tasks, Journal, or Notes feature.

Note: Microsoft also has plans to add the Microsoft Conference Server to its BackOffice suite of servers. The Microsoft Conference Server will allow users to launch real-time conferencing applications (such as NetMeeting).

Figure 13.2 shows the Outlook Calendar, in which you can create, edit, and view appointments and meetings, create and edit your to-do list, and even send invitations to colleagues to any scheduled meeting or appointment in your calendar.

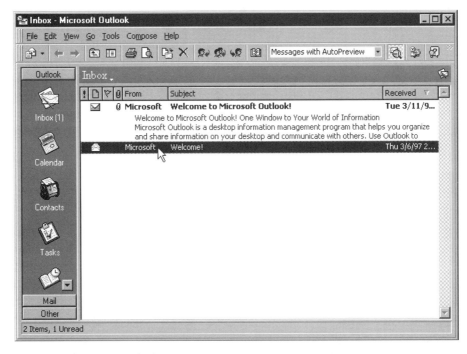

Figure 13.1 Use Microsoft Outlook for e-mail.

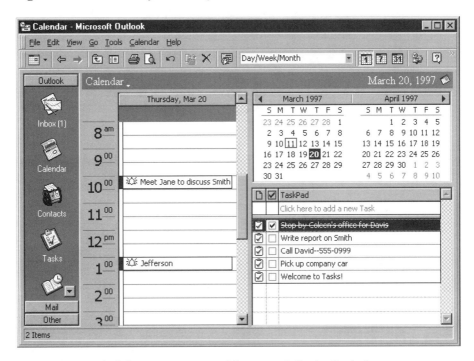

Figure 13.2 Schedule appointments and keep a task list in Outlook.

Lotus Products

Lotus offers e-mail and scheduling products—such as Organizer and cc:Mail—but more importantly, Lotus produces Notes. Used in corporations all over the world, Notes is the most comprehensive groupware product on the market today. This section introduces Notes, as well as Organizer and cc:Mail.

Lotus Notes/Domino

Lotus Notes and Domino are probably the most popular, and important, full-fledged groupware product on the market today. Notes can handle all five of the basic technologies of groupware, as previously described. Those who have used Notes successfully are great proponents of the product. The only problem you will find with Notes is that it is difficult to administer, often requiring a full-time administrator just to handle Notes, Domino, and its processes.

Figure 13.3 shows Notes 4.5 on a Windows 95 client; the workspace displays the Mail tab with mail databases and address books. In Notes, even the mail win-

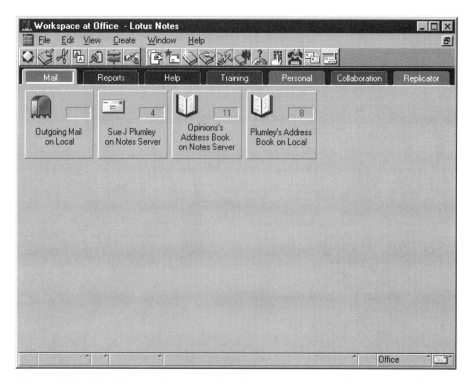

Figure 13.3 *The Notes workspace enables the user to organize document databases on various tabs.*

dow is a database, or collection of documents; in the case of the mail database, the documents are mail messages.

Note: Notes is the long-time name of the groupware product; however, in the latest version of Notes—version 4.5—Lotus chose to call the server application Domino and the client application Notes. Notes was renamed to Domino to emphasize its new connectivity to the world wide web (WWW); Domino inlcudes an HTTP server, translates Notes into HTML, enables you to access Notes databases and views via a Web browser, create and edit Notes documents, read and reply to Notes mail, and more.

Figure 13.4 shows a training document database in which document titles are listed in various categories. These documents are stored on the server and available to all network users. Users may also add documents to the database, print documents, copy documents, and so on. Only users with permissions (granted through Notes) can add or change documents in the database.

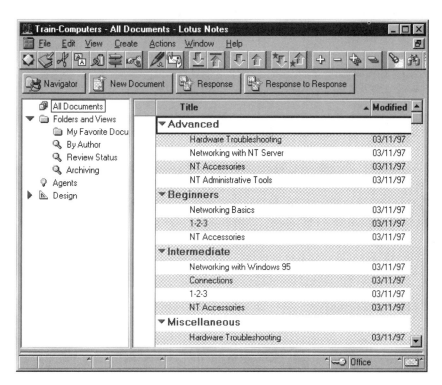

Figure 13.4 *Notes databases are an excellent document management and distribution tool.*

Notes enables users to share information, e-mail, and interact using the following functions:

- Document database server that stores and manages documents that include text, images, audio, and video.
- E-mail server that manages multiuser client access to mail, including e-mail features such as type-ahead addressing, collapsible sections, prevent copying items feature, and so on.
- A backbone server that supports mail-routing and database replication. Notes features synchronous replication between servers and between clients and servers, including mobile users.
- Distributed services, such as electronic signatures, security, and access control.
- Server-based agents that run when scheduled to distribute mail and perform other workflow operations.
- Internet integration through SMTP support, TCP/IP connectivity, for HTML browsers, and so on.
- Included is a bulletin board service for conferencing and a calendar for scheduling.

Figure 13.5 shows an informational document that introduces one of Notes discussion databases. Users can read, reply, and post new messages to the database for easier, more efficient collaboration between colleagues.

Internet Access with Lotus

TIP: Additionally, Lotus supplies integrated Internet access for Notes with Inter-Notes Web Publisher and Notes 4.5 Web Navigator. The Web Navigator is a Web browser built-in to Notes 4.5 you can use to browse the Web, save Web pages to a Notes document, send Web pages to other Notes users via Notes mail, retrieve previously viewed Web pages without reconnecting to the Internet, and much more.

The InterNotes Web Publisher is a server application that converts Notes databases into HTML files and copies them to the HTTP server so people browsing the Web can retrieve them. The Web Publisher enables you to convert Notes documents, publish Notes database as HTML pages, maintains HTML links, extends a full-text Notes search capability to Web users, and much more.

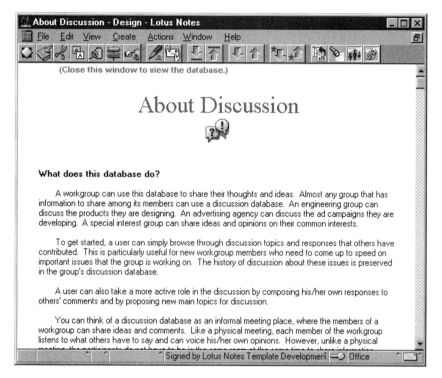

Figure 13.5 *Use Notes' discussion database to collaborate over the network.*

cc:Mail

cc:Mail is another Lotus product that supplies e-mail capabilities to networks. It enables the users to read, reply, and forward mail, use an address book, organize and store mail, archive messages, attach files, import and export text, use an included bulletin board, and more.

Lotus currently has several versions of cc:Mail on the market. Version 6 displays an interface more in tune with Windows NT 3.51, although you can easily use it on a Windows 95 or NT computer. Many of the dialog boxes and windows look as if they belong in an older version of Windows, such as Windows for Workgroups, but the program works well with NT Server 4.0 and is easy to administer and run.

cc:Mail 7 is Lotus' integration product to help users change over to Notes. The version 7 interface is very similar to that of Notes and administration is more difficult than with version 6 of cc:Mail. The version 7 interface is built for Windows 95 and NT.

Organizer

You can purchase Lotus Organizer separately, with Lotus SmartSuite, or you can get a copy with cc:Mail. Organizer is a scheduling and calendar program that enables the user to schedule appointments, meetings, and create and use to-do lists, similarly to Microsoft's Outlook program. Using Organizer with a mail program, such as Notes or cc:Mail, you can also send invitations to meetings and receive responses from the invitees.

Organizer has long been a scheduling standard in businesses and corporations. Since it is a common and long-time Lotus product, you can expect that it is intuitive, easy to learn and use, and works perfectly with other Lotus products.

Multitasking and Applications

Multitasking, the simultaneous execution of two or more programs and/or processes in one computer, is one of NT's capabilities. During multitasking, applications borrow CPU time for short bursts before relinquishing control to other applications. Some applications, however, tie up the CPU for longer periods of time while others never relinquish control. NT uses pre-emptive multitasking to manage multiple applications. The CPU cycles through all processes running to ensure all processes and programs get a chance, thus making it unlikely that any one program or process will tie up the CPU for too long a time.

Applications running on NT are assigned a priority, from 1 to 31, with 7 being the standard value. The priority determines how much attention the process or program gets from the CPU. Only 32-bit applications can start at a priority higher than 7.

By default, NT assigns the highest priority to the applications working in the foreground (the one in the active window) and the least priority to the applications in the background. By switching windows from one open application to another, however, you switch priorities. You can change multitasking priorities so that you specify foreground and background priority levels.

Open the Control Panel, double-click the System icon, and choose the Performance tab. In the Application Performance area, you can slide the selector between None and Maximum. To optimize the performance of applications running in the foreground, slide the slider all the way to Maximum; to assign a better performance for background programs but still give the foreground apps more processor time, set the slider to the middle. Setting the slider to None gives foreground and background equal amounts of processor time.

Working with NT and the Internet

Windows NT Server includes several applications you can use with the Internet; three in particular are the Internet Information Server, the Internet Explorer, and FrontPage. The Internet Information Server (IIS) is a network file and application server. You can use the Internet Information Server to administer Web pages, ftp (file transfer protocol) services, and gopher services on your Web server either on the Internet or in your corporate intranet.

The Internet Explorer is a Web browser used to view Web pages, send and receive e-mail, view news groups, and so on, either over the Internet or on your corporate intranet. FrontPage is a set of tools you can use to author and format Web pages in HTML format. You can create Web pages to publish to the Internet or to an intranet, advertising your company or your services, distributing important company data, or for social or entertainment purposes.

Understanding the Internet Information Server

The Internet Information Server (IIS) is an application you run on a computer that already runs the NT Server operating system; IIS enables you to distribute files and documents over a Web service (Internet or intranet) so others can view those documents using a Web browser. Using the IIS with your network enables you to share information with others—information about your company, products, services, employees, customers, company policies, and so much more.

One important factor about IIS is that it transmits the data in HTML using HTTP over a TCP/IP network. HTML is the format of the document, including fonts, type size, page color, and the links that connect one document to another. HTTP is a protocol that manages the links between one hypertext document and another. And TCP/IP is one method by which your computer communicates with another computer over your intranet. So IIS transmits data in HTML format, including links, over your network from server to client.

The Internet Information Server includes an Internet Service Manager that enables you to administer the program from a single location. It also includes a WWW service that uses HTTP as its protocol. The Internet Information Server also includes the ftp and Gopher services; both of these services enable the transfer of files over the Internet.

The Internet Information Server uses the same directory database of user and group accounts that NT Server uses, thus eliminating the need for additional user administration. You can also use NT tools—such as the Event Viewer, SNMP, and TCP/IP configuration—with the IIS to make administration easier.

> ### Intranet versus Internet
>
> The Internet, as you know, is made up of hundreds of thousands of networks, connected together to share information and ideas. The different networks rely on every kind of network technology from local area networks to phone lines to fiber optics to satellites that enable the transfer of information from one computer to another.
>
> Many people use the Internet for traditional network functions like sharing documents and transferring files; but the Internet is really meant for sharing information—for business, entertainment, and social interaction—in the form of text, images, sound, and video. The tools used to enable this sharing of information are many and varied, but you can use NT to create and view data on the Internet. NT's Internet Information Server, Internet Explorer, and Front Page enable you to publish information for anyone connected to the Internet to see and to view your company's information as well as others.
>
> An intranet is similar to the Internet but on a much smaller scale, extending only among those users connected to your business network. An intranet is a private network that uses Internet tools, software, and protocols to distribute information and data to the computers connected to the network. An intranet may or may not be connected to the Internet.
>
> On a network used for an intranet, there should be at least one server, a powerful computer running the NT Server 4.0 software. You may have additional servers, running NT Server or another network operating system (such as Novell NetWare), but you will need to identify one NT server as your Web server for your intranet.
>
> You place electronic copies of documents—such as reports, employee handbooks, forms, letters, schedules, and so on—on the Web server in the form of HTML documents that can be accessed by users on your network. Users access the Web of information using the Internet Explorer or some other Web browser on their workstations; thereby sharing data and information that helps the users collaborate over the network and improving communications, morale, and the quality of work in your office.

Following is a list of services you can supply to your intranet or your Web page on the Internet with the Internet Information Server:

- Publish a number of Web pages.
- Publish a newsletter, sales information, employee handbook, and other pertinent data for all to see and use.

- Provide access to databases across the network.

- Customize workgroup applications so that information-sharing is more efficient.

- Provide dial-up access to an intranet for employees who are out of the office.

You can install the IIS using the Network dialog box on the NT Server computer. Choose to add a service in the Services tab; in the Select Network Service dialog box, select the Microsoft Internet Information Server and choose OK. You will need your NT Server installation CD to complete the task.

For the most part, IIS runs without too much management; however, the Internet Service Manager enables you to configure and manage the Web site and other services on the server. The Internet Service Manager supplies the tools to manage, among other things, the following:

- Who can use your server and what resources they are permitted to access. You can block certain individuals or groups, or even certain computers from gaining access to the server.

- Logging of the server's activities that you can view and study. You also can specify how often a log is created and where the log is stored.

- The traffic on the server. You can control the maximum amount of traffic so as to better serve those who visit the Web sites.

- Services such as the Web, Gopher, and ftp. You can start, stop, and/or pause the services—WWW or Web services are available on intranet or Internet, but Gopher and ftp are only used over the Internet.

TIP: Use of the IIS is beyond the scope of this book; however, you can find more information about the Internet Information Server in NT on-line Help.

Understanding the Internet Explorer

NT Server comes with the Internet Explorer, a tool you can use with the IIS to take full advantage of the Web services. The Internet Explorer, as previously mentioned, is a Web browser—a tool that enables you to view HTML documents and hypertext links. You can use the Internet Explorer to view, or browse, the Internet or an intranet within your corporation or office. Figure 13.6 shows the Internet Explorer on an NT member server, accessing the corporate intranet.

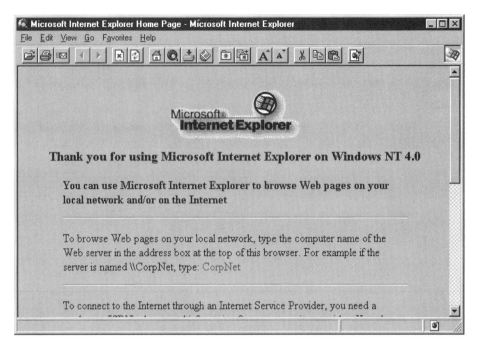

Figure 13.6 *Use the Internet Explorer to browse Web pages.*

TIP: The Internet Explorer also comes with a Windows 95 operating system and you can even download a version of the Explorer for a Windows for Workgroups client from Microsoft's Web site.

Advantages of the Internet Explorer

The Internet Explorer (IE) is the perfect Web browser to use with NT and Windows 95, mainly because the program ships with the two operating systems. In addition, there are other benefits to using IE, as follows:

- The Explorer looks similar to Microsoft's Office products in that it includes a title bar, menu bar, toolbar, document area, status bar, and so on. These similarities mean less time spent by your users, since they're already familiar with Windows and most likely one or more of the Office applications.

- Your users can use the Internet Explorer to access intranet Web pages, send e-mail, access corporate databases, and so on; thus the users feel more comfortable using a single application for several major tasks.

- If you use links to non-HTML files, the IE automatically displays the file with the proper viewer or downloads it to the local hard drive. So, if your users come across a file they need but cannot view with the Web browser, the IE will take care of accessing that file for them.

Configuring the Internet Explorer

Before you can use the Internet Explorer, either on a computer running NT or Windows 95, you must prepare by adding some hardware and software. Following are some general steps to take before you can connect to the Internet or an intranet. See Appendix C for more information about installing and configuring TCP/IP.

1. Install and configure a modem or configure access to a modem over the network. Use the Modem icon in the Control Panel to access the Add Modem Wizard.

2. If you plan to use the Explorer for the Internet, acquire an ISP (Internet Service Provider) or other access to the Net. You will need to know the following: username, password, access phone number, host's name and domain name, the Domain Name Server (DNS) server address, IP adress, authentication procedure, Subnet mask, and Default gateway. Choose a PPP (point-to-point) account, if your provider offers it.

3. You must install the TCP/IP protocol to the computer from the Network icon in the Control Panel. Choose the Protocols tab, Add button, select TCP/IP.

4. Select the TCP/IP Protocol and choose the Properties button. You will need to specify an IP address and enter the other information required. If you plan to use the connection for the Internet, you will need to install Dial-Up Networking first. When you're prompted to restart the computer, choose No, then go to step 5. If you plan to use the Explorer with an intranet, you're ready to restart the computer, so choose Yes; when the computer restarts, you can access the Internet Explorer.

5. To use the IE with the Internet, install Dial-Up Networking if it's not already installed. Open the Control Panel and double-click the Add/Remove Programs icon. You will need the NT installation CD to complete the process.

6. After you install Dial-Up Networking, open My Computer and double-click the Dial-Up Networking icon. Follow the directions in the Wizard for setting up your connection to your access provider. This is where you will need to know the phone number to dial, server type, terminal window information, and so on.

After you complete the steps, you can open the IE and access either the Internet or your intranet. Before you can access the intranet, you may need to know the address of the Internet Information Server and of the home page on the Internet Information Server; see Windows NT Help for more information or check out *Building Your Intranet with Windows NT 4.0* by Stephen Thomas and Sue Plumley (John Wiley & Sons, Inc., 1997).

Using the Internet Explorer

Depending on the version of Internet Explorer you're using, you will see various menus and toolbars containing shortcut buttons you can use to maneuver around the Explorer and find information over the Internet or intranet. Menus enable you to open various Web pages, print data, view tools, customize the look of the program, get help, and keep a list of favorite Web page sites you like to visit regularly.

Toolbar buttons provide shortcuts to many of the menu commands. Clicking a toolbar button displays a dialog box or performs an action. If you're in doubt about the function of a toolbar button, position the mouse pointer over the button and wait a second or two. A small box will appear with the name of the button or its function.

In addition to toolbars and menus, another excellent tool featured in most Web pages is the HTML link, as shown in Figure 13.7. A link is a connection, or bridge, between two Web pages. Most Web pages contain many, various links to other pages on the Internet or on an intranet; links enable you to view information, often related, on the original Web page topic.

The mouse pointer changes to a pointing hand when you place the mouse on a link. Links are usually underlined and in a different color text than the rest of the page. In the figure, these links are actual Internet addresses; however, links

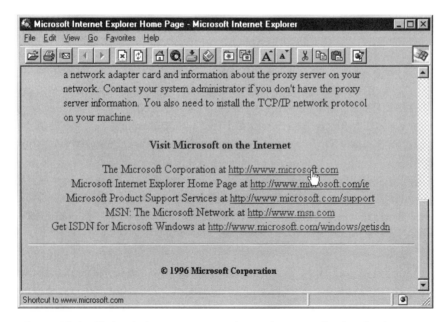

Figure 13.7 Click a link to jump to another Web page with related information.

may also be a word, phrase, or even an image or graphic on which you click to jump to another Web page.

Note: Windows 95 version B includes not only an Internet Explorer but also Internet Mail and Internet News applications you can use to send and receive e-mail and to visit and join newsgroups on the Internet.

Understanding Front Page

NT also comes with FrontPage, a tool for authoring Web pages and formatting them in HTML for use with the Internet or an intranet. Front page includes the tools you can use to create and maintain a Web site—such as managing the links and building Web pages. Included with FrontPage are four components you can use to construct and manage a Web: the Personal Web Server, the FrontPage Explorer, the Editor, and the To-Do List. These components work separately and together to accomplish their specialized tasks.

The FrontPage Editor is an instrument you use to create and edit Web pages in the HTML format. The Editor includes many formatting features you find in a word processor—including a formatting toolbar, Format menu, status bar, and many page-layout features—that you can use to create a page using HTML standard tags, so it can be viewed by any Web browser.

Figure 13.8 shows the FrontPage Editor with text added to start a Web page. Notice the formatting toolbar you can use to change the size, alignment, and style of the text you add to the page. You also can use special built-in templates on which to build your Web pages.

The FrontPage Explorer is a tool you use to create, manage, and maintain a Web site. The FrontPage Explorer looks similar to the Windows NT Explorer in that it contains two window panes, each offering a view of the files in your Web site. You can view all of the pages belonging to a Web site and the links each page contains in both an outline format and a graphical representation of the Web contents.

A third component, the Personal Web Server (PWS), enables you to build a Web site on a standalone PC. You don't have to work on the host server while you're creating your Web pages, thus slowing the server and keeping it from its daily tasks with your users. The PWS works in conjunction with the FrontPage Editor and the Explorer.

Finally, the FrontPage To Do List enables you to create and manage a list of tasks you need to complete to manage a Web site. Using the To Do List, you can organize your tasks by noting to whom you've assigned the tasks, a priority code

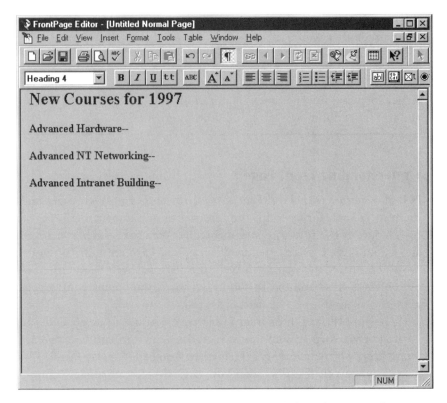

Figure 13.8 *Create a Web page and format it similarly to formatting documents in a word processor.*

of importance, the page to which the task is linked, and a description of the task. When you open a task that's linked to a page, the page or file automatically opens so you can complete the task. You also can sort the tasks and indicate when a task is completed.

Summary

In this chapter, you've been introduced to various groupware and communications applications—such as Lotus Notes, Microsoft Exchange, Internet Information Server, and the Internet Explorer. You will find detailed installation and implementation instructions about any of these programs in the documentation that comes with the product. This chapter is meant to introduce some possible routes to enhancing your corporate network with NT and available applications.

PART
VI

Advanced NT Server

14 Expanding the Network

As your business grows, so grows the amount of data, number of users, and requirements for a successfully run business. You will probably need to add one or more servers to your network, which will add to your administration responsibilities, as well. Also, you will need to add more workstations. You should plan for the expansion so that administration, security, and system management is orderly and efficient.

Without the proper foundation and knowledge, your network could easily become out of control before you know it. NT facilitates network expansion by providing tools and features that enable you to seamlessly add servers and workstations to the system. This chapter contains advice for planning network growth and steps for using NT's tools to add and manage additional servers and workstations on the network. This chapter focuses on the following:

- Planning for expanding your network
- Adding and managing users and groups
- Managing servers, directories, and users on the network
- Replicating data from computer to computer

Planning for Expansion

As your company grows, you will need to add workstations for additional employees, then add servers to take care of the needs of your users. Planning for expansion by estimating the number of machines to add, carefully widening your directory structure, reviewing user rights and security policies, and so on, will mean a smoother transition for your users and easier administration for you.

If you have not yet trained and implemented network assistants who can help you with administration of such tasks as printing management, file organization, user and group additions, and so on, consider adding those assistants now. If you have people to help you administer the network, meet with them and ask for suggestions, problems, and requirements they have in mind for network expansion. Each department head, for example, knows what his or her staff needs and can identify any deficiencies in the present system to help you plan for the future.

System Considerations

If you've followed the advice in this book thus far, your NT network follows the client/server model. Expansion from a peer-to-peer model is not acceptable; you will never be able to administer a large network unless it's client/server. You should also be using a domain as opposed to a workgroup plan. You most likely have only one domain in your current setup; Chapter 15 explains more about managing multiple domains.

If you're not using client/server and domain models in your current setup, make the necessary changes now, before you try to expand your system. If you continue to use workgroups and/or peer-to-peer, the security breaches, network traffic, crashes, and user complaints will soon convince you to make the change. Other system considerations include the following:

- *File System*: If you didn't install your first server (primary domain controller) using the NTFS file system, you should consider changing to NTFS before installing and configuring new servers to your network. If all servers utilize NTFS, security and services for a single domain and multiple domains are more useful.

- *Protocols*: If you're currently using NetBEUI or IPX/SPX-compatible instead of TCP/IP, your network can reasonably expand with little or no problem. However, if you're considering eventually moving to the Internet or creating a corporate intranet, you would be better off changing over to TCP/IP now before adding multiple workstations and servers. See Appendix C for more information about TCP/IP.

- *Workstation Hardware*: If you're planning to purchase new workstations to add to your network or upgrade existing computers, invest in equipment that will run either Windows 95 or Windows NT. Using the higher-end client software will enable users more access to services over multiple servers and domains.

- *Server Hardware*: If you're planning to purchase or upgrade additional computers for servers, invest in the best computer you can afford. Buying powerful, memory-loaded, expansive hard drives in the first place is much easier and more efficient than trying to upgrade equipment later, while multiple users are attached to and using the server.

- *Cabling, Routers, Network Cards*: Check with your hardware person for advice about your current networking hardware configuration and what will be needed to expand.

- *Peripherals and Printers*: In your planning, make sure you will have enough UPS, tape devices, modems, and printers to service all of your workstations and servers. Consider the number of users, amounts of data that will be backed up, usage of the Internet or dial-up networking, and so on; and make sure you add a UPS for each server. As for adding printers, consider how fast each printer can print, resolution needed for various print jobs, specialized printing needs, and so on.

Licensing

Licensing for the operating system and various software programs you use on your server is another item you need to plan for. For your software programs, check with the application's documentation to discover how licensing works. Applications usually grant network licensing to specific numbers of users or workstations; if you expand your network, you must purchase additional licenses.

For NT, licensing is very specific. Each server requires a separate license and each client computer accessing a server requires a separate license; Microsoft's licensing model enables you to add only what you need to your network. Microsoft also includes two client licensing modes with NT (and certain other BackOffice server products): Per Server and Per Seat.

With Per Server licensing, each Client Access License is assigned to one server and allows one connection to that server. Services on a Per Server licensed computer include file and/or print services, Macintosh connectivity, File and Print Services for NetWare, and Remote Access Services.

With Per Server licensing, you must have at least as many Client Access Licenses on the server as the number of clients that can attach to that server. When you install the operating system, you specify the number of concurrent connections. If you add users, you must purchase additional Client Access Licenses; if the number of concurrent connections exceeds the specified amount, no more clients will be allowed to connect to the server until enough users disconnect to get below the specified limit.

With Per Seat licensing, a Client Access License is assigned to each specific computer that accesses the server; so with Per Seat mode, a client can access any network server running NT. This is the best licensing mode for networks where multiple users can access multiple servers.

TIP: Users with a Per Seat Client Access License will not be allowed access to a server with a Per Server licensing mode, if the Per Server computer has reached its limit of connections.

You will use Per Seat mode with multiple domains and servers; for example, using the NT Server software on a computer for file and print sharing and on other servers in the domain or domains as intranet or database servers makes the Per Seat mode appropriate so clients can legally access the various servers. Using NT Server on a Remote Access server, on the other hand, you could choose the Per Server mode for more efficient use of the licensing agreement.

So, if you have only one server, choose Per Server; you can change the licensing once, later, to the Per Seat mode if you add more servers or domains. If you have multiple servers, choose the Per Seat mode. Within one or multiple domains, you can mix the licensing mode so that the mode suits the server.

Microsoft's Client Access Licenses are required separately from any licensing you receive with Windows 95 or Windows NT Workstation. You must purchase the Microsoft Client Access License separately from the desktop operating system to connect to a Microsoft server product, such as NT Server.

Check List

Before expanding the network, there are some general tasks and procedures you should make sure you are currently practicing. The following check list reviews some groundwork you will want to lay before going any further with your network expansion plans:

- *Backups*: Make sure you perform a complete system backup of programs, data files, user and group information, Registry files, and other data on the server and workstations. Augment your backups daily, especially throughout the transition phase.

- *Event viewer*: Check the events logged in the Viewer for any equipment failure, application errors, or system problems; before you make any changes, correct all problems. Also, make sure you're logging all possible events and continue to do so throughout the transition. See Chapter 11 for more information about the Event Viewer.

- *Security policies*: Review your security policies, including group rights and resource permissions, account policies, and so on, to make sure only those who need access are granted access. As the network expands, servers and the data they contain are harder to police.

- *Files and Folders*: Check your directory structure, available hard disk space, current file and folder names, and locate and delete any extraneous files and folders. Clean up the server before adding more machines to the network.

One or Multiple Domains

As you know, NT uses a domain structure to organize users in the database for naming and organizational purposes. You can use a domain to define one computer, a department or office, a building, city, or any other site designation you want to use in your network. Using a workgroup model, you will not be able to effectively expand your network.

You can easily expand your network using one domain or many. Technically, up to 26,000 users and groups can be successfully managed in a single domain, if you have enough servers capable of handling the network resources. Alternatively, multiple domains enable ease of administration, better organization of departments, and more efficient use of resources. Here are a few things to remember about domains:

- There is only one primary domain controller per domain and the first NT Server you install in a domain must be designated as the primary domain controller.

- There should be at least one backup domain controller in each domain to help ensure the safety of the user database, in case something happens to the primary domain controller.

- Member servers may also be added to a domain. Member servers can be used as workstations, file servers, print servers, and so on.

- The computers that belong to one domain share common security policies. Computers that belong to multiple domains can either share security policies or be limited in access to certain resources, as designated by the administrator.

- A user, with permissions, can access multiple servers and resources that reside in different domains.

- The network and resources are easier to view and recognize by both users and administrators when a network is grouped into domains.

One Domain

If your network consists of one or two servers and less than 200 users, you will probably want to continue to use one NT domain for your entire system. Install one primary domain controller and at least one backup domain controller. You can split the file, print, Web, and other services between the two servers or you could install member servers to help handle multiple services. This single domain model enables you to centralize the management of your user accounts. You can administer all network servers and domain accounts on the PDC.

You can certainly add new users to an existing domain as opposed to creating multiple domains. As previously mentioned, up to 26,000 users can be members of one domain as long as your networking hardware can support them. As you add more users to a domain, you must consider the traffic, access rates, software licenses, and other factors affecting your users and your hardware.

First, the more users that must be authenticated, the more power, memory, and disk space you need on the primary domain controller. A server that doesn't have the necessary power and memory will authenticate users slowly and create bottlenecks if used for other services, such as file and print services. A good rule of thumb is to double the RAM when you add a significant number of users. The only real way to know if you need to add memory is to assess the speed at which the server works. If logon is slow, if users complain about the server, if there seem to be a lot of bottlenecks when users access any server in particular, then you should add more RAM.

As for disk space, NT enables you to add multiple hard disks to a computer; using the Disk Administrator, you can manage disks, volumes, stripe sets, and so on, of all disks attached. Keep in mind that you not only need disk space for adding new users, files, programs, or other data to a server, but also adequate disk space for the operating system to work. A nearly filled disk will prevent certain processes from completing, so if you find errors or problems with applications, administrative tools, or other processes, you need to expand your hard disk space.

Another problem with using one domain for a growing network of users is traffic to and from one server. You may be able to alleviate some of the traffic problem by changing your cabling system, depending on the type of cabling you're using. You also could add routers and/or switches to help direct traffic flow. See Chapter 3 for more information and contact the person you've hired to take care of your hardware for help, as well. Another solution to heavy network traffic is to add servers, as discussed in the next section.

Multiple Domains

The advantage of adding multiple domains to your network is in the administration and organization of your company. Using one domain can be difficult to administer because all users are massed together on one primary domain controller.

NT's Performance Monitor

NT's Performance Monitor (Start, Programs, Administrative Tools, Performance Monitor) is a tool for measuring performance on the server or other computers on the network. You can monitor processors, memory, cache, threads, and processes for information about device usage, delays, and other elements that affect how the server is handling network traffic and system processes.

With the Performance Monitor, you can collect data from the current session or from multiple computers simultaneously. You can view that data in any of the four views offered in the program: Chart, Alert, Log, or Report. Chart view enables you to create a chart to view data for easy analysis; Log view stores the information in a file for later use; Report view displays a report of events for analysis, printing, charting, and so on; an Alert view offers data about events that exceed user-defined limits.

After collecting data in the Performance Monitor, you can analyze the information in several ways. You could export data to a spreadsheet, for example, or use Report data in a chart. The Performance Monitor doesn't give you advice on how to improve performance of the server; it just tracks and records data for you.

For more information about the Performance Monitor, use Windows NT Help or see John Ruley's *Networking Windows NT 4.0*, (John Wiley and Sons, Inc.).

With multiple domains, you can separate users into logical divisions, such as offices, buildings, departments, job descriptions, workgroups, or some other designation that fits into your corporate strategy.

TIP: One great advantage to dividing users and groups into domains is that you can also divide administration responsibilities among your network assistants, managers, supervisors, or other appointees.

There are other advantages to using multiple domains. Each domain, remember, uses its own primary domain controller, plus any other servers you've added to the domain; therefore, authentication and other network traffic is also divided. Resources may also be assigned to various servers within various domains, thus alleviating bottlenecks for popular printers, much needed files, or other resources.

NT also enables you to set security policies so that users can access resources across domains. For example, a user in the first domain can, if she has permission, use a printer in the second domain. Similarly, a group in the third domain can access, with permissions, files and folders in the first and second domains. You also can limit access by any group or individual to any resource within the multiple domains. Chapter 15 describes some domain models you can use to set up multiple domains in your organization as well as security issues related to multiple domains.

As for hardware, you may consider the requirements of multiple domains a disadvantage. Instead of upgrading one computer to superpower status, you must install one fairly well-equipped computer as a primary domain controller to each domain. Naturally, you will also want a backup domain controller in each domain and probably at least one member server as a file, printer, intranet, CD-ROM, database, or other resource server. Since users can access resources in each domain, one member server per domain will likely be sufficient, depending on the resources available.

So establishing multiple domains will cost you more for hardware and operating systems. The cost of workstations, however, would remain the same as if you were using a single domain. You should weigh the possibilities and choose the solution that best fits your situation. You can, of course, change your mind after establishing a single domain by adding domain controllers; however, it's best if you can save yourself the extra work by deciding on a course of action first.

TIP: There are two common methods of organizing multiple domains: the single master domain model and the multiple master domain model, the easiest being the single master domain. For more information about domain models, see Chapters 4 and 15.

User and Group Considerations

Adding users to a network affects much more than your user list in the User Manager for Domains. You must also think about the users' access to servers and other resources, network traffic, and ease of administration. You want your expanded network to work smoothly, providing quick access and efficient use of your resources, while spending as little time as possible managing the network.

You may find, as you expand network services, more and more remote users—those people who work from home or on the road. NT provides a Remote Access Service (RAS) for the server to enable remote users to connect and access network resources. Client computers running Windows 95, NT Workstation, or NT Server include a dial-up networking utility that enables users to access RAS on the server.

A Few Basics

Before you add new users to your network, consider some organizational matters. For example, will the new users require new groups and new security policies or will they fit into existing groups? Are you going to use only one domain in which to place all users or multiple domains for a division of users and groups? Do you want significant control over what the user can see and do on his or her computer or will you give the most control to the user? Will all users be in the office or will there be remote users as well? Making these decisions before adding new users will influence other factors, such as whether you need new servers and other decisions affecting the network configuration, such as cabling, server types, physical setup of the network, and so on.

When you add users to your network, you will want to organize them into groups to make security administration easier. If you're using a single domain, you probably will add new users to existing groups; but you also can create new groups in the User Manager for Domains. If you're adding new users and groups to a domain, remember you can copy user and group accounts to make creating new ones easier by building from a base set of configurations. See Chapter 6 for more information.

Another consideration for your network users and groups is to make sure the rights you assign are appropriate to the group. Check existing group rights before assigning new users to that group, in case you've forgotten about an existing right or ability. When you add more users to the network, security becomes even more important. You cannot constantly monitor the use of network resources, so you must let the operating system limit access for you.

Additionally, you can choose the amount of control you want to exert over your users by supplying user profiles and/or logon scripts. You may, for example, choose to set some or all of the users' desktop, application, and other configurations so that workstations running NT or Windows 95 look and act the same. On the other hand, you may want to allow the users to customize their own desktops and applications, thus exercising less power over their work space. NT enables you to create and apply both user profiles and logon scripts for workstations running NT Workstation, NT Server, or Windows 95.

Remote Services

NT provides excellent tools for remote services to help users who telecommute to attach to the server and use network resources. Dial-Up Networking is a feature that enables one computer to attach to the network over a phone line, connecting to remote servers and networks. A person working from home, for instance, or from on the road, could dial up the office network to access resources using Dial-Up Networking. Remote Access Service is an NT utility that enables remote users to dial in to the office, connect to their office computer, then access the server and network.

Dial-Up Networking on the Client

To use remote services, your computer must have a network adapter card and/or modem. Additionally, if you're on an X.25 network, you will need an X.25 smart card. If you're using ISDN, you will need an ISDN adapter. Dial-Up Networking is a feature included in Windows 95 and Windows NT Workstation and Server.

If you didn't install Dial-Up Networking when you installed the client operating system, you can install it using the installation disks or CD-ROM. The Dial-Up Networking icon is located in the My Computer window. If the utility isn't installed, double-clicking the icon results in a dialog box that prompts you to install Dial-Up Networking. Follow the directions in the resulting dialog boxes.

If Dial-Up Networking is installed, double-clicking the Dial-Up Networking icon results in the Add Phonebook Entry Wizard, if there are no entries for connection to a remote network (see Figure 14.1). Windows enables you to use the Wizard for setting up a connection item with all the information you need to dial the remote network.

Follow the instructions to setting up the phonebook entry. Name the entry, or accept the default name; specify the type of connection and password and logon

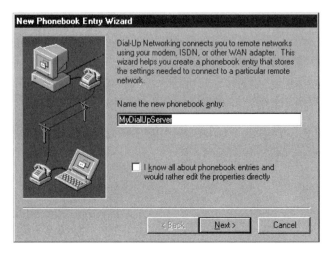

Figure 14.1 *Configure a dial-up connection.*

information; select the modem or other device to dial out; enter the phone number; and enter other information depending on the options and devices you choose. You may need to choose ports, protocols, and other information, as well.

Also, if you choose to configure a connection that uses TCP/IP, such as an Internet connection, you must first install TCP/IP to your computer. See Appendix C for more information.

Next, the Dial-Up Networking dialog box appears in which you choose the phonebook entry you want to dial. Each time you double-click the Dial-Up Networking icon after the first time, the Dial-Up Networking dialog box appears (see Figure 14.2). You can choose to dial the current phonebook entry, click New and add an entry, or click More and select any other entry you've created. When you choose the Dial button, Windows dials the connection item for you.

What happens after connection depends on the type of connection you've made. For example, you may need to enter a password and username to connect to the network, or you may simply connect to the host with no other dialog boxes to fill in.

Installing and Administering RAS

To effectively connect remotely to a work computer, the user installs Dial-Up Networking on the home or remote computer, and RAS on the computer at work—usually the user's workstation. RAS enables the user to connect via dial-up networking to the workstation, then to the server and network resources.

Install RAS from the Network icon in the Control Panel (Start, Settings, Control Panel). In the Network dialog box on the workstation, choose the Services tab

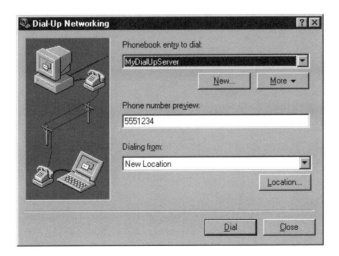

Figure 14.2 *Dial the entry you created.*

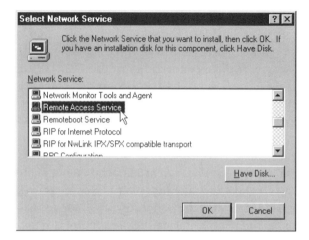

Figure 14.3 *Select the network service to install.*

and the Add button. In the Select Network Service dialog box, choose the Remote Access Service (see Figure 14.3) option and choose OK

The user will need the installation disks or CD-ROM to complete the installation. After installation, the service appears in the Services tab of the Network dialog box. To configure RAS, select the service in the Services tab and choose the Properties button. Figure 14.4 shows the Remote Access Setup dialog box on a computer running NT Workstation.

You can add a port for a newly installed modem or X.25 PAD, remove a port, change port settings, configure RAS settings for the network, and otherwise configure RAS settings in the Remote Access Setup dialog box.

After installing RAS to the workstation, you can manage the RAS service, users, ports, and other elements using the Remote Access Admin tool. Use the ad-

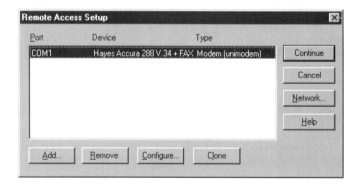

Figure 14.4 *Install drivers, select ports, and otherwise configure RAS.*

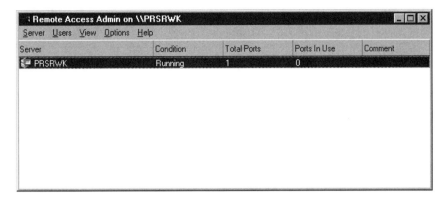

Figure 14.5 *Administer the remote access computer.*

ministration tool to give rights and permissions to users to dial in to the RAS computer, call-back rights, user account details, and so on.

To start the Remote Access Admin, choose Start, Programs, Administrative Tools, and Remote Access Admin. Figure 14.5 shows the Remote Access Admin with the workstation displaying in the window. Select the workstation to be managed, and choose Server (in the case of RAS, the workstation or server with the RAS installed is the "server"). Use the commands to start, stop, or pause the service, set the communications ports, and exit the Remote Access Admin. Use the Users menu to set permissions and call-backs for users, and to designate remote users who can call the RAS server.

Note: Use dial-up networking to mostly get files or for communications; dialing in to run applications from a remote station isn't productive. Running applications—like database, accounting, and so on—is very slow and likely endanger the integrity of your data, since telephone lines aren't reliable. If you're using ISDN, the connection will be faster.

Managing Users

A user profile contains configuration information that includes such settings as network connections, printer connections, personal program groups, desktop arrangement, screen colors, screen savers, window size, and so on. You can create user profiles for one user, a group of users, or all users on the network. These profiles reside on the server and apply to a user each time he or she logs on to the network.

When creating the profiles, you can set up a default user profile and assign it to all users to identify network connections and printer connections; then you can let the user define the rest of the profile him or herself, such as screen colors, window size, and so on. On the other hand, you can create a mandatory user profile that applies to all users, a group of users, or just one user. You set the configuration so that the user has no choices in the matter.

Note: You can manage the user's work environment through user profiles on Windows NT computers and on Windows 95 computers, if user profiles is enabled (see the sidebar later in this chapter).

As soon as a user logs on to the workstation, NT creates a user profile for that user starting with the default user profile that's stored on every computer running Windows NT Workstation, Windows NT Server, and Windows 95. With each setting the user customizes, his or her profile changes. In NT, user profiles are made up of changes the user makes to the Explorer, Taskbar, Printer settings, Control Panel, Accessories, and in NT-based applications. Changes, or modifications, to these settings might include options for mouse and keyboard settings, network configurations, drive mappings, network printer settings, where the Taskbar appears on-screen, and so on.

Logon Scripts versus User Profiles

You can use logon scripts in NT to perform such tasks as creating network connections, starting applications, and controlling the user's working environment. You also can control these things with the User Profiles; both perform similar functions so use the tool that's most comfortable for you.

NT provides several special parameters you can use to specify the user's home directory, processor type, operating system, domain, username, and so on. After creating the logon script in a text file, you enter the path to the file in the User Manager For Domains, User Environment Profile dialog box, on the server; the default path is \WINNT\SYSTEM32\REPL\IMPORT\SCRIPTS. You can name the text file with the user's username. At logon, the domain controller authenticates the user and runs the logon script.

Additionally, you can replicate logon scripts to ensure they are always available for the user. If you set up the primary domain controller as the export server, you can replicate the logon scripts to any backup domain controllers, as explained Chapter 15.

Default User Profile Folder

Generally, each user profile is located in the \WINNT\PROFILES directory. Additionally, the default user profile folder and the all user profile folders are also located in this directory. The default user folder contains an NTuser.dat file and a directory of links to desktop items.

Within a user's profile folder are subfolders containing shortcuts to the desktop (Desktop folder), the Favorites folder, the Network Neighborhood (NetHood folder), most recently used items (Recent folder), templates (Templates folder), program items (Start Menu folder), and so on. Figure 14.6 shows a Windows NT user profile folder in the Explorer. Windows NT Workstation contains one extra folder that Windows 95 does not: the Application folder.

Note: Some folders, such as the NetHood, Recent, and Templates folders are hidden and therefore do not show up in the user's profile folder unless you choose to show all files in the Explorer (View, Options, Show All Files).

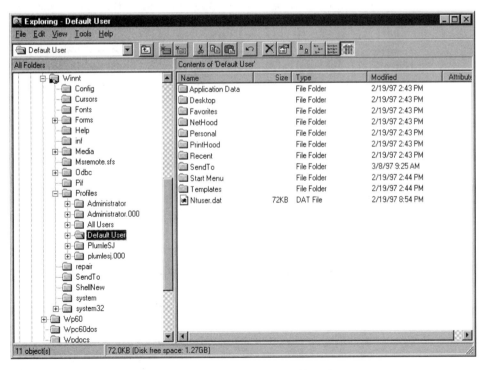

Figure 14.6 *The Default User folder contains user profile information.*

For each new user that logs on to a workstation, NT copies the default user profile folder as that user's profile, makes a copy of the NTuser.dat file (the Registry portion of the user profile), and copies a directory of links to add to the user's profile folder. When the user logs off, any configuration changes are saved to the user's profile folder.

Roaming User Profiles

You can enable a user to create his or her own user profiles, you can create a preconfigured user profile for each user account, or you can create a mandatory user profile for each user. For users to create their own user profiles, you need not change a thing; each time the user logs off, the changes he or she made are saved to the profile and that profile applies when the user logs on again.

Creating the Profile The easiest method for creating a profile is to log on to a computer running NT Workstation or NT Server as a new account and create the profile you want the users to use. You might log on as Profile 1, for example, and set application, desktop, Network Neighborhood, and other settings the way you want them. Log off to save the settings and create the NTuser.dat file. Next, you can copy the file to the appropriate location on the server.

Note: User profiles can restore network connections at logon that were established prior to logging off; however, they cannot create new network connections at logon.

One thing to keep in mind when you're creating user profiles is the hardware on the various workstations. Differences in monitors, video cards, and so on may cause a problem from one machine to the next. You can avoid the problem by creating one profile for a group of users who have the same hardware configurations; create the profile on one of the workstations for which you're designing the profile to be used.

Copying a Preconfigured Roaming Profile To copy a preconfigured roaming profile, you save the user profile to a centralized location (and shared folder) on the server. There are two steps to copying the roaming profile after you create it: Assign the server location to the user's account from the server and copy the file from the workstation on which you created it to the server location.

Assign server locations for specific user profiles in the User Manager for Domains. Figure 14.7 shows the User Environment Profile dialog box in the User

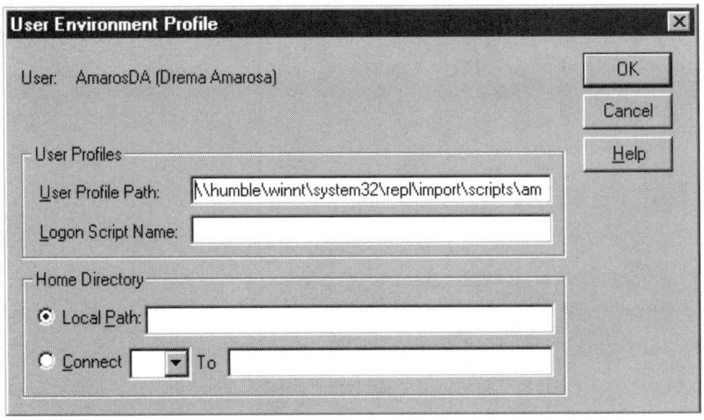

Figure 14.7 *Assign a specific user profile folder to the user.*

Manager for Domains. Open a User Environment Profile dialog box by selecting the user in the User Manager for Domains and choosing File, Properties; in the User Properties dialog box, choose the Profile button. The network path in the text box must be in the following format: *servername**profilesfoldername**username*, as shown in the figure.

After assigning a location on the server, open the System option in the Control Panel on the workstation (Start, Settings, Control Panel). In the System folder, choose the User Profiles tab (only in computers running NT, not those running Windows 95). Figure 14.8 shows the User Profiles tab of the NT Server; NT Workstation tabs look much the same. Select the Copy To button and copy the preconfigured profile to the server.

Note: You cannot copy a user profile in the Explorer or My Computer. The only way you can copy a user profile is in the System option of the Control Panel in the User Profile tab.

This profile becomes the roaming user profile and is available wherever the user logs on. When the user logs off, the roaming user profile is saved to the local machine and a copy is saved to the server. Each time the user logs on, the roaming profile from the server is opened, providing the server is available. If the server isn't available, the local copy of the roaming user profile is used. If the user has never logged onto the computer before, a new local user profile is created. If the server is unavailable and the local copy is opened, the next time the user logs on, NT uses the most recent profile.

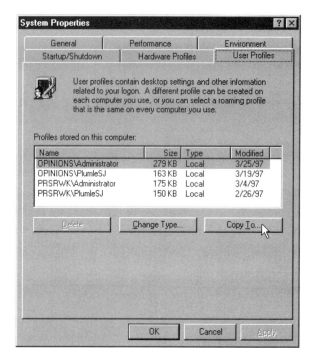

Figure 14.8 *User profiles are listed in the System Properties dialog box.*

Making the User Profile Mandatory To create a mandatory user profile, create the preconfigured roaming user profile as previously described and assign the location on the server. In NT Explorer, rename the NTuser.dat to NTuser.man by selecting the file and choosing File, Rename, then typing in the new name. When you press ENTER to complete the renaming process, NT labels the file as a MAN (mandatory) file. Figure 14.9 shows a default NTuser.dat renamed as a mandatory file; the MAN extension makes the file read-only. Note that you may not see the extension in the Explorer if you have chosen to hide file extensions (View, Options, View tab).

Note: Important: Don't assign a roaming user profile path to a group unless you make the user profiles mandatory. Each time a group member logs off, his or her profile overwrites the user profile on the server; thus, the group's profile would constantly be changing.

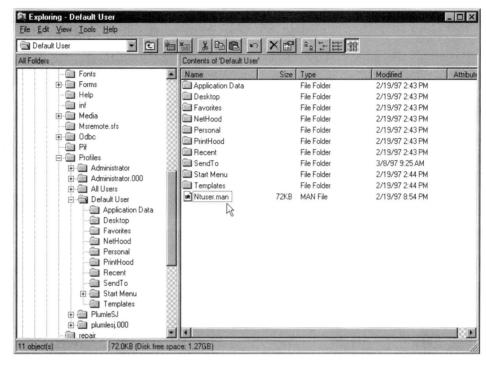

Figure 14.9 *Any changes made by the user are not saved to the NTuser.man file when the user logs off.*

Enabling Windows 95 User Profiles

You can create and apply Windows 95 user profiles similar to those you create in Windows NT Workstation. The differences between Windows 95 and Windows NT user profiles are as follows. Windows 95:

User profiles do not contain all desktop items, only shortcuts and program information files.

Doesn't support the centralized default users profile.

The roaming path comes from the user's home directory instead of the server.

In Windows 95, two files store the contents of the Registry file and folders containing the contents of the Start menu, Desktop, Network Neighborhood, and the Recent

(continues)

Enabling Windows 95 User Profiles (*Continued*)

Documents list that you can choose to save with the user profiles: User.dat and System.dat.

To enable user profiles in Windows 95, open the Passwords icon in the Control Panel and open the User Profiles tab. Choose Users Can Customize Their Preferences and Desktop Settings options. Additionally, you can choose to include the desktop icons and Network Neighborhood contents and the Start menu and Program groups in the user settings. Choose OK. You must restart the computer to create the profiles folder (\WINDOWS\PROFILES).

As in NT, Windows 95 user profiles are normally stored on the local drive. You can, however, store the profile on the network drive, in the user's home directory, to create roaming user profiles.

Additionally, you can create and enforce mandatory user profiles in Windows 95. Create the user profile on a workstation, then logoff; then rename the User.dat file to User.man and copy the user profile folders to the home directories of all users on the primary domain controller. Once again, the MAN extension makes the file read-only.

Using the Server Manager

NT's Server Manager tool enables you to monitor the network, including shared resources, user access, and relationships between servers. Specifically, you can select the domain, workgroup, or computer, then view connected users, shared and open resources, and you can manage directory replication, administration alerts, services and shared directories. You can even send messages to connected users from the Server Manager.

Additionally, you can add or remove servers from the domain, promote a backup domain controller, synchronize servers, and add and remove computers to a domain. Since you can use the Server Manager to manage domains and computers, this chapter discusses managing computers and Chapter 15 discusses using Server Manager to manage domains.

Server Manager enables you to administer only computers running NT Workstation and NT Server. Although you can see Windows 95 computers in the Server Manager, you cannot administrate them. You cannot see Windows for Workgroups or MS-DOS computers in the domain in Server Manager. You can, however, see NT computers from other domains that are active in the current domain.

Starting and Exiting the Server Manager

Only members of the following groups can open and administer the network from the Server Manager: Administrators, Domain Administrators, and Server Operators; Account Operators can add computers to the domain using the Server Manager but cannot perform any other tasks.

TIP: You cannot run the Server Manager remotely unless you expressly copy the needed files using the Network Client Administrator and you have appropriate rights and permissions.

To start the Server Manager, on a domain controller choose Start, Programs, Administrative Tools, and Server Manager. Figure 14.10 shows the Server Manager window with several computers listed.

TIP: Icons located to the left of the computer's name in the Server Manager indicate the type of computer—server, workstation, and so on. Dimmed icons are not currently connected to the server.

In the Computer column, the computer's name appears as assigned to it in the domain. The domain name appears in the title bar of the Server Manager. The type of computer is assigned by Windows, but you can always enter a description—such

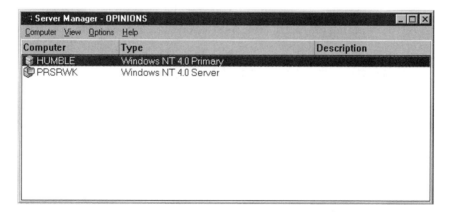

Figure 14.10 *Only NT computers can be administered in the Server Manager.*

as the location of the computer, the user's name, or other designation—to display in the Description column.

You can view servers only, workstations only, or all computers in a domain by choosing the View menu and selecting one of the following: Servers, Workstations, or All. Additionally, you can choose View, Show Domain Members Only if you do not want to view computers that are visiting the current domain.

To exit the Server Manager, choose Computer, Exit; alternatively, click the Close (X) button in the title bar of the Server Manager window.

Viewing Connections and Resource Usage on the Server

You can select any computer in the Server Manager Computer list to display more information about that computer's connection and resource information. Select the server, for example, and choose Computer, Properties. The computer's Properties dialog box appears, as shown in figure 14.11.

In the Usage Summary area of the dialog box, you see the following figures:

- *Sessions*: Displays the number of remote users currently connected.

- *Open Files*: Displays the number of currently open files from the computer.

- *File Locks*: Displays the current number of file locks on the computer by connected users. Files are normally locked to prevent replication; see the section later in this chapter.

- *Open Pipes*: Displays the current number of pipes being used; a pipe enables communication between processes, both local and remote.

The Description text box is optional; you can enter a description if you want or there may already be a description of the computer. Use information such as the location, brand, speed, and so on for the descriptive text.

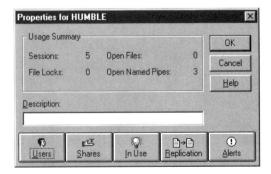

Figure 14.11 *The Properties dialog box summarizes the usage for the selected computer.*

Each button at the bottom of the dialog box enables you to view more information about the selected computer. Following is a brief description if each button; subsequent sections describe each button in more detail.

- *Users*: View the users connected to the server and the resources opened by a selected user; you can disconnect any or all of the users.

- *Shares*: View shared resources and the users who are connected to the resource; you can disconnect any or all of the users.

- *In Use*: View all open shared resources on server; you can close any or all of the resources.

- *Replication*: Manage directory replication, as described later in this chapter.

- *Alerts*: View the list of users and computers that are notified when administrative alerts occur.

Viewing User Sessions

In the computer's Properties dialog box, choose the Users button to view all users connected over the network to the computer and the resources any selected user has opened. Figure 14.12 shows the User Sessions on the selected server.

In the list of Connected Users, you may see the user's name and you do see the computer's name. The list of Opens is the number of resources currently open by that user; resources could be files, directories, printers, CD-ROM drive, and so on. The Time column describes the hours and minutes since the beginning of the current session; Idle displays the hours and minutes that have elapsed since the user last initiated an action. The Guest columns states either Yes, the connected user is a guest or No, the connected user is not a guest.

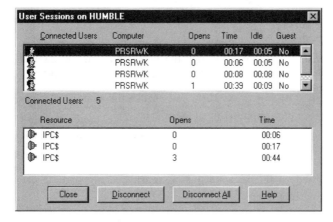

Figure 14.12 *View the connected users and the shared resources currently being used.*

The Resource area of the dialog box lists the shared resources, such as directories, pipes, printers, and so on, that are currently being used. The IPC$ you see listed in the figure as a resource is a special share created by the system; see the sidebar for more information.

To disconnect a user, open the User Sessions dialog box and choose the user you want to disconnect. Choose the Disconnect button to disconnect one user; choose the Disconnect All button to disconnect all users attached to the selected computer. You might disconnect users, for example, if you need to bring the server down or perform some procedure that necessitates all of the server's resources. Make sure you warn users before disconnecting them to prevent data loss; see "Sending a Message" later in this chapter.

Special Shares

Normal shares are resources, such as directories or printers, that the user or the administrator has designated as shared. Special shares are shares created by the system during installation and each share has a specific use. Depending on the computer's configuration, all or only some of the following shares may appear on the computer.

Special shares cannot be deleted or modified. Special shares are listed with a dollar sign ($) in the name so they can be easily identified. Following are a few of the special shares you will see in the Server Manager. In an NT Workstation computer, only Administrators and Backup Operators can connect to a drive share; in NT Server computers, members of the Administrators, Backup Operators, and Server Operators can connect to a special share.

IPC$ shares the named pipes that are essential for communication between programs. While you're remotely administering another computer, your user account is listed as a user connected to an IPC$ resource; you will not be disconnected if you disconnect all others.

ADMIN$ is a share used by the system during remote administration. The path is always the path to the Windows NT system root, usually C:\WINNT.

driveletter$, such as A$ or C$, is a share that enables the administrator to connect to the root directory of a computer or storage device.

NETLOGIN is a share used by the NT Server computer to process logon requests.

PRINT$ supports the use of shared printers.

REPL$ is located on the replicator export server and supports replication, as described later in this chapter.

Figure 14.13 *View the list of users and the resources they're using.*

Viewing Shared Resources

In the computer's Properties dialog box, choose the Shares button to see available resources on the selected computer, and for any resource see a list of connected users. Figure 14.13 shows the Shared Resources dialog box for the server.

The Sharename lists the available resources. Uses list the number of connections to shared resources and the Path shows the path to the resource. Select any resource in the Sharename list and view the connected users in the Connected Users area of the dialog box. In addition to the name of the user, view the time in hours and minutes, that the user has been connected and whether the resource is currently in use.

You can select a user and choose to Disconnect one or Disconnect All users connected to any resource; however, make sure you warn the users before disconnecting them so they do not lose data.

Viewing Resources in Use

Open resources describe the resources currently in use. To view these resources, choose the In Use button in the computer's Properties dialog box. Figure 14.14 displays the currently open resources on the server.

The Open Resources for the selected computer lists the number of open resources, the number of locked files, the permissions granted the user, and the path to the open resources.

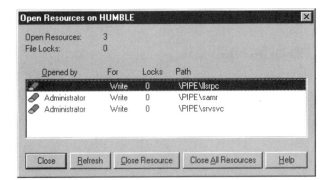

Figure 14.14 *Check for open resources before shutting down the server, for example.*

Note: Directory replication is a method by which shared files on the server are duplicated for easy access by many users, then updated to master files periodically so all files contain current information. Directory replication is covered completely in the following section.

Viewing Alerts

To view or set information about which computers are notified with Administrative alerts, choose the Alerts button in the selected computer's Properties dialog box. Administrative alerts are generated by the system and serve as warnings for the servers and resources; problems with security, access, user sessions, server shutdown, UPS services, and so on, are included in alerts issued by the system.

TIP: To be able to send an administrative alert, the Messenger service and the Alerter service must be enabled. Check the services by choosing Computer, Services for the server and for the computer, in the Server Manager.

Figure 14.15 shows the Alerts dialog box, in which you can add the computer names (or user names) you want to alert. Enter a new name in the New Computer or Username text box and choose the Add button. To remove a name from the Send Administrative Alerts To list box, select the name, and choose the Remove button.

Viewing Resources of Selected Computers

In addition to viewing resource usage and current users for the primary domain controller server in the domain, you also can view information about any con-

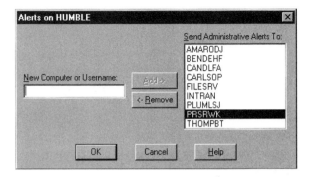

Figure 14.15 *Consider listing all servers and workstations in the domain to receive administrative alerts.*

nected computer on the domain in the Server Manager. You might want to check member servers, for example, to see if bottlenecks appear around any specific resource. You could also check workstations to see if others are accessing resources or causing problems with limited resources.

Shared Directories

To view shared directories for any selected computer, follow these steps:

1. To view any connected computer's shared directories, select the computer in the Server Manager and choose Computer, Shared Directories. The Shared Directories dialog box appears (see Figure 14.16).

2. In the Shared Directories dialog box, select a directory, then choose the Properties button to modify the properties, such as share name and user limit, of any share. The Share Properties dialog box appears, as shown in Figure 14.17.

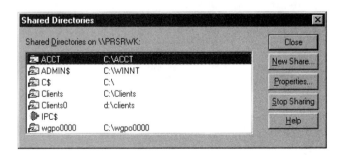

Figure 14.16 *View the directories that are shared on a selected computer.*

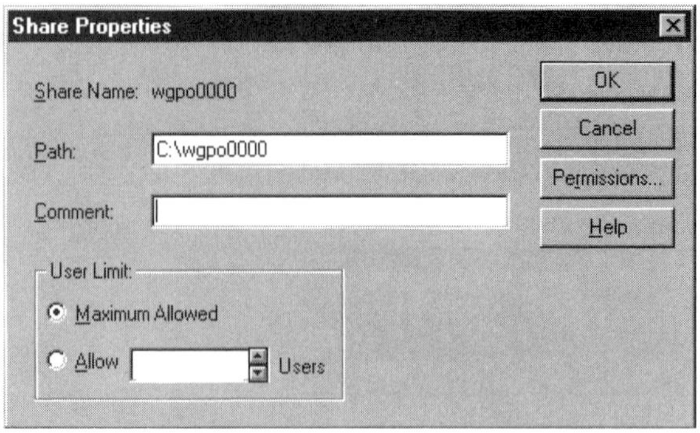

Figure 14.17 *Set permissions and user limits for any shared directory.*

3. In the Shared Directories dialog box, choose the Stop Sharing button to stop sharing the selected directory; make sure no users are attached before you stop sharing.

4. Select the New Share button in the Shared Directories dialog box to create a new share on the selected computer. The New Share dialog box appears (see Figure 14.18).

   In the New Share dialog box, you can do the following:

   Enter a new share name and path.

   Optionally enter a comment.

   Set a user limit.

   Choose the Permissions button to limit access of certain groups and/or users.

5. Choose OK to close the New Share dialog box when you're finished, to re-turn to the Shared Directories dialog box.

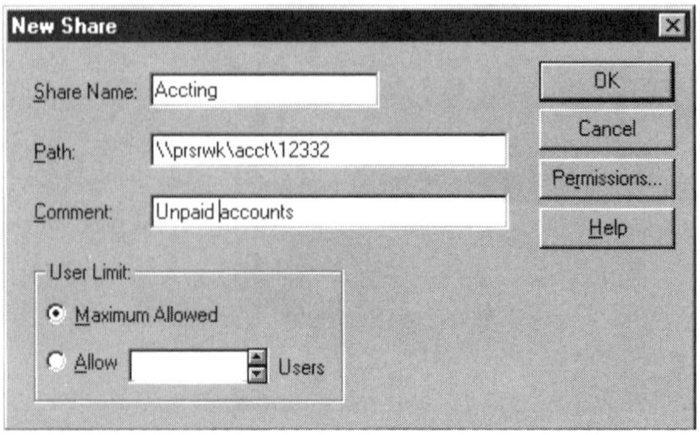

Figure 14.18 *Create new shares on any selected computer.*

Properties

To view the properties information for any shared directory, follow these steps:

1. In the Server Manager, select the connected computer about which you want to view information and choose Computer, Shared Directories. The Shared Directories dialog box appears.

2. Select the directory you want to examine and click the Properties button. The Share Properties dialog box appears, as shown in Figure 14.19.

3. Optionally, you can add a comment about the directory that others will see when they view shared directories on the computer.

4. Choose the Permissions button to display the Access Through Share Permissions dialog box and to set permissions on the shared directory.

5. In the User Limit area of the dialog box, set the number of users that can access the directory, if you want.

6. Choose OK to close the dialog box and return to the Shared Directories dialog box; choose Close.

Services

You can set services—such as Alerter, Plug and Play, Remote Access Server, TCP/IP, UPS, and so on—for any selected computer. This is the same Services option found on any NT computer in the Control Panel. To set services, follow these steps:

1. In the Server Manager, select the computer and choose Computer, Services. Figure 14.20 shows the Services dialog box.

2. Scroll through the list of services, select the service you want to control, and choose any of the following buttons:

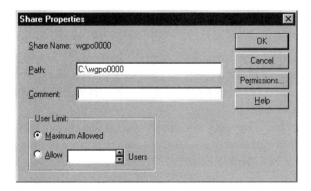

Figure 14.19 Set permissions for any directory.

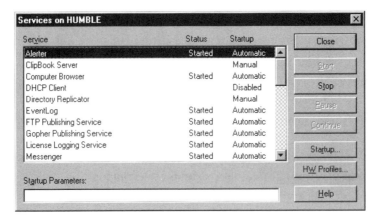

Figure 14.20 *Control the services for any connected computer.*

Start: Starts the selected service for this session only.

Stop: Stops the services for this session only.

Pause: Suspends the service.

Continue: Continues a paused service.

Startup: Enables you to view and/or change a startup type: Automatic, Manual, or Disabled.

HW Profiles: Enables or disables the service for a specific hardware profile.

3. Choose Close when you're finished.

Directory Replication

When working on a network, users often share data files stored on the server. For shared files to remain effective and useful, all users must have updated files on which to work. Directory replication is a method of creating a duplicate of the master set of directories and files on the server for other computers on the network to use. When you replicate directories, you can also replicate the files contained within those directories.

The server on which the master set resides is called the export server; all computers to which the duplicates are replicated are called import computers. Import computers must use the NT Workstation or NT Server software. The export server and the import computers are dynamically linked so that when changes are made

---

Sending a Message to a Computer

When you're connected to computers through the Server Manager, you can send a message to any selected computer. You might want to warn someone you're shutting down the system or tell him or her about a deleted share, for example.

To be able to send a message, the Messenger service must be running on both computers. The services is, by default, started automatically but you can check it in the Services dialog box (Computer, Services).

To send a message, select the computer in the Server Manager to which you want to send the message. Choose Computer, Send Message. The Send Message dialog box appears. Enter your message and choose OK to send it.

---

to a directory or file on the master set, the changes are automatically reflected in the duplicates on the import computers.

In addition to ensuring that everyone is working with the same information, directory replication can also help relieve bottlenecks at the server. Suppose you have data files that all workstations need access to. If all workstations access the server at one time for these files, network traffic becomes slower and perhaps even stops periodically. However, you can replicate the directories containing the needed files to another server and direct some of the workstations to access the files from there to help balance the workload.

Requirements for Replication

Only computers running NT Server (domain controllers and/or member servers) can export directories. Import computers include computers running NT Server or NT Workstation.

Creating the Subdirectories

The export server uses a default export path: *SYSTEMROOT*\\SYSTEM32\\REPL\\EXPORT; all subdirectories to be exported reside in this directory. The import computer uses the default import path, to which all imported subdirectories and their files are automatically placed: *SYSTEMROOT*\\SYSTEM32\\REPL\\IMPORT. The replication procedure creates the import directories automatically; you must create the export subdirectories yourself. Additionally, you must copy the files to be replicated into the subdirectories on the export server. You can use the Explorer on the export server to complete these tasks.

Creating Replicator Accounts

Before you can replicate directories and files you must configure the Directory Replicator service for each participating export server and create a special user account for the service. In the User Manager for Domains, create an account for the service on each export server and set the following user options:

Check the Password Never Expires option.

Enable the user to access the network during all login hours.

Enter a password.

Assign the user to the Backup Operators group.

Additionally, in the Server Manager, configure the Directory Replicator service for the export server to start up automatically and to log on under the newly created user account, by following these steps:

1. Open the Server Manager and select the export server. Choose Computer, Services and select the Directory Replicator service in the list.

2. Choose the Startup button and in the Services dialog box, choose Automatic, as shown in Figure 14.21.

3. In the Log On As area of the Services dialog box, choose This Account and enter the user's name you created for the replicator service.

4. Enter the password, confirm the password, and choose OK. The Server Manager notifies you it's adding the user to the Replicator group and returns to the Server Manager window.

Figure 14.21 *Configure the replicator service on the selected export server.*

You also must configure the service for the import computer. In the Server Manager, select the computer that will be the import computer, then follow these steps:

1. Choose Computer, Services and select the Directory Replicator service in the list.

2. Choose the Startup button and in the Services dialog box, choose Automatic.

3. In the Log On As area of the Services dialog box, choose This Account and enter the domain name and the user's name you created for the replicator service, for example: *DOMAIN\SRepl*.

TIP: If you're in doubt about the exact account name, choose the browse button (...) and find the user account in the dialog box that appears. Choose OK.

---

4. Choose OK to return to the Server Manager.

Configuring the Export Server

You can configure the primary or backup domain controller, or a member server, as an export server for the replication service. You will need to create the directories you want to export as subdirectories of the replication export path: *\SYSTEMROOT\SYSTEM32\REPL\EXPORT*. You can accomplish this in the Explorer. Additionally, copy any files you want to replicate to the subdirectories you create.

To configure the export server in the Server Manager, follow these steps:

1. Open the Server Manager (Start, Programs, Administrative Tools, Server Manager).

2. Select the server that will be the export server and choose Computer, Properties.

3. In the computer's Properties dialog box, choose the Replication button. The Directory Replication dialog box appears, as shown in Figure 14.22.

4. Choose the Export Directories option. In the From Path text box, the default export directory path appears.

5. Choose the Manage button to view and manage individual directories. The Manage Exported Directories dialog box appears (see Figure 14.23).

6. Select any subdirectory in the list and choose to Add Lock or Remove Lock; you lock the subdirectory when you do not want to replicate it.

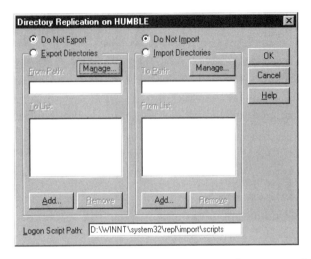

Figure 14.22 *Enable the export server and set options for the process.*

Replication on a locked subdirectory doesn't take place until you unlock the subdirectory.

7. Choose the Wait Until Stabilized check box. Stabilize a subdirectory to indicate the export server should wait two minutes after changes before exporting, just in case additional changes need to be recorded.

8. Choose the Entire Subtree check box if you want to export the subdirectory and any directories it contains; deselect the check box if you just want to replicate the first-level subdirectory.

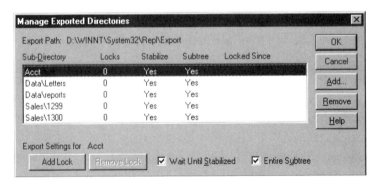

Figure 14.23 *The Manage Exported Directories dialog box displays the subdirectories in the Export directory.*

TIP: If you choose the Add button in the Manage Exported Directories dialog box, you can add subdirectories to the list; however, the Add button doesn't create subdirectories. You must create subdirectories in the Explorer.

---

9. Choose OK to close the Manage Exported Directories dialog box and return to the Directory Replication dialog box.

10. Below the To List, choose the Add button to add the computer to the list that will receive exported files. Select Add a second time and enter the domain name in the text box; you must also add the domain name to the To List.

TIP: If you're replicating over a WAN, you can just add the computer names in the To List instead of the domain names and computer names.

---

11. Choose OK to close the Directory Replication dialog box and choose OK again to close the export server's Properties dialog box. If the REPL$ share doesn't already exist on the server, the system will start the Directory Replicator Service, if it hasn't already been started.

Note: Before closing the Directory Replication dialog box, enter the path for login scripts in the Login Script Path text box if you want to replicate scripts as well as directories and files (if the default path is not correct). Replicate login scripts from a primary domain controller to a backup domain controller; only servers that authenticate users need to keep a copy of the login scripts.

Configuring the Import Computer

You can configure a computer running NT Workstation or NT Server as an import computer; you can even use an export server as an import computer to create a local backup, for example. You don't need to create the subdirectories used for replication on the import computer; the Directory Replicator Service will create them for you. To set up the import computer, follow these steps:

1. In the Server Manager, select the server or workstation that will be the import computer.

2. Choose Computer, Properties. Choose the Replication button and the Directory Replication dialog box appears.

3. Choose the Import Directories option.

4. In the To Path, check to make sure the path is correct; the default is WINNT\SYSTEM32\REPL\IMPORT.

5. In the From List, choose the Add button to add the export server to the list from which this computer will receive exported files.

6. Choose the Manage button to review the Manage Imported Directories dialog box (see Figure 14.24).

7. After the first replication, you can select any directory in the Sub-Directory list and choose to Lock or Remove Lock on the directory. A locked directory cannot be overwritten by a new exported, or replicated, directory. Manage locks to prevent importing subdirectories or to lock a subdirectory so it replicates to only one import computer and no other import computers.

Note: Important: Do not try to examine or set permissions for the import directory: SYSTEM32\REPL\IMPORT using the Explorer; you can damage or even lose the permissions set by the service if you even look at permissions in the Explorer.

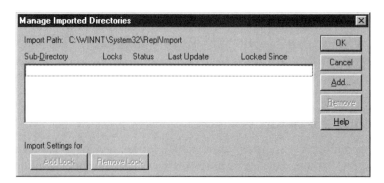

Figure 14.24 If you've never replicated to this computer, the Manage Imported Directories dialog box will be empty.

You can view the time and status of replicated directories in the Manage Imported Directories dialog box at any time. In the Sub-Directory column is the name of the directory that was replicated. The Locks column indicates any locks on the directory. If you've locked a directory, the Locked Since column lists the date and time the directory was locked. View the Last Update column for date and time of the most recent replication.

Finally, the Status column indicates the success or failure of the replication. Following are the possible entries in the Status column:

OK: Replicated subdirectory received and is identical to the exported subdirectory.

No Master: Subdirectory is not receiving updates (export server locked or not running).

No Sync: Subdirectory not updated (communications failure, open files, permissions problems).

No entry (blank): Replication didn't occur for that subdirectory (improper configuration).

Summary

This chapter has covered information about expanding your network, managing and adding users, managing servers on the network, and replicating data as a backup. As your network grows, your administrative duties will also increase; NT includes many tools and utilities that can help you effectively manage the network. As your network expands, you may want to add multiple domains; Chapter 15 discusses adding and managing multiple domains.

15 *Using Multiple Domains*

Thus far, you've worked with only one domain on your network and may find that that is all you need. However, if your network starts to grow, or if you attach to another network, you may find that multiple domains are a better tool for organizing and managing the network.

When working with multiple domains, the main concern is security. NT offers several security features; some may be familiar, and others may be new. This chapter explains how to set up multiple domains and manage security across two or more domains. Also included is information about how users will view the domains, how to access another domain's printers, and how to map drives for user access to other domains. Finally, this chapter includes steps to adding computers to your domain, promoting and demoting domain controllers, and synchronizing the domain controllers in your domain. Specifically in this chapter, you will learn the following:

- Learn the benefits of multiple domains
- Set up trust relationships
- Administer users and groups in other domains
- Access printers in other domains
- View resources in other domains
- Add a computer to your domain
- Promote and demote domain controllers

Single versus Multiple Domains

A domain is an administrative unit containing network servers and workstations that share common security and common user account information. For each user on the domain, there's an account that enables the user to log on to the network and, from the logon, access any server and any resource on the domain for which the user has rights and permissions.

Computers within a domain may be in the same office building, connected by a LAN; or computers within a domain could be cities, states, even continents apart and connected over a WAN, through dial-up networking, ISDN, fiber, satellite, or other physical connection.

Single Domain Components

Within one domain, a primary domain controller is necessary to manage interactions between users, groups, and resources. All members of the domain share a directory database that's stored on the domain controller(s) and identifies all users and groups within the domain.

There is only one primary domain controller in a domain. One domain may have additional domain controllers, however, in the form of backup domain controllers. Additionally, a domain can include multiple member servers and workstations. All computers in the domain are centrally administered and managed within the domain and only one user account exists for each user within the domain.

In addition to making network administration easy, users benefit from being members of a domain, as well. Users can browse available network resources and access any resources for which they have permission.

Security in a domain is based on discretionary access control. Some users can access a resource whereas other users cannot, depending on permissions and rights. User rights determine whether a user can log on only to one computer or to the entire domain, and which resources the user can access after logging in.

Organizing the users into groups makes it easier for the administrator to control access to resources. Instead of assigning rights to each user, an administrator can create a group and assign the rights to that group. Then, the administrator can add specific users to the group.

Multiple Domain Considerations

When you start adding more and more users, servers, and resources to a network, you start having more and more organizational, administrative, and security problems. Consider the following questions: How will each workstation know what resources are available? By what name are the resources identified? Where are those resources actually located? Another problem is how to enable some users to access some resources without allowing everyone on the network access. NT takes care of both of these problems with the use of multiple domains.

Trust Relationships

When you add a second domain to the mix, you also add the problem of how users from one domain access resources on the second domain. You could make each user a member of the second domain; assign a password, create a user account, and define rights and groups for the user in the second domain. But this causes some problems.

First, making each user a member of the second domain is an administrative nightmare; trying to update and manage two sets of users would be difficult to say the least, but what happens when you add a third domain, a fourth, and so on? Second, the user now has to remember a username and password for an additional domain and the user must log off of one domain before logging on to another. In addition to time-consuming, this is not a very effective way for users to navigate between domains.

NT has come up with an easier answer: trust relationships. With trust relationships, NT can supply security across multiple domains. There are two types of trust relationships: one-way trust relationship and two-way trust relationship.

In a one-way trust relationship, one domain trusts the users of another domain to use its resources. The *trusted* domain authenticates its users and the users, in turn, access the resources on the *trusting* domain. However, users on the trusting domain cannot access the trusted domain, since this is only a one-way relationship. In a two-way trust relationship, each domain trusts users accounts in the other domain and both domains share their resources, depending on applicable rights, of course.

Naturally, the accessibility of resources on any domain is subject to permissions associated with those resources. The great thing about trust relationships is the universal access to resources; one domain user account and password is all a user needs to access resources from multiple domains.

Multiple Domain Models

When a company is small, a single domain model works well. The network has just one primary domain controller, perhaps a backup domain controller, a few member servers, and workstations for everyone who needs it. Microsoft states that 26,000 users and groups can make up a single domain; however, reasonably, that's too many elements for an administrator to handle in one domain. Instead, the users and groups can be divided into multiple domains using departments, locations, offices, jobs, or some other natural divisions as guides for the domains.

It's more efficient to set up multiple domains from an administrative point of view than to group all of your users into one domain, especially if you have a large network or a network separated by natural boundaries, such as department or buildings. The major advantage to having multiple domains is delegating administrative duties. You can assign one person within each domain to manage that domain—creating users and groups, controlling files and other resources within the domain, backing up data, and so on.

Note: It's difficult for me to say you should or should not use multiple domains; you will have to decide for yourself. If you have 10 servers, for example, (used for file and print services as well as for authentication) and perhaps no more than 100 users, one domain might fit your network perfectly. On the other hand, you may have five servers and 25 users, all separated geographically so that management by a single administrator is impossible. In this case, two or more domains would make the job workable.

In Chapter 4, I discussed multiple domain models, particularly the single master domain and the multiple master domain. In these models, each domain has one primary domain controller (PDC), one or more backup domain controllers (BDC), then various combinations of member servers and workstations.

One tried and true method of organizing multiple domains is to place the authentication server, a primary domain controller, for all domains in a domain to itself—often called the master domain. The master domain enables centralized administration for all user and group accounts. Other domains within the model, then, control the various resources of the network.

Say you have six domains in your network. One domain, the master, controls all user and group accounts for the network. Two other domains control the printing services for the entire network and another two domains control all files and directories. You have users attached to each domain, but all users are authenticated in the master domain and all users access one or more of the resource domains for printing and file services.

Note: Each domain must have a primary domain controller and should have at least one backup domain server. You can add other computers running Windows NT Server 4.0 software as member servers that supply files, or printers, or other resources within each domain. If you're using the master domain/resource domains model, member servers in each domain contain the resources, but all users are authenticated from the master domain.

Single and Multiple Master Domains

The single master domain model consists of a master domain and one or more resource domains. The master domain contains all user and group accounts and the resource domains share their resources—such as printers and file servers. All users log on to the master domain. All resources are located in other domains.

In a single master, the resource domains establish a one-way trust with the master domain which enables the users access to the resources. Using the single master domain model, users only need to log on to the domain once but can still use all resources on the network.

You could also use the multiple master domain model, in which you establish two or more single master domains to serve as user and group account domains. Other domains on the network are resource domains, as in the single master domain model.

In the multiple master, the trust relationships differ from the single master domain model in that every master domain is connected to every other master domain in a two-way trust relationship. All resource domains have a one-way trust with each master domain, as well. With this model, every user account can use any master domain and any resource domain. For information about and Figures illustrating various domain models, see Chapter 4.

Generally with a single domain, you use fewer than 25,000 users per domain and centralized account and resource management. When instituting a single master domain, you use fewer than 40,000 users per domain, centralized account management, but decentralized resource management. For a multiple master domain, you can use any number of users, both centralized and decentralized resource management, and decentralized account management.

Logging On Multiple Domains

As you know, logon security is the first means of security for a network. When a user logs on, his or her username and password are checked against the directory database in the primary domain controller.

Note: Logon security is only utilized by computers running Windows NT Workstation, a Windows NT Server, or Windows 95.

If the user logs on to one of multiple domains, a similar authentication process takes place. The domain controller processes the request using the Net Logon service, which initiates discovery, a secure communications channel, and pass-through authentication.

Discovery is when the Net Logon service attempts to locate a domain controller in the trusted domain. The secure communications channel is a verification of the computer accounts in preparation to pass the user identification data. Finally the pass-through authentication passes the user's identification on to the appropriate domain controller, if the computer being used for logon is not the domain controller in the domain where the user account is defined. Naturally, both domain controllers must share a trust relationship for pass-through authentication to work.

The Net Logon service uses pass-through authentication depending on the domain name the user enters. If the domain name isn't the domain the domain controller belongs to, the domain controller checks trusted domains and passes on the user data if it locates the appropriate domain. If the user data is authenticated, the logon succeeds; if the domain controller cannot find an appropriate trusted domain or the trusted domain cannot authenticate the user's name and password, the logon fails.

Note: If you have multiple administrators, each should use two domain accounts for his or her local domain: one as a member of the Administrators local group used to perform local network management tasks and one in the Users local group to perform the same tasks as other users. This way your network will be more secure. Members of the Administrators group can accidentally change configurations, introduce viruses, and so on; these accidents will be less likely to cause major damage if administrators log on as users instead of as Administrators most of the time.

Administering Multiple Domains in the User Manager

The first thing you must do to set up multiple domains is install the primary domain controller (PDC) for each domain. When installing Windows NT Server 4.0 software, you choose the type of server you want to set up: primary domain controller, backup domain controller, or member server. Since each domain must have a primary domain controller, you set up that server first. When creating the PDC, make sure you assign a unique name to the new domain. See Chapter 5 for information about installing Windows NT Server 4.0 and changing domain names in the Network dialog box.

After you install the PDC, you can create client software, attach workstations, add users and groups, install printers, perhaps install a backup domain controller and a few member servers, as well. Additionally, you can create as many domains as needed for your network; you can always add more domains later, as well. Now you're ready to set up a trust relationship.

You configure trust relationships in the User Manager for Domains on the computer running NT Server; however, to set up trust relationships, the other domain involved must participate as well. You can set up trust relationships, then manage users and groups of multiple domains in the User Manager for Domains, if you have the Administrator rights on all domains.

Setting Up Trust Relationships

You must have the cooperation of the other domain(s) in order to set up a trust relationship, no matter if the relationship is one-way or two-way. Make sure you're logged on as a member of the Administrators group; if you're not logged on as the Administrator, then make sure your name is added to the second domain's user list and is a member of the Administrators group. It's easier if you keep the same password for all domains.

One-Way Trust Relationship

To set up a one-way trust relationship, the trusted domain adds a domain to its trusting list; then the trusting domain adds the first domain to its trusted list.

TIP: Remember, the *trusted* domain is the one accessing resources from the *trusting* domain.

To set up a one-way trust relationship, follow these steps:

1. Open the User Manager for Domains (Start, Programs, Administrative Tools, User Manager for Domains).

2. Choose Policies, Trust Relationships. The Trust Relationships dialog box appears (see Figure 15.1).

3. Choose the Add button to the right of the Trusting Domains list box and the Add Trusting Domain dialog box appears (see Figure 15.2).

4. Enter the name of the Trusting Domain and the password you will use for that domain; confirm the password and choose OK.

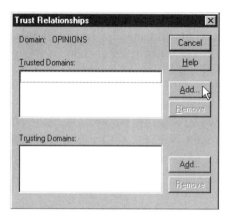

Figure 15.1 *The Trust Relationships dialog box lets you add trusting and/or trusted domains.*

5. Move to the server in the second domain and open the User Manager; you should be logged in as a member of the Administrators group.

6. Choose Policies, Trust Relationships. The Trust Relationships dialog box appears.

7. To add the trusted domain, choose the Add button to the right of the Trusted Domains list. The Add Trusted Domain dialog box appears (see Figure 15.3).

8. Enter the name of the trusted domain, then enter your password to that domain; choose OK.

Two-Way Trust Relationship

To perform a two-way trust relationship, the first domain must add the second domain to its trusting list and its trusted list. The second domain must also add the first to its trusting list and to its trusted list. You must do the steps in the following order for the two-way trust to work; if you don't follow the steps, you will receive an error message that says the trust relationship could not be verified. If that happens, remove all trust relationships and follow the order of the following steps.

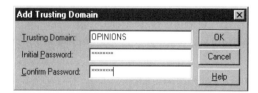

Figure 15.2 *Enter the trusting domain name and your password.*

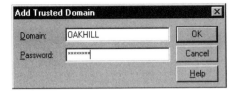

Figure 15.3 *Enter the trusted domain name and your password.*

To set up a two-way trust relationship, follow these steps:

1. On the first computer, open the User Manager for Domains (Start, Programs, Administrative Tools, User Manager for Domains).

2. Choose Policies, Trust Relationships. The Trust Relationships dialog box appears.

3. Choose the Add button to the right of the Trusting Domains list box and the Add Trusting Domain dialog box appears. Enter the name of the Trusting Domain and the password you will use for that domain; confirm the password and choose OK.

4. Move to the server in the second domain and open the User Manager; choose Policies, Trust Relationships. The Trust Relationships dialog box appears.

5. Choose the Add button to the right of the Trusting Domains list box and the Add Trusting Domain dialog box appears. Enter the name of the Trusting Domain and the password you will use for that domain; confirm the password and choose OK.

6. On the same server, you can now choose the Add button to the right of the Trusted Domains list. The Add Trusted Domain dialog box appears. Enter the name of the trusted domain, then enter your password to that domain; choose OK.

7. Move back to the first server and choose the Add button to the right of the Trusting Domains list box. Enter the domain name and your password, and choose OK.

Figure 15.4 shows the Trust Relationships dialog box with one trusted domain and two trusting domains. The trusted domain (OAKHILL) can access the resources from this domain (OPINIONS). OPINIONS can access the resources for both the trusting domains (BECKLEY and OAKHILL). Therefore, OAKHILL and OPINIONS have a two-way trust relationship; whereas BECKLEY and OPINIONS have only a one-way trust relationship.

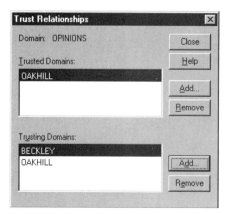

Figure 15.4 Results of a two- and a one-way trust relationship in the Trust Relationships dialog box.

TIP: It's a good idea to set the Audit policy (Policies, Audit) on your own domain to track events, since you're now allowing other users to access your resources. You can view the audit log in the Event Viewer.

Removing Trust Relationships

Removing trust relationships is also a process that you must perform in both domains. The trusted domain must remove the second domain from its list of trusting domains and the trusting domain must remove the first domain from its list of trusted domains. To remove trust relationships, follow these steps:

1. In the User Manager for Domains on the first server, choose Policies, Trust Relationships.

2. Select the domain you want to remove from the relationship and choose the Remove button. The User Manager displays a message dialog box, as shown in Figure 15.5.

3. Choose OK to confirm the removal of the domain.

4. Repeat steps 1 through 3 on the server in the second domain.

Administering Users in Multiple Domains

In the User Manager for Domains, you can select users and groups in other domains and administer them as if they were in your domain. Additionally, you can

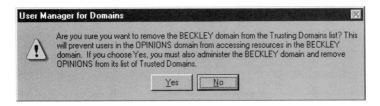

Figure 15.5 *A confirmation dialog box verifies your choice to remove the domain from the trust relationship.*

set policies for users in other domains with which you have a trust relationship, as long as you have administrative rights in that domain.

You can display an individual computer running NT Workstation, NT Server as a member server, or a Microsoft LAN Manager server. If you select a primary or backup domain controller, the domain is displayed instead of the computer. To display a computer instead of a domain, enter double slashes and the computer name, for example \\MANAGEMENT.

Changing Domains

To change domains and administer users and groups in that domain, follow these steps:

1. In the User Manager for Domains, choose User, Select Domain. The Select Domain dialog box appears (see Figure 15.6).

2. Choose a domain to administer, or select a specific computer.

3. Choose OK and the User Manager accesses the users and groups on the selected domain. Figure 15.7 shows the BECKLEY domain in the OPINIONS User Manager for Domains.

TIP: Use the Low Speed Connection option if connections to other domains seem slow to you; however, using this option prevents you from seeing the users and groups. Although you can still administer local groups, you cannot administer global ones.

After choosing the domain, you can add, modify, remove, and otherwise manage users and groups, change account policies and user rights, and so on.

Figure 15.6 *You can select a domain or double-click a domain to display computers in the domain.*

Username	Full Name	Description
Administrator		Built-in account for administering the comp:
AlisonJ	Alison Johnson	Training
BevB	Beverly Barker	Training
DebD	Debbie Davis	Training
Guest		Built-in account for guest access to the con
HughB	Hugh Bender	Sales
IUSR_HOSERVER	Internet Guest Account	Internet Server Anonymous Access
JimS	Jim Smith	Hardware
JohnT	John Tuttle	Training
JudyT	Judy Terry	Hardware
KipG	Kip Garten	Sales
SueP	Sue Plumley	Director
TammyB	Tammy Berry	Sales

Groups	Description
Account Operators	Members can administer domain user and group accounts
Administrators	Members can fully administer the computer/domain
Backup Operators	Members can bypass file security to back up files
Domain Admins	Designated administrators of the domain
Domain Guests	All domain guests
Domain Users	All domain users

Figure 15.7 *The domain name appears in the title bar of the User Manager for Domains window.*

Global Groups Revisited

In Chapter 6 you were introduced to local and global groups but you may not have been too concerned with the concept at that time. Since you're getting ready to work with multiple domains, however, you now need to understand the difference between the two. Basically, a local group is used within one domain and global groups are used when the network is set up in multiple domains.

Remember, you can put users and global groups into a local group; however, you cannot put one local group into another. Global groups are groups that can only contain users and these users can only be from the domain in which the global group was created.

The three built-in global groups include:

1. Domain Admins: A member of the Administrators local group; a member can administer the domain, the primary and backup domain controllers, and all other computers running both NT Server and Workstation in the domain.

2. Domain Users: A member of the Users local group for the domain and of the Users local group for every NT Workstation and member server on the network; have normal user access.

3. Domain Guests: Members of the domain's built-in Guest user account—have limited rights. You could move any Domain Users to the Domain Guests group if you want to limit their rights and permissions.

In addition, remember these guidelines when working with global and local groups. If you need a group that can contain users from multiple domains, you must use a local group. Local groups can only be used in the domain in which they're created, so if you need to grant this local group permissions in more than one domain, you will have to manually create the local group in every domain in which you need it.

You can group the users of one domain into a single unit for use in other domains; this would be a global group. Global groups can be put into other domains' local groups and can be given rights and permissions directly in other domains.

If you have a group that needs to be in more than one domain, then create two groups: a local and a global.

User accounts should be members of global, not local groups, to enable them to access multiple domain resources. Place people with administrative privileges in the Domain Admins group instead of the Administrators; place new users in the Domain Users group instead of Users.

To create global groups, open the User Manager for Domains and choose User, New Global Group. The New Global Group dialog box appears. Enter the name for the new group and assign rights as explained in Chapter 7.

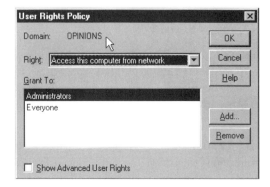

Figure 15.8 *Set rights for users and groups using resources in your domain.*

Managing the User Rights Policy

You already have a user rights policy for the groups and users on your domain. When you add new domains to your network, you may need to assign rights to the new users or groups for your domain. The user rights policy enables you to grant rights to individuals and/or groups. To manage rights for users and groups from other domains, follow these steps:

1. Choose Policies, User Rights. The User Rights dialog box appears (see Figure 15.8).

2. In Right, select the right you want to grant to the user and/or group.

3. Choose the Add button and the Add Users and Groups dialog box appears.

4. Choose the List Names from the drop-down list box and select the domain, as shown in Figure 15.9.

5. To view the members of any group, select the group and choose the Show Users button. The users are displayed at the end of the groups list in the Names list box, as shown in Figure 15.10.

6. Select any names of users or groups you want to add and choose the Add button. When you're done, choose OK to return to the User Rights Policy dialog box.

Using Domain Resources

Now that you can see how to secure your domain when working with multiple domains, you may be wondering how users browse the domains and access resources. An important point is: Only computers running Windows NT Worksta-

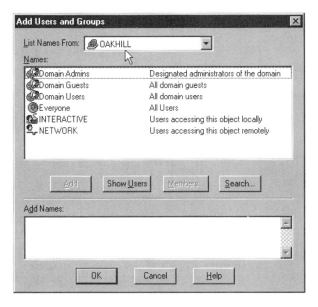

Figure 15.9 *Choose a domain, then choose the groups to add.*

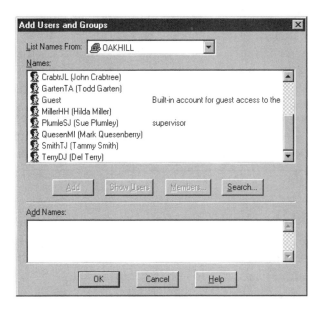

Figure 15.10 *Choose individual users and/or groups.*

Figure 15.11 *Users access the domains from the Network Neighborhood.*

tion, Windows NT Server, or Windows 95 can browse and access the resources of domains other than the one on which they are a member. Windows for Workgroups and MS-DOS clients can only access the resources from their own domain.

Browsing the Domains

Users browsing the network see resources grouped in domains rather than just a listing of multiple servers and printers. Viewing resources in this manner makes it easier for the users to locate the resources and identify resources.

Clients can use the Network Neighborhood to view available resources. Figure 15.11 shows the Neighborhood window with all three available domains, as well as a workgroup, for resource sharing. To view the resources on any domain, the user double-clicks the domain name, then continues to expand from computer to folder to access files and directories.

TIP: Users can also access the domains from the Explorer window. They locate the Network Neighborhood, then double-click to expand the domains and resources.

Mapping Drives to Domains

Users can map drives to other domains similarly to the way they map drives to their own domain. Additionally, users can choose to reconnect the mapped drive automatically at logon. To map drives to another domain, follow these steps:

1. In the Network Neighborhood, choose View, Toolbar to display the toolbar if it is not already showing.
2. Select the Map Network Drive icon, as shown in Figure 15.12.

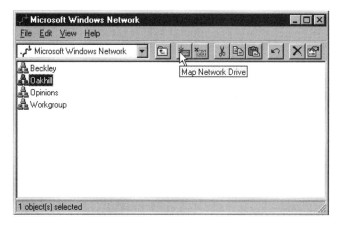

Figure 15.12 *Use the Map Network Drive icon to quickly connect to another domain.*

3. In the Map Network Drive dialog box, expand the domain to which you want to map a drive; continue to expand the drive until you find the folder you want.

4. Select a Drive from the drop-down list, then select the folder in the Shared Directories list. The path to the folder appears in the Path text box, as shown in Figure 15.13. Choose Reconnect at Logon to connect to the selected drive each time you log on.

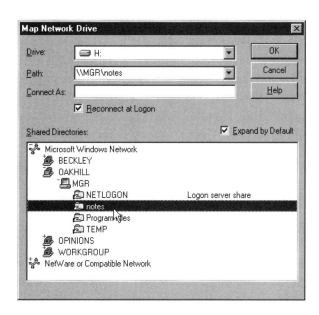

Figure 15.13 *Locate the folder on the domain to which you want to map a drive.*

5. The user enters his or her username in the Connect As text box and chooses OK. The mapped connection shows in the My Computer window and in the Explorer.

Note: The administrator can also map drives in this manner for user profiles. On a workstation, the Adminstrator sets up the drive mappings and any other environment settings for the user, then saves the configuration as a user profile. See Chapter 14 for more information.

Sharing Printers

Before the users can access a printer on another domain, you must add the printer as a network printer to a server in the users domain. Add a printer to the domain as you would any network printer, then administer the print queue in the same manner as well. See Chapter 8 for more information about setting up printers and managing print queues. Briefly, to set up a printer in another domain for use in your domain, follow these steps:

1. Choose Start, Settings, Printers. The Printers window appears.

2. Double-click the Add Printers option and the Add Printer Wizard dialog box appears.

3. Choose the Network Printer option and choose the Next button. The Connect to Printer dialog box appears.

4. Expand the domain containing the printer by double-clicking first the domain name, then the server name. Available printers display below the server, as shown in Figure 15.14.

5. Select the printer and choose OK. Follow the directions on-screen to complete setting up the printer. Users then access the printer the same as they would any other printer on the server in their own domain.

Managing Servers and Domains

In Chapter 14, you learned about the Server Manager and how to manage your domain. As your network enlarges, you will find there are a few additional tasks you need to know. For example, when you add workstations or servers to your network, you must tell the server and the network that you've added another computer. You can accomplish this task in the Server Manager.

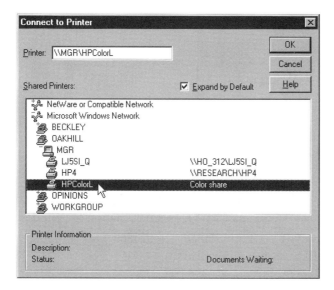

Figure 15.14 *Display available domain printers.*

Another task you will need to perform at some point is promoting a domain controller. You may, for example, have trouble with your primary domain controller and need to shut it down for servicing. Rather than shutting down the entire network, you can promote a backup domain controller to primary, and let the users continue with their work. This section shows you how to further manage your servers and domain.

Adding Computers to the Domain

Add a computer—a workstation, member server, or backup domain controller—to the network at any time. When you add a computer, you must identify the domain and the name of the computer to the server; then you must set the computer to the appropriate domain and restart the computer before it becomes a member of the domain. You must be a member of the Administrators or Account Operators group to add a computer to the domain. To add a computer to the domain, follow these steps:

1. On the primary domain controller of the domain, open the Server Manager (Start, Programs, Administrative Tools, Server Manager).

2. Choose Computer, Add to Domain. The Add Computer to Domain dialog box appears (see Figure 15.15).

3. In Computer Type, choose one of the following:

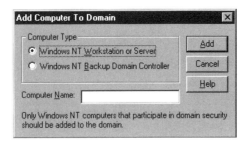

Figure 15.15 *Identify the computer type to the server of the domain.*

Windows NT Workstation or Server. This computer can be running NT Server as a member server, NT Workstation, or Windows 95.

Windows NT Backup Domain Controller. This computer must be set up as a BDC (through installation).

4. In the Computer Name text box, enter the computer's name.

5. Choose Add. You can add more computers at this time or close the dialog box.

On the workstation or server you're adding to the domain, follow these steps:

1. Open the Control Panel (Start, Settings, Control Panel).

2. Double-click the Network option to display the Network dialog box.

Note: If you are just installing the software to the client computer, you can enter the domain name and the computer name as you set the computer up. See Chapter 5 for information.

3. In the Identification tab, choose the Change button. The Change dialog box appears (see Figure 15.16).

4. Choose OK. NT prompts you to restart the computer. When the logon dialog box appears, the correct domain appears.

Note: You can move member servers and/or workstations from one domain to another simply by removing the computer from its current domain and adding it to another domain. You cannot, however, move a backup domain controller unless you reinstall the Windows NT Server 4.0 software.

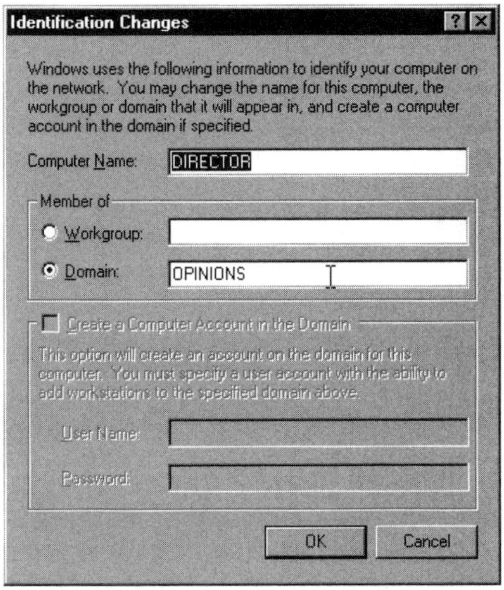

Figure 15.16 *Change the domain name and the computer's name to match those entered in the Add Computer to Domain dialog box on the server.*

Promoting a Domain Controller

If you have a problem with your primary domain controller, such as a crash or major hardware failure, you can assign any backup domain controller in your domain to take over as primary domain controller by promoting the server. The data on the BDC is up-to-date, due to the automatic directory replication between the two domain controllers. For user and group information, rights, permissions, files, even trusting domains, the BDC is a perfect replica of the PDC.

If the current PDC is still active when you promote the BDC, the current PDC is demoted to a BDC automatically. If the current PDC is not available when you promote the BDC but you return it to service later, you must demote the former PDC to a BDC else it will not run the Net Logon service or participate in authentication of user logons. To promote a BDC to a PDC, follow these steps:

1. Open the Server Manager by choosing Start, Programs, Administrative Tools, and Server Manager.

2. Choose Computer, Promote to Primary Domain Controller as shown in Figure 15.17.

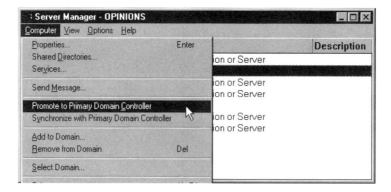

Figure 15.17 *The Promote to Primary Domain Controller command promotes the BDC.*

Note: When you select a former PDC in the list of computer in Server Manager, the Promote to Primary Domain Controller command changes to Demote to Backup Domain Controller command.

---

3. The User Manager carries out the change.

Synchronizing Controllers

Usually, the system takes care of all synchronization of backup and primary domain controllers; however, if the BDC is unable to establish a connection for some reason, you can do it manually. The BDC will send an administrative alert to the PDC if it cannot, for some reason, synchronize. Make sure the Alerter service and the Messenger service are set to automatic on both the PDC and BDC.

To manually synchronize domain controllers, follow these steps:

1. Open the Server Manager by choosing Start, Programs, Administrative Tools, and Server Manager and select the BDC you want to synchronize.

2. Choose Computer, Synchronize with Primary Domain Controller. The User Manager takes care of the task.

If you have more than one BDC in your domain and you want to manually synchronize all of them, select the PDC in the domain and choose the Computer menu. The Synchronize with Primary Domain Controller command changes to Synchronize Entire Domain. Choose that command and choose OK.

Summary

This chapter shows how to plan, add, and manage multiple domains. You must consider users, groups, and servers as well as workstation computers when you expand your network. Appendix A offers a glossary of terms used in NT and networking. If you have problems with any NT process or task, or with your applications, hardware, or network configuration, check out Appendix B for some probable solutions to common problems. Finally, if you need some clarification with installing and configuring TCP/IP, see Appendix C.

A Glossary of Terms

Account. For administrative, security, and communication purposes, as well as for use of on-line services, a user account identifies a subscriber by name, password, server or domain, and information about the groups to which the user belongs.

Account Operators Group. This NT group has the ability to manage and create accounts for users and groups using the User Manager for Domains. An Account Operator cannot however, modify the Administrators, Servers, Account Operators, Print Operators, or Backup Operators local groups or any local groups that are members of these local groups.

Account Policy. A set of rules that defines whether a new user is permitted to access a system and its resources; also defines the way passwords are used in a domain or on an individual computer.

Adapter. A circuit board that plugs into a computer to provide added capabilities; common adapters include display, memory expansion, input/output, and network interface cards.

Administrators Group. A group whose members have full control access of the network to its members, by default. Administrators can access workstations, files, and folders; manage and control users and groups; choose which resources to share, such as printers, CD-ROM drives, and so on. The Administrator has all rights and abilities on the NT Server and Workstation.

Application Layer. The seventh, and highest, layer in the OSI model for NT architecture. This layer uses services provided by the lower layers but is insulated from the details of the network hardware. The application layer describes how applications interact with the network operating system.

API (Application Program Interface). The complete definition of all of the operating system functions available to the application. In a graphical user interface,

419

the API also defines functions to support windows, icons, pull-down menus, and other components of the interface.

Architecture. The overall design and construction of the computer, especially how the system is constructed, how its components fit together, and the protocols and interfaces used for communication and cooperation among the components.

ATM (Asynchronous Transfer Mode). A method of transmitting voice, video, and data over high-speed LANs and WANs.

Attach. To access a server from a workstation; often to access additional servers after logging in to one server. Also, a NetWare 3.x workstation utility used to attach to an additional server after login.

Auditing. Tracking certain network events—such as security breaches, application errors, or system problems. Results are stored in a security log file which can be viewed only by users with special rights and/or permissions. In NT, view audit logs in the Event Viewer.

Authentication. The process of validating a user's login information by comparing the user name and password to a list of authorized users of the network.

Authentication Server. At least one network server must validate users' login information. Authentication usually involves comparing the username and password to a list of authorized users. If a match is found, the user can log in and access the system in accordance with the rights and permissions assigned to the user's account. NT designates the Primary Domain Controller (PDC) as the first server of the network, the server that authenticates users.

Backbone. That portion of the network that manages the bulk of the traffic; it may connect several locations or buildings, or even several smaller networks. The backbone uses a high-speed protocol, usually higher-speed than the rest of the LAN.

Backup. An up-to-date copy of your files that ensures against possible hard-disk failure and protects against accidental deletion of files.

Bandwidth. In networking, the transmission capacity of a computer or communications channel, stated in megabits per second (Mbps).

Backup Domain Controller (BDC). The backup domain controller contains a copy of the database and periodically and automatically updates it with the PDC.

Backup Operators. This group has the control over the server they need to perform backup and restores.

Backup Server. In NT, you can use a Backup Domain Controller as a backup for authentication of users. The Backup Domain Controller keeps updated copies of all user accounts, rights, and permissions listed on the Primary Domain Controller so that in case the PDC computer goes down, the BDC can continue services without disturbing the network or the users.

Basic (ClearText) Authentication. An authentication method in which the user's name and password are encoded during transmission; cleartext or basic means the base-64 encoding can be decoded by anyone with a decoding utility. *See* **encryption**.

BIOS (Basic Input/Output System). A set of instructions that lets the computer's hardware and operating system communicate with applications and peripherals devices, such as hard disks, printers, and video adapters.

bps (bits per second). The measure of speed at which data is transferred over a network.

Boot. The process of loading the operating system into memory.

Bridge. Equipment that connects different LANs together. Bridges are independent of protocol but hardware-specific.

Built-in Groups. The default groups provided with the software. Each group defines a collection of rights and abilities for members that provide access to commonly used network resources.

Cabling. The medium that connects nodes on a LAN—twisted-pair, coaxial, or fiber optic, for example.

Campus Network. A network that connects LANs. Even though a campus network may extend several miles, it does not include WAN services.

Card. A printed circuit board or adapter that plugs into the computer to add support, such as a network adapter card.

Category 3, 5. Also Cat 3 or Cat 5; The Electronics Industry Association/ Telecommunications Industry Association of standards. Cat 3 is for UTP cable for use at speeds up to 10Mbps; the basic minimum requirement for 10BaseT. Cat 5 is also for UTP cable for use at speeds up to 100Mbps.

Client. A device or application that makes use of the services provided by a server. A client may be a PC, or workstation, on a network using services provided from the network server.

Client/Server Network. Also called a dedicated server LAN, uses a central, often dedicated computer as a server that is specially configured to enable easy storage and sharing of files and resources. A server is a data management center from which clients can access applications, files, directories, and other resources. *See also* **Peer-to-peer network**.

Coaxial Cable. A type of electrical cable in which a solid piece of metal wire is surrounded by insulation, then surrounded by a tubular piece of metal; can carry voice, video, and data simultaneously.

Communications Server. A type of gateway that translates the packetized signals of a LAN to asynchronous signals, usually used on telephone lines, and enables nodes on a LAN to share modems or host connections.

COM Port. The device name used to denote a serial communications port.

Computer Network. Physically connected PCs that enable your employees to share files electronically, use e-mail, and share expensive equipment, such as CD-ROM drives and printers.

CPU (Central Processing Unit). The part of the computer in which mathematical operations are performed; the heart of the computer.

Creator Owner. For permissions sake the creator of a file or directory is a member of this group.

CTRL-ALT-DEL. A three-key combination used on most IBM-compatible computers to restart or reboot the machine; however, with NT, this combination is used to display the logon dialog box.

Database. A collection of related items, such as tables, forms, queries, and so on, organized by a database management system, and containing related information, such as lists of names and addresses, customer information, images, and so on. Data is usually indexed or sorted in a logical order; users can access the data they need using the index.

Database Server. Software that doles out database data to PCs on a LAN. A database application that follows the client/server architecture divides the database application into two parts: a front-end running on the client computer and a back-end running on the server. The front-end collects and displays data while the back-end performs the computations, analysis, and storage of the data. An application server.

Data-Link Layer. The second of seven OSI layers for computer-to-computer communications. The data-link layer validates the integrity of the flow of data from one node to another by synchronizing blocks of data.

Data Packet. One unit of information transmitted from one node on the network to another node.

Dedicated Line. A communications circuit used for one specific purpose, not used by or shared between other users.

Dedicated Server. A computer on the network that functions solely as a server by performing such tasks as storing files, printing, and managing users.

Default Gateway. In TCP/IP, the gateway is the intermediate network device on the local network. The default gateway has knowledge of the network Ids of the other networks in the Internet, so it can forward packets to other gateways until the packet is eventually delivered to the correct destination.

Device. A general term used to describe any computer peripheral or hardware element that can send or receive data, such as modems, printers, serial ports, disk drives, routers, bridges, and so on.

Device Driver. A program that allows a computer to communicate with and control a device.

Device Fonts. Fonts that reside in the print device or a font cartridge.

DHCP (Dynamic Host Configuration Protocol). A server that automatically administers client TCP/IP addresses and related settings for a network.

Dial-Up Networking. A Windows NT and Windows 95 component that enables users to connect to remote networks, like the Internet.

DIP (Dual In-line Package). A DIP switch is an "on-off" or "yes-no" switch mounted on a printed circuit board and used to configure various options for a device.

Directory. In a hierarchical file system, a method of organizing and grouping files and directories on a disk. In NT, directories are also called folders; subdirectories are also called subfolders.

Directory Database. A system used to track and maintain user accounts.

Directory Services. A listing of all users and resources on the network.

Disk Controller. The electronic circuitry that controls and manages the operation of floppy disks or hard disks installed to a computer.

DLL. *See* **dynamic-link library**.

DNS (Domain Name System). A static, hierarchical name service for TCP/IP hosts.

DNS Name Server. In the DNS client/server model, the servers containing information about a portion of the DNS database, which makes computer names available to clients querying for name resolution over the Internet.

Domain. A single computer, entire department, complete site, etc., used for naming, grouping, and management purposes.

Domain Admins. A member of the Administrators local group; the built-in Administrator user account is a member of the Domain Admins global group. An Administrator can administer the domain, the primary and backup domain controllers, and all other computers running both NT Server and Workstation in the domain.

Domain Guests Group. A group that contains the domain's built-in Guest user account; the rights are limited.

Domain Users. A member of the Users local group for the domain and the Users local group for every NT Workstation and member server on the network. Domain Users have normal user access.

Download. In communications, to transfer a file or files from one computer to another over a network or by using a modem.

Downloadable Soft Fonts. Fonts installed to the computer for use with applications; when you're ready to print, the fonts are downloaded to the printer before the document can actually be printed.

Drive Mapping. Assigning a drive letter to represent a complete directory path statement.

Dynamic-Link Library (DLL). A feature of Windows that enables executable routines that serve a special function to be stored separately as files with DLL extensions. DLL files are loaded only when needed by the program that calls them.

Encryption. The process of modifying data to protect it from unauthorized viewing or use. The modification makes data indecipherable as it's transmitted over a network or stored on a magnetic medium.

Enterprise. Describes an entire business group, organization, or corporation and all local, remote, and satellite offices associated with the group.

ESDI (Enhanced Small Device Interface). A popular hard disk, floppy disk, and tape drive interface standard.

Ethernet. One of the most popular network protocols and cabling scheme with a transfer rate of 10 megabits per second. Ethernet provides computers with network access on a transmit-at-will basis and runs on either coaxial cable or twisted-pair wiring.

Everyone. Anyone using the computer is a member of this group.

Fault Tolerance. A method of ensuring continued system operation in the event of individual failures. Backups, UPS (uninterrupted power supply), disk duplexing, disk mirroring, and so on are methods of providing fault tolerance.

FDDI (Fiber Distributed Data Interface). The specification for fiber-optic networks transmitting at a speed of up to 100 megabits per second over a token-ring topology.

Fiber-Optic Cable. A data transmission medium, consisting of glass fibers, that sends pulses of light along specially manufactured optical fibers. Fiber optic offers immense bandwidth and absolute protection from eavesdropping.

File Allocation Table (FAT). An operating system table that lists all disk space available on the disk in blocks. The table lists the location of each block, whether it's being used or available for use, disk damage, and so on. NT can run on a FAT system or NTFS file system.

File Server. File servers store data—documents, images, drawings, accounting files, and so on—that clients can request over the network. The files on a file server are shared among the clients; shared files can be read, reviewed, and updated by more than one individual. Access to the files may be regulated by password protection or account or security clearance.

File Sharing. The sharing of files over the network file server; shared files can be read, updated, printed, copied, and so on by more than one person.

Flashing-point Processor. A special-purpose, secondary processor designed to perform floating-point calculations faster than the main processor.

ftp (File Transfer Protocol). A TCP/IP protocol used to transfer files between computers; this is an older protocol used mainly on the Internet, now.

Frame Relay. A standard for a packet-switching protocol running at speeds of up to 2 megabits per second.

Gateway. A shared communication between two networks, often between a LAN and a larger system. A gateway permits two networks using different protocols to communicate with each other.

Global Group. An account granted server rights in its own and in other domains.

Gopher. A hierarchical system for finding and retrieving information over the Internet or from an intranet, using a menuing system and links to other servers.

Group. A set of network users who have been assigned to a network user group so they all have the same level of security.

Groupware. Network software designed for use by a group of people all working on the same project or sharing the same data.

Groupware Servers. Groupware applies to the distribution of mail, bulletin boards, images, and workflow to place people in direct contact with other people. Lotus Notes is an excellent example of a groupware application. Often, not only a specialized server is needed to manage groupware information but a specially trained manager or administrator may also be needed. An application server.

Hard Disk Controller. An expansion board that contains the necessary circuitry to control and coordinate a hard disk drive.

Hardware Interrupt. A request, or interrupt, for a service provided by a hardware device, such as a video card, keyboard, or other device.

Home Page. The primary page containing information for a collection of pages, on the Internet or an intranet. Usually the starting point for a Web site.

HTML (Hypertext Markup Language). A simple language of formatting and tags used to create hypertext documents used on the World Wide Web.

HTTP (Hypertext Transport Protocol). The protocol used for communication between WWW clients and servers.

Hub. A device that allows the network to be extended to accommodate additional workstations. The center of a star topology network or cabling system. A file server may act as the hub of a LAN because it houses the network software and direct communications within the network.

IDE (Integrated Drive Electronics). A popular hard disk interface standard.

Interactive. Anyone using the computer locally is a member of this group.

Interface. A demarcation between two devices; carries out the procedures, codes, and protocols that enable two devices to interact.

Interface Card. A printed circuit board fitting in the expansion chassis of a computer to make the physical connection between the computer and LAN cable. *See* **Network Interface Adapter**.

Internet Information Server, (Internet Information Server) A network file and application server that supports multiple protocols, but primarily supports transferring HTML information using the HTTP protocol.

Intranet. An internal web site you can create for your company's use only. Just as with an Internet site, an intranet site can include text, images, and links to other documents. You can create an intranet with Windows NT.

I/O (Input/Output). The transfer of data between the computer and a peripheral device.

IP Address. A number used to identify a node on a network and to specify routing information. The address is usually represented in dotted-decimal notation of four period-delimited octets consisting of up to 1`2 numerals (such as 142.57.0.27).

IPX/SPX Compatible. In NT, a protocol compatible with NetWare's IPX/SPX for communications between NT computers and NetWare servers.

IRQ (Interrupt ReQuest). A signal that tells the hardware that an event has taken place that requires the processor's attention.

Jumper. A small connector that completes a circuit, usually to select one configuration from a choice of configurations on a card or adapter.

Kernel. A fundamental part of the operating system, loaded into memory and hidden from the users. The kernel manages system memory, the file system, and disk operations.

LAN (Local Area Network). A group of computers and associated peripheral devices connected, spanning a limited geographical area, by way of a communications channel and capable of sharing files and other resources.

LAN Manager. A network operating system created by Microsoft.

LANtastic. A peer-to-peer network operating system from Artisoft, Inc, that runs with DOS or Microsoft Windows.

Local Group. A group granted rights to just the resources on the servers of its own domain.

Local Printer. A printer attached to a workstation rather than to the file or print server.

Logical Drive. A smaller unit resulting from the division of a large hard disk.

Log in/Log on. In NT "log on," but both mean the same thing—the process of identifying oneself to the computer system by establishing a connection and by entering a username and password.

Mainframe Computer. A large, fast, multiuser computer, usually supplied complete with peripherals and software by a vendor, designed to manage huge amounts of data. Almost always use dumb terminals connected in star configuration; dumb terminals are workstations that don't have a computer processor in them, just a screen and keyboard.

Map. *See* **Drive Mapping**.

Medium. The hardware equipment used to connect computers in a network, including cables and network cards.

Megabits Per Second (Mbps). A measurement of the amount of data moving over a network in one second.

Member Servers. Servers running NT Server software that do not contain the database of users, can be used as workstations, file servers, print servers, and so on. A member server can be used as a workstation, file server, and/or print server.

Migration. A movement of one operating system to another, including user and group information, resources, rights, files, directories, and so on.

MIME (Multipurpose Internet Mail Extensions). A mechanism for specifying and describing the format of Internet message bodies; enables the exchange of objects, character sets, and multimedia in e-mail on different computer systems.

Minicomputer. A small or medium computer accessed by dumb terminals; it is bigger, usually more powerful, than a PC.

Motherboard. The main circuit board of a computer that contains the CPU (central processing unit), coprocessor, memory, device controllers, and other devices.

Multiprocessing. The capability of an operating system, such as NT, to use more than one processor (CPU) at a time in a single computer.

Multiserver Network. A network that uses two or more servers.

Multitasking. The simultaneous execution of two or more programs in one computer. Enables users to recalculate a spreadsheet, for example, while writing a report.

Multiuser. The ability of a computer to support multiple users while providing a full range of capability to each one.

NDIS (Network Driver Interface Specification). A device driver standard that is independent of the network interface card and the protocol being used. Enables multiple protocol stacks to be used at the same time within the same computer.

NetBEUI (NetBIOS Extended User Interface). A network device driver used in LAN Manager, Windows for Workgroups, Windows 95, and Windows NT to communicate with the network interface card.

NetBIOS (Network Basic Input/Output System). A protocol that manages data exchange and network access. Applications use NetBIOS to gain access to computer resources over a network.

NetWare. A network operating system made by Novell.

Network. A group of computers and associated peripherals connected by cable and capable of sharing files and other resources.

Network Adapter (NIC). An interface card that enables communications between a computer and the network cable to which it is connected. Also called a Network Interface Card, network card, adapter.

Network Administrator. The person who operates and manages the network, including such tasks as adding and removing users, troubleshooting problems, planning for future expansion, installing hardware and software, monitoring the system, backing up the system, and so on.

Network Group. In NT, all users connected over the network are members of this group.

Network Layer. The third layer in the OSI that defines protocols for data routing.

Node. Any device attached to the network capable of communication with other network devices. Node is sometimes used interchangeably with workstation; however, a node can also be a hub, a gateway, or other device capable of communication over the network.

NOS (Network Operating System). In the client/server architecture LAN, the software that runs on the file server and coordinates functions, such as creation and management of user accounts, resource sharing, information sharing, security, error detection, and so on.

NTFS (New Technology File System). In NT, the native file system that supports long file names, permissions for sharing files, a transaction log, and the FAT file system.

OSI (Open Systems Interconnection). A network model that divides communications between computers into seven layers, or a protocol stack. Each successively higher layer builds on the functions of the layers below. *See* **Application Layer**; **Presentation Layer**; **Session Layer**; **Transport Layer**; **Network Layer**; **Data-link Layer**; and **Physical Layer**.

Packet. A group of bits, including address, data, and control elements, that are switched and transmitted together. Data exchanged over a network.

Packet Switching. A method of data transmission using packets, whereby a channel is occupied only for the duration of transmission of the packet. The packet switch sends the different packets from different data conversations along the best route available in any particular order; at the other end, the packets are reassembled to from the original message and sent to the receiving computer.

Partition. A portion of a hard disk that the operating system treats as if it were a separate drive.

Peer-to-Peer Network. A group of PCs linked together, each with the same status as the other, each sharing its resources with the others. *See also* **Client/server network**.

Permission. Authorizations given to certain user accounts to access files and directories.

Physical Layer. The first layer of the OSI model that defines the mechanism for communicating with the transmission medium and interface hardware.

POP (Post Office Protocol). The protocol that permits a workstation to dynamically access a mail drop on a server in a useful fashion. POP3, or version 3 of POP, is used to allow a workstation to retrieve mail that is being held for it in an SMTP server.

POST (Power On Self Test). A set of diagnostic programs loaded from ROM before the operating system is loaded.

Presentation Layer. The sixth layer of the OSI, defines the way data is formatted, converted, and presented over the network.

Primary Domain Controller (PDC). A domain's master security database (that approves or rejects requests for resources on the network) is located on the primary domain controller. Also, any and all changes made to user accounts for the domain are made to the PDC; there is only one PDC per domain.

Printer. The interface between the operating system and the print device.

Print Device. The actual printer.

Print Operators. This group can log on to the server and shut the system down. The only ability granted a Print Operator is the ability to create, edit, delete, and manage printer shares.

Print Queue. A list of documents in line to be printed on any network printer. In NT, create a queue by first creating a printer to represent the print device.

Print Server. A server that handles the printing for all users and all printers on the network. The server collects the print jobs and places them in a print queue on the hard disk, then routes them to one or more printers attached to the server or the network. The print queue is a list of documents waiting to be printed and one queue normally exists for each printer on the network.

Protocol. A set of rules for communicating between computers. Protocols govern format, timing, sequencing, and error control.

Protocol stack. Several layers of software that define the protocol used between computers and between a computer and a network.

Queue. A line of tasks, usually printing but could refer to jobs or messages, waiting for service. A task in a queue is assigned a priority so that important tasks jump ahead of the others.

RAM (Random Access Memory). A collection of chips where data can be entered, read, and erased. RAM speeds your computer processing; RAM is the fastest memory device. It also loses its contents when you lose or turn off power, as opposed to the way ROM works.

RAS (Remote Access Service). In NT, a service that can be used by remote clients to dial into the NT Server for services such as Internet access, file and printer sharing, e-mail, scheduling, and so on.

Remoteboot. A technique used to boot a workstation from the file server rather than from the workstation.

Replicator Group. In NT, this group does not have actual users as members; instead, the only member of the Replicator group is an account used to log on the Replicator services of the primary domain controller and the backup domain controllers of the domain.

Resources. Equipment or data on a network such as printers, CD-ROM drives, modems, files, and directories.

Rights. Privileges granted to a user or group by the network administrator. Rights determine the operations a user can perform on the system.

Ring Network. A topology in the form of a closed loop or circle with each node connected to the next. Data moves in one direction around the ring; the more

PCs on the ring, the slower the response time. Loss of one PC may disable the entire network.

RIP (Routing Information Protocol). A routing protocol used on TCP/IP networks that maintains a list of reachable networks.

RISC (Reduced Instruction Set Computing). A processor that recognizes only a limited number of assembly-language instructions, commonly used in workstations.

ROM (Read-Only Memory). A memory system that stores information permanently, retaining its contents when the system is shut down.

Router. An intelligent connecting device that can send packets to the correct LAN segment.

Routing. The process of directing message packets from one node to another by choosing the best path through the LAN.

RPC (Remote Procedure Call). A set of procedures used to implement client/server architecture in distributed programming.

Screen fonts. Those fonts you see on-screen; screen fonts are installed to the computer for use with applications and are not necessarily sent to the printer.

SCSI (Small Computer System Interface). A high-speed parallel interface that allows up to seven peripheral devices to connect at a time to just one port.

Server. A computer that makes access to files, printing, communications, and other services available to users of the network. Usually a combination of hardware and software.

Server Operator Group. This group grants its members the rights and abilities needed to administer the primary and backup domain controllers: logging on locally to the server, shutting down the system, backing up and restoring files, locking and unlocking the server, sharing resources, and so on.

Session Layer. The fifth layer of the OSI architecture that coordinates communications and maintains the session for as long as it's needed.

Sharing. A method of designating a resource—such as a directory or printer—as available for network users to access.

Shielded Cable. Networking cable protected against electromagnetic interference by metal-backed mylar foil and plastic.

Shielded Twisted-Pair Cable (STP). Networking cable with a foil shield and copper braid surrounding pairs of wires so that the electrical signals from outside the cable cannot interfere with transmission inside the cable. Shielded cable provides more protection against interference and is more expensive than unshielded cable.

SMTP (Simple Mail Transfer Protocol). A TCP/IP protocol used to exchange mail on the Internet between two SMTP servers.

SNMP (Simple Network Management Protocol). A standard protocol, part of TCP/IP, used to manage nodes over a network.

Spanning Tree. A topology that builds on the star topology by interconnecting two or more hubs and nodes in a branching tree-like configuration. There is only one route between any two nodes on the network, thereby protecting all nodes in case one cable or node goes down.

SQL (Structured Query Language). A database query and programming language widely used for accessing data in relational database systems.

SQL Server. A server running on a PC that uses the structure query language to query, update, and manage a relational database.

Star Topology. A network topology in the form of a star in which the center is a hub.

Subdirectory. A directory within another directory, also a subfolder in NT.

System Administrator. The person responsible for the day-to-day management and operation of the network. *See* **Network Administrator**.

10BaseT. An Ethernet standard over unshielded twisted-pair wiring based on the start topology.

T1 or T3 Connection. Standard measurements of network bandwidth.

TCP/IP (Transmission Control Protocol/Internet Protocol). A set of communications protocols that encompasses media access, packet transport, session communications, file transfer, electronic mail, and terminal emulation.

Token. A combination of bits passed around a LAN that gives a workstation permission to transmit.

Token-Ring Network. A topology with a ring structure that uses token passing to regulate traffic on the network. Token Ring is IBM's implementation of the token-ring network architecture.

Topology. Description of the physical connections of a network, including the placement of cables and nodes, routers, gateways, and other components. *See* **Ring**; **Star**; **Token-ring**; **Spanning tree**.

Traffic. The flow of messages and data over the network.

Transport Layer. The fourth layer of the OSI, defines protocols for structuring messages and takes care of error checking.

True-Type Fonts. True-Type fonts ship with most Windows versions, including NT. They are device-independent; the font you see on the screen can be duplicated in any print device.

Twisted-Pair Cable. A networking cable that twists together two or more pairs of insulated wires. The cable may be shielded or unshielded.

UNIX. A 32-bit, multiuser, multitasking operating system that uses the TCP/IP set of protocols. Originally developed by AT&T and works on some personal computers.

Unshielded Twisted-Pair Cable (UTP). A networking cable that contains two or more pairs of twisted copper wires. The advantages of UTP is its low cost and ease of installation; however, UTP has limited signaling speeds and can use only short maximum cable-segment lengths.

UPS (Uninterruptable Power Supply). A set of batteries used to power a computer system if the normal power service is interrupted. UPS provides uninterrupted power for around five minutes, to give you time to save files and shut down the system in case of a power failure.

URL (Uniform Resource Locator). A naming convention that uniquely identifies the location of a computer, directory, or file on the Internet—such as http://www.microsoft.com.

User. Any person accessing a computer system or network.

User Account. A security measure used to control access to a network by identifying users by a name and password.

Users Group. This group has no rights on the server and no abilities either, unless you assign them.

Vertical Application. An application created especially for a narrow market or profession, such as real estate software or a horse registry program.

Video Adapter. Hardware that plugs into the computer and provides the text and graphics output to the monitor. Some video adapters, such as VGA, are included on the motherboard as opposed to a separate card.

Volume. The highest level of the file server directory and file structure.

WAN (Wide-Area Network). A network that connects users across long distances, such as cities, states, even countries. Designed to serve an area of hundreds or thousands of miles; public and private packet-switching networks and a nationwide telephone network are good examples of WANs.

Web Browser. A software program, such as the Internet Explorer, that retrieves a document from a Web server, interprets the HTML codes, and displays the document to the user.

Web Page. A WWW document.

Web Server. A Web server is a server that supplies documents to clients when requested. The Web server may provide services to your internal intranet of users, those attached to your LAN (local area network) only. A Web server may additionally or separately be attached to the Internet, thus serving clients over the World Wide Web. An application server.

WINS (Windows Internet Name Service). A name resolution service that runs on NT Server. WINS resolves NetBIOS computer names to IP addresses for WINS clients on a routed network.

Wireless LAN. A networking method of connection in which infrared beams or radio signals are used.

Workgroup. In NT and other Windows versions, a group of users who work together and share files and databases over a LAN.

Workstation. A personal computer attached to a network which you can send data to or receive data from. *See* **Client**.

WWW (World Wide Web). The software, protocols, conventions, and data that enable hypertext and multimedia publishing of resources on different computers all over the world.

B *Troubleshooting Guide*

You may be able to save your server from disaster by performing a few preventative measures as outlined in this appendix. Following are some preventative measures you can take that will help you in case of a crash or other problems. Also, there are some problems outlined with possible solutions in the following pages.

Preventative Maintenance

First and foremost, you should establish some sort of procedures for regularly checking each server for the following:

- Available disk space
- Database storage space
- Mail box or post office storage space
- Event viewer for potential problems

You might want to check the server every morning or every evening; but make sure you check it at least twice a week. Avoiding potential problems is the best method of providing better service to your users and reducing the number of complaints and annoyances.

Regular Maintenance

Schedule a regular time each month to perform regular maintenance checks. Make sure your users know about the scheduled down time so they can plan their work day around it. Be careful to consider other important office procedures when planning a maintenance check; for example, you don't want the network to be down while accounting is trying to pay bills or write payroll checks.

TIP: Consider changing the hours the network staff works on the maintenance days. Instead of having the network staff work from 9 to 5, change their hours to 11 to 7 or 1 to 9 only on maintenance days; this prevents a lot of overtime and means down time won't be as adverse as it would be during the regular work day.

Clean hard drives regularly, removing unnecessary files and folders. Archive data that's not accessed regularly to clear space. Keep a check on hard drives, network adapter cards, video cards, and so on, replacing the hardware when necessary. Rebuild databases or mail systems regularly.

Anticipate Needs

You can anticipate your needs by creating an emergency repair disk, if you did not create one during installation of NT or by updating the disk each time you make a software or hardware change. Additionally, you can save your configuration in the Disk Administrator and make backups regularly to help anticipate problems down the road.

Emergency Repair Disk

The emergency repair disk contains all of the initial setup information of your system and can help you in case of a server crash and with several other problems. Each time you make significant changes in your configuration, hardware, or software setup, create another emergency repair disk or update the original one.

To create an emergency repair disk, choose Start, Run. In the Open dialog box, type **rdisk** and choose OK. The Repair Disk Utility dialog box appears, as shown in Figure B.1. Choose the Create Repair Disk if you do not have a disk or Update Repair Info and insert the disk you created during installation. You should

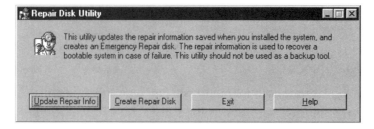

Figure B.1 *Update configuration information on your emergency repair disk.*

only update the repair information if your system is running properly; if you update while the system is faulty, you won't be able to use the repair disk.

TIP: You can also use the Setup Boot Disk, the same one you used during installation, to boot NT if it's not cooperating.

Save Configuration

As another precaution, you can save your configuration *before* you run into a problem. The procedure saves assigned drive letters, volume sets, strip sets, stripe sets with parity, and mirror sets. If you haven't changed your partitions to include these items, it's not necessary for you to save configuration. If you have changed your partitions, however, this can be a valuable aid for ensuring that you don't lose system configuration information.

Open the Disk Administrator by choosing Start, Programs, Administrative Tools, Disk Administrator. If it's the first time you've run the Disk Administrator, the system configuration will be automatically updated; NT displays a dialog box telling you this. You can choose OK to continue. After the system updates, the application opens, as shown in Figure B.2.

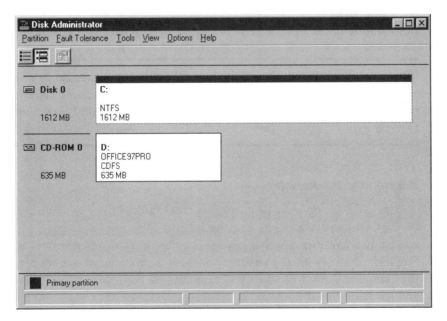

Figure B.2 *Use the Disk Administrator to update your configuration.*

Choose Partition, Configuration, Save. Insert a disk to save the configuration to and choose OK. Follow directions, then choose OK when you're done. Keep the disk safe in case you need to restore the configuration at some point.

If you should need to restore your disk configuration, open the Disk Administrator and choose Partition, Configuration, Restore. You are prompted for the disk and warned that the configuration will overwrite your disk configuration information. Choose Yes to continue.

TIP: One of the handiest NT features is the Event Viewer. If you have any problems—security, application, printing, and so on—first view the logs in the Event Viewer (Start, Programs, Administrative Tools, Event Viewer). These logs may contain important information you can use to help you solve your problem. Chapter 11 covers opening and viewing logs in the Event Viewer.

Backups

As always, creating backups of the server and important files and applications is a must for any network. If you have a backup domain controller on the network, then all the better for you; the backup domain controller stores copies of all user and group profiles, permissions, rights, and so on, but does not store files, directories, applications, and the like. Choose your favorite software and tape drive, CD drive, or other storage device, and make a backup now and often in preparation for a disaster.

Note: As a global reminder, make sure that in NT you're logged on as a member of the Administrators group (or other group with appropriate rights) before you panic about being denied access to a tool, program, or utility on the server or on a workstation.

Backing Up the Registry

You should back up your Registry files to a floppy disk or to some other location, perhaps on the network, in case the Registry becomes corrupted or in case you add hardware or software that impairs the system. You can copy the backups of the Registry files back to the server if you have a problem; this restores the server to the configuration it had when you made the backups. Naturally, if you successfully add hardware or software to the server, you should update the backup of the Registry files.

To back up the Registry files, open the Explorer and choose View, Options; in the View tab, choose Show All Files and choose OK. Open the Winnt\System32 folder and save the entire contents of the Config folder to a floppy disk or to another folder on the network. This is your backup of the Registry. To restore the backup, copy the files back to the Winnt\System32\Config folder, then restart the computer.

TIP: The System.alt file, located in the Winnt\System32\Config folder is the Registry's own backup copy.

Problems and Solutions

Following is a list of problems you may run into while working with NT Server, users and groups, installation of the application, and so on. If you don't find a solution in this appendix, check the NT documentation and the on-line Help for more information.

Installation Problems

Following is a list of possible problems and solutions that you may run into during installation of the operating system.

Floppy Disk

If you have a 2.88M 3.5-inch floppy drive and use a 2.88M formatted disk for creation of the emergency repair disk during installation, you may have problems creating the disk. Use a disk formatted to 1.44M instead and the disk should work fine.

CD-ROM

If you have trouble with NT recognizing the CD-ROM device after using the third Setup floppy disk, check the hardware compatibility list to see if the device is listed as compatible. If your CD-ROM is not listed, you may want to install NT Server from the network instead of from CD. To do this, copy the CD to a directory on the network, access the network from the server to which you will install NT, and enter the winnt command at the DOS prompt or in the Run dialog box. See Chapter 5 for information about installing NT.

Formatting the Hard Disk

When choosing to format or partition your disk before installation of NT, be careful if your hard disk contains stripe sets, volume sets, or mirrors. NT's Setup screen displays these elements as Windows NT Fault Tolerance. If you delete any of these elements, or if you delete a partition, you will lose the data in that area.

Disk Compression

If you're having trouble installing NT, make sure the drive to which you are installing is not compressed with any compression utility other than an NTFS compression. NT cannot install to the drive if that's the case.

Restarting Trouble

While installing NT, Setup reboots the computer several times. Often it takes a while to start the system again; be patient. If it seems like the system gets stuck somewhere and you don't think it will continue after it reboots itself, turn the computer off, wait 10 seconds, then turn the computer back on. Setup should continue from where it left off. If it does not, insert the first Setup disk—the boot disk—and start the computer again. Setup may need to start over completely or it may pick up where you left off.

Server Crashes

If your server crashes or refuses to boot because of something you've done to your system configuration, such as changing a video card, you can try several things to get the configuration back before you try reinstalling NT. Reinstalling most always works; however, you will have to reconfigure users, groups, print servers, and other important settings that make the process time-consuming.

Try the following solutions when you have a server configuration problem:

- As your computer boots, it displays a message "Press spacebar now to evoke the Last Known Good Configuration." Press the spacebar and choose to start the computer using the configuration that was used the last time you successfully booted the machine.

- Use the emergency repair disk you created during installation. Place the disk in the floppy drive, reboot the computer, and follow the directions on-screen. The repair disk has information based on your initial setup; now users, permissions, or other changes you've made to the system will be applied.

- If you changed video drivers and have a hard time seeing the screen and choices because of it, restart the system. When the computer displays the options for starting NT Server, choose the option NT Server 4.0 (VGA drivers). The system will boot with generic video drivers; go to the Control Panel and double-click the Display icon, then choose the appropriate driver.

Screen Savers

Don't use a screen saver on any server computer; screen savers often cause crashes or other erratic behaviors, plus they take away from the server's memory and usage.

Problems with Users and Groups

The primary problem you will find with users and groups occurs when someone thinks he or she has rights to perform certain tasks but does not. Confirming group membership and understanding the rights and abilities assigned to each group will help you if you have any problems in this area. See Chapter 6 for information about editing, adding, and managing users and groups. See Chapter 7 for help with assigning rights and permissions to users and groups. Following are a few common problems you may run into.

Recreating a User Account

User and group accounts each have a unique SID (Security Identifier) number assigned to them. Internal processes in NT user, the account's SID instead of a group or username. If you change your mind after deleting a user or group, you must recreate the account from scratch, assigning rights, adding groups, and so on. Just recreating a group or username doesn't retrieve the SID and the properties attached to that SID.

Unavailable Features in the User Manager for Domains

If your computer communicates across a connection with low transmission rates—such as a Remote Access Service connection or overseas connection—you can reduce delays in the display of accounts, groups, and so on in the User Manager for Domains by choosing Low Speed Connection in the Options menu. If you use the Low Speed Connection option, however, you'll find that some features are not available to you, including the Refresh command, Select Users command, the ability to create new or modify global groups, and so on. Change the Low Speed Connection to make these features available again.

Deleting a Group

You cannot recover a group once you've deleted it; the SID (Security Identifier) for the group is deleted as are the resource permissions associated with the group.

To recreate the group, you must start from scratch. You do not, however, delete the users in a group simply by deleting the group.

Home Directories

When assigning home directories to a user's profile (User Manager for Domains, User dialog box, Profiles button) remember you cannot use a file or directory name longer than the 8.3 DOS convention unless you're using the NTFS file system. FAT file systems restrict the file and directory names. You also cannot use the wildcard %USERNAME% when creating a home directory.

Sharing Resources, Rights, and Permissions

If you have problems with rights and permissions, check the group memberships first. See Chapter 7 for information about rights, abilities, and permissions. Following are a few other problems you might run across.

Sharing Problems

If you choose to stop sharing a directory while users are connected to that directory, the users can lose their data. Make sure everyone is disconnected from the directory before stopping sharing.

Default Permissions

If you revoke default permissions for any directories created by NT Server and/or NT Workstation, you could create problems for the operating system. If this happens, you can try to reset the permissions, using the NT documentation as a guide to the defaults; if all else fails, you will have to reinstall the software.

Do not open or change permissions on the SYSTEM\REPL\IMPORT directory; even opening the permissions could change or damage settings in this replication directory.

Printing Problems

In general, if you have a printing problem, there are several questions you can ask yourself in an effort to find a solution. Chapter 8 explains creating and configuring printers and print devices. Before listing specific printing problems, I'll offer a list of questions you can ask that may help you discover your print problem.

Is the correct printer port specified?

Is the correct printer driver installed? If the answer is yes, you might try deleting and reinstalling the printer driver in case the file is corrupted in some way.

Have you tried printing to another printer? Perhaps the application is at fault. Can you print to the printer from another application?

Is the printer cable bad? Try using another cable.

Will the printer print when attached to another port?

You might try turning on the logging of spooling events, as well. Choose File, Server Properties in the Printers window, then choose the Advanced tab in the Print Server Properties dialog box. By default the log spooler option is activated, but make sure the check box is checked. Note the Spool Folder in which the log is stored, for example C:\WINNT\System32\spool\PRINTERS.

Next, open the Event Viewer (Start, Programs, Administrative Tools, Event Viewer) and choose Log, Open. In the Open dialog box, go to the spool folder and open any files that appear there. Viewing the files in the Event Viewer may give you a hint to the problems you're having.

Parallel Port Problems

Even though most personal computers support three parallel ports, they usually only have one installed. If you have trouble locating or connecting to LPT2 or LPT3, check installed ports first. Additionally, when configuring parallel ports, you might have to set hardware jumpers or switches. Refer to the device's documentation for instructions.

Serial Port Problems

Serial ports can be set for flow control through the Ports icon in the Control Panel. Default settings are typically 9600 baud, no parity, 8 bits, 1 stop bit, and hardware handshaking. If you change these settings and have trouble, change back to the default settings or check your print device's documentation to confirm these settings.

Unsupported Printer

If NT doesn't list a printer driver for your specific print device and you don't have a disk containing the driver, you can often use a different supported driver instead. When using an HPPCL (LaserJet)-compatible laser printer, for example, try a Hewlett-Packard LaserJet Plus driver. For a PostScript compatible printer, try the Apple LaserWriter Plus driver.

If you're using a 9-pin dot matrix printer that's IBM-compatible, try an IBM Proprinter driver; if the printer is Epson-compatible, try the Epson FX-80 (for narrow) or FX-100 (for wide) carriage. For a 24-pin dot matrix printer, you can try the IBM Proprinter X24 for an IBM-compatible and the Epson LQ-1500 for an Epson LQ-compatible.

If you have another type printer, call the manufacturer or refer to the printer's documentation for emulation types.

Printing from DOS-based Applications

If you're printing from a DOS-based application through the command prompt window on an NT computer and going to an NT print server, you will have trouble if you don't first issue the NET USE command. At the command prompt (Start, MS-DOS Command Prompt), type **NET USE /?** to get help entering the switches and parameters that suit your situation.

Printer Memory Errors

If you frequently receive memory errors, check the Device Settings page in the printer's Properties dialog box. Make sure the amount of memory listed is the amount of memory in your printer; NT may assume there is more memory than there actually is and that could cause the memory error.

Troubleshooting Help

This section describes both solutions to problems you may encounter with the Help feature in NT and the troubleshooter Help feature in NT that helps you find answers to common problems.

Help Problems

If you click the Find tab in the Help Topics window and get an error message, such as Unable to display the Find tab, your GID (General InDex) or FTS (Full Text Search) file is corrupted. The answer is to delete these files, then the next time you start Help, NT regenerates them. The files are located in \WINNT\HELP, as shown in Figure B.3.

Often, people who need more space on the computer delete files, such as HLP files, then find they needed those files after all. If you deleted some of the files in the Help feature, specifically CNT files, you will notice you cannot see a Contents tab in the Help feature. While you can rebuild GID, FTS, and FTG files to regenerate the Index and Find tabs, you cannot rebuild CNT files. You can only restore the Contents tab if you recover the CNT file from the Recycle Bin; or if you've already emptied the bin, you will need to reinstall the application.

Using the Troubleshooter

NT's Help includes a troubleshooter that offers solutions to many problems you may encounter. In the troubleshooter, you choose a statement that best describes your problem; this takes you to another set of statements from which you choose

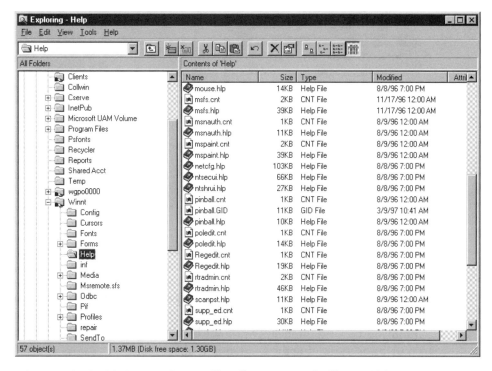

Figure B.3 *CNT, GID, and HLP files all represent Help files in NT.*

again. Figure B.4 shows the network troubleshooter. To find a troubleshooter in Help, choose Start, Help, then click the Index tab. Type **trouble** in the text box; a list of troubleshooting subjects appears, including network, modem, memory, printers, and so on.

Migration Problems

Although this book doesn't cover migration from NetWare to NT Server, you may want to try migrating your users and files. If you plan ahead, then perform a trial migration, you should be able to work out all of the kinks before performing the final migration. Here are a few problems you may run into; however, you might take a look at my book *Migrating from Novell NetWare to NT Server,* (John Wiley and Sons, Inc., 1997) for help in planning and performing a migration.

Migration Tool Won't Start

To run the Migration tool, the Windows NT server computer must be running the NWLink IPX/SPX Compatible Transport (Control Panel, Network option,

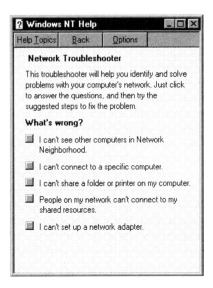

Figure B.4 *Find the statement that describes your problem in the troubleshooter.*

Protocols tab). Additionally, you must have installed the Gateway Service for Net-Ware prior to running the Migration tool.

Can't Select NetWare Server

If you cannot see a NetWare server when selecting servers for migration, you may not be logged onto the NetWare server as a Supervisor.

Can't Select NT Server

If you have trouble selecting the NT Server in the Migration tool window or you cannot transfer data to the NT server, check to make sure you're logged on as a member of the Administrators group.

Gateway Services

You may try using the Gateway services to connect an existing NetWare server to your NT server. This is also addressed in my migration book. If you're having trouble getting the Gateway Service to start, first check your configuration of the network card. Configure the network card in the Control Panel, Network option. Following are some additional problems and solutions.

Access Denied

If you are denied access to a Windows NT Server computer while you're trying to configure it as a file or print gateway, you may not be using a NetWare user account that is a member of the NTGATEWAY group or that group may not have appropriate rights. Create the group. Using SYSCON, NETADMIN, or NWADMIN from a NetWare-attached workstation, create a user on the NetWare server that matches the user that will log on from the NT computer. Set the password for the user. Next, create a NetWare group called NTGATEWAY and place the newly created user in that group.

Gateway Service Unavailable

If the Gateway Service is unavailable in the Network dialog box, Services tab, you may not have removed the NetWare redirectors first. To remove existing NetWare redirectors, open the Network icon in the Control Panel and choose the Network Settings dialog box, Services tab; select the existing redirector—such as NetWare Services for NT from Novell—and choose the Remove button. Confirm the choice and choose OK to close the dialog box. You'll have to reboot your computer.

Service Startup Problems

If the Gateway service doesn't start or starts then abruptly stops, you should first check your adapter card configuration (Control Panel, Network option). Next, check the Event Viewer. If you cannot find a problem, delete the Gateway Service from the Services tab of the Network dialog box, then reinstall it. The service may have been installed or configured incorrectly.

File Attribute Problems

It's important to understand that when using the Gateway Service for NetWare, some NetWare file attributes are not supported, specifically Read Write, Shareable, Transactional, Purge, Read Audit, Write Audit, and Copy Inhibit. Only the Read Only, Archive, System, and Hidden file attributes are preserved.

Application Problems

Windows NT can run MS-DOS, Windows 3.x, Windows NT and Windows 95, 16-bit OS/2, and POSIX applications. Applications not designed specifically for

Windows NT or Windows 95, however, need a device driver designed to run with NT. If you have applications that do not supply an NT-compatible driver, contact the manufacturer of the application to see if there is an updated driver for that program. NT prevents the application from running properly without a compatible driver. Applications such as fax cards, scanner cards, and disk maintenance applications fall into this category as well as applications that rely on their own graphics device drivers or disk device drivers.

Windows 3.x Application Problems

If you're running several Windows 3.x applications at one time and in the same memory space, one application crashing can result in all Windows 3.x applications locking up. You can avoid this problem by running a Windows 3.x–based application in its own memory space. Running several Windows 3.x–based programs, each in its own memory space, will use more NT memory and may slow the system. See Chapter 12 for more information.

Windows for Workgroups Password Problem

If you have a password problem when logging onto a Workgroups client, you can delete the PWL file with your username (found in the Windows directory) to get rid of your password list. The next time you log on, you enter a password, thus starting a new list.

PIFs

You can modify the PIF (program information file) file for MS-DOS applications by right-clicking the file in the Explorer (Start, Programs, Windows NT Explorer) and choose the Properties command. Changing the properties creates and modifies the PIF file. If you have problems locating a PIF file for any MS-DOS application, you can use the NT-supplied PIF for most DOS-based applications. NT's PIF is named _DEFAULT.PIF and is located in the *%SystemRoot%* folder. See Chapter 12 for more information.

TSRs

NT supports TSRs (Terminate-and-Stay-Resident) programs; however, do not place TSRs in your AUTOEXEC.NT or CONFIG.NT files. Since the AUTOEXEC.NT and the CONFIG.NT files run each time you open a Command Prompt window, the TSR would also start each time you open a new window, thus you would have several copies of the TSR running at one time and that would tax your system memory. To run a TSR, use the Run command (Start, Run). See Chapter 12 for more information.

Command Prompt

You can make adjustments to the way the Command Prompt screen looks, but re-alize that if you don't use the defaults, you may have some problems with the screen. Following are a few possible problems.

Distorted Text On-Screen

If the text in your Command Prompt window looks distorted, you may need to change your screen font, colors, or screen size. Use the Control menu to open the Properties dialog box within the Command Prompt window. If making changes doesn't work, go back to the defaults: Font-Raster Fonts, Size 8 x 12; Screen Colors-Back background with gray (192 for Red, Green, and Blue) letters; Screen Buffer size is Width 80 and Height 25; Windows Size is 80 X 25.

Note: Important: Don't change the Command Prompt settings using the Control Panel's Command Prompt icon because you could easily cause errors with your screen; instead, use the Command Prompt Properties dialog box.

Computer Slowed

If you've altered the buffer size in the Options tab of the Command Prompt Prop-erties dialog box, you may notice your computer has slowed somewhat. Since a buffer is reserved in memory, a large setting could affect your computer's speed and memory usage. The default buffer size is 50 and default number of buffers is 4.

Using Switches with Commands

Be careful when you use parameters and switches with commands you use in the Command Prompt window; since some commands have as many as 15 or 20 switches, using the wrong one could result in an inappropriate action. To verify a switch before you use it, type the command name followed by a space, the forward slash, and a question mark (copy /?) to get help about a particular command.

Other help commands to use in the Command Prompt window are as follows:

help	Lists commands with a brief description of each.
help command	Lists help for that command, including syntax, switches, parameters, and so on.
net help	Lists the network commands.
net help command	Lists help for that command, including syntax, switches, parameters, and so on.
command /?	Lists syntax for that command.

Memory Problems

If you receive a virtual memory error message, you need to create some space on your hard drive to increase the size of your pagefile. When an application or process starts in NT, NT supplies a memory space. Each process would like to have 2 to 4G of space available; but since that much available space is unlikely, NT creates a virtual pagefile to help simulate 4G for each process. The virtual pagefile lets NT use more memory than is actually available by enabling data to be stored temporarily and to be swapped between the pagefile and RAM.

The virtual pagefile is an actual file—pagefile.sys. If the pagefile isn't large enough, you need to create more space on the hard disk to enable the pagefile to expand; do this by deleting unnecessary files from the computer. Depending on the processor, the size of a pagefile block of data is 4096 bytes; there may be more than one block of data within a pagefile. Note, if you're running out of space on the server, it's time to get a second drive or a larger drive to replace the one you have.

You may need to manage your server's memory if you receive the not enough memory message when starting applications, if the computer seems sluggish, or if there is significant hard drive activity when you're not specifically using the hard drive.

You can configure the pagefile yourself. Generally, use the following equation: initial pagefile size = physical RAM+11M. So if you have 64M of RAM, the pagefile could be as much as 75M. Set the pagefile value by opening the Control Panel, System icon, Performance tab. In the Virtual Memory area, you see the total size of the pagefile, as shown in Figure B.5

Click the Change button to display the Virtual Memory dialog box (see Figure B.6). Following is a description of the items in the Virtual Memory dialog box.

Drive/Paging File Size	Shows the current and maximum sizes for the paging file, in megabytes.

Paging File Size for Selected Drive area

Drive	Current drive.
Space Available	Disk space available on current drive.
Initial Size	Set the initial size to equal or greater than the Recommended size.
Maximum Size	Set the maximum size for the pagefile, then click Set.
Total Paging File Size for All Drives area	Specifies the minimum allowed pagefile (always 2M), the recommended pagefile size, and the currently allocated pagefile size.

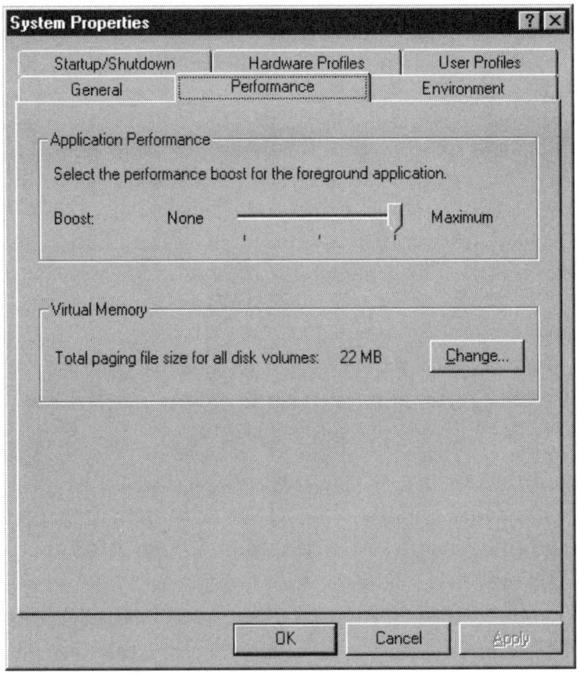

Figure B.5 *If the default pagefile is not enough, you can change it.*

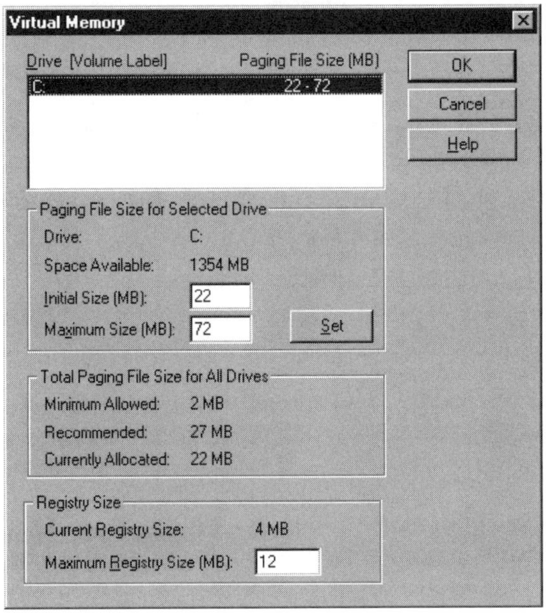

Figure B.6 *Configuring the virtual memory on the NT Server.*

Registry Size area

Current Registry Size	Shows current value.
Maximum Registry Size	The size you set limits both the page pool size and the amount of disk space that can be used by the Registry; all of the allotted space may not be used.

The Registry

The NT Registry is a database of configuration information that replaces previous Windows versions INI, SYS, and COM files. When NT starts, the Registry feeds the system information about device drivers, hardware, and user information. The Registry also assists OLE-enabled applications to share information by storing data about each application. Applications also store other information in the Registry, such as defaults and file locations.

You can change the Registry's contents using the REGEDT32 command in the Run window (Start, Run); however, be very, very careful. One wrong move, however minor, can cause the entire system to shut down and the only way out most likely will be to reinstall NT. The Registry does not consist of one file but of many files, located in many different folders; so backing up the Registry as you might have backed up INI files is not nearly as easy. For information about backing up the Registry, see the Windows NT Workstation Resource Kit.

The Registry is a hierarchical database divided into five sections, or keys:

HKEY_CLASSES_ROOT: Consists of data on file type associations and OLE (Object Linking and Embedding).

HKEY_LOCAL_MACHINE: Contains data about the local computer: hardware, drivers, system parameters, and startup options.

HKEY_CURRENT_USER: Includes information about the current user logged onto the system.

HKEY_USERS: Contains information about all User Profiles on the server.

HKEY_CURRENT_CONFIG: Consists of data about hardware configuration settings.

Each of the previous keys is divided into additional keys, which may also be divided again and again. Each key also has a unique name and one or more associated values; each value has three parts: a name, a data type, and an actual data value. Following are the five possible data types for those associated values:

REG_BINARY: Contains raw binary data.

REG_DWORD: Includes a 4-byte value.

REG_EXPAND_SZ: Consists of a text string that contains replaceable parameter(s).

REG_MULTI_SZ: Contains several text strings, separated with a NULL character.

REG_SZ: Includes a text string often used for description values or program names.

Viewing the Registry

You can view the Registry using the Start, Run command. Enter Regedt32.exe to search for keys and subkeys in the Registry. Enter Regedit.exe to search for strings, values, keys, and subkeys.

Note: Important: Do NOT change data in the Registry; if you must change any information in the Registry, use the Control Panel icons: Services, Devices, Network, SCSI Adapters, and so on, to change Registry information.

Figure B.7 shows the Registry Editor started with the Regedt32.exe command. The menus may provide an easier method of viewing the components of the Registry.

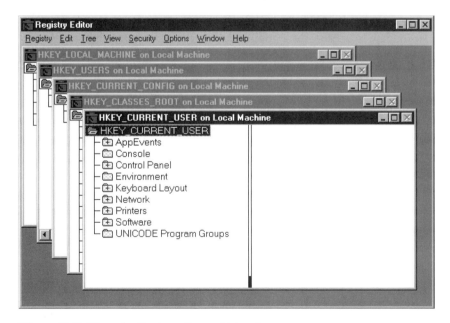

Figure B.7 *View the Registry for troublshooting purposes.*

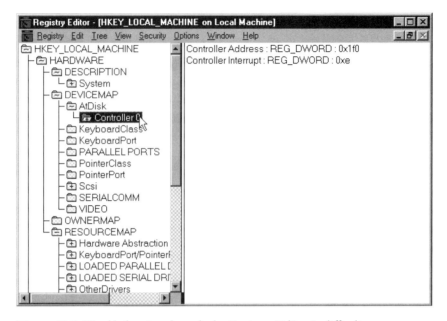

Figure B.8 *Troubleshooting through the Registry Editor is difficult.*

Troubleshooting with HKEY_LOCAL_MACHINE

The HKEY_LOCAL_MACHINE key contains no data about software or users; only data to specify the configuration of the computer. Often you can trace problems with services, device drivers, or startup control data to this key. The HARD-WARE and SYSTEM keys are the most useful for troubleshooting.

The HARDWARE key is configured each time the computer boots and contains data about what NT needs to boot the computer; this key is rewritten each time the computer boots. The HARDWARE key describes the physical hardware in the computer, including mappings and related data that link Kernel-mode drivers with user-mode code. Figure B.8 shows the Registry Editor with the HARDWARE key and its many subkeys displayed.

Since the HARDWARE key stores data in binary form, the best way to view the data is by using NT Diagnostics (Start, Programs, Administrative Tools, Windows NT Diagnostics). Figure B.9 shows the same information but in a more readable form. This information was found by choosing the Resources tab in the Diagnostics dialog box, then selecting the hard drive (AtDisk, in this case) and choosing the Properties button to view the Bus and Settings for that device.

Another key within the HKEY_LOCAL_MACHINE key is the SAM (Security Account Manager database) which contains user information and is modified

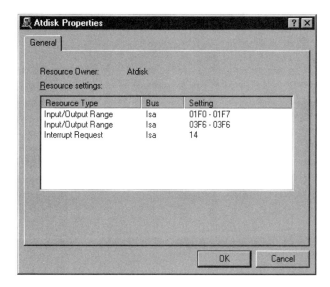

Figure B.9 *The NT Diagnostics may be easier to read than Registry settings.*

through the use of the User Manager for Domains. The SECURITY key contains user rights, passwords, and so on, also changed through the User Manager. The SOFTWARE key includes information about the software installed to the computer. Finally, the SYSTEM key controls system startup, device driver loading, NT services, and operating system behavior.

The SYSTEM key contains many subkeys that store all startup-related data, such as the ControlSet001, CurrentControlSet, DISK, Setup, and so on. A control set contains the system configuration information. There are at least two control sets and often more. The SYSTEM\Select subset describes two of the control sets that are used.

The SYSTEM key contains multiple service and device subkeys you might use to troubleshoot your computer. Use these subkeys to see which devices and services load when you start your computer. Under the SYSTEM key, CurrentControlSet subkey, you see four subkeys: Control contains the startup data, Enum contains Plug and Play hardware tree, Hardware Profiles enables you to define and select the configuration for startup, and Services lists all Kernel device drivers, file system drivers, and Win32 services drivers that can be loaded by the system.

Figure B.10 shows the list of Services in the CurrentControlSet subkey. You also can view services in the Services option from the Control Panel. Viewing services in this utility shows you which services have started automatically, which have been disabled, and so on.

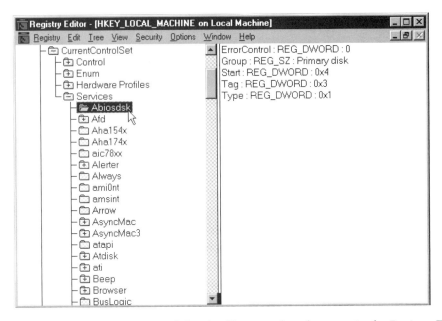

Figure B.10 *View services and details of how or when they start in the Registry Editor.*

Working with the Registry and viewing it using the Registry Editor is extremely complex. As you can see, you can view services, hardware, devices, applications, and other problems elsewhere in NT; however, if you're brave enough to learn the Registry, you will find a wealth of information for the taking. For more information about the Registry and its components, see the *Windows NT Resource Guide.*

TCP/IP Problems

If you're having trouble with the TCP/IP protocols over the network, you might try to use some of NT's diagnostic tools for TCP/IP. Generally, configuration of the protocol is the most likely culprit to any problems or errors. Make sure you've entered the correct addresses, subnet masks, gateways, and other settings before doing anything else. Not only check for the appropriate addresses, make sure you've correctly defined the DNS server, WINS server, and so on. For more information, see Appendix C.

Ping

Ping, probably the most useful diagnostic tool, is a command that verifies the protocol is correctly configured and communicating with a remote system. When you issue the Ping command, you're sending an echo request from a host to a remote or vise versa. To use Ping, open a Command Prompt window and type **ping** ***IP_address***. The IP_address is the address of the computer you're targeting.

TIP: To check the local machine to see if TCP/IP is installed and configured correctly, use the following command at a command prompt: **ping 127.0.0.1**.

After you enter the command and press ENTER, you will either see a successful map of the TCP/IP route or an error. If you see an error, make sure you restarted the computer after installing and configuring TCP/IP; then check to make sure the IP address is correctly entered.

Other Tools

You can also use any of the following tools to troubleshoot TCP/IP connections. Type the following command(s) in at the command prompt:

TIP: Some of these commands include switches and/or other parameters; for more information about any command, type the command name followed by a space, hyphen, and a question mark—for instance, **hostname -?**—then press ENTER. Switches are case-sensitive.

---

hostname: Displays the name of the host on which the command is issued.

ipconfig: Displays the current TCP/IP network configuration values, such as the host name, DNS servers, node type, and addresses for the IP, subnet mask, default gateway, DHCP server, WINS server, and so on.

nbstat: Displays protocol statistics and current connections if you're using NetBIOS over TCP/IP (NetBT); switches enable you to list local NetBIOS names, display both workstation and server sessions, and more.

netstat: Displays protocol statistics and current connections; you can use switches to display Ethernet statistics, all connections or server connections, and/or addresses and port numbers in numerical form instead of by name.

For a list and descriptions of more diagnostic tools you can use with TCP/IP, open Windows NT Help (Start, Help) and in the Index tab, type **TCP/IP: utilities**. Help displays a list of utilities and services that will help you diagnose your TCP/IP problems.

C TCP/IP Configuration

TCP/IP (Transmission Control Protocol/Internet Protocol) is a set, or suite, of communications protocols that includes media access, packet transport, session communications, file transfer, electronic mail, and terminal emulation. TCP/IP is supported by numerous hardware and software vendors and is available on various types of computers.

You can use Microsoft TCP/IP with NT Server to perform several different tasks: communicating over the network to other servers and clients, printing to UNIX printers, communicating over the Internet, and so on. This appendix presents an overview of TCP/IP and related services for Windows NT.

TCP/IP Structure

Microsoft's TCP/IP provides many of the TCP/IP protocols and services, including Transmission Control Protocol (TCP), Internet Protocol (IP), User Datagram Protocol (UDP), and so on. It also provides support for Point-to-Point Protocol (PPP) and Serial-Line IP (SLIP) for access by modem to TCP/IP networks, such as the Internet. Microsoft's TCP/IP also includes basic utilities—such as finger, ftp, telnet, tftp, and so on—that enable users to connect and use resources of other hosts, such as UNIX.

Figure C.1 illustrates the Microsoft TCP/IP structure as it is incorporated into the Windows NT architecture.

Additionally, Microsoft's TCP/IP supports tools and utilities for setting up Internet and Intranet Web sites, including the following:

- DHCP (Dynamic Host Configuration Protocol) to automatically configure TCP/IP

- WINS (Windows Internet Name Service) for dynamically registering and querying computer names on an internetwork

- DNS (Domain Name System) for registering and querying DNS domain names on an internetwork
- TCP/IP printing for accessing printers on computers running UNIX

Microsoft's TCP/IP for NT doesn't include a complete suite of TCP/IP utilities or server services; however, many third-party vendors produce such applications and utilities that are compatible with Microsoft TCP/IP, such as Http, WAIS, NFS, and so on.

TIP: For more detailed information, see the Microsoft Windows NT Resource Kit Networking Guide.

Common TCP/IP Protocols

TCP/IP is a suite of protocols that work together to connect computers and enable communication between them. The most common of the protocols in the TCP/IP suite are TCP, UDP, IP, ARP, and ICMP. This section briefly explains those common protocols.

- TCP (Transmission Control Protocol) is the part of TCP/IP that guarantees the delivery of packets and the accuracy of the data. TCP secures proper sequencing of the data, which also requires additional network traffic.

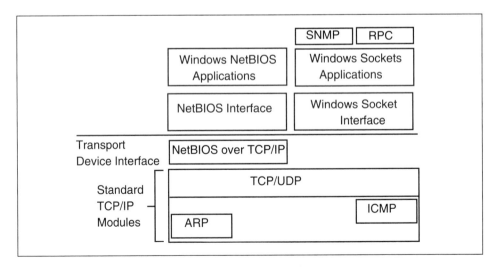

Figure C.1 *NT uses TCP/IP to enhance its networking abilities.*

- UDP (User Datagram Protocol) works hand-in-hand with TCP to exchange data without any guarantees of delivery or correct sequencing. UDP doesn't require the additional network traffic or time that TCP does so it can be more efficient, even if it is less secured; therefore, UDP depends on TCP and other higher-level protocols to provide consistency and accuracy.

- IP (Internet Protocol), like UDP, transfers data without a guarantee and relies on higher level protocols for the data's sequencing. Its purpose is it's quick and inexpensive (in system resources).

- ARP (Address Resolution Protocol) A maintenance protocol that requests an IP address from the network, then sends the reply packet containing the address and stores the address in the ARP cache for subsequent use.

- ICMP (Internet Control Message Protocol) is a maintenance protocol that enables two systems to share status and error data; ICMP works with the IP network. The ping utility, that checks an IP system to see if the network is functional, uses the ICMP echo request and reply packets.

TCP/IP Utilities

You can use Microsoft's TCP/IP within an enterprise network, incorporating many clients and networks to provide connectivity and server support. Among the Microsoft networks, TCP/IP is compatible with Windows NT Workstation and Server, Windows 95, Windows for Workgroups, and Microsoft LAN Manager. Various utilities are supported for each network type as described in Table C.1.

Table C.1 TCP/IP Connectivity

OPERATING SYSTEM	SUPPORTED UTILITIES
Windows NT Workstation	WAN, TCP/IP printing, FTP, Telnet, DHCP, WINS, DNS client software, Windows Sockets, and extended LMHOSTS file
Windows NT Server	WAN, TCP/IP printing, FTP, Telnet, DHCP and DHCP Server, WINS and WINS Server, DNS client software, Windows Sockets, extended LMHOSTS file, and Internet Information Server
Windows 95	WAN, DHCP, WINS, DNS client software, extended LMHOSTS file, and Windows Sockets
Windows for Workgroups using TCP/IP-32	Windows NT, LAN Manager, DHCP, WINS

Additionally, using TCP/IP, Windows NT can communicate with many non-Microsoft systems, including Internet hosts, Macintosh systems, IBM mainframes, UNIX systems, and others.

Installing and Configuring TCP/IP

To use TCP/IP for the Internet, communicating with other operating systems, or for network communications, you must configure an IP address, a subnet mask, and a default gateway. You can manually configure the addresses.

Each device attached to a TCP/IP network has a unique IP address; one IP address is assigned to each network adapter in the computer. An IP address is represented in dotted-decimal notation, for example: 122.59.2.25. The IP address contains a network ID and a host ID; each is a unique address that identifies which packets the computer receives.

Subnet masks distinguish the network ID and the host ID portions of the IP address. A subnet mask is created by assigning 1s to network ID bits and 0s to host ID bits, then converted to dotted-decimal notation. A subnet mask might look like this: 255.255.255.0. All computers on a logical network must use the same subnet mask and network ID.

IP routing connects the devices from one network to another and enables the IP packets to transfer. Generally, a default gateway router, a computer connected to the local subnet and to other networks, is used for IP routing. The default gateway is also written in dotted-decimal notation: 198.33.34.1, for example.

Adding TCP/IP

You can install TCP/IP protocol in NT during installation or after setup is complete. See Appendix A for information about installing NT. To add TCP/IP, follow these steps:

1. Choose Start, Settings, Control Panel.

2. In the Control Panel, double-click the Network icon. The Network dialog box appears.

3. Choose the Protocols tab (see Figure C.2).

4. To add TCP/IP protocol, choose the Add button. The Select Network Protocol dialog box appears (see Figure C.3).

5. Choose the TCP/IP Protocol in the list of **N**etwork Protocols and choose OK. NT may prompt you for the Windows NT CD-ROM so it can copy files. When copying is complete, NT returns to the Network dialog box.

Choosing an IP Address for Your Network

If you'll be using the Internet and that's why you're configuring TCP/IP, you should use the IP address, subnet mask, and other information as given to you by your Internet Service Provider. However, if you're using TCP/IP to set up your network, you probably don't have an IP address in mind for the server and/or for your workstations.

Any IP address that begins with 172.16, among others, is for private use (not for use over the Internet); therefore, you can use this address for your private network. No one is allowed to use this address over the Internet, however. So, if you ever move your system to the Internet, you will need to obtain an IP ss from your ISP and make the necessary changes.

You might then use the IP address 172.16.1.100 and assign IP addresses for your workstations as follows: 172.16.1.101, 172.16.1.102 172.16.1.103, 172.16.1.104 172.16.1.105, and so on. With each of these IP addresses, you would use the same subnet mask, 255.255.255.0, for example.

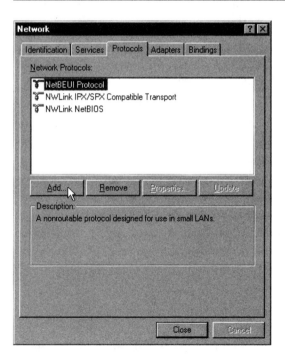

Figure C.2 *Use the protocols tab to add TCP/IP.*

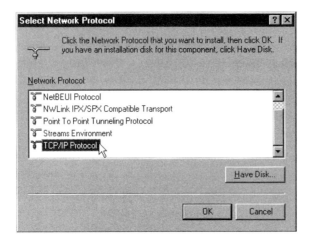

Figure C.3 *Add the TCP/IP protocol to the list of Network Protocols.*

Configuring TCP/IP

To configure TCP/IP, you will need to know the IP address, subnet mask, and the default gateway of your network. To configure the protocol, follow these steps:

1. In the Network dialog box, Protocols tab, select the protocol in the Network Protocols list and choose the Properties button. The Microsoft TCP/IP Properties dialog box appears.

2. In the IP Address tab (see Figure C.4), select the adapter you're configuring with TCP/IP.

3. In the Specify an IP address area of the tab, enter the IP Address, Subnet Mask, and the Default Gateway.

4. You can choose the Advanced button to configure additional gateways, addresses, and subnets, and other settings as described in Table C.2. Figure C.5 shows the Advanced IP Addressing dialog box.

5. Choose OK to close the Microsoft TCP/IP Properties dialog box and OK again to close the Network dialog box. You will be prompted to restart the computer for the configuration changes to take place.

DHCP Configuration

A DHCP server provides automatic TCP/IP configuration, prevents address conflicts, and makes centralized management of address allocation easier for the administrator of the intranet. You can configure a Windows NT Server 4.0 to act as a

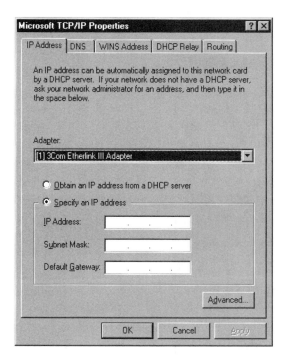

Figure C.4 *Use the IP Address tab to enter the data needed to configure TCP/IP.*

Table C.2 Advanced IP Addressing Options

OPTION	DESCRIPTION
Adapter	A server can contain multiple network adapter cards and each one can be configured differently; select the adapter card you want to configure.
IP Addresses Area	Add up to five additional IP addresses and subnet masks for any selected adapter; Edit any selected item in the IP Address or Subnet Mask list; or Remove the selected item.
Gateways area	Add up to five gateway routers; Edit any selected gateway; or Remove any selected gateway in the list. Choose Up or Down to move the selected gateway in the list.
Enable PPTP Filtering	Enables Point-to-Point Tunneling Protocol filtering so users can access corporate networks securely over the Internet (when enabled, no other protocols can be used on the selected adapter, only PPTP).
Enable Security	TCP/IP security lets you control network traffic, typically for Internet servers.
Configure	Use to add, remove, and permit TCP ports, UDP ports, and IP protocols.

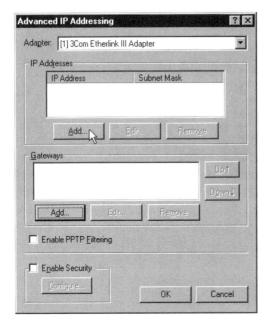

Figure C.5 *Configure advanced options for the IP addressing.*

DHCP server. As a DHCP server, the computer would automatically configure client computers using the TCP/IP protocol and choosing to enable the DHCP server to configure the protocol automatically. The server "leases" the configuration to each client for a specified amount of time and automatically updates any address or data changes the administrator makes to the protocol. (You must manually configure a server for DHCP; you cannot use DHCP configuration when installing as a DHCP server.)

To add the DHCP service to your NT Server, choose the **A**dd button in the Services tab of the Network dialog box. In the Network Services list, choose Microsoft DHCP Server and choose OK. You will need the Windows NT CD-ROM or you can enter a path to the NT files, if they're stored on the network. Next, install TCP/IP manually as described in the previous section. When you restart the computer, the DHCP data will be ready to use.

You use the DHCP Manager (Start, Programs, Administrative Tools) to add the DHCP server to the DHCP scope, to define properties of the scope, and to configure DHCP option types and values of the lease duration. Figure C.6 shows the DHCP Manager. For more information about setting up a DHCP server, see NT Server on-line help and the *Microsoft Windows NT Resource Kit Network Guide.* For more information about how to use the DHCP Manager, see on-line help in the DHCP Manager.

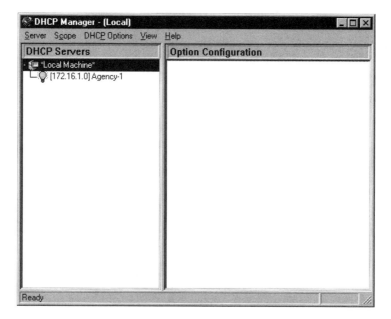

Figure C.6 *Use the DHCP Manager to set options and configurations.*

Note: A client Windows NT Workstation or Server computer can make use of the DHCP automatic configuration by opening the Network dialog box and choosing the Protocols tab. Select the TCP/IP protocol, choose the Properties button, and in the IP Address tab of the Microsoft TCP/IP Properties dialog box, select the option: Obtain an IP Address From a DHCP Server. Other clients—Windows 95 and Windows for Workgroups 3.11—can also take advantage of the DHCP automatic configuration; see the documentation of the operating system.

WINS Configuration

WINS (Windows Internet Name Service) is a replicated, dynamic database that registers and queries NetBIOS computer names in a routed network environment. The more complex a network is, the more you will need a WINS service for name resolution. WINS enables users to quickly and easily locate systems on remote networks and updates changes to IP addresses through DHCP addressing automatically.

Consider these facts before installing the WINS service:

- Do not assign a fixed IP address to a WINS server.
- Do not make a WINS server a DHCP client.

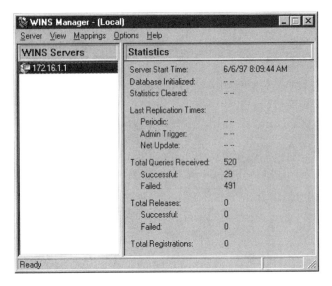

Figure C.7 *Use the WINS Manager to configure the WINS service.*

To install a WINS server, Open the Network dialog box and choose the Services tab. Choose the Add button and from the list of network services, choose Windows Internet Name Service and choose OK. Insert the Windows NT CD-ROM or enter a path to the NT files and choose Continue.

After installation of the WINS files, you must configure TCP/IP as described in the previous section. After you restart the computer, the WINS software will be ready to use.

Use the WINS Manager (see Figure C.7) to administer WINS. Access the WINS Manager through Start, Programs, Administrative Tools, and then choose WINS Manager.

Note: You can start and stop the WINS Server service by opening the Services option in the Control Panel and selecting the Windows Internet Name Service in the list and choosing Start, Stop, Pause, or Continue.

Domain Name System (DNS) Server

The DNS is a database that identifies hosts information and resolves names to IP address mapping queries from clients or from DNS name servers. The Windows

NT DNS name server can use WINS for host name resolution, thus allowing more efficient name resolution.

Small networks and/or single networks do not really need a DNS server; your Internet Service Provider maintains a DNS server and you could use the DNS client software to query their DNS server instead. If, on the other hand, you want to access DNS from your LAN, you will need to provide your own DNS server. A DNS server system is large and involved. You may want to use two computers—a primary and a secondary name server—with replicated data to the secondary server for backup purposes.

Note: The DNS naming system can be compared to a filing cabinet. Each domain is a drawer in the cabinet; and a subdomain compares to file folders within the domain drawer. When writing out the domain name, periods are used to separate each part of the name; for example, the DNS domain name *humble.com* defines *humble* as a subdomain of the parent *com* domain. You're probably familiar with the seven organizational domain name abbreviations: com (commercial), edu (educational), gov (government), org (noncommercial), net (networking), mil (military), and int (international).

To add the DNS server service, open the Network dialog box (Control Panel, Network icon) and choose the Services tab. Choose **A**dd and select the Microsoft DNS Server; choose OK. You will need your NT CD-ROM or a path to the NT files. Restart the computer to enable the DNS server software.

You can use the DNS Manager (Start, Programs, Administrative Tools) to administer the name servers. For more information about DNS, see on-line help. NT supplies a complete help file specifically for Microsoft TCP/IP; to get help, choose Start, Help and in the Index tab type **dns**. In the list of help topics that appears, double-click "DNS Servers, installing and configuring". NT displays the specialized TCP/IP help contents screen.

TCP/IP Utilities and Services

TCP/IP utilities provide diagnostic tools for connecting to other systems, for network administration, and for troubleshooting the network. You use TCP/IP utilities at an MS-DOS command prompt (Start, Programs, Command Prompt); some applications are configured with the Control Panel. It is important to note that NT's TCP/IP utilities are not full-blown applications; many are only basic, even simple, tools that may or may not serve your needs. Following is a brief description of TCP/IP utilities and services available with Windows NT Server:

The *Telnet* client application is a tool you can use to connect to a remote host, along the lines of a basic terminal application.

The *Finger* client is a way to query a remote system for information in the form of text. Use Finger to identify users.

RCP (remote copy) is a command for exchanging files with a remote host or copying files from one host to another using a trust between systems.

FTP, a simple command line utility in NT, lets you establish a connection, log in as a user, and transfer files from the host.

Gopher server is a distributed menu system that can provide a menu of files, links to other menus, or links to other servers' menus.

SNMP (Simple Network Management Protocol) provides basic administrative information about a device so you can monitor the system; you must install the SNMP service from the Network dialog box to take advantage of this utility.

Index